Saving Power

Saving Power

THEORIES OF ATONEMENT
AND FORMS OF THE CHURCH

Peter Schmiechen

William B. Eerdmans Publishing Company
Grand Rapids, Michigan / Cambridge, U.K.

© 2005 Wm. B. Eerdmans Publishing Co.
All rights reserved

Wm. B. Eerdmans Publishing Co.
255 Jefferson Ave. S.E., Grand Rapids, Michigan 49503 /
P.O. Box 163, Cambridge CB3 9PU U.K.

Printed in the United States of America

10 09 08 07 06 05   7 6 5 4 3 2 1

ISBN 0-8028-2985-6

www.eerdmans.com

To

Timothy Carl and Nathan John
Schmiechen

Contents

Preface

Issues relating to atonement are the point of continuity through all of my theological study and work. I left seminary with more questions than answers and welcomed the challenge of graduate school. For the first three years I also served a congregation and preached every Sunday. The repetition of themes of judgment and grace in the lectionary provoked consternation. Are these themes to be alternated from one week to the next, or included every Sunday? But how are they to be resolved? That presupposes clarity regarding atonement, which at the time seemed to be an area of large uncharted waters. Gustaf Aulén appeared to have mapped these unknown lands, dividing them very neatly into three areas. But a careful reading of Anselm, assisted by Herbert Richardson, who at the time was translating Anselm's treatises, led me to a very different conclusion regarding this great medieval theologian. My long-standing interest in Luther was enriched by the perspective of Heiko Oberman on late medieval theology and the Reformation. Richard R. Niebuhr introduced me and fellow students to a new and liberating interpretation of Friedrich Schleiermacher. By 1970 it was apparent that theology must deal with a host of social/political issues, but traditional categories did not seem to be adequate. The writings of Jürgen Moltmann, James Cone, Gustavo Gutiérrez, and feminist writers offered new approaches as well as new conclusions.

In 1975 I accepted an opportunity to serve as academic dean at Elmhurst College, primarily because it seemed essential to determine whether the church-related, liberal-arts college could be responsive to educational challenges and the pressing moral and religious needs of society. Ten years later, Lancaster Theological Seminary called me to be president. As a theologian, the college experience required one to deal with the relation of theology and the world, as represented by the many disciplines. What interested me about the seminary role was the opportunity to deal with issues pertaining to the faith and life of the church itself. In this context I came to see that the malaise of the church was directly tied to lack of clarity regarding Christological issues, which is to say, atonement and the basis of the church. This inspired me to reflect on Paul's theology of the cross in 1 Corinthians 1–2, first as a theory of conversion, then as a comprehensive theory of atonement, published in 1996 under the title, *Christ the Reconciler: A Theology for Opposites, Differences and Enemies*. It also prompted me to continue reading H. Richard Niebuhr, partly because of his approach to faith and religion, but also for his perspective on Christ and our knowledge of God. After years of reflection I became convinced that he represented a distinctive form of atonement dealing with the transformation of our knowledge of God.

Entry into the tradition of the Mercersburg Theology at Lancaster prompted further study of John Williamson Nevin and that long tradition running from the Gospel of John through Athanasius and Schleiermacher, where Incarnation was the crucial doctrine. Those years at Lancaster also provided opportunity for two related endeavors: one was the need for theological reflection on the current state of the church in the midst of all the confusion and conflict that beset mainline denominations; the other was the opportunity to develop, with a grant from the Lilly Endowment, a program on leadership renewal for pastors attempting to be catalysts for renewal in congregations. This endeavor convinced me that the renewal of the church must proceed from clear and confident proclamation of the gospel, rather than the use of organizational theory and management techniques. This basic conviction was reinforced by years of working with pastors who were willing to explore new ways for the gospel to reform contemporary church life.

The goal of a systematic study of theories of atonement was nurtured through all of these stages, though not actually possible until the last two years. The immersion into major texts and studies, with serious discussion with colleagues, has allowed me to draw all of these strands together. The faculty of Lancaster Theological Seminary has offered advice and encouragement along the way. In particular I wish to thank Dean Anabel Proffitt, Frank Stalfa, Ann Thayer, Julia O'Brien, John Payne, Robert Webber, Sally Brown (now at Princeton), Jennifer Lord, Rollin Russell, Bruce Epperly, and my successor, President Riess Potterveld. Greg Carey and Lee Barrett offered extensive comments on several chapters and the general scope of the project. As always, they supplied a wealth of knowledge. A friend of many years, Steven Crocco, Librarian at Princeton Seminary, has made helpful suggestions regarding the chapter on H. Richard Niebuhr — a subject on which he excels.

The Assistant Librarian at Lancaster, Christopher Beldan, kindly assisted on many technical matters in the composition of this manuscript. I am, of course, grateful for the rich resources of the Philip Schaff Library at Lancaster Seminary, overseen by Richard Berg, Director.

The writing has been possible because of work carried out at earlier points, though each of these parts has gone through major revision in light of new studies and changes in my own thinking over time. In a real sense, this study was never far from my mind, since the work of theological education in the service of the church hinges on Christological questions. While publication brings the process of writing to completion, I assume it will allow the discussion that has been so much a part of my life to continue in new ways.

Introduction

This is a book about interpretations of the life, death, and resurrection of Jesus Christ for the church today. The thesis is that atonement has to do with the saving power of God in Jesus Christ. The New Testament and later traditions reveal how such saving power is interpreted in many ways. The life and work of the church depend on claiming the richness of these many witnesses to saving power.

This perspective is confounded by confusion and lack of confidence, much to the detriment of the church's preaching and mission. If there is no clarity regarding the richness of these many theories, then preaching and piety are shaped by a single view of atonement. While this may appear to have the advantage of single-mindedness, it ignores a wide range of other ways saving power addresses different human needs. For example, forgiveness of sins is a quite different theme from that of the victory over death or the reconciliation of divided parties. Persons held captive to shame do not need to be forgiven but released. Given the diverse spiritual needs of people, focusing on but one aspect of saving power really amounts to confusion regarding atonement. By contrast, if there is no confidence regarding the proclamation of saving power in Jesus Christ at all, then ministry and mission live under a cloud of gloom. The heart may yearn for the proclamation of the power of the cross, but the will to do so is absent. Much of the lack of clarity and loss of nerve stems from the fear that atonement is the weak point in the Christian message because there is but one theory (namely, penal substitution) and it is flawed. Whether one openly subscribes to such a view, or quietly fears that it is true, in either case the drive to proclaim the cross is undercut. This paralysis regarding the cross, however, leads to a general shutdown of all systems: If one cannot find a way to confess the saving power of the cross, then Jesus becomes irrelevant and the church has no good news. The situation is not improved, as we shall see, by substituting the threefold outline of Gustaf Aulén. While he appears to recognize three theories rather than one, in the end the three are reduced to only one acceptable theory, i.e., Christus Victor. Against the imperialism of those who argue that atonement is but one general theory or that everything can be squeezed into three theories, this study shall present ten distinct theories, thereby demonstrating the breadth of Christian witness to the fullness of Christ.

A. Method

Given the nature of this study, there will inevitably be a heavy reliance on biblical and historical study. But the primary methodology is that of theology, for two reasons: First, the study seeks to identify and analyze distinctive theories as interpretations of Jesus. This obviously requires the use of material from the Bible and the history of theology. Anyone who is familiar with these sources knows that they present a wide range of ideas, with multiple variations, in written word, art, hymnody, and liturgy. But here the purpose is not to present the full spectrum, or all the variations within one general type, but to construct a coherent and viable formulation of each particular theory. To be sure, such an approach requires that one step back from the myriad of historical detail in order to capture what might be called the basic idea of a theory. This is in fact the way preachers and teachers actually operate. Preachers usually rely on their personal summary and idealized version of a particular theory of atonement. A sermon might refer to the conquest of sin or death, but hardly ever take a timeout and present the exact formulation of Irenaeus, Athanasius, Luther, or Gutiérrez. Likewise, when teachers are asked what is the theory of Christus Victor, they probably first give a general definition that represents a composite of many versions and then proceed to compare and contrast particular versions. The organization of the first ten chapters reflects this theological concern for defining theologically ten distinctive theories.

Second, the study is theological in the attempt to determine the viability of these theories of atonement for the life and work of the church today. On the one hand, this requires a clear statement of each theory. To accomplish this, each chapter will include a brief outline of each theory and then witnesses of faith involving one or more primary texts. This assumes that if a theory is once outlined in its basic logical form, such a formulation is best served by examining a particular author who gives us a strong and coherent affirmation of it. These case studies will be presented in considerable detail so that the reader may examine the way a theory is constructed and moves towards its conclusion. Only by seeing how a writer builds on certain assumptions and makes critical decisions can one comprehend fully the Christology that emerges. The advantage of this approach is that it puts the reader in touch with a detailed presentation of major primary sources. The fact that the greater part of the study is dedicated to the case studies obviously reflects my commitment to these major texts, as well as how contemporary theology must be in dialogue with them. It is amazing how they continue to surprise and enrich our attempts at finding viable expressions for Christology. While the presentations cannot claim neutrality, I have tried to respect the distinction between description and evaluation. On the other hand, this goal requires that the values used for analysis and criticism be clearly stated to the reader. The evaluation of these theories is an extremely controversial area of theology. Just as it would be naïve to suggest that this study is neutral, it would be just as erroneous to conceal the critical perspective employed to assess the theories. Therefore the values used at the outset of the study, with respect to selection, organization, and evaluation, will be outlined below. In the Conclusion, the critical values developed from the study will be presented and used for further discussion. Each chapter will also include analysis and critical evaluation.

Having stated in positive terms how the primary theological method will incorporate biblical and historical study, it may be helpful to indicate what this approach excludes. More than one reader will probably assume that this study intends one of the following. (1) This study is not a history of the doctrine of atonement. Such an approach would have to track the development of theories, from origin to full expression, and then their journey through the history of many different traditions. This study makes no attempt to do this because it is primarily a theological study. (2) The case studies are not intended to present a comprehensive view of the total theology of a particular writer. For example, in analyzing Calvin's presentation of the priestly office of Christ, our purpose will be to provide an example of the sacrificial theory, rather than present a complete assessment of Calvin's Christology. In a similar way, the use of Luther on justification by grace is not meant to imply that this is the only theory of atonement he employs in his whole theology. The case studies are examples of particular theories, but not a review of each author's complete theology. Likewise, it must also be said that the study could not seek to resolve all of the critical issues connected with each writer. Readers are expected to seek out historical studies that provide either background on general periods or specialized study of individual authors. (3) The case studies were not chosen as a definitive list of the most important theologians. There are some obviously great figures who are not included (e.g., Augustine, Aquinas, and Edwards).

The purpose of this study is a theological examination of ten theories of atonement, and the case studies were chosen because they are excellent examples. In some cases, the person chosen is in fact identified with the theory (as in the case of Anselm). (4) As a study of theories of atonement, the study does not seek to resolve the full spectrum of theological issues that bear on a full systematic theology. To complete this study it has been necessary to restrict the discussion to the primary goal and not move beyond it.

With several exceptions, most chapters in Part I will follow a similar format: (a) examination of the central image as the basis for the theory; (b) an outline of the basic theory; (c) the presentation of one or more case studies or witnesses of faith; (d) theological commentary. Part II will consist of two concluding chapters, one analyzing the ten theories and the other demonstrating the connection between theories of atonement and the formation of the church.

B. From Images to Theories

The theories considered here are highly developed and comprehensive interpretations of Jesus' life, death, and resurrection. They have developed over time and have passed through generations of use. Some possess a certain simplicity, where key phrases may summarize in the manner of code language. Some have been revised and adapted so many times, that it is often difficult to ascertain their genealogy. They draw upon the history of interpretation of who Jesus is and what he does, as well as the life and worship of particular periods of Christian faith. Each seeks to answer, by appeals to authority, common experience or reason, the very questions raised by the New Testament itself: Who is Jesus? Why was he rejected and killed by his own people? If he was the Christ and/or Son of God, why did God allow him to die? Why did he not use divine power to save himself? What is the meaning of his death and resurrection? In short, how does this story reveal the saving power of God?

The New Testament raises these questions and also offers multiple answers in various stages of development. The fact that so many explanations appear in the process of formation in the New Testament itself, and then undergo further development in the next three centuries, indicates two things: One is that there was no primary story that answered all of the questions posed — either in the first two generations or in the following centuries. If all questions had been answered, Christian teaching, preaching, and apologetics would simply have used the one, primary explanation. We must be reminded again that while the church officially adopted creedal statements regarding

Trinity and Incarnation, it did not adopt one official theory of atonement. There is something inherently complex and diverse about the subject that resists the restriction of a single answer.

The other point, closely related to the first, is that the signs and wonders in Jesus' life, death, and resurrection are not self-explanatory. Contrary to the conservative view that the signs and wonders are self-evident and constitute irrefutable proofs, just about everything in the story of Jesus requires an explanation. Even the most dramatic and powerful sign — namely, the resurrection — requires interpretation: it could be one of the most unusual and inexplicable events in history, or the work of the devil, or a fabrication by the disciples, or a sign of God's deliverance. But it is not, as we see with the disciples on the road to Emmaus, self-explanatory.

Theories of atonement, then, attempt to provide an internally coherent explanation of Jesus' life, death, and resurrection. Their purpose is fundamentally evangelical in nature, even though they may not always appear in the form of sermons. Their intent is to draw the listener/reader into the saving power of Christ. To accomplish this, the theories do several things, which become the basis for three values:

First, a theory employs an image that has the potential of being the cornerstone for an interpretation of Jesus. As such it will have to *symbolize something about Jesus that connects saving power with some form of human need.* An image might be a metaphor (e.g., Lamb, Bread, Vine, Shepherd) or a title (e.g., Lord, Word, Suffering Servant). It could also be a proper noun (e.g., Teacher), a word describing some thing or event in the story of Jesus (e.g., cross) or a phrase (e.g., "Jesus died for us."). The New Testament overflows with images and testifies to the creative energy at work in the earliest period as the church sought to name Jesus and explain the meaning of the crucial events. Images, then, are usually the starting point for theories, providing a key idea that catches the imagination. By contrast, theories build on images and expand them, as is the case with the tightly woven argument of penal substitution or the dramatic narratives of Christ's conquest over Satan. They make connections, seek to explain, and place the originally inspired idea into a comprehensive view. While most theories use biblical images, some work from new ones, as in Anselm's use of the image of honor. The use of images may be called the *symbolic* value of theories, i.e., their ability to catch the spiritual imagination with an image that expresses something essential about Jesus and supports a comprehensive theory regarding sin and redemption, God and humankind.[1]

---

1. I make the distinction between image and theory in this study as an interpretative device

Not all images possess this symbolic value, and for this reason images in themselves are not theories. Thus it is quite understandable that some images, while brilliant in their suggestive power, never become the basis for theories, or even fade into the background. Perhaps the best example is the title Teacher (Rabbi): while used in the gospels as a title for Jesus, it fades from use in later affirmations because it does not have the ability to express the church's estimate of Jesus' person or of what he does. The redemption by means of death and resurrection could not be contained in what we normally mean by teacher. A somewhat similar problem lies with the image of Good Shepherd: by itself it is not a theory of atonement, though when coupled with Jesus' death it can be added to various theories. So it can be said that by themselves some images fail to possess the symbolic value.

Second, in order to offer a comprehensive and compelling interpretation of Jesus, a theory will have to connect Jesus with God. This may be called its *theological* value. The theory, with its initial image, will have to appeal to essential affirmations regarding God as well as interpret the agency of God in the story of Jesus. To do this, the theories will inevitably draw upon the history of redemption as recorded in the Old Testament, appealing to the teachings of Jesus or the broad theological affirmations at the heart of the creeds. Theories of sacrifice and substitution will search the scriptures for images and support. Other theories, such as those of Irenaeus and Athanasius, will draw upon basic images of Jesus in the New Testament and the early church's proclamation: the *conquest* of demonic powers and the renewal of creation by the incarnate Word.

The *theological* value of a theory also requires that it be consistent with the essential affirmations regarding God at a given time and place. This, of course, is a difficult task, since these affirmations undergo considerable development and in different centuries the emphasis might change. Anselm objects to previous approaches because they rely too heavily on metaphors, whereas he proposes to present a theory with rational necessity derived from the very nature of God. Yet his theory was opposed by Abelard and many in succeeding generations, precisely because of affirmations that appeared to violate the love of God. The same can be said of the theory of penal substitu-

---

without identifying with one or more theories of language in the broad theological and philosophical discussions. It may be noted, however, that we find in different discussions of language (e.g., science and religion) similar distinctions between an originating image, symbol, or metaphor and a theory. Cf. Ian Barbour, *Myths, Models and Paradigms: A Comprehensive Study in Science and Religion* (New York: Harper and Row, 1974), and Sallie McFague, *Metaphorical Theology: Models of God in Religious Language* (Philadelphia: Fortress, 1982), pp. 1-29.

tion in its literal form, where the requirement for blood becomes an end in itself, making God to appear vindictive.

Third, theories connect the story of Jesus with the believers in a new time and place. By identifying the needs of their own context, the authors portray the saving power of Jesus in ways that draw a new generation into the believing community. This means, however, that the theories will display the freedom to interpret the story of Jesus in terms applicable to new situations. We see this already occurring in the New Testament. Paul interprets the meaning of Christ in relation to problems of sin and the law in quite different ways when dealing with Jewish and Gentile Christians. Likewise, when faced with the spiritual conflict of the Corinthians, he again breaks new ground in developing a gospel of reconciliation. Another dramatic example is the merger of the language of sacrifice for sin with the Passover imagery of the Exodus experience. In its original setting, the Passover celebration is not a sacrifice for sin, though Christian liturgy has united the two in an inseparable way.

The ability to connect Jesus with a new time and place might well be called the *contextual* value of theories. Each theory grows out of a particular culture with its needs and concerns. Could any theologian be more governed by a particular form of brokenness, and its overwhelming anxiety, than Martin Luther? But such particularity is found in all of the great exponents of atonement theory, be it Irenaeus, Athanasius, Augustine, or Anselm. At times the embrace of images and arguments is so bound to a personal and social context that it appears impossible to comprehend. This may well explain why certain theories rise and fall in recognition and use. But having noted this contextual character, one must still recognize why these basic theories continue in use. The theories we shall discuss have endured over time. They are not like the daily newspaper that is so important today, but discarded in a week, or even like the great sermon that from the distance of a later time has lost its power. Their persistence is best explained by their boldness in naming elements of the human condition that signify our fallenness (i.e., bondage, guilt, death, alienation, idolatry) in relation to the saving power of Christ. In light of this enduring character of the theories, it is more appropriate to speak not simply of their *contextual* value, but rather their *evangelical* value. By providing a cogent and powerful interpretation of Jesus, the great theories proclaim good news.

This discussion suggests that the *evangelical* value contains two elements: context and gospel. To propose that the *evangelical* value is achieved when good news is proclaimed to specific people assumes one knows what is the good news. It also raises the question whether context can control or destroy the formulation of the good news. The identification of Christianity with all manner of evil reminds us that being contextual is not always legitimate.

Thus the *evangelical* value requires that the gospel proclaimed be *faithful* as well as *relevant*. Such faithfulness must be tested by the witness to Jesus in the New Testament, by the creeds, and by the worship, faith, and life of a variety of Christian communities. That this is a complex task does not lessen the need for such critical reflection on context and gospel.

A corollary to the *evangelical* value of theories is that since they intend to connect Jesus with particular times and places, there will be many theories with endless revisions. Thus we have theories that relate to the issues of sin as disobedience and failure, with the grace of forgiveness the answer. In others, captivity and liberation tell the story. Anselm uses the issue of God's honor to deal with human violation of the creation and God's intent to restore it. For Athanasius, the primary issue is ontological: bondage to death and the possibility of the new creation. The list goes on. What this means is that we need to recognize and celebrate this diversity. It is part of the fullness of Christ that the salvation he brings relates to so many forms of human need. This also gives us a vantage point for recognizing that the theories speak to different issues and that they do not necessarily contradict one another. With such a rich and varied offering of interpretations of Jesus, it is no wonder that the church never codified one official interpretation.

C. Classification of the Theories

When one examines the many ways the traditions have defined the saving power of Christ, it soon becomes apparent that they do not all focus on the same issue. The reason is twofold: First, there is a variety of human needs and interests taken up in the drama of sin and redemption. Human sin, as an act for which one is guilty, is quite different from the overwhelming sense of being in bondage to powers beyond one's control. The moral sense of failure is also quite different from the longing for the true knowledge of God or the hope for a world reconciled. It is quite appropriate, therefore, that images and theories should focus on distinctive issues that relate to specific aspects of the human problem and the saving power of God. Second, very often the overriding issue is not the resolution of a particular human problem but an affirmation regarding God. What drives some theories is something in God, and the outcome is something far exceeding a single aspect of salvation. It is more appropriately called a revealing of God's purposes. For such theories, Christ represents something about God's relation to the creation.

Since atonement theories are not all about the same thing, I have grouped them into several categories. There is nothing final about this alignment, and from other perspectives one could organize them in a different way. The organizational plan used here does express the assumption, to be demonstrated as we proceed, that more than one or three categories are needed to differentiate the many theories of atonement. Therefore the organization presented here first notes four broad headings, under which ten specific theories are grouped. In one case, one heading includes only one theory (Liberation). While this may seem to be a flaw in the outline, the theory of liberation could easily be subdivided, given its many versions over the centuries and its current usage throughout world Christianity.

It should also be noted here that an outline functions to list distinct positions. As best as I can determine, the four headings cannot, or should not, be reduced to one another. Likewise, each of the ten theories possesses a distinct purpose that is best not collapsed into another theory, or considered merely as a subpoint of one of the others. Most important, I have tried to present four headings and ten theories as viable positions. Some theories are not simply presented for the purpose of denunciation or as a foil for the *one and true* theory of atonement. To be sure, I have great difficulty in accepting the theory of penal substitution and believe that it is in need of major reconstruction. But because it is affirmed in major branches of the church, it must be taken very seriously and therefore is included. The magnitude of the current debate over this theory indicates the need for further study as well as conversation between both sides. This will not happen if it is excluded from the discussion.

The four headings or sections used to organize the ten theories are:

1. *Christ Died for Us*

The first group of theories pertains to sin, the moral life, and the impact of sin on the relation of humanity to God. These theories deal with sin by reference to the law, human failure, guilt, and redemption. In all of them salvation involves forgiveness and freedom from sin. But they differ by virtue of their focus and the dominant images they employ: sacrifice, justification by grace, or penal substitution.

2. *The Liberation from Sin, Death, and Demonic Powers*

Like the first group, this approach is also concerned with sin, but expands the problem to include the powers of evil, death, and Satan. The tension, therefore, is between God and all of the destructive powers: sin, death, and demonic power. The key categories here will be liberation and the conquest of all the powers. The affirmation of liberation appears in the earliest Christian witness and throughout the New Testament. The theme is found in all periods of Christian proclamation and has had a major revival in the last part of the twentieth century. The cases include Irenaeus, Jürgen Moltmann, James Cone, Gustavo Gutiérrez, and feminist writers.

3. The Purposes of God

Some theories include affirmations of forgiveness and new life, but treat them as subordinate themes to a larger drama. This has to do with God and God's eternal purposes. The subthemes are caught up in a revealing of a greater glory as represented by the renewal of the creation, the restoration of creation, or even the final goal of creation.

The selection of three theories and their representatives under this heading will no doubt surprise many readers. What do Athanasius, Anselm, and Schleiermacher have in common? All three of these writers are theologians of the incarnation. They are gathered together here because in each case, the dominant theme has to do with the revealing of God's purpose or glory. This conclusion may be easy to accept regarding Athanasius, the great exponent of the Incarnation and the Trinitarian affirmation regarding God. With Anselm, the case will be made that the issue at work in his classic text is not penal substitution but the restitution of the honor of God, precipitated by the violation done to the creation. With words that echo Athanasius, Anselm presses the question: What was God to do? As will be argued, it is all about God and God's faithfulness to a divine purpose. Finally, few figures have been vilified more than Friedrich Schleiermacher. Our reading of his major text will argue that it is God's eternal purpose that ordains the redemption brought by Christ. Something new is happening that far exceeds the forgiveness of sins. The primary concern is with God and the new life Christ brings. To be sure, this new life overcomes the problems of the fall. But it is not simply dictated by human need and it is more than the forgiveness of sins. The story of Jesus Christ is really about God and God's divine intention for the world.

4. Reconciliation

Some theories, while acknowledging the value of everything mentioned above, nevertheless see Christ as the Reconciler. This broad category easily subdivides into variations on the theme. One form of this has to do with the restoration of the true knowledge of God. Given the unique way Jews and Christians understand such knowledge, the healing of our minds involves an act of reconciliation. In Augustine, Calvin, and H. Richard Niebuhr, Jesus is the Way to the true knowledge of God and ourselves. A second form deals with reconciliation between conflicted groups. In this formulation (1 Corinthians 1–2), Jesus is the Reconciler creating unity and peace. Finally, there is the oft-repeated affirmation that Jesus is the demonstration of the wondrous love of God, thereby drawing us back to God. The basic form of this view is presented by Abelard, but two variations are included: one is the way John and Charles Wesley use the wondrous love of God as the motivation and overarching theme for the saving work of Christ; the other is the suffering of the crucified God in the writings of Jürgen Moltmann. In all of these cases the problem is alienation, and the solution is reconciliation.

The ten theories gathered under these four headings are:

    I. Christ Died for Us: Sacrifice

    II. Christ Died for Us: Justification by Grace

    III. Christ Died for Us: Penal Substitution

    IV. Liberation from Sin, Death, and Demonic Powers

    V. The Purposes of God: The Renewal of the Creation

    VI. The Purposes of God: The Restoration of the Creation

    VII. The Purposes of God: Christ the Goal of the Creation

    VIII. Reconciliation: Christ the Way to the Knowledge of God

    IX. Reconciliation: Christ the Reconciler

    X. Reconciliation: The Wondrous Love of God

Part One   Theories of Atonement

A. Christ Died for Us

For I handed on to you as of first importance what I in turn had received: that Christ died for us for our sins.

1 CORINTHIANS 15:3

Introduction

All Christian proclamation relates the life, death, and resurrection of Jesus to the forgiveness of sin. The three theories presented in Section A attempt to name that relation by interpreting cross and resurrection from different perspectives: sacrifice, justification by grace, and penal substitution. In terms of the controlling image and general theology, the three represent very distinctive approaches. But there are similarities in structure and language. The language of the three is often intertwined in Scripture, liturgy, hymnody, and preaching. Indeed, many Christians would assume that all three are part of one common theme. All move to the same conclusion: on the cross Jesus died for us and for our salvation.

We have, then, reasons for treating these three theories together and separately. Recognizing the value of both procedures, we have placed them together in this section, with a common introduction. Many of the things we need to say about one must be said of all. It would be both repetitive and confusing to introduce and review each theory separately. But some differentiation is needed, and they will be examined separately in this order: The theme of sacrifice, with its appeal to the tradition of sacrifice in Scripture and Jewish traditions of the first century, stands in marked contrast to the other two theories, which approach the cross from the standpoint of legal imagery and the overriding concern for the righteousness of God. Therefore, the theme of sacrifice will be considered separately in Chapter One. The use of legal imagery appears to unite the two other major theories relating to the forgiveness of sin — justification by grace and penal substitution. But in fact they are quite different and require separate treatment. Therefore, they will be presented separately in Chapters Two and Three.

Though the three theories are well known by Roman Catholics and Protestants, nevertheless, they have had a stormy history. For those in favor of the theories, the imagery of Christ dying for us defines their theology as well as their liturgy, hymns, and preaching. Advocates find in these theories indispensable articles of faith: Christ's atoning death, redemption by his blood, and the cross as the means of salvation. For those troubled by the theories, the graphic presentation of sacrificial death and/or penal substitution constitutes an unpardonable distortion of the very good news the theories seek to present. Instead of embodying *theological* and *evangelical* values central to faith, they repel some people from faith.

As a consequence, we must acknowledge at the beginning that these theories have something of a double life. One or more can be a wonderful solution to the need to interpret Jesus, or one or more can be a contentious problem. Part of our task, then, is to try to unravel this ambivalence. Is the problem in the root images themselves, in the way they are developed, or only in some errant formulations? Like so many doctrines with a long history, it is not hard to imagine that they could develop in unfortunate ways, or even be distorted. But shall we reject certain distortions or the entire theory? The ultimate question will be to determine in what sense these three theories are viable today.

Let us begin by asking the general question: Why have these theories persisted over time, with such great impact on Christian faith? One answer is that these theories portray the human situation in radically honest terms and represent the deep need for reconciliation with God and one another. If we consider the biblical narrative from Genesis 3 onward, human life is marked by self-centeredness, disobedience, anger, and violence. Such acts are interpreted as breaking faith with the covenants of God and with one another. From priest and prophet there is the persistent call to repent, to atone for one's sins and to reclaim the covenant of God. The theories before us stand in this broad tradition, describing the human situation as alienated from God by the barrier of sin. By their interpretations of the cross, they heighten our awareness of our estrangement, but also open before us the possibility of forgiveness. In the final sense, each theory intends to be an image of grace in a broken and bitter world. Thus it can be said that for those partial to these theories, they possess great *symbolic* value, i.e., they symbolize something about Jesus that connects saving power to our needs.

A second answer is that they maintain, against human optimism and self-centeredness, a view of God where love can never be separated from holiness. If there is realism in the Bible regarding the human condition, there is a boldness to speak of the sovereign God in ways that far transcend our interests and needs. The issues of sin and forgiveness must always be worked out in the presence of a holy God. To affirm that God is gracious and loving only heightens the tension, since now any reconciliation between God and Israel must involve the tension between the divine justice and love. In one sense the entire Old Testament is the story of this tension, played out on two levels: the interaction between God and humankind and the tensions within God between justice and love. That there is a wide range of solutions testifies to the complexity of the matter. At this point it is too early to look at ways this dilemma is resolved. Instead it must simply be recognized that the very scriptures accepted by the early Christians require them to think about God in a particular way, namely, as the sovereign and holy God who has covenanted with Israel. Jesus himself sets the tone when, in his first utterance in Mark, he calls for repentance in the presence of the Rule of God (1:15).

The two answers easily merge to create a mindset where human sin cannot be merely dismissed and the tension between the divine justice and love is not easily resolved. All three theories before us assume that we cannot ignore the problem. To deny the divine holiness (and its troublesome expression: *wrath*) in favor of an all-accepting love inevitably leads to distortions in both the view of God and human life. It would also involve discounting major portions of both Testaments. These three theories are attempts to affirm redemption by the cross without compromising the divine love or justice. In spite of the fact that we may ultimately be dissatisfied with one or more of these theories, we need to respect the commitments they bring to the interpretations of Jesus.

Having described the general context, let us now turn to the interpretation of Jesus. But instead of proceeding directly to passages in the New Testament, let us attempt to set the stage. We need to remember that the New Testament already represents a complicated development and the interface of multiple traditions. Let us step back and consider in our imaginations the earliest Christians prior to the written letters and gospels. What did these women and men know and assume in that time when faith was in the process of formation? Here I shall risk several statements.

First, that this was a post-resurrection community. All of their memories about what Jesus did and said, about how they related to him, were now in the process of reconsideration in light of the resurrection. If Jesus has been raised to be Lord, then everything must be reevaluated. This cannot be emphasized enough. Everything — God, Jesus, the scriptures, as well as their own lives — had to be rethought in light of Jesus' resurrection.

Second, the resurrection must be interpreted in light of his life and death. It is always Jesus, the teacher from Nazareth, the worker of signs and wonders who proclaimed the Rule of God, who was crucified, who has now been raised. But remembering Jesus' life and death was not easy to do, given the multiple interpretations:

a. Their opponents saw Jesus' death as a sign of defeat and presented a very different interpretation of his life.

b. The disciples themselves did not understand either his life or his death. The gospels quite clearly make this point by portraying the disciples in their resistance and fear prior to Good Friday, as well as their depression and confusion afterwards.

c. The only one who connects the mission of Jesus with his suffering is Jesus. Such a judgment opens the door to the long and continuing debate as to how many of the sayings regarding imminent suffering and death are from Jesus. Indeed it is precarious to base theological arguments on highly complicated and contested readings of Scripture. But it may not be necessary to wait until this matter is resolved (if it ever is resolved!). We will proceed by assuming that there is some connection between these sayings as a group and Jesus himself. There is no doubt that some of these statements are post-resurrection sayings or have been embellished in light of the resurrection. But it is doubtful that all of these sayings have no connection to Jesus. To reject all of them, in their current form or even in seminal form, would posit a Jesus who did not see any connection between his purpose and his suffering and death. That would mean that his death came as a complete surprise to him and that the disciples were justified in opposing it. For the purposes of this discussion, therefore, we are only assuming some link between Jesus and these sayings. If this is correct, it would suggest that the disciples' reconsideration of Jesus' death was in part prompted by remembrance of Jesus' own teaching. This is said even though in Luke, it is the risen Jesus who interprets the meaning of his life and death according to the scriptures (24:27).

Third, the task facing the early Christians, therefore, was to reinterpret from the beginning to the present their encounter with Jesus. To do this, they turned to their scriptures and their religious practices and traditions. These were used in the context of their new freedom and power in the Spirit, the tensions with Jewish authorities, as well as the new crisis created by the admission of Gentiles.

The purpose of this exercise of imagining that time between resurrection and resolute preaching and teaching (as well as written documents) is to make the point that the early Christians had to come to terms with Jesus' death. To be sure, the resurrection was the pivotal event. But it could not be given meaning apart from Jesus' death. There is no evidence in the New Testament for claiming the resurrection while ignoring the crucifixion. On the contrary, there is the overwhelming assumption that everything that happened for the good in this encounter with Jesus stems as much from his death as his resurrection. In some way it is a causative factor essential to the story.

There is no getting around his death. Even far more important, they do not seem to want to relegate his death to inconsequential details. Thus they begin to gather together their memories of Jesus and begin to explore names, titles, images, and metaphors that would enable them to interpret both the death and resurrection of Jesus.

The perspective suggested here may well be applied to all theories of atonement and not just the three theories immediately before us. But it constitutes a way of understanding these three theories, namely that of sacrifice, justification by grace, and substitutionary atonement. Whatever we say about the way the three theories develop, let us remember that each was an attempt to see in Jesus' death the saving grace of God: in one case, a sacrifice; in the two other cases, a demonstration of God's righteousness.

Chapter 1 Sacrifice

The Letter to the Hebrews

A. General Background

Several very powerful sacrificial images are used to interpret Jesus in the New Testament (e.g., Mark 14:22-25; John 1:29; Rom. 3:25; and the Letter to the Hebrews).[1] These images require that we examine the tradition of sacrifice in

---

1. The issue of the authenticity of sayings attributed to Jesus or other figures, such as John the Baptist, requires some explanation of our procedure in this study. At the level of *presentation* of identifiable theories that rely on New Testament passages, it is not necessary to determine in every case the origin of such passages. For example, whether the words of institution are actually from Jesus (Mark 14:22-25), or whether John the Baptist actually uttered the words in John 1:29 are appropriate and significant issues for understanding Jesus and John. But at the level of presentation of the theories it is not necessary to enter into the complicated discussions regarding authenticity. At another level, however, such issues can be highly relevant. When we engage in *evaluation* of theories, then the issue of authenticity may need to be discussed. This is especially the case if a theory seeks to justify its images and conclusions by reliance (be it implied or explicit) on the New Testament. But even here we must note that the theories develop a life of their own. While the use of language, images, or quotations from the New Testament always carries with it an implied claim of approval, in actual fact a theory may rely equally upon the experience of the Christian community, past and present, as the justification for certain images. Thus, for example, the viability of sacrificial language may appear to derive from Jesus' words in Mark 14. But in actual fact it may rely more on the experience of the suffering of the innocent the world over, who substantiate Jesus' words through their own loss. In such a case, historical-critical evidence that Jesus may not have uttered the specific words does not alter what some believers might claim to be true about such a passage: Jesus was broken and his blood poured out, just as we have experienced such brokenness in our lives. Such a situation does not make the issue of authenticity irrelevant. In those cases where a theory relies primarily on the authenticity of key passages, it will be crucial. But in those cases where a theory appeals to the New Testament and broader experience within the community of faith, the issue of authenticity in and of itself will not determine the outcome of an evaluation of the theory.

both ancient Israel and the time of Jesus. For our purposes, we shall restrict this discussion to sin offerings, which occur from the earliest times down to the more structured patterns in postexilic Judaism. These offerings were a ritual of atonement for sin, involving the death of an animal and the shedding and pouring of blood. But a great deal of caution is needed in connecting Jewish sacrificial practices to the interpretation of the New Testament, as well as in general theological application. One reason is the general lack of clarity as to how the wide range of sacrificial traditions (e.g., thank offerings, food offerings, and offerings for sin) developed over time. Even in the later Priestly stage there is an absence of a rationale for specific aspects of different types of sacrifice.[2] Another reason is the confusion created by what we bring to the texts. If, for example, thank offerings are offerings *to* God, it is easy for us to assume that sin offerings are also offered *to* God. Even worse, knowing a little or much about sacrificial traditions in Greco-Roman religions or in ancient cultures around the world, it is easy to assume that such practices give us clues for interpreting the language in Old or New Testament.

We can identify several important characteristics of sin offerings, keeping in mind that sin offerings are quite different from other types of sacrifice in the Old Testament. The first point is that sin offerings deal with purification of the sinner and/or the community.[3] They are not an exchange between humans and God. The sin offering must be seen in the context of the general view of sin itself. As a violation of covenantal law, sin breaks relation with God and other people. As a break in harmonious relations, it is seen as a stain or contagion that infects the person and the entire community.[4] Therefore there is the need for purification. To be sure, the broken relation must be restored, but sin itself is a burden that must be removed.

Second, the use of animal sacrifice relied on the idea of identification be-

---

2. Compare discussions of sacrifice in: Frederick Buchsel, "hilasterion," in *Theological Dictionary of the New Testament*, ed. Gerhard Kittel, trans. Geoffrey W. Bromiley (Grand Rapids: Eerdmans, 1965), vol. 3, pp. 319-23; B. Lang, "kipper," in *Theological Dictionary of the Old Testament*, ed. G. Johannes Botterweck, Helmer Ringgren, and Heinz-Josef Fahry, trans. David E. Green (Grand Rapids: Eerdmans, 1995), vol. 7, pp. 289-98; Gerhard von Rad, *Old Testament Theology*, trans. D. M. G. Stalker (New York: Harper and Row, 1962), vol. 1, pp. 251-70; T. H. Gastner, "Sacrifices and Offerings, Old Testament," in *The Interpreter's Dictionary of the Bible*, ed. George Arthur Buttrick (New York: Abingdon, 1962), vol. 4, pp. 147-59; G. Nagel, "Sacrifices: Old Testament," in *A Companion to the Bible*, ed. J. J. von Allmen (New York: Oxford University Press, 1958), pp. 378-80; James D. G. Dunn, *The Theology of Paul the Apostle* (Grand Rapids: Eerdmans, 1998), p. 218.

3. Compare Gastner, pp. 151-52; Dunn, p. 214; and Joseph A. Fitzmyer, *Paul and His Theology: A Brief Sketch*, 2nd ed. (Englewood Cliffs, N.J.: Prentice Hall, 1989), p. 65.

4. Cf. Lang, pp. 245-97; von Rad, p. 265.

tween the sinner and the animal.[5] This required several things: (a) since the purpose was purification, the animal needed to be pure, whole, and unblemished;[6] (b) to connect the sinner with the animal, the priest laid his hands on the animal, symbolizing the identification of humans with the sacrifice.

Third, the central act involved the blood of the animal, poured out and smeared on the altar.[7] For the Israelites, blood was the symbol of life. It was this life-bearing power of blood — not the death of the animal — that resulted in a change (cf. Lev. 17:11). The life of the unblemished animal represented the power to restore the defective life of the sinner. The key word for atonement literally means *to cover*. In effect, sin is covered by the life of the sacrifice. Having covered the offense that divides, the barrier is removed and the way is open for a renewal of relations between the two parties. When the Hebrew *kipper* is translated as atonement, or as in several cases in the New Testament as expiation, the original meaning of cover is lost. Such a loss prevents us from connecting references to blood in the New Testament with the covering (as well as sprinkling and smearing) of blood in the Jewish rituals. Only when we realize the full meaning of atonement as *covering* can we grasp the idea that the blood is directed toward sin and not an appeasement of God, i.e., it involves purification for sin.[8]

Fourth, the major exception to this basic form of animal sacrifice is, of course, the scapegoat in the ritual for the Day of Atonement. In this case the animal (note that it was a goat, not a lamb) became the bearer of the sins of the people and was literally led out of the city to the wilderness, dying not by ritual slaughter but falling from a cliff.[9] But this practice retains continuity with the basic concept of cover/remove: the scapegoat removes the sins from the people, thereby allowing for purification. It must also be noted that while sins are transferred to the scapegoat, the victim does not die vicariously for sinners; the death of the victim is not a substitute for a death penalty pronounced against a sinner.

---

5. Cf. Lang, pp. 295-97; von Rad, p. 265; J. C. Rylaarsdam, "Day of Atonement," in *The Interpreter's Dictionary of the Bible*, ed. George Arthur Buttrick (New York: Abingdon, 1962), vol. 1, p. 315; Gastner, p. 152.

6. This point is used repeatedly in Christian applications. Cf. the Letter to the Hebrews.

7. Cf. Lang, pp. 293-97; Fitzmyer, p. 64; Dunn, p. 214; Gastner, pp. 152-58.

8. Here we should note that the Hebrew *kipper* (atonement) connects with the word ransom, which *covers* or *removes* sinners from their sinful state. While ransom is usually associated with rescue from bondage and even military intervention, it has linkage with sacrificial traditions. In this regard one can only wonder about a connection between these words and a verse in 1 Peter 4:8: "love covers a multitude of sins."

9. Cf. Rylaarsdam, p. 315.

Fifth, there is strong agreement that the practice of sin offerings was given by God, who in grace and mercy initiates a means for the removal of the very sin that corrupts human beings and disrupts covenantal relations.[10] God is not the object of appeasement nor the recipient of payments in the form of valuable commodities. If the priests speak for God or act in God's name, it is because God has so appointed them to be agents of divine mercy. Here we can note that it is God who ransoms Israel, and this divine agency is consistently affirmed in New Testament uses that involve sacrificial imagery.

Finally, it must be noted that the Passover celebration is not a sin offering, but the festival marking the deliverance from Egypt. The Passover lamb is indeed slain, but not as a sacrifice for sin. Given this, we will have to deal with the fact that the New Testament presents us with an already accomplished *new* development, where the imagery of the Passover lamb is merged with the lamb sacrificed for the removal of sin. This is a major development, and its significance is overlooked by the general Christian reading of the New Testament that assumes that the two traditions were always united. The merger is present in the words of Jesus in presenting the bread and wine of the Lord's Supper. It is also present in the declaration attributed to John the Baptist: "Behold the Lamb of God, that takes away the sin of the world" (John 1:29).

When we turn to the New Testament, two things stand out. First, these writings indicate that the early Christian community has already incorporated sacrificial imagery in its understanding of Jesus. There we discover specific references as well as formal usage. While it is correct to see all of these uses as the basis for later development, this should not cause us to overlook the fact that the material has already undergone considerable development. Whether we can get behind the text of the New Testament and reconstruct that development is an open question. Second, outside of the fifteen references to sacrifice in the Letter to the Hebrews, the remaining references are limited in number. But these are highly significant uses of sacrificial imagery and related words, which have had tremendous impact. We shall review them by reference to key words.

1. Sacrifice

We shall omit discussion of passages that use the word sacrifice in reference to the general practice of sacrifice or to offerings we should make (cf. Rom. 12:1; Phil. 2:17 and 4:18; 1 Peter 2:5). Ephesians 5:2 affirms that Jesus gave himself

---

10. Cf. von Rad, pp. 269-70; Fitzmyer, pp. 64-65; Dunn, p. 214; Nagel, p. 378.

"for us, a fragrant offering and sacrifice to God." But no comment is offered on the meaning of such use, and the writer proceeds directly to moral admonition. It is, of course, in the Letter to the Hebrews that sacrificial imagery is worked into an extended argument describing Jesus as the true and final sacrifice. Since we will use Hebrews as a major example of this theory of atonement in the case studies that follow, we will defer further comment until that point. Outside of Hebrews, the important passages use related words but not the actual word sacrifice itself.

2. Hilasterion (Expiation/Atonement)

The word *hilasterion* appears in Romans 3:25 and 1 John 2:2 and 4:10. But the English translation is problematic: sometimes being rendered expiation (RSV and New English Bible) or atonement (NRSV). In the Septuagint *hilasterion* is used to refer to the lid of the ark of the covenant on the Day of Atonement, when it was covered with blood (Exod. 25:16).[11] Such usage connects with the idea of atonement as a covering of sin.

Romans 3:25 is a key passage involving *hilasterion.* While we are struck by the fact that the word sacrifice does not appear, it is clearly implied by the use of *hilasterion* and the word blood, emphasizing that atonement was effected by the shedding of blood: "Christ Jesus, whom God put forward as an expiation by his blood, to be received by faith" (RSV). Though the word blood is in the text, the New English Bible translates the phrase: "For God designed him to be the means of expiating sin by his sacrificial death, effective through faith." In this translation, blood is incorporated into an image *(sacrificial death),* which is implied but not actually spelled out in the Greek text. These variations in translations are emphasized, not to question whether Paul meant to use sacrificial imagery, but to illustrate the problem of interpreting this verse. The conclusion of verse 25 incorporates further reference to atoning sacrifice, when Paul says: "This was to show God's righteousness, because in his divine forbearance he had passed over former sins" (RSV). The word *paresin,* which literally means pass over, can be taken to mean letting go unpunished or remitting.[12] Such usage connects with the covering of sin offerings and/or the remitting of sins on the Day of Atonement and even with Passover.[13]

11. Cf. Buchsel, p. 319.

12. William F. Arndt and F. Wilbur Gingrich, *A Greek-English Lexicon of the New Testament* (Chicago: University of Chicago Press, 1957), p. 631.

13. The word *paresin* (pass over, remit) is used in the Septuagint in Exodus 12:11-12.

What then can we make of Paul's statement in Romans 3:25? Paul appears to be affirming that by the death on the cross ("by his blood"), God has removed our sin and brought us into a new relation.[14] Since blood was necessary as the decisive element in sin offerings, reference to Jesus' blood in this passage allowed Paul (and presumably the early church) to comprehend Jesus' death as a part of the saving event and to insist that it cannot be forgotten or minimized.[15] The point is not that Jesus changes the mind or heart of God, but that the event of Jesus' death is comparable to the means of atonement in the tradition of sin offerings and even on the Day of Atonement — all given by God for the deliverance from sin.

If we interpret Romans 3:25 in light of the tradition of sin offerings, then this passage should not be understood as appeasement of God, nor as a price to be paid to change the mind of God.[16] We also need to recall that the means of expiation was not a vicarious death, but the giving of life for the removal of sin/renewal of life. Such an interpretation is supported by the general view of Jesus' death in Romans and the other Pauline letters. Nowhere is God the object of appeasement, nor is Jesus' death, in and of itself, seen as something required by God to balance the scales of justice.

Such an interpretation need not overlook the fact that Paul does adapt the traditions in new ways. One is the integration of sacrificial language with the imagery of justification by faith (cf. 3:25) and its attendant legal imagery. Paul must have known that they are separate, yet he weaves them together: the death of Christ removes sin and reveals a righteousness that accepts or justifies sinners. The language of sacrifice and justification are so intertwined that the reader easily assumes they represent one theme.[17] A second innovation is the use of Paschal imagery, which is merged with sacrificial imagery (cf. 1 Cor. 5:7).[18] Here again we see a development that appears to be fully accepted by the early church, and we now move to that issue.

3. Lamb of God

There are six verses that name Jesus as the Lamb (John 1:29; 1 Cor. 5:7; 1 Peter 1:19; Rev. 5:6; 5:12; and 13:8). The point has already been made that the Paschal

14. Cf. Fitzmyer, pp. 59-65; Dunn, pp. 212-17, 231-33.
15. Cf. Buchsel, pp. 321-23; Fitzmyer, pp. 64-65; Dunn, pp. 214-15.
16. Cf. Buchsel, p. 320.
17. Dunn emphasizes that Paul freely uses multiple metaphors and combines them because no one image is adequate to express the full meaning of Christ. Cf. Dunn, pp. 231-33.
18. Dunn, p. 217.

tradition is separate from that of sacrificial sin offerings. This obviously requires a reorientation in our thinking, since Christians have been accustomed to think of the Paschal Lamb as being connected to atonement. In the references cited here, we see that the early church has made the transition to the merger of the Paschal tradition with that of sacrifice for sin. How and when this occurred will be difficult to assess. In John's gospel we see it clearly at work, though the date for this gospel is usually set quite late and probably reflects more of an accomplished fact, rather than an original idea. John 1:29 presents the declaration of John the Baptist: "Behold the Lamb of God, who takes away the sin of the world!" The notion of *taking away* is, of course, the primary image of the sacrifice in sin offerings noted above, which is accomplished only by the shedding of blood.[19]

But more to the point of origin regarding this merger of Paschal traditions with the removal of sin is the Last Supper in the synoptic gospels. There the crucial element of blood poured out for sin is connected with the making of a new covenant, all in the context of a Passover meal. As we have seen, blood shed/poured out was a key for the sin offering. Thus, while Jesus does not use the image of the Lamb, the general imagery of sacrifice is present in his words of institution, as well as in the decisive statement regarding "a ransom for many."

4. Ransom

In Mark 10:45 and Matthew 20:28 we have the major declaration that the Son of Man came to give his life as a ransom for many. In a decisive way Jesus connects his purpose with suffering, leading to deliverance. The only other reference to ransom appears in 1 Timothy 2:6. Ransom is a word that moves in more than one direction. In the Old Testament, ransom is used of God's rescue of Israel from bondage in Egypt (Isa. 43:3) as well as the return of Israel from exile (Isa. 35:10). Christians are accustomed to understanding ransom in terms of intervention leading to rescue, especially in ransom theories that take on the imagery of warfare between God and the devil. But ransom has connections with sacrifice, since the word itself is derived from the word for covering, used in sacrificial sin offerings.[20] Thus, these passages point to a sacrificial understanding of Jesus' death as well as the conquest of demonic powers.

---

19. For an extensive discussion of the interplay of themes from the Exodus Passover, the Suffering Servant of Isaiah, and the sacrificial use of the lamb, see Raymond E. Brown, *The Gospel According to John* (Garden City, N.Y.: Doubleday, 1966), vol. 1, pp. 58-66.

20. Cf. Lang, p. 293.

To conclude, the New Testament presents us with a variety of passages relating to sacrifice. Some powerful images are presented without further interpretation (e.g., ransom and Lamb). In the case of *hilasterion,* the image is used and connected with other images such as justification (Rom. 3:25). In Hebrews we have a fully developed argument regarding the meaning of Jesus in light of sacrifice and priesthood. Such variety suggests that the New Testament itself is more than a source, prior to serious reflection on the use of sacrifice, but already represents such a development. Moreover, it combines sacrificial imagery with the Passover tradition, thereby creating new imagery for a general theory of atonement. If there is any surprise in this development, it is that sacrificial imagery has not been used more. Perhaps its most powerful and abiding influence is in liturgy, hymnody, and Eucharist. In these broad areas, it continues to inspire art, words, music, and ritual.

B. The General Theory in Outline

There is, as with most general theories, considerable variation in the form of this theory. At the center is an argument consisting of a comparison based on likeness or similarity. If parts of the story of Jesus' life, death, and resurrection are like the basic structure and outcome of ritual sacrifice, then the image of sacrifice can be attributed to Jesus. Such a thought process might begin with the beginning or end of the crucifixion/resurrection cycle: If the former, his death is compared to the death involved in sacrifices for sin, leading to the conclusion that it results in a similar outcome. If the latter, the outcome of Jesus' death — a new relation with God — is likened to the outcome of ritual sacrifice, leading to the conclusion that his death was a sacrifice or expiation for sin. And of course, the two can be combined, producing the double claim that Jesus' death is a sacrifice because it results in a new covenant *and* Jesus died (i.e., had to die) because it was a sacrifice. In the Letter to the Hebrews, this type of reasoning proceeds from the basic positive comparison to the superlative, i.e., what happens in Jesus is even greater than the traditional ritual of sacrifice (7:15; 7:28; 8:6; 9:11; and 9:13). Here then is a basic outline for the sacrificial theory of atonement:

1. Created for life together in obedience to the holy and loving God, human beings rebelled and have violated the Law of God. Sin has corrupted the relations between human beings and with God.
2. To restore the relation, Jesus as the chosen one offers his life as a sacrifice for atonement with God, i.e., the innocent and obedient Son of God

27

takes upon himself the sins of the world in order to reconcile humanity with God. This image of sacrifice can take a variety of forms, depending on which classic source is made primary: e.g., the Suffering Servant imagery of Isaiah 53, the Passover image of the Lamb of God, the image of ransom in Mark, or the highly structured appeal in Hebrews to Jesus as the fulfillment of the priestly office. At this crucial point, theories divide:

   a. Jesus' action can be portrayed as the gracious will of God, who, according to John, sends and gives the beloved Son for the salvation of the world.

   b. Or, the theory can move in the opposite direction, namely, that Jesus' sacrifice is offered to God as a means of appeasing God and/or gaining salvation. This version will obviously provoke serious debate.

3. As a sacrifice in the tradition of sin offerings, the shedding of his blood removes sin and draws believers into a relation with God by faith, represented especially by the Eucharist, the sign of the new covenant in his body and blood.

C. A Witness of Faith: The Letter to the Hebrews

In our review of sacrificial imagery in the New Testament, we deferred discussion of the Letter to the Hebrews so that we might examine it as a case. Indeed, no writing has had a greater impact on the use of sacrificial imagery in Christology and liturgy than this work. Hebrews is a complex yet highly organized affirmation of Jesus Christ as the Son of God, who in his suffering and death inaugurates a new covenant and is now seated at the right hand of God (1:1-4). The argument is both a vigorous defense of Christian faith in the face of the loss of converts and a powerful exhortation for struggling Christians to remain faithful. In style, Hebrews is tightly woven together, using memorable visual images that have come down to us in liturgy and preaching. A first-time reader would be surprised to discover the origin of images already quite familiar. But what elevates this work is the unity or coherence between the Christological claims and the exhortations. All of the arguments about Christ relate directly to the admonitions to look to Jesus, remain faithful, and to trust God's promise of reaching the heavenly Jerusalem (12:22).

What attracts us at this point is the reliance on imagery of sacrifice. Hebrews describes the major work of Christ as the creation of a new covenant, providing new access to God. Salvation is repeatedly defined as redemption or purification from sin through the atoning sacrifice offered by Christ. It is Jesus who is the high priest, only in this case the sacrifice is Jesus himself, in his obedience, faithfulness, and blood. As priest and sacrifice, Jesus replicates the basic requirements for ritual sacrifice, but also surpasses them. The writer thus draws us to the conclusion that Jesus both fulfills the requirements for sacrifice for sin and sets them aside by providing, in the now famous phrase, *a once-for-all* sacrifice (7:27; 9:25; 10:10).

While this highlights the dominant theme of Hebrews, it should not be overlooked that it is not the only theme. There are at least two other themes that elevate the priestly work of Jesus. One is the theme of the incarnation of the Son of God, whom God "appointed the heir of all things, through whom also he created the world" (1:2). This one, who is the revelation of God in "these last days" (1:1), reflects God's glory and "bears the very stamp of his nature, upholding the universe by his word of power" (1:3). He is now seated at the right hand of God. As an introduction for what is to come, the author could not have made greater claims for Jesus, with respect to authority, power, or honor. These statements, in and of themselves, already constitute good reason for *looking to Jesus* (12:2). Whether the author was in contact with Pauline or Johannine traditions is unknown, but the reader can see connections with a variety of texts (e.g., Phil. 2 and John 1). Moreover, the author anticipates the arguments of Athanasius against Arius in his claim that the Son became one of us in order to destroy death (2:14), was tempted in order to help those who are tempted (2:18), and to sympathize with our weakness (4:15). What all this means is that the priestly office and work of Christ — the central point of the letter — are placed in a rich theological context involving incarnation and God's design for salvation.

A second theme that also complements the sacrificial motif is the defeat of the devil. In 2:14-15 the author declares:

> Since therefore the children share in flesh and blood, he himself likewise partook of the same nature, that through death he might destroy him who has the power of death, that is, the devil, and deliver all those who through fear of death were subject to lifelong bondage.

To add this theme with that of incarnation only strengthens the author's claim regarding Jesus and the need to keep faith in him. While redemption as purification will preoccupy the author in most of the letter, here it is clear that Jesus also brings redemption by the defeat of death and the devil. Note also that is not by a payment to the devil but by the devil's defeat.[21] All of this

---

21. Craig R. Koester, *Hebrews: A New Translation with Introduction and Commentary*, vol. 36, *The Anchor Bible* (New York: Doubleday, 2001), pp. 412-13.

adds strength to the author's claim that the Jesus who suffers and dies is this Jesus: Son of God, the agent of creation, the Victor over death.

There appears to be no agreement as to the outline of the letter, in spite of the fact that Hebrews is perceived as a tightly constructed argument.[22] Such disagreement may stem from the fact that the letter is made up of many arguments and exhortations that can be organized in numerous ways.[23] For our purposes we need not resolve this. Craig Koester identifies three arguments, though they are more like themes that cannot be contained in the identified chapters because the author moves back and forth between them.[24] But what holds the many themes together is the general argument that we must attend to Jesus, the pioneer of faith and the mediator of the new covenant through his sacrificial death. We will organize our interpretation of the letter around the three themes identified by Koester.

1. The first theme is that Jesus, as the Son of God, is made perfect through his suffering and death. This is, indeed, a paradoxical statement and typical of the New Testament's attempt to interpret Jesus. To claim that Jesus is Son of God, Word and Christ, *and* at the same time the rejected and crucified constitutes an essential problem for Christian proclamation. Instead of ignoring the contradiction, the author of Hebrews boldly resolves the tension in the first four verses. It is by the design and will of God that the agent of creation should also be present among us, making purification and offering a new covenant. Why should the one who is superior to the angels and Moses, who now sits at the right hand of God, endure suffering and death? The intensity of this question was no less for the first readers than it is for our time, when objections are raised against extolling suffering and death.

In one sense the author's answer is found in the introduction of the image of sacrifice as a way of explaining Jesus' death. Once again we must bear in mind that the author, like the early church, is faced with an accomplished fact: salvation has come through the life, death, and resurrection of Jesus. But to answer the question, Why did he suffer?, by simply introducing the concept of sacrifice is to move in circles. In what sense does sacrifice, as an interpretative device, answer the question?

22. Cf. the review of the many ways the letter is outlined: Koester, pp. 83-86.

23. For example, Koester isolates 7:1–10:25 as the second argument regarding Jesus' suffering leading to a new covenant (Koester, p. 85). It is in this section that the major comparison of Melchizedek, the Levitical priesthood, and Jesus takes place, with all the comparisons and contrasts. But Melchizedek has already been introduced in 5:6 and referred to in 5:10 and 6:20. Thus there may well be something about the author's style itself that resists the strict isolation of themes.

24. Koester, pp. 84-86.

The author provides two ideas to justify Jesus' suffering, though each requires further explanation. One is *fitting* (cf. 2:10; 7:26), the other is *made perfect or completed* (2:10; 5:8-10). They appear together in 2:10-11:

> For it was fitting that he, for whom and by whom all things exist, in bringing many sons to glory, should make the pioneer of their salvation perfect through suffering. For he who sanctifies and those who are sanctified have all one origin.

To say something was *fitting* only raises the question: Fitting according to what? Certainly not according to the ideas of divine transcendence in Gnosticism or even Arius, where the eternal Word cannot become flesh and blood. Nor was it fitting for a Jew to be rejected and crucified. Similar questions arise with the second image, that Jesus is *perfected* or *made complete* in his suffering. This image is repeated in 5:8-10:

> Although he was a Son, he learned obedience through what he suffered; and being made perfect he became the source of eternal salvation to all who obey him, being designated by God a high priest after the order of Melchizedek.

There is no indication in the letter that suffering is an end in itself, nor that God demands suffering or death in payment for sin. In what follows, Hebrews remains within the general boundaries of our review of Old Testament practices, i.e., sacrifice relates to purification for sin and is not a payment to appease God. Just as God gave the practice of sacrifice in order to make atonement possible, so in Hebrews 1:1-4, God is the one who sends and appoints the Son to effect salvation. Given this initial declaration, it is more appropriate to understand Jesus' suffering from the standpoint of this divine purpose for the redemption of the world. Jesus is perfected in his suffering and obedience if we presuppose that it is the will of God to create the world for a holy purpose and to redeem it in love. Likewise, only on these terms is it *fitting* for the Son to be like us *in every respect* (2:17; 4:15). If it is the very nature of God and God's anointed to redeem the world, then the images *fitting* and *perfection* make sense.[25]

This interpretation is supported by the fact that the means of this perfection relate to the very nature of the redemption. Jesus' obedience and faithful-

---

25. One of the lines of influence that extends from Hebrews is the use of the word *fitting*. As we shall see in our discussion of Athanasius' *On the Incarnation of the Word*, the word appears there as a way of understanding the incarnation.

ness must be seen in light of: (a) Adam's disobedience and that of the readers; (b) the sin and the violence of all of the world's powers. In the context of such disobedience, the shedding of his own blood for us embodies the life of obedience that becomes "the source of salvation" (5:9) and makes him the "pioneer and perfecter of our faith" (12:2). The exhortation directed to the readers regarding obedience and faithfulness is based on the new way of obedience Jesus offers to those who believe in him. We have, then, in this first theme, an answer to the question: Why did Jesus, as Son of God, die on the cross? For Hebrews, the answer is clear: for our salvation and God's glory.

2. The second theme goes to the matter of what actually happens, as well as how this happens in his death. Hebrews portrays Jesus as the mediator of a new covenant, who claims the office of high priest and gives his life as a sacrifice. There then follows a complicated and extended argument involving comparison with the Levitical priesthood. As noted above, the argument consists of establishing the likeness between Jesus and the sacrificial tradition. But since Jesus' death is in many ways different from the sacrifice of sin offerings, such a comparison leads to as many contrasts as similarities. This requires the author to find a point of comparison other than the Levitical system, which is done by the introduction of Melchizedek. As a result, the argument in Hebrews is complicated by a double comparison of Jesus with Melchizedek and the Levitical system, leading to a double conclusion: first, that Jesus' suffering is a sacrifice for sin, and second, that it surpasses the entire Levitical system. The main points can be summarized as follows:

1. If Moses is the servant of God, Jesus is the Son of God (3:5-6).
2. Levitical priests originate from Aaron, serve limited times, and are many in number; Jesus is the sole priest serving forever, in line with Melchizedek, who is a priest forever (7:3).
3. The Levitical priests serve an imperfect system where disobedience persists; Jesus is made perfect in his obedience (7:11-25). The order of Melchizedek represents a new order, apart from the order of Aaron, based not on descent from Aaron but "the power of an indestructible life" (7:16). The old law is set aside because the "better hope is introduced, through which we draw near to God" (7:19).
4. The priests offer daily sacrifices of blood from animals; Jesus offers his own blood, once and for all. But just as the animals for sacrifice were unblemished, so Jesus was blameless and can be in his own body a sacrifice for purification from sin.
5. If the high priest enters the Holy of Holies each year, Jesus enters a more perfect tent once for all (9:6-12).

6. If the earthly tent is but a copy or shadow of heavenly things, Jesus enters the true and heavenly tent and is now seated at the right hand of God (8:4; 9:23; 10:1).
7. If Moses is the mediator of the old covenant based on Law, Jesus is the mediator of a new covenant in his own blood (7:15), based on the promises of God in Jeremiah 31 (8:6-13) and achieving the perfection promised in the old law (10:1).

These comparisons are woven together and always press the point that Jesus was appointed by God to make sacrifice for sin. In one important case, the likeness is a simple or positive comparison: as the animal sacrificed must be unblemished, so Jesus was blameless. But in most cases, the comparison proceeds to the superlative: whatever the old system did or possessed, Jesus is *more or greater* (cf. 7:15; 7:28; 8:6; 9:11; and 9:13). Taken as a whole, the extended argument gives legitimacy for understanding Jesus' suffering and death in the language of sacrifice. As such, Jesus' obedience and the shedding of his blood is a purification for sin and provides access to God, just as on the Day of Atonement. But the emphasis on the superlative goes well beyond this basic comparison: Jesus surpasses the Levitical priesthood in authority, permanence, and access to God. He abolishes the old system and offers purification and sanctification by faith (cf. 10:1-25).

3. The third theme extols Jesus as the pioneer and perfecter of faith — both his and ours — as we journey to the city of the living God (12:2 and 22). Therefore, as we remember the saints who journeyed in faith (ch. 11), and as we ourselves struggle to find and/or keep faith, we look to this Jesus, the faithful and obedient servant of God (ch. 12). The groundwork for this theme is laid in the chronicle of saints in chapter 11 and concludes with the exhortation to seek the heavenly Jerusalem (12:22). This pilgrimage is not easy and is filled with hazards and affliction. The imagery of the pilgrimage envisions many dangers, since even God will shake earth and heaven (12:26). Hard-pressed on every side, pilgrims are called to go outside the security of the city/camp, for Jesus was crucified outside the camp (13:16). But in their search for the heavenly city, they shall be led by Jesus, the pioneer of faith. The vision of the heavenly Jerusalem harks back to the references to seek the true rest (3:18; 4:9; and 4:11). From beginning to end, Hebrews connects the plan of God with the crucifixion and exaltation of Jesus, joining Christological affirmations with a vision of the Christian life.

The Letter to the Hebrews is the first attempt to take isolated references to sacrifice and/or ransom and develop them into a broader Christological statement. The fact that it was included in the New Testament testifies to its impor-

tance in the early church as well as its continuing influence to this day. Hebrews presents a general theory of atonement: an image becomes the basis for
understanding the meaning of Jesus' life, death, and resurrection. It takes the
horrible event of Jesus' death and brings it into the known world of Jewish rituals, making it comprehensible as a saving event. Indeed, there is irony here,
since the curse and defilement of Jesus' death outside the gate are removed by
redefining his death with the very language from the temple within the gate.
Moreover, all of the comparisons regarding Jesus and the Levitical priesthood
are placed in the broader context of God's plan for salvation and are finally
connected with the precarious situation of early believers. The benefits of Jesus' sacrifice are communicated through repentance, faith, and obedience, as
followers take up their pilgrimage in a world where there is no security.

As a general theory, however, the main argument regarding sacrifice leads
to a conclusion that is far more complex and even paradoxical. The conclusion moves in two opposing directions, each representing a different evaluation of sacrifice: (a) Jesus fulfills the requirements of priestly sacrifice, i.e., by
his death he brings purification for sin and opens a way for us to God; (b) Jesus so surpasses the Levitical system that sacrifice is actually abolished. If the
former honors the ritual of sacrifice by employing it in Christological interpretation, the latter brings it to a complete end in the once-for-all sacrifice of
Christ, replacing it with the spiritual acts of repentance and purification by
faith in Jesus Christ. Whereas the former keeps the door open for continuity
with Jewish traditions, the latter appears to close that door, sometimes quite
harshly.

The use of Melchizedek illustrates the tension present in this twofold appraisal of sacrifice: Melchizedek is introduced as a priest with whom Jesus can
be identified; yet Melchizedek is outside the tradition of Levitical priesthood.
The author can thus make his double point: Jesus is truly a priest, but not like
the Levites. There is at work here in the use of Melchizedek a rhetorical move
broadly similar to Paul's use of Abraham in Romans and Galatians. In those
letters, Paul uses Abraham to demonstrate that someone was declared righteous by faith apart from the Law, thereby establishing scriptural authority
for affirming salvation apart from the Law. Here in Hebrews, the author
wants to affirm priestly sacrifice yet justify a priestly role outside of the
Levitical tradition. With Melchizedek, the author has scriptural authority for
affirming both the tradition of sacrifice, yet rejecting the Levitical tradition.
The fact that at times the comparisons are strained and overextended, with
considerable hyperbole, makes it difficult to accept the argument in all of its
details. For example, there is actually nothing in the Melchizedek story to require the end of sacrifice. The real argument for suspending Levitical sacrifice

rests squarely on the finality of the redemption brought by Christ's death and resurrection (cf. 8:6 and 13; 9:11-15).

There is another important example that represents a counterargument against the continued use of sacrificial imagery. This has to do with Jesus' being crucified outside the *camp* (13:11). In the main argument, the author pointed out that the sacrifices (i.e., those made daily and on the Day of Atonement) took place within the camp and/or tent. But here in the last chapter he reminds readers that the bodies of animals, whose blood was used within the tent, were burned outside the camp. So with Jesus: he was crucified and his blood was shed outside the gate of Jerusalem. Christians are called, therefore, to leave the sanctity of the city and the tent and to go outside the gate where Jesus suffered (13:12). This connects with chapter 11, where the saints lived by faith in the promises of God, though never receiving the promises. It also connects with chapter 12, where they are exhorted to "lift up their drooping hands and strengthen their weak knees" in the pilgrimage toward Mount Zion and the heavenly Jerusalem. God will shake earth and heavens, but what is unshakable will remain, namely, the heavenly sanctuary where Jesus has made a once-for-all sacrifice for our salvation. Here again, as with the Melchizedek example, we have affirmation of like and unlike. Jesus is like the practice of sacrifice in ways that allow him to be called a priest and his death a sacrifice, but the actual facts of his crucifixion virtually shatter the official practice. His sacrifice is offered outside the gate in the face of defilement and abuse.

On careful analysis, therefore, Hebrews reveals a complex use of the sacrificial image. The positive use brings the horrible event of Jesus' death into the known world of Jewish rituals, making it comprehensible as an act of atonement. But at the same time, the author makes it clear that Jesus brings to an end the entire system because the work of Christ is ultimate and stands forever. The ritual of sacrifice therefore ends, with its imagery incorporated into a new covenant where the cross of Jesus becomes the focal point and proclamation of his death calls hearers to obedience and faith in the promises of God.[26]

D. Critical Issues in the Use of the Image of Sacrifice

Two things stand out when we step back to assess the image of sacrifice. First, sacrifice provided the early Christians with an image from their authoritative

---

26. Koester, pp. 439-42.

tradition and practice for interpreting Jesus' death and resurrection. Since the image itself was drawn from cultic rituals dealing with sin and forgiveness, it was a natural way to see in Jesus an atoning event. When the traditions of sin offerings and the Paschal sacrifice were combined and then connected to the Lord's Supper, all of the rich meanings from the Exodus experience of redemption as well as the regular worship of the community were made available for seeing in Jesus the saving power of God.

Second, the image quickly entered the theological and liturgical traditions of the church and continues to be a major category for interpreting Jesus. The concept of sacrifice is virtually a constant in Christological discussions of the work of Christ down through the Reformers. Even in figures such as Athanasius, where it is subordinated to other themes, it is included as a minor theme in his interpretation of Christ. The same constancy appears in the liturgical practice of the Lord's Supper. From the liturgies of the early centuries to the reform of Gregory in 604 and through the Middle Ages, the image of sacrifice is at the heart of the Eucharist. Indeed, it is difficult to separate the formation of the doctrinal tradition from that of the liturgical tradition. The two are so intertwined that it would be precarious to suggest that one came first, or that one is cause and the other effect. The reason for this is that both Christology and liturgy give expression to the evangelical proclamation that Jesus is Lord and Savior. If Nicea and Chalcedon insist, against much opposition, that it is truly God present in Jesus, the liturgy of the Eucharist insists that such divine presence is for our salvation.

To recognize the high status and persistence of the image does not, however, deny its problematic character. Whereas Hebrews stays clearly within the tradition of sin offering for purification, given by God, later developments too easily move in the direction of sacrifice as something given to God for the sake of gaining salvation. In some respects, this difficulty is foreshadowed in Hebrews, where on the one hand, the details of Jesus' passion do not exactly fit the details of the practice of sin offerings, and on the other hand, the practice of sacrifice is abolished by the once-for-all sacrifice of Jesus. The problems are exposed in the Reformation's rejection of the Roman Mass and the ensuing tendency to subordinate *sacrifice* to other atonement themes. Luther continues to use it in speaking of the work of Christ, but his critique of the Roman Mass required a revised understanding.[27] His basic charge that the Mass had become a work, offered by humans to God to effect their salvation, called into question any use of the word *sacrifice* that implies a human or up-

27. Cf. Martin Luther, "The Babylonian Captivity of the Church," trans. A. T. W. Steinhauser, *Three Treatises* (Philadelphia: Muhlenberg Press, 1960), pp. 123-78.

ward movement rather than a divine or downward movement. As we shall see, Calvin uses it as one of three Christological categories (Prophet, Priest, and King), but with great difficulty. In the twentieth century, both Karl Barth and Emil Brunner use it only by subordinating it to the themes of restoration of humanity, justification, and a strong emphasis on the love of God.[28] The Roman Catholic tradition, in spite of such criticism, continues to hold the image of sacrifice as essential to its theology and liturgical practice. As we shall see, from the Council of Trent to twentieth-century interpreters, the use of sacrifice in the Roman Mass is strongly defended.

To illustrate the problems, we shall look briefly at two striking examples of sacrificial imagery: Calvin's treatment of Christ's priestly office and the Roman Mass. In both cases, sacrificial imagery lies at the heart of the proclamation of the gospel, yet the language derived from it always carries a certain ambiguity that has the potential for subverting the intended evangelical message.

1. Sacrifice in Calvin's Institutes

In Book II of the *Institutes,* Calvin describes the priestly office of Christ, following descriptions of the prophetic and kingly.[29] To make the case that a divine/human mediator is required, Calvin reminds the reader that sin has divided us from God, that we are rightly judged to be guilty and face condemnation. Sin bars us from access to God, but just as important, the God who is righteous cannot accept us in our sin. Since God's wrath cannot arbitrarily be withdrawn, there can be no reconciliation without appeasing God's wrath.[30] Calvin repeatedly affirms that the defilement of creation is so great a matter that God must stand over against us as our enemy.[31]

The separation of God and humanity is resolved only by the descent of the divine/human mediator, who makes expiation for sin. With references to the tradition of sacrifice in the Old Testament and Hebrews, Calvin emphasizes the terms of this intervention: there can be no expiation without the

---

28. Cf. Karl Barth, *Church Dogmatics,* vol. IV: *The Doctrine of Reconciliation, Part I,* ed. G. W. Bromiley and T. F. Torrance, trans. G. W. Bromiley (Edinburgh: T. & T. Clark, 1956), pp. 273-83; and Emil Brunner, *The Mediator: A Study of the Central Doctrine of the Christian Faith,* trans. Olive Wyon (Philadelphia: Westminster, 1947), pp. 475-535.

29. John Calvin, *The Institutes of the Christian Religion,* ed. John T. McNeill, trans. Ford Lewis Battles, vol. 20 of The Library of Christian Classics, ed. John Baillie, John T. McNeill, and Henry P. Van Dusen (Philadelphia: Westminster, 1960), pp. 482-534.

30. Calvin, p. 503.

31. Calvin, pp. 504 and 506.

shedding of blood and death. The death must be voluntary and clearly offered as an expiation. He dies in our place, with our guilt transferred to him and the curse directed toward us now laid upon him. Thus Christ offers his life for us to God as an expiation to remove the wrath of God. In his death the old Adam (i.e., sinful humanity) dies; in his resurrection righteousness and life are restored.[32]

This summary is intended to emphasize: (1) that Calvin fully embraces a sacrificial view of atonement (along with several other theories); (2) that he does not refrain from using all of the language that is problematic for so many today: divine wrath and anger; God the enemy; and the ambiguous verbs *appease, propitiate, and expiate.* While Calvin will attempt to place all of this in a broader context that affirms an eternal love, we need to acknowledge that all of this language is there. While Calvin may not be responsible for latter-day readers who take a sentence or chapter out of context, or fail to see his final conclusion, nevertheless the fact is that his initial presentation of atonement as sacrifice is quite harsh. The impact of such language by one of the leading Reformers upon the history of Protestantism cannot be overestimated. Taking Calvin's presentation without any qualification, it exemplifies two dangers contained in sacrificial language.

The first is the issue of the primary agent. When Jesus offers his life as a sacrifice, is he acting on behalf of God or toward God? Stated in another way: Is God the subject or the object of Jesus' activity? If the former, then God is the active agent, but if the latter, then God is passive and the object of Jesus' activity. For purposes of our discussion, I shall name the problematic alternative in this contrast as *retributive atonement.*[33] Such a view operates on the as-

32. Cf. Calvin, pp. 501-25.

33. The choice of words to describe what has been considered a negative development in atonement theology is quite difficult. I have deliberately not chosen to name such a theology by the highly charged words *appeasement, propitiation, expiation,* or *satisfaction.* First, these words do not have precise meaning and are widely used in the tradition by so many writers, many of whom represent the antithesis of what I have called *retributive atonement.* For example, propitiate is used in some translations of Romans 3:25, but one could not imagine retributive atonement, as defined here, to be Paul's meaning. Likewise, it would be misleading to name the negative option *satisfaction atonement,* because the word satisfaction runs throughout Christian theology, with many writers using satisfaction in positive ways (cf. the discussion of Anselm in Chapter Five). Second, they are words so highly charged with negative meanings in other cultural contexts that it would be hard to take seriously a viewpoint so designated, even though one wishes to reject it. To refer to what I have identified as the negative option by the title *appeasement atonement* makes it difficult to have any serious discussion. Even though one wishes to reject the substance of such a view, it needs to be carefully considered, given its persistence through Christian history.

sumption that God cannot forgive or be reconciled with sinful humanity until retribution is made, either in the form of a punishment or in the form of an appeasement of the divine anger or holiness.

The second issue is the valuation given to the death of Jesus. Is the death of Jesus the cause of our salvation, because God demands it as some kind of payment or satisfaction for sin? Or, is Jesus' death to be evaluated in very different terms, for example, the consequence of Jesus' fidelity or a demonstration of solidarity with fallen humanity? If we take the former position that the death is itself the cause, this would imply that his death is the means to change God. Such a view adopts a *retributive* concept of the divine justice, i.e., God cannot love until the sacrifice is offered to balance the scales of justice or appease the anger of God.

Before we proceed, further explanation is needed as to why the idea of retribution is theologically a problematic concept. In human justice, the idea of retribution appeals to our basic sense of fairness as proportionality: punishment should equal the crime, and in the best of all worlds, provide compensation or restitution. But in reality, punishment seldom equals the actual financial loss or the personal distress. In serious acts of violence, punishment does not compensate or make actual restitution. In what sense can imprisonment or even capital punishment restore health or lost life? The only thing punishment appears to achieve is: (a) fulfill the appearance that some price is being paid to quell our anger and the desire for retaliation; (b) in cases of imprisonment, remove the offender from society for a period of time. These results of punishment should not be minimized or ignored. For those who are victims of violence, the mere idea of nothing being done is a great torment. In cases of extremely brutal murder, multiple murders, and large-scale crimes of genocide, many people support the death penalty not because it equals the crime but because it appears to be the least one can do to affirm justice. It can probably also be argued that while the death penalty does not prevent murder, it may prevent the taking of life in retribution, or what is called blood vengeance.

These comments suggest not that retribution is always wrong, but that in the realm of human justice it presents us with less than satisfying results. If, then, this is the case in human justice, in what sense can retribution be applied to the issue of atonement? There is no way that the punishment can equal the violation of God's purpose, nor can it provide compensation or restitution. But if the punishment cannot equal the offense, then that leaves us with the idea that the punishment per se is somehow satisfying to God. (One is struck by the double meaning of *satisfy*, implying a legal requirement as well as a psychological requirement.) Such an idea has repeatedly come under criticism for making God passive as well as vengeful: God will not relent from the divine wrath until punishment is exacted. We must be clear here that in the matter before us, what is offered to God is not obedience or a new holy life that inaugurates the new creation, but a penalty exacted for no reason than to meet the demand of punishment. It is this idea of retributive atonement that I consider problematic because it makes God passive as well as vengeful.

Most of the objections to sacrificial theories (as well as Anselm's theory and the legal theory known as penal substitution) involve these two issues. When divine passivity and death as an end in itself are combined, then Jesus' death becomes an action by Christ offered to God and required by retributive justice. But that is not the claim of the major New Testament texts that use sacrificial imagery. As we have seen in Paul and Hebrews, God is the active agent. The same can be said of confessions that Jesus dies on the cross for us. Compare, for example, Peter's sermon in Acts 2 and in general Paul's theology of the cross. In both cases the cross is a witness to the love of God. It is also difficult to find support for a divine passivity in the gospels. For example, in the parable of the householder whose son is killed by the tenants, it is the householder who sends his son as a messenger (Matt. 21:33-41). Or again, Jesus' fidelity is not presented as a payment to God but as his response to his own teaching of the Rule of God. So he sets his face to Jerusalem, and prays "not my will, but thine be done." Salvation does not come against, in spite of, or without the will of God, but is fully the expression of the divine will. The irony of the matter is that when sacrificial theories make God the object, they tend to violate the very *theological* and *evangelical* values they wish to affirm. If God is made the passive object of a transaction, then the gospel is irreversibly compromised. The same can be said for the isolation of the death of Jesus as the cause of salvation. At another place we will discuss the psychological impact that graphic images of the bleeding, crucified Jesus have on people, or the way they shape the form of Christian piety. Here our concern is that the emphasis on the death per se makes God appear as a vindictive deity, who requires the death of an innocent person as retribution for the sins of the world. That this crucified one is called the Son of his heavenly Father makes the entire story worse, and in our time evokes again objections on moral grounds.

There is one attempt to avoid these criticisms, which might be called the *Trinitarian defense.* Using the language of Father and Son, it can be argued that since the Father sends the Son into the world to make sacrifice to the Father, therefore God is the active agent: first as the Father who sends the Son, and second, as the Son who offers sacrifice or satisfaction to the Father. Aside from making the human Jesus a marginal figure in such a transaction, the problem with this attempt to escape the criticisms is that it simply transfers the problem to the internal life of God. At this point greater clarification is needed. On the one hand, if the intention in using the Trinitarian language is simply to transfer an exchange required by retributive justice to the Father and Son, little is gained. Why does the Father need the Son to offer sacrifice or satisfaction? If the Father needs sacrifice or satisfaction, why does not the Son? Is holiness the sole position of the Father and love the sole position of the Son? Such questions undercut the attempt to rescue divine initiative by recasting the saving event into the language of Father and Son. Instead of Jesus appeasing a passive God, we now have the Son appeasing the Father within the Godhead. This is the burden of the heavy-laden words *appease, earn, and propitiate,* which negate the affirmation of God's faithfulness in Old and New Testaments. Thus the moral force of the original criticisms still stands, namely, the theory has destroyed God's intention to redeem the world.

On the other hand, invoking the language of the Trinity could illuminate the whole matter of Jesus' death if the issue is not the payment of a death to a vindictive Father but an expression of the tension of holiness and love in God. This tension runs throughout the Bible and witnesses to God's holiness and mercy, finding expression in the concepts of wrath and judgment. In Exodus 32 the tension between holiness and fidelity to the promises of the covenant are literally acted out in the debate between God and Moses, with Moses reminding the outraged Sovereign of promises made to Abraham.[34] In this

---

34. The encounter of Moses with God on Mount Sinai in Exodus 32 is a wonderful indicator of our approach to the Bible. For those who claim to read it literally, the story is taken in a straightforward manner: God is angry at the sin of the Israelites, who have so recently entered into a sacred covenant to be God's people. Moses, who formerly pleads incompetence at public speaking, now rises to the occasion and persuades the Almighty to set aside the divine anger, though there will be judgment. In the encounter with the idolatrous people who have made the golden calf, Moses calls upon the sons of Levi to wage war. There is a violent battle with three thousand killed. In the end, Israel is taken back and the covenant is renewed. For those inclined to modern sensitivities, the passage offends in a variety of ways: The narrative is totally anthropomorphic: God is portrayed as one who talks with Moses and is subject to all manner of human emotions: anger, vengeance, forgetfulness, and change of mind. We are asked to suspend our critical judgment by the suggestion that a human being can persuade the Almighty God to calm down and relent, on the assumption that God had forgotten about the promises to Abraham. Then there is the bloodbath in the name of Yahweh. From the standpoint of modern rationality, the passage is an embarrassment and is best ignored. A completely different reading occurs if one sees in this story a sophisticated attempt to affirm that sin creates an almost insurmountable tension within God. The holy God cannot accept moral evil, but that same God has pledged to Abraham and Israel to create on earth a people in holiness and love. The crisis cannot be solved by letting Israel reap the consequences of its idolatry or by destroying Israel. God cannot abandon the

sense the Trinitarian defense could be helpful by emphasizing that God is opposed to sin and evil, that God cannot forgive sinners unless sin is removed/covered, which is also to say, that holiness is honored. What this means is that given the frequent use of the Trinitarian defense, one must discern whether the purpose is simply to reaffirm appeasement of a vindictive deity, or to affirm the painful struggle within God, who wills life for the creation.

Where then do these criticisms leave Calvin's portrayal of Jesus' priestly office? In the end it can be said that Calvin does not affirm a *retributive* view of the atonement: salvation is the work of God and it is accomplished by the obedience of Christ, rather than his death as an isolated act. But the road to that conclusion is so circuitous and filled with such crucial revisions that, when all is said and done, the sacrificial imagery has been drastically recast.

To survey that road, let us begin by recognizing that Calvin considers the redemption in Jesus Christ, from beginning to end, as a work of God. Building on Nicea and Chalcedon, Calvin affirms the incarnation of the eternal Word for our salvation. Humanity is locked in sin and death, and has no power to ascend to God, but God in mercy descends to earth for us.[35] Moreover, the mercy and love of God are eternal, prior to the creation. Mercy and love are the sole grounds for our reconciliation. Calvin explicitly denies the notion that the cross of Christ causes the love of God.[36] Indeed, he never diverges from the theme that Christ, dying for us and in our place, is ultimately the very presence of God for us and for our salvation.

But why then employ with such vigor all of the ambiguous language of satisfaction and appeasement? There are clear indications that Calvin is aware of the precarious nature of the sacrificial imagery. Two themes stand out for discussion. The first represents a moment of candid reflection (cf. Book II, Chapter XVI, Sections 1-4). Calvin acknowledges the apparent contradiction in claiming that God is the source of our salvation and our enemy.[37] He quickly cites Romans 5:10, Galatians 3:10 and 13, and Colossians 1:21-22 lest someone claim the matter is without scriptural warrant. But then he opens a line of discussion that could be taken in several ways. He suggests that the strong contrasts in the portrayal of God's wrath and the grace revealed in the death of Christ are an *accommodation* to the limits of the hu-

---

project. But how can holiness and love be reconciled? By bringing this struggle in the mind and heart of God out into the open by constructing a debate between God and Moses, the author points to a profound truth that is central to Israel's faith. God will be faithful to the promises, but Israel must learn the meaning of being in covenant with a holy and loving God.

35. Calvin, p. 464.
36. Calvin, p. 506.
37. Calvin, p. 504.

man mind and heart.[38] On first glance one wonders if he is suggesting that all of the imagery of wrath, death, and appeasement might be mere hyperbole borrowed only to motivate repentance and faith. He explains that the human heart cannot truly respond to the grace of God unless it is overwhelmed by the divine wrath and our eternal damnation. This is a surprising idea, coming immediately after his presentation of the priestly office, where there is no hint that the language is to be qualified in any way. Indeed, the reader looking for some relief would gladly seize Section 2 as the very opening needed to counter the seemingly negative force of the sacrificial imagery. But then Calvin quickly cuts off this possibility at the opening of Section 3, by declaring that while the vivid contrast of wrath and grace "is tempered to our feeble comprehension, it is not said falsely."[39] In other words, while Calvin appears to be aware of the problems in the language, the problem will not be solved by a linguistic solution.

This leads to the second theme, which ultimately is Calvin's major solution to the problem. The necessity of sacrifice for sin points to the tension between God and the evil of sin, reflected in the opposing demands of holiness and love. What is at stake is the eternal will to create a world where holiness and love are revealed and embodied. Sin has alienated God from God's very creation, a separation that is so severe that it cannot be overcome without judgment and punishment.[40] Following Augustine, Calvin affirms that this tension can only be expressed in the contradiction that God loves us as a divine creation and hates us as sinful creatures. There cannot be access to God or reconciliation with God unless sin is removed and righteousness restored. All of the harsh language about wrath, anger, and God the enemy is not mere hyperbole, but testimonies to the sovereignty of God.

But how then shall this gulf between the holy God and sinful humanity be bridged? Calvin's answer is the mediator, Jesus Christ, who in his obedience abolishes sin and reconciles us to God. At this point (Chapter XVI, Sections 5-18), he emphatically states that the atoning work is the entire life, death, and resurrection of Jesus, beginning with his baptism. From the point when he is anointed by the Spirit, Jesus becomes the agent of reconciliation "by the whole course of his obedience."[41] The point is again made by arguing that only a voluntary death given in obedience to God can reconcile (in contrast to death by murder or accidental death). By these statements, one could

38. Calvin, p. 505.
39. Calvin, p. 505.
40. Calvin, p. 504.
41. Calvin, p. 507.

conclude that Calvin does not see the death per se as the sole cause of salvation or that it is an end in itself. This does not prevent Calvin from emphasizing the death of Christ. In fact, he finds support for emphasizing the cross in Scripture and human nature:

> Yet to define the way of salvation more exactly, Scripture ascribes this as peculiar and proper to Christ's death. . . . But because trembling consciences find repose only in sacrifice and cleansing by which sins are expiated, we are duly directed thither; and for us the substance of life is set in the death of Christ.[42]

We have then a view of Christ's priestly office that develops by stages, though not necessarily in a linear way. At the initial stage, Calvin joins the image of priest with those of prophet and king in order to create a comprehensive view of the work of Christ. The presentation of Christ's priestly work follows the pattern in the New Testament, though the emphasis on wrath, appeasement, and satisfaction far exceeds the Letter to the Hebrews. Calvin boldly sees the sacrifice of Christ offered to God to remove the divine wrath. Once set forth, the theory bristles with nuances and implications that can contradict Calvin's very own evangelical intention. To keep this from happening, Calvin must expand the argument in ways that go beyond the concept of sacrifice. First, the relation of God to sin is developed in a much broader way, based on the traditional concepts of God's holiness and righteousness. The divine wrath and God's role as enemy become expressions of God's opposition to sin and evil. Second, the affirmation of holiness leads to the tension between God's love and holiness, i.e., the divine will to claim humanity and the will to oppose sinful humanity. Such a tension can only be resolved by God, who sends Christ as the mediator to redeem humanity and to restore righteousness.

From this perspective we can now see that Calvin is constantly struggling with the paradox that God can be both redeemer and judge:

> . . . we must see in passing how fitting it was that God, who anticipates us by his mercy, should have been our enemy until he was reconciled to us through Christ. For how could he have given in his only-begotten Son a singular pledge of his love to us if he had not already embraced us with his free favor? Since, therefore, some sort of contradiction arises here, I shall dispose of this difficulty.[43]

42. Calvin, pp. 507-8.
43. Calvin, p. 504.

But instead of disposing of it, it would seem more correct to say that Calvin affirms it. Calvin wants to affirm the paradox of the God who simultaneously judges and redeems the world according to God's divine purposes. Against the power of sin Christ appears as the incarnate Word in human flesh, to restore humanity by his obedience. Christ *satisfies* or *appeases* the divine wrath by creating a new humanity: he takes the guilt and curse of the old humanity upon himself and shares with humanity his righteousness. Christ's victory is over death, but also over the old Adam, against which God assumed the role of enemy. By amplifying the sacrificial work of Christ into this broader redemptive work, and by drawing on images of justification and the conquest of sin, death, and the powers, Calvin avoids having the priestly work be a form of retributive justice. Indeed, there is good reason why Calvin, much later in the *Institutes,* speaks of the Lord's Supper as a sacrifice of *praise and thanksgiving.*[44]

The twenty-first-century reader is tempted to expect Calvin to be aware of all of our concerns and moral outrage. But even if we try hard to let Calvin live in his time, one can still ask why he opened the door so widely in his initial presentation of the priestly office to what appears as a retributive approach to atonement. Even when we restrict ourselves to the evangelical values and concerns of his time, he is vulnerable to attack. His very criticism of the medieval Mass, following Luther, has no place for sacrifice offered to God as a work that merits salvation. Yet his initial presentation of the priestly office brims over with the language of a sacrifice offered to God. Only when he moves to unravel the paradox of God as judge and redeemer, revealed in the obedience of Christ, does he make his intention clear. But perhaps at this point we have come full circle: the idea of obedience, as the true sacrifice, is already in the Letter to the Hebrews, wherein Christ as the true Adam becomes the pioneer and perfecter of the new humanity.

2. *The Roman Catholic Mass*

Turning from the Geneva Reformer to the Roman Catholic tradition, we find the image of sacrifice at the center of the Mass. However, major changes have taken place regarding the theology of sacrifice in the Roman Catholic Church in the past fifty years. We will look first at an older point of view and then at a more current one, represented by the new *Catechism of the Catholic Church.* In search of a broadly representative and traditional interpretation of the

---

44. Calvin, pp. 1441-45.

Mass, let us review the article by J. H. Miller in *The New Catholic Encyclopedia,* published in 1967.[45] Miller affirms the continuity of the present-day Mass with the early Eucharistic traditions of the second century, which received definitive form under Gregory the Great in 604 and was then revised and reaffirmed at the Council of Trent in 1570. For Roman Catholics, the Mass is not simply a theological statement, nor merely a liturgical form, but the very heart of the Christian faith. In the Mass the Paschal mystery is made present to the people of God.[46] Miller interprets the Mass by three categories, which appear repeatedly in various theological works.[47]

First, it is a memorial *(anamnesis)* or remembrance, which dramatically reenacts what is recalled. In the sacrament, the salvation brought by Christ is made present.[48]

Second, against those who would define the sacrament as only a memorial, it is the sacrifice of Jesus as our Paschal Lamb. The eternal sacrifice of Christ is made present through the miracle of transubstantiation, whereby the bread and wine become the body and blood of Christ. As Jesus once offered his life as a propitiation for the sins of the world to God, so the people of God have opportunity to join with Christ in offering themselves with Jesus as a sacrifice to God the Father.[49] Just as Jesus, the Word incarnate, offered his humanity to the Father, so the church now makes its offering to God, who will accept it if it is made in a worthy manner and with the proper disposition.[50]

Third, the Mass is a sacred meal, filled with images of the Paschal supper and the messianic banquet. In remembrance and thanksgiving, the church celebrates our incorporation into Christ as the new humanity, which requires our personal sacrifice and love.[51]

These three themes used by Miller to interpret the Mass run through Roman Catholic teachings, past and present. Thomas Aquinas declares that divine

---

45. J. H. Miller, "Roman Mass," in *New Catholic Encyclopedia,* ed. William J. McDonald (New York: McGraw-Hill, 1967), vol. 9, pp. 414-26.

46. Miller, p. 415.

47. Cf. Joseph A. Jungman, *The Mass of the Roman Rite: Its Origin and Development,* trans. Francis A. Brunner (Westminster, Md.: Christian Classics, 1986), vol. 1; Joseph M. Powers, *Eucharistic Theology* (New York: Herder and Herder, 1967); H. M. Feret, *Eucharist Today,* trans. Aimée Bourneuf (New York, Paulist, 1966); Bertrand Fay, *The Church as Eucharist* (Milwaukee: Bruce Publishing Co., 1966); Lucien Deiss, *It's the Lord's Supper: The Eucharist of Christians,* trans. Edmond Bonin (New York: Paulist, 1975); François Amiot, *History of the Mass,* trans. Lancelot C. Sheppard (New York: Hawthorn Books, 1959).

48. Miller, p. 415.

49. Cf. Miller, pp. 415 and 425.

50. Miller, p. 415.

51. Miller, p. 418.

justice can only be satisfied by a sacrifice of obedience and love.[52] God can be propitiated only by an offering of homage that is due to God.[53] In suffering death, Christ overcomes death and washes away the sins of the world.[54] His sacrifice is received by God as sufficient for the sins of the world because it is offered in pure love by the divine/human agent of salvation: because Jesus is human, he can give his life; because he is divine, his sacrifice is sufficient for all.[55] The saving merit gained by Christ flows to humankind not through natural propagation, but "by the zeal of good will in which a man cleaves to Christ."[56]

This theology of sacrifice is repeated in the Council of Trent, where the efficient cause of salvation is the mercy of God, but the meritorious cause is the death of Christ, who "merited Justification for us by his most holy Passion on the wood of the cross, and made satisfaction for us unto God the Father."[57] When speaking directly of the Mass, Trent immediately appeals to Hebrews, with its contrasts between the Levitical priesthood and Christ. To transmit his saving work to the faithful, the Mass represents the once-for-all sacrifice of Christ.[58] The Mass is the new Passover given to the church, which the church through the ages offers to God. As such it is

> truly propitiatory, and that by means thereof this is effected, that we obtain mercy, and find grace *in seasonable aid, if* we draw nigh unto God, contrite and penitent, with a sincere heart and upright faith, with fear and reverence. For the Lord, appeased by the oblation thereof, and granting the grace and gift of penitence, forgives even heinous crimes and sins. For the victim is one and the same, the same now offered by the ministry of priests, who then offered himself on the cross, the manner alone of offering being different.[59]

The Council of Trent also includes a reaffirmation of the efficacious nature of the sacrament by the performance of the act.[60]

---

52. Thomas Aquinas, *On the Truth of the Catholic Faith: Summa Contra Gentiles,* Book Four: *Salvation,* trans. Charles J. O'Neil (Garden City, N.Y.: Image Books, 1957), pp. 240-42.

53. Thomas Aquinas, "Summa Theologia," in *Documents of the Christian Church,* ed. Henry Bettenson (New York: Oxford University Press, 1947), p. 208.

54. Aquinas, *Summa Contra Gentiles,* p. 243.

55. Aquinas, *Summa Contra Gentiles,* p. 244.

56. Aquinas, *Summa Contra Gentiles,* p. 246.

57. John Leith, ed., *Creeds of the Churches: A Reader in Christian Doctrine from the Bible to the Present* (Garden City, N.Y.: Anchor Books, Doubleday, 1963), p. 411.

58. Leith, p. 438.

59. Leith, p. 439. Italics in text.

60. Leith, p. 426.

A variety of works in the last part of the twentieth century reappropriate these themes. For example, in Jungman the Mass is defined as an offering presented to God.[61] To say the Mass is a reenactment means that Christ is offered again to the Father, only in this case, Christ's oblation becomes our offering.[62] If baptism is God's act toward us, the Mass is our action toward God.[63]

While Protestants incorporate sacrificial images as a part of their theology and liturgy, it would appear fair to say that for Roman Catholics, such images dominate theology, liturgy, and the practice of piety. The Mass was and continues to be the focal point of such theology and the practice of faith. The brief review of Roman Catholic writings illustrates both the power of the sacrificial motif as well as its problems. The emphasis in deed and word is on the propitiation of God and the meritorious significance of Jesus' death. The multitude of visual symbols within the typical Roman Catholic sanctuary only tends to heighten this emphasis on suffering and death. We are confronted again, therefore, with the two problems already highlighted: theories of sacrifice are in danger of making God the passive recipient of Christ's work and extolling suffering and death.

There are themes that could be used to counter both of these problems. For example, Thomists can reply that since the entire discussion of sacrifice is within the context of the Incarnation, whatever happens in Jesus Christ is also the activity of God. But it is not clear whether this reply, which I have called the *Trinitarian escape,* can actually outweigh all of the language of propitiation, with the strong emphasis on something offered *to* God by the humanity of Jesus. A stronger defense of the Mass could be made by appealing to those passages in Aquinas where he expressly states that the satisfaction given to God is not the death per se but the obedience of Christ.[64] What is efficacious is not the death but the voluntary giving of a life that possesses virtue and charity. This offering of humility comes, not from Jesus' divinity, but his humanity, and it signifies the transition from fallen Adamic humanity imprisoned in pride and love of the world to the new humanity of Christ, marked by the love of God.

This turn from Jesus' death as a transaction to his obedience offered to God becomes the dominant theme of the new *Catechism of the Catholic Church,* published in English in 1994. The presentation of the work of Christ and the Eucharist clearly show the influence of the twentieth-century biblical

61. Jungman, p. 175.
62. Jungman, p. 184.
63. Jungman, p. 193.
64. Aquinas, *Summa Contra Gentiles,* pp. 242ff.

and ecumenical theological revolutions that affected Vatican II and Roman Catholic theology since then. From first to last God is the active agent, with the emphasis always on God's economy of salvation.[65] The preoccupation with death as a transaction demanded by retributive justice is pushed to the background. In the foreground is the affirmation of Christ as the incarnate Word who actualizes on earth the obedience and love that were lost in Adam's fall. There is a strong emphasis on the union of the Paschal tradition of redemption in the Exodus with the Suffering Servant theme, wherein the chosen one gives his life for others. By accepting his role as the agent of reconciliation, Jesus freely offers a life of love and obedience to God. His death brings liberation from sin, reconciling us to God, while his resurrection opens the way for the new life in Christ. This new life can only be a communal existence in Christ, as the Body of Christ created and sustained by baptism, confirmation, and Eucharist.

In the presentation of the Eucharist, the *Catechism* places the emphasis upon the church in God's plan of salvation, which embodies and witnesses to the redemption in Christ from God the Father. The Eucharist is treated under three headings: first, as an act of thanksgiving to the Father; second, as a memorial of Christ's sacrifice; third, as the Presence of Christ on earth and in the church. As a memorial, the sacrament offers to God what God gives us.[66] It is a recollection and proclamation of God's saving action, which in the sacrament becomes present again. It is a sacrifice because it re-presents the sacrifice of the cross,[67] now united with our sacrifice offered to God. For Jesus and for the church, it is a sacrifice of love: it contains Jesus' pledge of love for us and our praise to God.

In substance and tone there is a major shift in the new *Catechism*. While Jesus' death is still the focal point, given the emphasis on the Paschal meal and the Suffering Servant, the death is placed in the context of God's plan of salvation and Jesus' obedience to God. The tone is that of a pastoral voice, where shades of language do not reflect older moralistic themes of guilt, sorrow, and punishment, but the joy and excitement of the people of God joining Christ in the work of salvation. But alongside what appears as a contemporary theological perspective, there are frequent references to the older tradition. At numerous points the document embraces the Council of Trent and thereby suggests that there really has been no change at all. For a church that changes by

---

65. *Catechism of the Catholic Church with Modifications from the Editio Typica* (New York: Image, Doubleday, 1995), pp. 172-88.

66. *Catechism*, pp. 378-83.

67. *Catechism*, pp. 380-81.

adding to the tradition, rather than subtracting from tradition, such claims are to be expected. But sometimes the continuity with the past appears so strong that one wonders which perspective dominates. For example, the description of the work of Christ does reaffirm the older images of an offering for reparation, of substitution and an offering for sin, of satisfaction for our sins, of a death that merits satisfaction.[68] Are we to understand these key words, along with the repeated affirmation that Jesus offers his life *to* God in the older way as part of a retributive act that appeases God, or in accord with what appears as the more dominant theme of the economy of salvation?

Another example of the older tradition is the discussion of the Eucharist, when the document affirms:

> Celebrated worthily in faith, the sacraments confer the grace they signify. They are efficacious because in them Christ himself is at work. . . . This is the meaning of the Church's affirmation that the sacraments act *ex opere operato* (literally: "by the very fact of the action's being performed"), i.e., by virtue of the saving work of Christ, accomplished once and for all. It follows that "the sacrament is not wrought by the righteousness of either the celebrant or the recipient, but by the power of God."[69]

Such language takes us straight back to the Council of Trent and leaves the Protestant reader unsure as to how much of a change has been made. This is especially the case when, breaking the pastoral tone, the document declares that the Eucharist is not open to Protestants.[70]

The theology of sacrifice in the older tradition, as represented by Trent and pre–Vatican II perspectives, is still subject to the Reformers' criticisms. Luther set the stage for a reevaluation of the idea of *sacrifice* by his broadside against a church system that included the Mass, the doctrine of transubstantiation, and the practice of indulgences based on the concept of merit. By interpreting the Eucharist from an evangelical point of view, Luther affirmed that the essence of the sacrament was the Word of promise offered to the believer by God in Christ, to which the only appropriate response is faith (i.e., trust of the heart).[71] Having staked everything on this understanding of the sacrament, it followed that the sacrifice could not be a human work offered to God, but only God's work offered to us.

---

68. *Catechism*, pp. 175-76.

69. *Catechism*, p. 319.

70. *Catechism*, p. 392.

71. Cf. Luther, *The Large Catechism of Martin Luther*, trans. Robert H. Fischer (Philadelphia: Fortress, 1959), pp. 91-101.

It is the common belief that the mass is a sacrifice, which is offered to God. . . . Over against all these things, firmly entrenched as they are, we must resolutely set the words and example of Christ. . . . When he instituted this sacrament and established this testament at the Last Supper, Christ did not offer himself to God the Father, nor did he perform a good work on behalf of others, but, sitting at the table, he set this same testament before each one and proffered to him the sign.[72]

The only meaning, therefore, that sacrifice could have for Luther in speaking of the work of Christ is to point to the cross, whereby the treasure of forgiveness comes to us. If, then, the gospel in Word and sacrament consists of this promise of grace, sealed by the blood of Christ, the notions of earning merit or seeking indulgences are also set aside.[73]

Calvin's disagreement with Luther on the way Christ is present in the Eucharist does not diminish the general agreement on the criticism of the Mass. At the outset, Calvin declares that God has given the sacrament to nourish our souls, which includes "his pledge, to assure us of this continuing liberality."[74] His attack on the Mass is no less vehement than Luther's. The chief error is summarized as "the belief that the Mass is a sacrifice and offering to obtain forgiveness of sins."[75] It is striking to note that whereas Luther, in rejecting the Mass as a sacrifice, also qualifies the meaning of sacrifice when speaking of the work of Christ. But as we have seen in the analysis above, Calvin offers a forthright rejection of the Mass as a sacrifice, but continues to speak of the work of Christ as a sacrifice in language that is not altogether clear.

We shall return to the dilemma that both the Mass and Calvin face in our general conclusion. Here we close this section with a general comment on the dilemma that sacrificial theories face. To the extent that these theories press the idea of sacrifice as a work offered to God because of sin, they move in the direction of retributive justice, which requires amelioration of the wrong by the offender, thereby endangering *theological and evangelical* values at the heart of the Christian faith. One way theories have tried to avoid this has been to utilize the two-natures theory of Christ (i.e., only humans must offer payment; only God can). But this solution has not always kept in the foreground that God is the primary agent and, as we have seen, too easily absolutizes the death of Jesus. The *wondrous* cross becomes instead the *horrendous* cross. A

72. Luther, *Babylonian Captivity*, pp. 171-72.
73. Luther, *Large Catechism*, pp. 93-94.
74. Calvin, p. 1360.
75. Calvin, p. 1429.

second approach to resolve this dilemma, while still using language of sacrifice, involves making an implicit or explicit revision. We saw this in Calvin and to a lesser extent in Aquinas and theologies of the Mass, especially in the new *Catechism of the Catholic Church*. This is the shift from the death of Jesus as the cause of salvation to Jesus' obedience. Much of the older theory remains in place in this revision: sin is still defined as disobedience and life curved in upon itself. What comes to the forefront, however, is the holiness of God as the divine will to restore the creation according to God's righteous will. On these terms, sin must be punished or judged, for how can God overlook that which violates the purposes of creation? Moreover, sin must also be replaced by righteousness. Within this context, Jesus' death is crucial, but not as an offering to God. There is a necessity to Jesus' death, as the inevitable result of his obedience in the face of evil, but not as a mandate from God for death per se. His death becomes that paradoxical event in which he bears the sins of the world and the judgment of God against sin. As the obedient one who proclaims the Rule of God, Jesus stands over against Adamic humanity and conquers sin and death. By incorporating humanity into his death, Jesus allows humanity to be born again to righteousness.

What this revision does is shift the emphasis from something paid to God to God's sovereignty, both as power to oppose sin and as power to restore the world to the divine purpose. The troublesome notions that God is passive, that God is immobilized by anger, or that death per se is the active cause of salvation — all these are ruled out. However, the attempt to save the sacrificial motif by this revision actually moves outside of it and comes closer to theories that this study classifies as the restoration of the creation as well as justification by grace. In the last century both Barth and Brunner made this revision of the sacrificial theory, recasting it in terms of God's judging sinful humanity and creating a new humanity based on the righteousness of God revealed in Christ.[76] It can be argued that such a revision is thoroughly consistent with the broad Calvinist commitment to righteousness on earth.[77] This may explain why Calvin persists in using the strongest language possible when speaking of the divine wrath as well as God the enemy. It may also reveal a point of convergence between the Roman Catholics and the Reformed traditions, in contrast to Lutherans.

76. See Note 28.

77. This point was suggested by my colleague Lee Barrett, and I think it is worth consideration, given the major concerns for the moral life and sanctification in the Reformed and Roman Catholic traditions.

E. General Use of the Term Sacrifice

For those immersed in Jewish and Christian traditions, where there is a knowledge of ritual sacrifice, it is inevitable that the use of the word sacrifice will draw us to traditions of sacrifice in the Bible. When, however, we speak of such biblical images with people who have no knowledge of the Bible, communication is difficult. This gap caused by biblical illiteracy could prompt us to avoid the image altogether, to reject all versions of the theory of sacrifice and look for more relevant images. But this overlooks one important aspect of this image. The word has more general use, and it may well be that all the cases discussed here (Hebrews, Calvin, and the Roman Mass) continue to have power because readers have firsthand experience with this more general usage. To speak of general usage is not meant to suggest that everyone in our culture or throughout the world has an archetypal image of sacrifice, or that they share the same common experience. It is simply to recognize that in European and North American cultures, the word sacrifice is used in many ways and has been associated by particular groups with specific historical events. These many uses are not all the same, but they do constitute a cluster of meanings in general culture, alongside of or even outside of religious use. Therefore it is not uncommon for people to bring these associations to the discussion of sacrifice regarding Jesus Christ. Such a position will, no doubt, disappoint those readers who want to affirm the primacy of the religious use of sacrifice, in the belief or hope that people will first comprehend the religious meaning of key concepts before they draw upon general experience. But it seldom works that way, even for religious people. We seldom encounter religious symbols with minds as blank tablets. Whether these prior or parallel encounters with the word sacrifice are helpful or hostile to the Christian message will have to be determined on a case-by-case basis.

Sacrifice is a word people use when they find themselves indebted to someone or some group for things that sustain life or rescue life itself. People speak of their parents making *sacrifices*. We honor explorers to unknown lands, or intellectual pioneers punished for their work, or persons who spoke the truth and suffered the consequences. In all of these cases we speak of their *sacrifice*. We describe the loss of life in war as a *sacrifice* made to defend a nation or made for a cause, such as freedom and justice. For some Americans, to stand on the beaches of Normandy is to stand on holy ground, for those stones have been washed with blood. Cemetery monuments at Colville-sur-Mer, France, evoke gratitude for *sacrifices* made. A similar experience may occur at the Gettysburg battleground, with quite different interpretations of the sacrifice by those from the North and South. In other words, the word sacrifice has these general uses when we wish to refer to something done for us, freely and without concern for self, which has given life or preserved life.

If, then, we have such general uses, it should not surprise us that the story of Jesus should prompt his followers, then and now, to use the word sacrifice in describing him. The reality of the Christian experience is that by his life, death, and resurrection, we are brought into a new relation to God. Once one begins to say: "Jesus died for me" it soon follows that one will also say that "He sacrificed his life for me." In the case of Hebrews, the impulse to make that move becomes the opportunity to utilize the imagery and authority of the Jewish sacrificial tradition. But in other cases, the impulse to use the word does not necessarily have to search the scriptures or the creeds. The use is authorized by the relation of the speaker to that which is sacrificed. It is substantiated, not by third-party authority, but by the profound sense of indebtedness and/or gratitude for what has happened.

This sense of indebtedness increases in relation to the nature of the sacrifice. A momentary favor at modest cost will not be valued in the same way as the remembrance of a lifetime of struggle, hard work, and saving that allowed children to find a new sense of self and/or opportunity. As the cost of the sacrifice escalates, so does the sense of indebtedness. When the sacrifice involves the shedding of blood, we reach a level that has power far beyond what we can estimate in words.

A most important thing about these cases is that in nearly every case, the emphasis is on the recipient's relation to the person who makes the sacrifice and the result of the sacrifice, rather than the question: To whom is the sacrifice given? The parent who makes sacrifices gives time, money, and energy in many directions, or perhaps primarily in the direction of hard work. The soldier who dies loses his/her life in a war with an enemy, but the sacrifice was not *to* the enemy but *for* his or her people or cause. The point is that the general use of sacrifice does not get involved in the hazardous questions: To whom is the sacrifice given? or, Was the sacrifice necessary? The troublesome questions that arise when we speak of Jesus' sacrifice do not seem to arise in this general usage.

This leads to the double conclusion: First, perhaps the image of sacrifice is so often applied to Jesus in the practice of piety through the ages because people understand it against the background of their general experience. Consider, for example, the fidelity and adoration given to Mary in her moment of sorrow as she holds the crucified Christ. This scene is depicted in paintings and sculpture in Roman Catholic churches everywhere. It is often the very focal point for prayer and adoration. But note who is praying: in most cases it is older women! Are not these women responding to Mary because they themselves have held a parent, husband, or child in their arms at the point of death? They come to Mary as fellow sufferers and mourners. Second, if the image of sacrifice is to be used in thinking of Christ, it might be helpful to keep the focus on what Jesus does and our relation to him. The tradition has indeed been led astray when the focus shifts to the question: To whom is the sacrifice paid? When the answer is God, we are then confronted with things that confuse and undermine the very evangelical purpose of the image. There is no doubt that sacrificial theories have been essential to the proclamation of the gospel. The dilemma the sacrificial imagery faces is whether it can be used without being diverted into an expression of retributive justice, thereby evoking justifiable protests.

Chapter 2 Justification by Grace

Martin Luther

A. Introduction: Biblical Sources

In the theories of justification by grace and penal substitution the focus is on sin and the righteousness of God. But unlike the theory of sacrifice, the solution is framed in the legal language of justification. These theories assume that God is righteous and that sin has created a barrier between humanity and God. They also assume that humans must take responsibility for sin, no matter how much they speak of the power of sin to enslave or the solidarity of original sin. The problem cannot simply be dismissed, since sin has both disrupted the covenant community and alienates humanity from God.

In preparation for both theories, it will be helpful to understand the word *righteousness*. In the Old Testament this word has multiple uses.[1] God is righteous and so are God's ways, deeds, and relations. God creates the world to reveal the divine goodness and calls Israel to be holy as God is holy. Interpreters repeatedly place the emphasis on righteousness as the relation between God

---

1. For an overview of righteousness in Old and New Testaments, consult general works such as Gottlob Schrenk, "dika," in *Theological Dictionary of the New Testament*, ed. Gerhard Kittel, trans. Geoffrey W. Bromiley (Grand Rapids: Eerdmans, 1965), pp. 176-215; Gerhard von Rad, *Old Testament Theology*, trans. D. M. G. Stalker (New York: Harper and Row, 1962), vol. 1, pp. 370-83; Paul Achtemeier, "Righteousness in the New Testament," in *Interpreter's Dictionary of the Bible*, pp. 91-99; and in general, E. P. Sanders, *Paul and Palestinian Judaism* (Philadelphia: Augsburg Fortress, 1977). For works dealing specifically with Paul, cf. James D. G. Dunn, *Romans 1–8*, vol. 38a of Word Biblical Commentary, ed. David Hubbard and Glenn W. Barker (Dallas: Word, 1988), pp. 176-82; and Dunn's *Theology of Paul the Apostle* (Grand Rapids: Eerdmans, 1998), pp. 218-23, 334-86; Joseph A. Fitzmyer, *Paul and His Theology: A Brief Sketch*, 2nd ed. (Englewood Cliffs, N.J.: Prentice Hall, 1989), pp. 31-66; and J. Louis Martyn, "God's Way of Making Right What Is Wrong," *Theological Issues in the Letters of Paul* (Nashville: Abingdon, 1997), pp. 141-56.

and Israel, rather than on an abstract concept that functions normatively. Because of this relational character, righteousness has a history. Israel learns the full meaning of righteousness through successive encounters with the righteous God in Exodus, conquest, monarchy, exile, and restoration. Righteousness receives form and substance through the encounter of God's covenant faithfulness with Israel's sin and infidelity.

If righteousness is tied to the covenant, then a person is righteous only in relation to that covenant, with its claims, obligations, and expectations. The righteous are those who trust God and do God's will. In this context, Torah or Law gives expression to righteousness in several ways: First, it points to the gracious calling of Israel, whereby God creates the covenant and draws Israel into God's righteousness. One does not earn righteousness but receives it as a gift from God. Second, Torah embodies righteousness as the structure of communal life, setting the goals for life (e.g., love, justice, mercy) and the limits against the chaos of sin (e.g., the restrictions of the Decalogue). The Law cannot be defined or understood only as rules, since such an approach reveals that one has already lost the personal bonds of love and trust that are at the heart of the covenant. Deuteronomy makes this clear in the double love commandment, as do the prophets in their insistence on spiritual compliance with the Law in contrast with external behavior.

Righteousness is also revealed in God's opposition to sin and to the sufferings caused by evil. Two images are important: One is the role of God as Judge, i.e., the one who will hold both Israel and the world accountable. The Day of the Lord in the prophets gives expression to the confidence that there can be no escape from judgment and that such judgment will be on God's terms. God will judge the heart as well as external action; God will vindicate those who are oppressed, the poor, the weak, and those who suffer for righteousness' sake. The other image is that of wrath, as the terrifying power of God against unrighteousness. Few images in the Bible evoke more discomfort, be it personal fear or theological opposition, than this symbol of divine anger against sin. Like the image of Judge, wrath moves into the realm of legal or forensic language: disobedience, violation of the law, and judgment.

While the New Testament contains many references to righteousness, Paul's Letter to the Romans became the primary reference for the theories before us. This is not to say that justification by grace is the only theme, or even the central theme, in Romans. Rather, it simply affirms that in numerous places Paul develops particular arguments using the theme of the righteousness of God. But here the reader must give serious attention to the fact that the English words *righteous, righteousness, justification, justify,* and *acquittal,* used in translations of Romans, all stem from a set of Greek words with one common stem.[2] But unfortunately, the different English words have different trajectories: references to the *righteousness* of God hark back to usage in the Old Testament, with strong overtones of covenant and even wrath, whereas *justify* and *acquittal* move in the direction of legal or forensic imagery. While use of these different English words has legitimacy, based on usage in first-century Greek, we need to remember that they all refer to God's righteousness and righteous activity. For this reason it is helpful to see translations that only use words with *right* in the stem.[3]

In Romans, Paul connects the theme of righteousness to Jesus in five crucial passages, which have had great influence in atonement theory. When we review these passages, we need to recognize that Paul is very much the theologian of the new life in Christ, which in Romans is placed in the context of God's plan to extend mercy to the Gentiles. In no case does Paul ever step back and analyze the death and resurrection of Jesus directly, i.e., as the initial subject for discussion. In all five cases, Jesus' death and resurrection are tied to a specific subject at hand. As a result, some of the things Paul says remain at the level of powerful images without extended development. Not surprisingly, many of our questions nearly two millennia later are not part of the discussion. The five passages are:

1. God's righteousness is revealed apart from the Law in Jesus' death (3:21ff.). In the opening chapters Paul makes the point that all (i.e., Jews and Gentiles) have sinned and that no one has advantage. After referring to the gospel in the introduction (1:1-6) and in the famous declaration of 1:16, he now returns to God's response to the state of humankind. In this new time ("But now . . ."), all are justified by grace, which is received as a gift. How does this happen? Paul provides two images:

a. God in Jesus Christ offers redemption as a gift of grace (3:23-24). The word redemption implies liberation from bondage, by saving action or ransom. It could suggest to Jews the Exodus event. The emphasis, however, is not on the ransom or payment but on the fact that God's action is a gift.[4]

b. God offers Jesus as a covering or removal *(hilasterion)* of sin by his blood (3:25). Here the image shifts from redemption/ransom to the removal of

---

2. The three words used most often, *dikaios, dikaiosune,* and *dikaioo,* which are variations of the common stem used in the form of a noun, adjective, or verb, appear over sixty times.

3. One interpreter who has tried to represent the unity of all these words in English is J. Louis Martyn (cf. his essay "God's Way of Making Right What Is Wrong").

4. Cf. Fitzmyer, pp. 41-67, and Dunn, *Theology of Paul the Apostle,* pp. 218-28.

sin by means of a sacrificial offering, which removes sin and allows new access to God.[5] The shift from redemption to sacrifice is important, since *hilasterion* draws on the language of sin as transgression, leading to removal, forgiveness, and reconciliation, whereas redemption denotes enslavement or bondage, with the hope of liberation.

Many interpreters consider the basic affirmations in 3:24-25 to be taken from material present in the early church.[6] This could mean: First, if Paul assumes that the readers already view Jesus with images of redemption and sacrifice, then he need not take time to explain their meaning. Second, when Paul does expand on them, he adds elements crucial to his basic argument regarding salvation for all by faith as a gift. Thus, Paul weaves the two images together as the basis for his claim that the righteousness of God has been revealed in Jesus, apart from the law.

A later reference in Romans 10:4 can be mentioned in this connection, though it requires careful interpretation. There Paul says: "For Christ is the end of the law, that everyone who has faith may be justified." If *telos* is taken to mean termination, then the verse echoes 3:21ff. But *telos* can also mean completion or goal, suggesting that Christ fulfills God's plan, first set forth by the law but now revealed in the new covenant open to all people. James Dunn argues that while the second interpretation of *telos* may be generally consistent with Paul's theme in Romans, it is probably beyond Paul's intention in 10:4. Instead, Dunn argues strongly that Christ is the end of the law as a means to righteousness, without implying a denunciation of the law, which Paul repeatedly upholds as good. From the perspective of salvation history, the stage of the law, as representing only the call of Israel, now ends with the extension of God's call to all people.[7] Consistent with this reading, Dunn

---

5. Cf. the discussion of sacrifice in Chapter One.

6. Cf. E. P. Sanders, *Paul* (Oxford: Oxford University Press, 1991), p. 78; Martyn, p. 142; and Dunn, *Romans,* pp. 181-83.

7. Dunn, *Romans,* pp. 595-98. A summary statement is especially relevant: "we should stress that Paul neither says that the law as such has been brought to an end in Christ. . . . Nor does he imply that the law was seen as a way of earning or meriting righteousness: that interpretation would not only give a picture of Judaism hard to square with what we know of Judaism contemporary with Paul from other sources. . . . Hence, what Paul thinks his people are ignorant of is not God's righteousness in general, but the *character* of that saving power, the terms on which it can be received and known. They knew God's electing grace well enough, but had failed to recognize the implications of their own original election, the implications of the facts already set out in 9:6-18 — that God's righteousness is extended to humankind not in terms of race, nor as a relationship dependent on or made firm by particular acts of men. God's righteousness is from faith to faith; it always was (chap. 4) and always will be" (pp. 595-96).

translates 10:4 as: "For Christ is the end of the law as a means to righteousness for all who believe."[8]

2. Justification by faith brings many gifts: peace with God, access to God, hope of sharing the glory of God, and the reign of life (5:1-21). To explain how these gifts occur, Paul offers two answers:

The first is the bold affirmation that God shows love in Jesus dying for the helpless, the ungodly, and the sinners. Therefore we are justified by Christ's blood (5:9), reconciled to God by his death (5:10) and, if all this is true, "much more, now that we are reconciled, shall we be saved by his life" (5:11). To this threefold affirmation of the saving efficacy of Christ should be added the words of 4:24-25, which conclude the discussion of Abraham and precede the great *therefore* of 5:1. There Paul says: "It will be reckoned to us who believe in him that raised from the dead Jesus our Lord, who was put to death for our trespasses and raised for our justification." In all of these references, justification by faith, with its many gifts, is linked to Jesus' death. As he died for our sins, so we are reconciled by his death and resurrected life.

The second answer is the dramatic portrayal of the contrast of Adam and Christ (5:12-21). While it builds on the earlier material in chapter 5, it lays the groundwork for the equally powerful description of our participation in Christ's death and resurrection in chapter 6. In 5:12-21 Paul contrasts Adam's disobedience, leading to death, with Jesus' obedience and righteousness, leading to justification and the free gift of life. By this contrast of Adam and Jesus, Paul begins to describe the double relation Jesus has to us, which will be further expounded in Romans 6: On the one hand, the obedience of Jesus places him over against Adam and us; but on the other hand, Jesus is the one cursed and rejected as if he were sinful as we are sinful. He is "put to death for our trespasses" (4:25). He dies because of his righteousness and that same righteousness leads to "the righteousness of life" (5:18).[9] Thus Paul presents Jesus as both different from us, or over against us, while at the same time introducing the theme of his participation in our life for our behalf. It is this theme that is explored again in Romans 6.

3. The call to new life and the death of sin (6:1ff.). The chapter begins with the rhetorical question whether we are to continue to sin that grace may abound?

8. Dunn, *Romans*, p. 579. Here we have a good example of how the text can be legitimately translated by means of the word righteousness, rather than the more common: "that every one who has faith may be justified."

9. This is an alternative translation of the close of 5:18, supported by Dunn, in contrast to the RSV: "so one man's act of righteousness leads to acquittal and life for all men."

The question really has two sides: First, if we are justified by faith, are we free from the power of sin? Second, the question also asks if we should keep on breaking covenant, knowing that grace has been poured out in Jesus Christ. Here we will only discuss the first side of the question (6:2-14), where Paul argues that we are free from sin and may walk in new life because:

a. In the death of Jesus, sinful humanity was crucified and the power of sin is broken. The same can be said for the power of death (6:9). Paul assumes a corporate humanity, in which we and Christ participate. His representative death is, as the sacrifice in Hebrews, once for all (6:10).

b. As Christ participates in our life and death, so we participate in his death and life through baptism. In baptism we die with him and are raised with him (6:4-5). We thus have new life and are free from the powers of sin and death.

By connecting the death of Jesus with freedom from the power of sin, Paul introduces a new idea, namely, participation. E. P. Sanders considers it the most distinctive contribution of Paul to Christology, even more important for Paul than justification.[10] Whether or not one accepts this view, we need to recognize that Paul links participation with sacrifice and liberation. Sacrifice requires identification between the sacrifice and the sinner. If sin is to die or be destroyed, there must be a process to do this. At the same time, the death of sin and death itself introduces the liberationist element into the same discussion. By making baptism the symbol of our participation in Christ's death and resurrection, Paul ties participation in Christ to the sacramental practices of the community. Henceforth, every baptism testifies to the death and resurrection of Jesus, as well as our incorporation into that death and life.

4. There is no condemnation in Christ, but only freedom (8:1ff.).

Having been set free from sin and death, Paul affirms the new freedom in Christ. If we ask how this has happened, Paul returns to the theme of chapter 6, namely, Christ as the representative of both God and humanity. In this formulation, Paul emphasizes the opposition between flesh and the Spirit: In the technical terms of Paul, flesh is not human nature envisioned at creation, but human life lived for itself against the will of God. Things of the *flesh* are not things of the earth per se, but things that we have allowed to control us and/or that we worship instead of the Creator. Freedom from sin

---

10. Sanders, *Paul,* p. 74.

and the flesh is achieved by God sending Christ "in the likeness of sinful flesh and for sin" (8:3) to bear the condemnation against sin and the flesh. The purpose of this, Paul states in 8:4, is "that the just requirement of the law might be fulfilled in us, who walk not according to the flesh but according to the Spirit."

The parallelism of Romans 6 is repeated: Christ's crucifixion is the destruction of the power of sin; his resurrection is the introduction of new life and righteousness in those who are in the Spirit (in contrast to the flesh). Moreover, to reinforce the distinction between the two ages in God's plan of salvation, God has done in Christ what the law could not do (8:3). Having established the cross and resurrection as the source of salvation, Paul can then enumerate the blessings that flow from God's action: those who suffer with Christ receive life in the Spirit (8:11 and 17); the God who did not spare the Son will also justify us, Jesus will intercede for us, and we receive a love from which nothing can separate us (8:32-39).

5. Salvation comes by confessing Jesus is Lord (10:9). While reference to Jesus' death is not actually included in this passage, it is implied. We shall be saved if we confess Jesus is Lord and that God raised him from the dead, i.e., the vindication of the crucified. The death and resurrection of Jesus have thus become for Paul the very symbols of justification and salvation, for both Jew and Gentile (10:12). This leads to the famous inspiration for missionary action: to call upon the Lord requires belief, which requires hearing, which requires preaching. Such connections are quite consistent with Paul's affirmation of justification by faith: salvation is transmitted not by cultic works of the law but by preaching and faith.

Having reviewed these key passages in Paul regarding the death of Jesus, we may now turn to the theory of justification; the theory of penal substitution will be considered in Chapter Three.

B. The Theory in Outline:

The theory of justification by grace can be outlined as follows:

1. This theory begins with the reality of sin as a violation of covenant law, thereby creating separation from God and incurring the judgment of God.
2. Human attempts to overcome this separation by obedience and fulfillment of the law prove to be inadequate: the law only continues to

reveal what we are to do as well as the reality of our sin. In this situation the law becomes a tyrant, reminding us of our bondage to sin and death.

3. But the gospel declares that while we were sinners, God sends Jesus to die for us, thereby revealing that God's righteousness is not the will to condemn (and maintain the purity of God's righteousness apart from us), but is instead the will to make righteous. Jesus dies for us on the cross and in his resurrection overcomes sin and death.

4. The new life revealed in Christ is shared with us, not according to human works or according to the moral demands of the law, but as a gift received by faith.

To illustrate this interpretation of the gospel, we turn to Martin Luther's *Commentary on Romans.*

C. The Witness of Faith: Martin Luther on Justification

Paul, a servant of Jesus Christ (Rom. 1:1)

The sum and substance of this letter is: to pull down, to pluck up, and to destroy all wisdom and righteousness of the flesh (i.e., of whatever importance they may be in the sight of men and even in our own eyes), no matter how heartily and sincerely they may be practiced, and to implant, establish, and make large the reality of sin (however unconscious we may be of its existence). Hence, Blessed Augustine says in the seventh chapter of his book, *On the Spirit and the Letter:* The apostle Paul "contends with the proud and arrogant and with those who are presumptuous on account of their works," etc.; moreover, in the letter to the Romans, this theme is almost his sole concern and he discusses it so persistently and with such complexity as to weary the reader's attention, yet it is a useful and wholesome wearying.[11]

With images from the prophet Jeremiah and a quotation from his Blessed Augustine, Luther opens his commentary on Romans. There are good reasons to begin our discussion here, since Paul's Letter to the Romans became the symbol of Reformation theology. This connection was personalized by Luther's own appeal to Romans as a basis for his personal breakthrough in

---

11. *Luther: Lectures on Romans,* trans. and ed. Wilhelm Pauck, vol. 15, *The Library of Christian Classics,* ed. John Baillie, John T. McNeill, and Henry P. Van Dusen (Philadelphia: Westminster, 1961), p. 1.

understanding the gospel as a message of grace, received by faith.[12] Moreover, the work on Romans comes early in Luther's public lectures and writings (1515-1516), right after lectures on the Psalms and before lectures on
Galatians.[13] In *Romans,* Luther's understanding of justification by faith is already in place, well before the ensuing controversies. All of the basic categories (sin, law, works, grace, justification, and faith) are formulated in a consistent manner. His presentation shows no tentativeness but instead brims
over with confidence. A clear sign of Luther's confidence is found in the contentious nature of the lectures. At every point, Luther is prepared to criticize
and reject the traditions of Scholasticism. There is neither caution nor concern, as one might expect from a newly appointed biblical scholar trying to
find his way.

What all this means is that two years before the Ninety-Five Theses (1517),
and five years before the three great treatises of 1520, Luther at age 32 had
found his way to the gospel of justification by faith in Paul's Letter to the
Romans.[14] The commentary also reveals the style that will characterize Luther throughout his life: he is contentious and assertive, seeing all things in
opposing terms. Having grasped what he considers to be the truth of Paul's
proclamation of justification by faith, he is prepared to reject anything that is
to the contrary. Luther resonates with the oppositions of Paul, where sin and
grace, law and gospel, flesh and spirit are set over against one another. There
is no irenic search for a mediating position. Instead, every page conveys his
confidence that his reading of Paul is the beginning of a new understanding
of the gospel. And every page is filled with tensions. We shall summarize Luther's view of justification by faith by means of three tensions that run

12. The dating of Luther's religious turning point has been a source of great debate. In later
life Luther himself referred to it as the pivotal event. But his references to the exact time, based
on his memory, never resolved the problem. The attempts to set the date focus on a period from
1509-1519. Much depends on whether one is looking for a singular conversion experience where
Luther first grasped the gracious character of God's righteousness or a set of ideas that represent the fully mature Protestant view of justification. Since there is clear evidence that development occurred with respect to Luther's understanding of justification during these formative
years, it is possible to see the change as a developmental process involving a series of insights. Cf.
Heiko A. Oberman, *Luther: Man between God and the Devil,* trans. Eileen Walliser-Schwarzbart
(New York: Doubleday, 1992), pp. 161-74. If one insists on the single event as a decisive conversion experience, it is difficult to place it after the lectures on Romans, since here the crucial ideas
are present and applied to the issue of our status before God.

13. Pauck, pp. xix-xx.

14. Pauck, pp. xxiii-xxiv. The irony of this statement is that Luther's lectures on Romans
were tucked away in several libraries for centuries, finally rediscovered at the beginning of the
twentieth century, with editions published in 1908 and 1938.

throughout the entire commentary: One is his interpretation of Paul (by means of Augustine) against the Scholastics; a second is the tension between the righteousness of God and sin; and third, the tension between true and false faith in the life of Christians.

1. Paul against the Scholastics

Luther had joined the Augustinian order in Erfurt in 1505.[15] Because he was formed by the spirituality of this monastic culture, it should not surprise us that Augustine came to play a major role in his reading of Romans. But this point should not be overdone. Luther's general training was in logic, rhetoric, theology, and philosophy, with the key figure being Aristotle. He was very much caught up in the nominalism of Occam and Biel, known as the *via moderna,* in contrast to the tradition of Thomas Aquinas. Two unusual things about his development also need to be noted: One is that Luther did not take up a serious reading of Augustine until 1509, four years after joining the order; the other is that when he was appointed to biblical studies in 1512, he worked entirely with the Latin Bible, which was standard practice.[16] It was not until 1516, right in the middle of the lectures on Romans, that Luther had access to the newly published Greek text, edited by Erasmus.

All of this suggests the convergence of multiple forces in the life of a newly appointed lecturer on the Bible. We know that he was struggling personally with the burden of a medieval piety that demanded that everyone, but especially those who had taken religious vows, fulfill the commandments of God. Since it was generally assumed that we become righteous by our good works, it followed that we shall be judged according to our righteousness.[17] Being part of an order committed to reform (i.e., genuine spiritual practice and high moral standards, for the sake of the renewal of the church itself) only tended to heighten expectations. Then he began to discover the discontinuity between Augustine versus Aristotle and the Scholastics — the very teachers who had formed him. But his major commitment of time went to the reading of the Bible and lectures on Psalms, Romans, and Galatians —

---

15. Oberman, p. 124. For the general background of Luther's education and late medieval nominalism, cf. *Luther* as well as Oberman, *The Harvest of Medieval Theology: Gabriel Biel and Late Medieval Nominalism* (Cambridge, Mass.: Harvard University Press, 1963).

16. Oberman suggests that Luther's choice of the Augustinian order was not based on a prior knowledge of Augustine, but because of its local reputation for monastic reform and openness to the new theology (*Luther,* pp. 130, 159).

17. Cf. Oberman's discussion of the monastic drive for righteousness, pp. 113-50.

three books important for the great debate between Augustine and Pelagius regarding sin and grace, faith and works.

But while Augustine was a major influence on Luther, it was Luther's encounter with Scripture itself, and especially Paul, that ultimately proved decisive. If Augustine was all that Luther needed to find himself and a viable theological position, he would not have needed the encounter with Romans. It was Romans that precipitated the crisis and its resolution. Indeed, this encounter reveals a teacher being changed by what is being taught.[18] It is very hard to accept a little of Paul. For Luther it was all or nothing, and he chose all. In fact, we will find that in some important respects Luther moved beyond Augustine because he could not reconcile the biblical categories with the philosophical language so important to the medieval church. Nevertheless, Augustine was important for Luther as a young teacher, since the former offered him protection as he set himself against the dominant theology of his day. Augustine opened the door and gave encouragement, but Paul provided the foundation for understanding sin and grace. In *Romans* we find Luther embracing both Paul's ideas and language regarding sin and grace.

The reason the commentary is so often a three-way discussion (Paul, Augustine, and Luther) is that the issue, in broad terms, is confidence in human capability. This goes to the heart of Augustine's debate with Pelagius and quickly places Luther on the side of Paul and Augustine, against the Scholastics. Here one must recall that Pelagianism, as a theological and spiritual tendency, joins together rationality with optimism.[19] Those taken by these tendencies have always felt that it makes no sense to imagine that God commands us to do things that we cannot do. Furthermore, views that suggest humans are incapable or enslaved in some way are far too pessimistic and depressing. Against all this Augustine held that sin was an act against God as well as a state of being, dominated by pride and self-love. The idea that sin was more than a momentary impulse, but a general state of being that even transcends the individual, ultimately led to the idea of the solidarity of the race and original sin. If sin, as the problem, were defined in such radical

18. One is tempted to compare Luther's immersion in the world of the Bible, against the general theological culture of the Scholastics, to the experience of Barth's discovery of a strange, new world in Romans. In both cases, a difference in the language of Paul and contemporary culture pointed to significant differences in substance.

19. Regarding Augustine's debate with Pelagius and the overall impact of Pelagianism, compare such standard texts as J. N. D. Kelly, *Early Christian Doctrines,* 2nd ed. (London: Adam and Charles Black, 1960); Reinhold Seeberg, *Text-Book of the History of Doctrines,* trans. Charles E. Hay (Grand Rapids: Baker, 1958), as well as discussions in volumes on historical theology such as Justo L. Gonzalez, *A History of Christian Thought* (Nashville: Abingdon, 1971).

terms, then the solution could only be defined in equally radical terms, namely, the primacy of grace. It was to this realism regarding sin, human bondage, and the primacy of grace that Luther appeals when he seeks support against the Scholastics. But though Augustine may have won the debate with Pelagius, the optimism and moralism of Pelagius run through the medieval discussions regarding human nature (nature) and the divine initiative (grace). This must have appeared both ironic and disappointing to Luther as he surveyed a church system committed to good works, merit, rewards, and indulgences.[20] It may also help us understand why Luther ultimately gravitated toward placing emphasis on Scripture rather than Augustine, since an appeal to the latter could too easily be countered by appeals to other teachers of the church.

Luther finds in Paul's description of the universality of sin, as well as our bondage to sin, a completely different way of understanding the human situation than that presented by the Scholastics. What he finds is consistent with what he has learned from Augustine: sin is self-love, or life curved in upon itself.[21] The tendency toward self-centeredness in heart, mind, and will is so great that everything is transformed into something to be used or abused by sin. Moreover, once this inclination or desire for the self reaches its full proportions, it cannot be defined simply as an isolated act, but must be viewed as a new state of being. Nor can sin be defined as a privation of the good, as claimed by the Scholastics (p. 169). In Romans, Luther discovers a new language for naming this bondage to self, namely, life *in the flesh* and *bondage to sin* (p. 183). Just as Paul uses *flesh* to refer to human life lived only for itself amidst all the desires of mind and body, in contrast to God's original intention at creation, so Luther uses *natural* and *nature* to refer to humanity having a new fallen nature in sin.[22] It is inevitable that Augustine and Luther should reach the same conclusion as Paul, namely, that the problem of sin far exceeds the tendency to occasional bad acts. When one moves in the direction

20. Oberman, p. 54.

21. *Luther: Lectures on Romans,* p. 218. Note: all future references to pages in Luther's *Lectures on Romans* will be included in the text. References with comment will be included in footnotes.

22. *Romans,* pp. 219 and 225. The use of language in this way has provided endless confusion in modern discussions of Paul as well as the general interpretation of Christianity. Taken literally, the words can suggest that it is human nature as created that is evil, rather than human nature under the power of sin. Such a negative interpretation has been encouraged by practices that denigrate physical life and/or theologies that blame physical needs and impulses as inherently sinful. Not only have these things produced a repressive moralism, but they have also driven many people away from Christian faith. Faced with the choice of a repressive moralism or a world-affirming secularism, they have chosen the freedom of the latter.

of sin as defiance against God, rooted in a turning away from God at the core of our mind and heart, one can no longer assess the problem with optimistic rationalism. For this reason, in the tradition that runs from Paul through Augustine to Luther there is a willingness to speak of sin in terms of bondage and sickness. For Luther, such categories reflect an honest appraisal of our situation and also represent the end of both naïve optimism and self-righteous hypocrisy (p. 183).

Once Luther entered the world of Paul, where sin and death dominate, where the law reveals God but is unable to liberate, and where hope is found only from beyond all human striving, then he could not coexist with his contemporary theological orientation. This can be illustrated by charting the trajectory of Luther's thinking on several crucial issues, each being a direct consequence of his new understanding of sin derived from Romans.

a. Late medieval theology accepted the dictum from Aristotle that good deeds make a person good, or as Luther states, that "righteousness follows upon and flows from actions" (p. 18). Such a principle was utilized in a variety of ways: it could mean that we have the capacity to do the good and therefore each person should seek, with proper intention, to do what was within him or her, as symbolized by the Latin phrase *facere quod in se est*. It was the advice that Luther received in the midst of his spiritual crisis, where he despaired of being able to do what was commanded in order to stand before God.[23] If that sounded too optimistic and opened the possibility that faith and/or grace were unnecessary, a further distinction was made between deed and intention: by our natural powers we are able to do good deeds, but only by grace are we able to do them with the right intention. Time and again Luther denounces all of these views, arguing that we can neither do righteous works nor love God by our own powers.[24] Nor will he enter into a calculation of degrees of cooperation between nature and grace, whereby sinful nature is aided by grace to do the good, all the while maintaining the identity of the old sin-

---

23. Cf. Pauck, pp. xxxiv-xlix; Oberman, pp. 175-79, as well as Philip S. Watson, *Let God Be God!* (Philadelphia: Fortress, 1947), pp. 15-27. While the Latin phrase may be unknown to popular religion in America, its meaning is quite prevalent in the optimistic advice handed out from many pulpits: "Do the best that you can and that will be acceptable to God."

24. *Romans*, pp. 108, 129, 218, and 222-26. Cf. the comment: "For this reason it is sheer madness to say that man can love God above everything by his own powers and live up to the commandment in terms of the substance of the deed but not in terms of the intention of Him who gave it, because he does not do so in the state of grace. O you fools, you pig-theologians! So, then, grace was not necessary except in connection with a new exaction over and above the law! For if we can fulfill the law by our own powers, as they say, grace is not necessary for the fulfillment of the law but only for the fulfillment of a divinely imposed exaction that goes beyond the law. Who can tolerate such sacrilegious opinions!" (*Romans*, p. 129).

ful self. The key here is that Luther no longer thinks in the framework of his theological culture: nature and grace, deeds and intentions, deeds leading to goodness, or degrees of cooperating grace. Instead, it is an either/or: either we live in the *flesh,* where all of life is consumed by self-love, pride, and rebellion, or we receive Christ in us, i.e., receive a new life not our own. Instead of cooperation between sinful nature and righteous grace, Luther hears Paul speaking of a death of the old self and a new birth in Christ. Instead of a gradual progress from sin to justification, Luther understands Paul to affirm that we are always in sin and grace. There is no final transition from one to the other in this life. And as we shall see, if there is a way from sin to righteousness, it is not by deeds but repentance and faith.

b. Luther totally rejects the idea of ordered love, a common idea in moral theology and contemporary spirituality (pp. 222, 262-63, 406ff.). It presupposed continuity between our self-love (i.e., our natural love for ourselves) and our love for others and for God. As we have it within ourselves to love, so we may progress from one love to another. Given his new realism regarding sin, Luther will have none of this. The issue, however, created a delicate problem for Luther, since on this matter the tradition appealed to Augustine. Luther even acknowledges how Peter Lombard quotes Augustine to defend ordered love (p. 406). Indeed, there are aspects of Augustine that emphasize continuity between the old self and the new self, between the restless heart that yearns for God and the heart that is finally at rest in the love of God. Luther's initial reaction is to condemn the idea of ordered love as "sheer madness" (p. 121). But finally, he must deal more directly with his spiritual father, Augustine, though not by name. In discussing the commandment that we love our neighbor as ourselves, he appeals to Gregory in arguing that this cannot mean that we love as we love ourselves, since our self-love is corrupt. With a virtual apology to Augustine, he proceeds to defend his view that self-love cannot be the basis for love of others or God. Here and earlier, he appeals to the realism in Paul: if we once adopt the view that the self is caught up in a closed world of selfishness and enmity against God, how can we propose that such a self can either will or accomplish the perfect love of God (pp. 223, 406-8)?

In one sense it can be argued that Luther is simply appealing to Augustine's realism on sin against those aspects in Augustine that support ordered love. But it is probably more accurate to say that Luther is moving closer to Paul and away from this tradition of medieval spirituality, even though it has ties to Augustine. This emerges in Luther's vigorous protest against making God one more object of our love for our own sake. He is appalled by the way the moral and spiritual traditions condone the love of God for our sake. By contrast, he repeatedly admonishes us to love God unconditionally for God's own sake.[25] Luther is so concerned about this that he seizes every opportunity to make the point. When, for example, Paul says that he would be willing to be "*anathema* from Christ for my brethren's sake" (Rom. 9:3), Luther interprets the passage as a model of Christian self-resignation. As Paul was willing to be damned for the sake of his brethren, so we must be willing to resign everything for the will of God. Here and throughout the commentary, the opposition is set forth in the strongest terms: love of self, coveting God, seeking our own righteousness vs. hatred of self, accepting God's judgment, forsaking all claims to righteousness (pp. 260-65). But of course, the true model of self-denial is Jesus, who abandons himself for the sake of God's will, loving God only for God's sake (p. 263). Here we see the emergence of a theology of the cross, which will become so important for Luther's entire theology.

c. Having seen the movement of Luther's thought thus far, it comes as no surprise that he has little patience for claims to freedom of the will (cf. pp. 217-19, 222, 226, and 276). Throughout his debate on this issue, including his treatise against Erasmus, Luther's position rests on one fundamental point: freedom of the will does not mean the ability to make simple choices, or even to will (i.e., intend) the good, but the ability to accomplish what is willed. Of course we can sit down and decide to eat or not eat, or even make decisions on crucial matters of importance, for which we are responsible and may take credit. We can even perform a particular good work. But Luther's concern is the overriding implication of our fallen nature, bound to the body of sin. If we are inclined to love ourselves more than we ought in all things, and are weighed down with the legacy of our personal and social life curved in upon itself, then it is for Luther preposterous to imagine that we can do what God wills. The sinner is not a person who simply lacks a good will or intention, needing an infusion of grace, but a defiant sinner who loves self above all else. As we have seen throughout this entire discussion of sin, what is needed is the liberation of the self, or the transformation of the self. If Romans 7 were not enough to clinch the argument, Jesus' teaching regarding the good and bad trees is offered to settle the matter (p. 228).

Luther's conviction that sinners need a change of heart, or a new spirit, should not be interpreted to mean that by the power of Christ we are so changed that sin no longer dwells in us. Justification brings freedom from condemnation and the domination of sin in our lives, but it does not remove sin (p. 194). It should be noted that Luther's concern here is not with sectarian holiness movements, but the Scholastics who imply that by an infusion of

25. *Romans*, pp. 160 and 163. With regard to Jesus as the example of the true love of God without regard for self, cf. pp. 263 and 410.

grace original sin is taken away or that we progress from sin to justification (p. 128. Cf. pp. 112, 124, 127, 140, 169, and 178). To the contrary, we remain sinners all our lives, but live in hope for final redemption. Here it is appropriate to insert one of Luther's vivid images of the church and the Christian life:

> So then, this life is a life of cure from sin; it is not a life of sinlessness as if the cure were finished and health had been recovered. The church is an inn and an infirmary for the sick and for convalescents. Heaven, however, is the palace where the whole and righteous live. (p. 130)

2. *The Righteousness of God and Sin*

The lectures on Romans gave Luther the opportunity to analyze and reflect on the very text that at one time had terrorized him, but then came to be his comfort in the face of personal anguish. What liberated him from despair regarding his unrighteousness before God was the simple but profound reversal of his understanding of Paul's affirmation of the righteousness of God. This he is quick to explain in the commentary on Romans 1:17: "For the righteousness of God is the cause of salvation. Here too, *'the righteousness of God'* must not be understood as that righteousness by which [man] is righteous in himself, but as that righteousness by which we are made righteous (justified) by Him, and this happens through faith in the gospel."[26]

We need to unpack this basic statement: first, if God is righteous in any way (i.e., intrinsic or in relation) then we are confronted with the opposition of the holy, righteous God against our sinfulness and unrighteousness. The Law, as an expression of God's righteousness, makes this clear. The Law reveals our unrighteousness; but even more, by commanding us to do the good the Law makes us aware just how much we do not want to comply with it (cf. pp. 100 and 106-7). But as much as the Law exposes unrighteousness, sinners resist such assessment and claim just the opposite. Therefore to know oneself

---

26. *Romans*, p. 18. Cf. pp. 67, 71, 77-79, and the comment: "The Scripture interprets 'righteousness' and 'unrighteousness' quite differently from the way the philosophers and jurists do. This is shown by the fact that they consider them as qualities of the soul. But, in the Scripture, righteousness depends more on the reckoning of God than on the essence of the thing itself. For a person who possesses only the quality of righteousness does not have righteousness, for he is an unrighteous sinner through and through, but that person has righteousness whom God mercifully reckons as righteous because he confesses his unrighteousness and implores the divine righteousness; it is such a man that God wants to regard as righteous. Thus we are all born in iniquity; i.e., unrighteousness, and we die in it, but we are righteous, through faith in God's word, only as he mercifully regards us as righteous" (*Romans*, p. 141).

as a sinner is not possible without the Word of God, for in our sin we are still content and claim to be righteous (pp. 79-80). Thus Luther concurs with Romans 4:15, namely, that the Law "works wrath" (p. 145). By this he does not mean that the law itself is negative, but that the violation of the Law produces wrath and condemnation (p. 148). Living under such judgment, which sinners resist, makes God appear as a tyrant and enemy (p. 233).

Second, if sin and our unworthiness mark the character of our status before God, how then shall we find mercy? While Luther's world readily admitted that God was merciful, it also placed on all people, but especially religious vocations, the expectation of seeking righteousness in this life before the final judgment.[27] If such moral realism is combined with a serious regard for God's judgment, how could one stand before a righteous God? Here the reversal of meaning regarding Romans 1:16 allows Luther to perceive God's intention as life rather than death. If the righteousness of God is revealed in Christ, then righteousness points to how God is in relation to us, namely, it is the will to create righteousness in the world for God's glory (p. 79). In this, God is proven to be truthful and faithful to the promises to Israel and truly righteous, as the giver of life rather than death (p. 75). With Paul, Luther sees this active righteousness of God as good news since it is conferred entirely as a gift, received by faith. It is *not* received by virtue of any work.

Third, Luther accepts Paul's judgment that the new paradigm in this matter is God's declaration regarding Abraham, prior to the Mosaic Law (cf. pp. 123ff.). Luther takes *reckon* or *impute* to mean God's act of making righteous apart from and against our moral action. We are *intrinsically* sinners having no claim on God, but *extrinsically,* i.e., in the sight of God, declared righteous by God's grace (p. 124). Thus Luther proceeds immediately to declare that by faith we are at one and the same time "*righteous and unrighteous . . .* they are knowingly righteous and knowingly unrighteous, sinners in fact but righteous in hope" (p. 125). But how can sinners be righteous in any sense when they are in fact sinners? By their works they cannot, but by faith they can receive the righteousness of God in them. So Luther writes:

---

27. Cf. Oberman, pp. 102-10, 175-79. Luther's reading of Paul is too easily discounted if Luther is portrayed as an exceptional or overly sensitive individual, or even worse, as an obsessive-compulsive person, immobilized by doubt and guilt. In general, Oberman overturns these accusations, but at the same time insists that Luther is not a modern person. Luther lived in a penitential world, where human sin and divine holiness framed the practice of religion. The fact that he was a member of an Augustinian order caught up in serious reform (i.e., strict observance of the religious life and the pursuit of spiritual goals) obviously heightened his awareness of unworthiness.

For God does not want to save us by our own but by an extraneous righteousness which does not originate in ourselves but comes to us from beyond ourselves, which does not arise on our earth but comes from heaven. Therefore, we must come to know this righteousness that is utterly external and foreign to us. That is why our own personal righteousness must be uprooted. (p. 4)

Fourth, the multiple oppositions between God and sin, grace and condemnation, faith and works, now make clear why Luther gives as much attention to humility and self-condemnation as to faith. To be justified by faith is to give up pride in ourselves. The great barrier to the gospel of justification is self-righteousness, born of pride, wherein we deny our sin and wish to stand before God on the basis of our own goodness. Luther's language, so vivid and extreme, is to be taken quite literally: the sinful self that defies God, that uses all things for itself and that rests content in its self-estimation must be destroyed and die.

Hence, when grace comes . . . there must be neither prayer nor any action on our part but only a keeping still. This is certainly a hard thing to do and casts us into deep affliction. For not to think and to will is for the soul the same as to go into darkness as though it were to be ruined and reduced to nothing, and this it seeks violently to avoid. So it comes about that it frequently deprives itself of the noblest gifts of grace. (p. 244)

If we have understood this truth, which lies at the heart of the gospel of justification, then we can understand why Luther's first words in the lectures used the powerful images from Jeremiah.

Finally, the full meaning of God's righteousness, for Paul and Luther, is that such righteousness is revealed apart from the law (Rom. 3:21). It is precisely at this point that Paul, in the midst of an extended argument framed by the legal language of justification, breaks out of the constraints of such legal language. Legal justice requires equity between action and status, offense and penalty. For such reason God's judgment against all humanity is just: all have sinned and all are under a fair judgment. Luther not only understands this in light of his entire philosophical training in logic and ethics, but he feels the full weight of this in his personal confession of sin before the holy God. Thus, Romans 1:16 tormented him. To declare, therefore, that righteousness is revealed apart from the Law is to open the possibility of another solution to the question of our status before God besides that of righteousness based on works. This new solution, apart from the Law, becomes all the more significant in light of Luther's interpretation of two related themes in Romans: one is the power of sin over mind and will (Rom. 7) and the other is the inability of the Law to bring about a solution within the terms of the Law (i.e., a moral command evoking action leading to positive judgment).[28] Both of these themes only heighten the tension before God: the former reveals that we ourselves are internally divided by the power of sin; the latter reveals that the Law cannot save us. There would be no hope if not for the fact that the righteousness of God is revealed in the cross of Christ.

Having outlined Luther's understanding of the righteousness of God, we can now ask how this relates to the death and resurrection of Jesus Christ. The first and obvious point is that Luther, following the text of Romans, incorporates into his lectures images of sacrifice and liberation. He discusses with approval the idea that sins are covered (pp. 124ff.) and that Christ's death "offers satisfaction for our sins" (p. 152). Regarding Romans 8:1-4, he can say twice that Christ took upon himself our sins and bore the punishment against sin (pp. 217 and 223). And he declares with Augustine that we need not fear death because of the *merit* of Jesus' death (p. 222). These elements are there, though they receive very little discussion. We also find strong liberationist images, again reflecting the text of Romans itself. Regarding Romans 1:3-4, Luther emphasizes how the Son of God emptied himself in the weakness of human flesh, to be glorified in his resurrection with power over all things (pp. 13-14). Paul's comparison of Adam and Christ also allows Luther to affirm in Jesus the power of righteousness that liberates us from sin and death (pp. 173, 178-83). This affirmation is anticipated by Luther's insistence that the human predicament is the loss of our freedom to the power of sin. At times he refers to the liberated state as a spiritual view, in contrast to a moral view, meaning that we are no longer discussing human possibilities but cosmic warfare between demonic powers and God (p. 193). In such a world, what is needed is precisely what God in Christ accomplishes, namely, the destruction of sin and death.

But having recognized the limited references to sacrifice and the more general appeal to liberation images, there is ample reason to say that all of these images are never developed as one might expect. For example, when dealing with Romans 3:23-25, Luther says nothing about the Christological affirmations contained in this confession. When he does use language of satisfaction and merit, which appears to have been shaped by medieval theology and liturgy rather than the biblical language of sin offerings, very little is said. In these passages Luther never speaks of punishment as a vicarious act assumed by Jesus to satisfy the demands of the Law, nor is the suffering of the

28. Cf. Luther's discussion of Romans 7 (pp. 193-216) as well as pp. 217-23.

cross offered to God as some kind of satisfaction. In fact, just the opposite seems to be the case. When Luther examines the idea of punishment it is clear that the punishment of sin is against sin, not against Jesus. Likewise, the merit of Jesus' death is our liberation from the dominion of the flesh and the gift of the Spirit to us, rather than a reward earned from God and now bestowed upon us by Jesus (pp. 222-23).

All of this suggests that the reason why the images of sacrifice and liberation are not developed by Luther in this commentary is that they are subordinated to the theology of justification. The fact is that justification involves a language of its own, but also quite different issues than sacrifice and liberation. Justification addresses the question of worth and status, be it righteous or unrighteous, innocence or guilt. Sacrifice overlaps with justification by addressing the issues of guilt and forgiveness, the removal of sin and access to God. But it does not speak as clearly to the issue of worth or standing, especially if *sin cannot be removed.* On the other hand, liberation speaks to the issue of freedom from bondage or sickness — and does play a major role in Paul's letter and Luther's interpretation. But while liberation speaks clearly to the issue of freedom from a third party (i.e., the power of sin or death), like sacrifice it leaves open the issue of the worth or standing of the liberated. What is the status of the liberated prisoner once freed from bondage? Our experience of the estrangement of liberated soldiers upon their return home points to the unresolved matter of status.

The Christology of Luther in *Romans* combines and recasts elements of sacrifice and liberation into the framework of justification. For Luther, justification means both the forgiveness of sin and freedom from condemnation, as well as from the powers of sin and death. It creates a new status before God and a new identity: I belong to Christ who died and rose for me. At this point we see the connection between justification and the death and resurrection of Christ. The general emphasis of Luther's interpretation of the entire letter points to the middle chapters, at the heart of which is Christ's participation in our humanity for our salvation.[29] In Romans 5–8 Luther finds that all the

---

29. Here we should note the parallel between Luther and Paul. Recent commentaries on Paul point out how Paul says very little about the traditional formula included in Romans 3:23-25. This is explained in several ways: Paul repeats a traditional formula in the expectation that it is shared by the listeners and needs no interpretation; the controversy Paul faces in Romans is not with the Christological titles but the mission to the Gentiles; the most important Christological theme for Paul, as well as his new contribution, is the idea of participation (Rom. 6). Cf. Sanders, *Paul,* pp. 74-79 and *Paul and Palestinian Judaism,* pp. 464-67, 497-503; Dunn, *Romans,* pp. 181-83. A similar explanation could easily be applied to Luther, even though Luther defines the general theme quite differently than current NT scholarship: his quarrel with the

many elements come together: the humility of Jesus in assuming our sinful humanity, his obedience and righteousness compared to the failure of Adam, his suffering on the cross for our sake, the overthrow of sin and death, the invitation to participate in his death and resurrection by baptism, and the new status (justification or righteousness) by faith. Thus for Luther there is an essential connection between the active righteousness of God that reckons us as righteous, even in the presence of our weakness and sin, *and* the crucified and risen Christ. What will become known as his theology of the cross will always have this multidimensional character. It will always be filled with tensions and will find expression in diametrically opposed affections. To this matter of the new life of faith we now turn.

3. The Christian Life: The Struggle between True and False Faith

For Luther, justification by grace is the doorway into a particular form of Christian life. Its primary characteristic is faith. Such faith is always faith of the heart directed to Christ, since it cannot exist except for the intervention of Christ, the Word, and the Spirit (pp. 154, 234, 235, 293, and 299). Apart from God's Word there can be no knowledge of ourselves as we in fact are, i.e., sinners (p. 308). Since faith is not a human work, but the very antithesis of all human works, it involves the transformation of the old self into the new self in Christ and the Spirit. Thus Luther repeatedly contrasts the spiritual person with other modes of existence. The use of the term *spiritual* is, of course, borrowed from Paul, and represents Luther's movement away from the philosophical language of Scholasticism. By entering into the language world of Paul, Luther begins to understand sin and grace in a new way. In one pointed reference against the philosophers, Luther says that they analyze and consider things according to their essence and accidents in the present, whereas Paul points to things "in terms of what they will be" (p. 235). Without using the word that we take for granted in reading the New Testament, Luther appears to grasp the *eschatological* tension present in the proclamation of the resurrection of Christ. The grace that awakens faith also opens new possibilities. Instead of works seeking to make the old self good, *Christ in us* creates the new being, from which good works shall arise (pp. 108 and

---

tradition is not over the Christological titles per se, but with the matter of sin and justification. Like Paul, Luther sees that justification involves ideas about Jesus Christ moving in a new direction (i.e., Rom. 6), which cannot be easily contained in ideas of sacrifice or liberation.

326). And as we have already noted, such faith is characterized by humility, since the believer has received all by the grace of God.

Now it is one thing to define the nature of faith. But to live in and with such faith places one in a constant struggle between sin and grace, flesh and spirit, temptation toward self-centeredness and trust in God. Luther describes this struggle with remarkable maturity of insight. In spite of his image as an inordinately troubled soul, there is only one reference to his own struggle. But even this is quite general and arises as an illustration of a point he is making (p. 128). Most often, themes are illustrated by reference to the Christian life. The language is personal and at times takes on the descriptive style used to speak of *everyman.* These comments display great discernment, perhaps developed by Luther's care of his fellow monks as deputy vicar of the monastery. For example, in commenting on tribulation (Rom. 5:3), he writes: "People who impute their anger or impatience to what injures or troubles them, talk foolishly. For tribulation does not make anyone impatient but it brings to light the impatience that was or is in him. Thus everybody can learn in tribulation what kind of man he really is, just as the glutton can when he itches, etc." (p. 156). Such realism causes Luther to say that for the believer "confessing is the principal work of faith. . . . For by confessing God and denying himself, he dies" (p. 294). In another passage Luther returns to the images of Jeremiah: "But, in reality, the word of God comes, when it comes, in opposition to our thinking and wishing. It does not let our thinking prevail, even in what is most sacred to us, but it destroys and uproots and scatters everything" (p. 298). Thus, one can only encounter God and be dissatisfied. Without making such dissatisfaction into a test or a required *new measure,* Luther says: "Hence, it is an infallible sign that one really has the word of God and that he carries it in his heart if he is not satisfied but only dissatisfied with himself and if he is troubled in all he knows, says, does and suffers, finding pleasure only in others or in God" (p. 298).

Luther cannot help but speak in oppositional terms: law and gospel, sin and grace (p. 301). For example, "God does nothing else than transform men's minds. But people who are self-complacent resist being so transformed" (p. 327). On speaking of hope, Luther distinguishes the false and true God: "The false gods are demons and as such they are the gods of tangible reality. . . . But he that depends on the true God has laid all tangible things aside and lives by naked hope. To call God the 'God of hope' is therefore the same as to call him the God of hopers. He certainly is not the God but the enemy and judge of people who despair easily and are unable to trust anyone" (p. 413). So the saints know they are sinners and therefore are justified before

God, whereas the hypocrites believe themselves to be righteous and therefore are sinners before God (p. 124). The faithful who trust only God

> have only the one concern to wash away their guilt and to restore the grace of God whom they have offended; they do not seek the Kingdom; they are ready to forego salvation and are freely willing to suffer damnation. . . . This is contrary to the ways of those who imagine that they have merits and who picture these to themselves while they seek their own kind of good; they shun evils but deep in their hearts they have nothing. For they go along blindly, wholly absorbed in the good they conceived and wished for themselves. (p. 265)

Finally, in one of his most imaginative comparisons, which also shuns all self-righteousness that may be attributed to the saints, Luther declares:

> There is, then, a difference between sinners and sinners. There are some sinners who confess that they have sinned but do not long to be justified; instead, they give up hope and go on sinning so that, when they die, they despair and, while they live, they are enslaved to the world. There are other sinners who confess that they sin and have sinned, but they are sorry for this, hate themselves for it, long to be justified, and under groaning constantly pray to God for righteousness. This is the people of God: it constantly brings the judgment of the cross to bear upon itself. (p. 120)

There is one powerful image where the truth is not simply set against falsehood, but is found in between two false options. This is the word picture of the royal road. Luther observes that some find such security in their progress that they no longer fear God; by contrast others are so driven by their desire to purge sin and please God that their continual failure only causes them despair. The way between these pitfalls is "the royal road, and the way of peace in the spirit: really to know and to hate sin and so to walk in the fear of God, lest he count it and permit it to rule in us, and at the same time to pray for his mercy that he free us from it and not impute it to us. The fear of God cuts off the way at the right which leads to security and vain self-satisfaction, and faith in the mercy of God cuts off the way at the left which leads to despair of self and despair of God" (pp. 137-38). The image of the royal road suggests the rich theme of pilgrimage, though in many respects it is not indicative of Luther's spirituality. There is a searching and striving throughout all of life, but it is a contending with sin and a yearning or quest for justification. While life offers the possibility of purging sin from our lives, Luther does not think in terms of slow or fast progress from our old life to the new. In this life we shall always face the struggle of sin and grace, evil powers and Christ, temptations to our own righteousness and the righteousness of God (pp. 118-19). As we conclude this description of the Christian life, it might be helpful to refer to an insight of Oberman, where he makes the point that Luther's discovery was that temptation and spiritual distress are not to be treated as a problem to be cured, either by religious practice (or in our day, psychological treatment). Neither are they things one can escape by a retreat from the world into the monastery. Rather, they are a part of human existence in this world, amid the struggle with sin and the devil. The only solution is in God, who in the suffering of Christ calls human beings to set aside all false claims and trust the crucified.[30]

The exposition of Luther's view of justification by faith offered here has focused entirely on the lectures on Romans. This has been done for several reasons: it allows the reader to turn to one text rather than many; it is a work that comes early in Luther's life, filled with all the excitement and energy of a new discovery; and finally, it contains in basic form and substance the pivotal idea of justification by grace, received in faith. But this approach leaves out the way that Luther develops the idea of justification from such an early writing to his later works, as well as reference to the great debates on indulgences, sacraments, Scripture, and church authority. Certainly the lectures on Galatians, given the issues at hand of legalism and libertarianism, allowed Luther to develop the idea of justification in ways not possible in the lectures on Romans. While these developments are crucial for a complete understanding of Luther, our purpose is achieved by focusing on a text where justification by grace is so clearly defined. The lectures on Romans already contain the fundamental distinction of intrinsic/extrinsic righteousness that will become the centerpiece of Luther's famous sermon in 1519, where the alien righteousness of God is set over against whatever righteousness we have.[31] We can still note, however, that interpreters see subtle changes in the development of the basic concept as Luther progresses from Psalms to Romans to Galatians, and then to the disputations and treatises.[32] Of special interest is the way Luther turns away from the discussion of humility as a precondition for justification, as well as the intricate discussions of contrition and attrition, to the complete focus on faith alone as the human response to the promise of God in the gos-

---

30. Oberman, pp. 175-79.

31. Cf. "Two Kinds of Righteousness," in *Martin Luther: Selections from His Writings*, ed. John Dillenberger (Garden City, N.Y.: Doubleday, 1961), pp. 86-96.

32. Cf. Oberman, pp. 145-65; Gordon Rupp, *The Righteousness of God* (London: Hodder and Stoughton, 1953), pp. 148-246; Watson, pp. 15-65; Heinrich Bornkamm, *Luther's World of Thought*, trans. Martin H. Bertram (St. Louis: Concordia, 1958), pp. 75-92.

pel. Thus, in his treatise on the *Freedom of a Christian,* Luther declares that faith alone stands in relation to the Word. It is by faith that we receive all the gifts of Christ through the union of Christ with and in us.[33] One can also note how confidently Luther speaks of faith in *The Large Catechism,* when he says: "trust and faith of the heart alone make both God and an idol. If your faith and trust are right, then your God is the true God. On the other hand, if your trust is false and wrong, then you have not the true God. For these two belong together, faith and God. That to which your heart clings and entrusts itself is, I say, really your God."[34]

Luther gave to Christians a theology of the cross that includes both judgment and grace. In Jesus Christ, God is both hidden and revealed: hidden in the judgment against sin and the weakness of the crucified; revealed in Christ's bearing the sins of the world for us and in our sharing his resurrected life. It is a multifaceted view of Christ, who is both sacrifice and liberator in his role as the agent of salvation. These themes are gathered together into the dominant theme of justification, which gives form and substance to Luther's thinking about the cross. Jesus is God's agent of forgiveness and liberation, but such acts allow Jesus to participate in our life and transform our life for what Paul describes as the new life in Christ. The key here is the transfer or exchange of all of Christ's gifts to us and the acceptance by Christ of all our weakness and sin. Thus in his later writings Luther draws on two images: first, the image of marriage, where bride and groom share their life; and second, the image of iron working, where the heated iron takes on the heat from the fire. By faith alone one receives the spiritual benefits of the crucified and risen Christ.[35]

While Luther stands in a tradition that runs from Paul through Augustine, in many respects he stands alone. His realism regarding human sin and his reliance on nothing else but God's grace results in a theology of paradox that few share. In Roman Catholicism, the Reformed traditions, the Anabaptist, Pentecostal, and Holiness traditions, one finds a variety of strategies to resolve the tensions embraced by the words *simul justus et peccator.* Thus Lu-

33. Cf. Martin Luther, "The Freedom of a Christian," in *Three Treatises,* trans. W. A. Lambert (Philadelphia: Muhlenberg Press, 1960), pp. 277-86.

34. *The Large Catechism of Martin Luther,* trans. Robert H. Fischer (Philadelphia: Fortress, 1959), p. 9.

35. For the image of marriage, see both "Two Kinds of Righteousness," pp. 89-90 and "The Freedom of a Christian," p. 286; regarding the image of the hot iron, see "Freedom of a Christian," p. 284. Compare also Oberman's discussion of what he terms the "joyful exchange," which he judges as the crucial image for the Christian life in "The Freedom of a Christian" (pp. 183-84).

ther's single-mindedness is both his strength and his weakness. In answer to the question of the ground and certainty of our salvation, Luther forever witnesses to God and God alone. This same trust resists all false claims and acts of self-justification from within and all temptations and threats from without. While the theme of justification by faith stems from Paul and has been used throughout Christian tradition, no one has been so identified with it as Martin Luther. But if Luther is the symbol of the theory, he also is the lightning rod that receives the criticisms directed against it. Some of the major issues will now be considered. While our concern is in part with their impact on Luther's position, our main concern is with their impact on the general theory of justification as an atonement theory. As stated from the outset, our primary purpose throughout this study has been on determining the viability of particular theories.

D. Summary and Critical Comment on the Theory of Justification by Grace

1. Summary

Let us begin by summarizing in broad terms the theory of justification by grace as an interpretation of the death and resurrection of Jesus. The aim is to develop a Christology based on the revealing of the righteousness of God. At the heart of the theory lies a fundamental paradox: While the language of righteousness and justification gives the theory a forensic framework, the basic affirmation is the nullification of human expectations regarding morality and God. God's righteousness is ultimately revealed not as vengeance or retributive justice (i.e., "we get what we deserve"). Nor is God's presence confined to the majesty and glory of heaven, but is revealed in the humiliation of the cross. The paradox, then, is that the theory so framed in the juridical language of law, guilt, and punishment overthrows the very moral passion that so often inspires interpretations of Jesus as the satisfaction of legal requirements. To say with Paul that salvation comes apart from the Law lays the foundation for the theory that overturns human moral expectations in the name of God's righteousness. Here we see that the theology of justification challenges both Pelagian moralism, with its demands for moral accountability, as well as Arianism, with its insistence that the true God is so transcendent that the divine cannot be incarnate in the crucified. The opposition to these two views is usually intense because each in its own way is destructive of saving faith.

This theory has always been noted for its realism regarding the human condition. The problem is sin, understood as defiance, rebellion, or disobedience, growing out of human pride and self-love. It is compounded by the fact that it has become a historical-social network of mistrust and alienation. While the concept of original sin is problematic in suggesting either condemnation prior to our birth or the notion of sexual transmission of sin, the concept does affirm that the individual was born into a world already at war with God, humanity, and nature itself. Caught in this environment of selfishness and social strife, individuals and groups are subject to forces beyond their control, whether they be named sin, death, demonic powers, cultural influences and ideology, or even the Law as moral judgment.

Against all of these forces of sin stands the affirmation of the sovereignty of God, revealing both the violation of the covenants and judgment. The gospel, however, is about God and God's righteous intervention. From beginning to end, the story is about the divine agency. If there is nothing within human powers to rectify the situation, all is not lost because it all depends on God. Once and for all the concern whether God is active or passive is laid to rest. Following Paul, Luther is unrelenting in his insistence that justification is God's act, revealing from first to last a divine grace. In Christ, God reveals righteousness (i.e., life-giving power) against human expectations regarding God and morality. Justification by grace, therefore, continually celebrates the divine activity in incarnation, crucifixion, and resurrection.[36]

The Christology that develops within this framework draws together elements from two major traditions in order to create something quite new: The tradition of sacrifice provides the elements of judgment against sin, human guilt, and forgiveness of sins; the tradition of liberation provides the element of the conquest of cosmic powers that enslave humanity. But what is distinctive about this theory is the incorporation of elements from sacrifice and liberation into the idea of divine participation (Rom. 6). Jesus Christ participates in our sin and suffering *and* is the agent for new life as the incarnate Word of God. It is at this point that the case can be made that the theory of justification moves beyond forgiveness as removal of sin, and liberation as freedom from the powers, to the affirmation of a new status before God. The

---

36. Since theology is communicated as much by images, stained glass, hymns, and music, here it may be helpful to refer to two great lines in sacred music that drive home this point. One is Brahms' *Requiem*, where the soloist declares: "Behold, all flesh is as the grass. . . ." The other is the crucial hinge in Handel's *Messiah*, where the description of Jesus' suffering and death comes to a close. The transition, when all is lost, is announced: "But Thou did not leave his soul in hell." No doubt the same point is made in countless hymns, but seldom is this truly profound evangelical claim made with such power.

sinner is declared righteous by the grace of God and accepted into the fellowship of Christ.

As an interpretation of the story of Jesus, the theory is usually played out in a double movement. There is, first, the terrifying judgment of God against sin and all that destroys our relations to God, one another, and nature. God's wrath, as the symbol of divine opposition to sin and evil, stands opposed to sin and the idolatrous attempts to justify ourselves. From Augustine down to Reinhold Niebuhr, there is always a critical edge directed against the self-deception involved in our best efforts to achieve goodness. Neither the individual nor society can escape the word of judgment; nor can religious institutions and the religious life. Such a radical declaration of judgment is matched by the radical affirmation of grace: Jesus Christ means forgiveness and freedom, as well as a new status before God. Both of these movements, judgment and grace, are revealed in *both* cross and resurrection. Jesus bears the sins of the world and dies because of sin, revealing both God's judgment and God's gracious will to be for us and with us. But Jesus' resurrection is also both judgment against the powers of sin and death, as well as the vindication of God's will to reconcile. Such judgment and grace relate to the moral problem of ill will, but also to the problem of knowing ourselves and God. Cross and resurrection reveal that when left to ourselves, we did not know God. God is not constrained by retributive justice, nor is God confined to the glory of heaven. In this theory, God is on the cross in Jesus, suffering and dying for the redemption of the world. Forsaking a theology of glory, the theory seizes the weakness of the cross to point to the way that God is both hidden and revealed in Jesus.[37] Such stress on the cross, however, does not mean that Jesus' death is an end in itself or something offered to God. In Paul and Luther, the action of God in Christ is directed toward sin and demonic powers. The means for the removal of sin and liberation from the powers is Christ's participation in our humanity, leading to the exchange of values in our death and resurrection with him. The only necessity for such

---

37. It should be noted that for the theology of justification, it is not only the cross that possesses a twofold character of God hidden and revealed. The Bible and sacraments are also understood in this way. Such a view is based on: (1) the distinction between God and the world, which means that nothing in the world is self-evidently a revelation of God; (2) the magnitude of sin, which means that from our perspective, we cannot see God in anything — even Jesus — without faith born of the Spirit. What this means, then, is that while the Bible is authoritative as the definitive revelation of the Word of God, it is not self-evident. Cf. Oberman's discussion of the Bible as good and evil (*Luther,* pp. 168-74). The same can be said for sacraments. On this, compare the Reformers' critique of the tendency to make the sacraments efficacious in the mere doing of them (*ex opere operato*).

participation lies in the magnitude of sin and the depth of God's love, revealed in the cross.

With so much emphasis on the activity of God, what then is the nature of Christian existence before God? The paradox of the cross (i.e., that the crucified is the Son of God) is matched by the paradox of the person's being judged a sinner *and* declared righteous in Christ. As we saw in the case of Luther, the new life in Christ is neither a nudge nor a push, neither a helping hand offered to those who try nor the enabling power that completes our efforts. Following Paul, the believer must die to sin in Christ and rise to new life. The new Pauline language, invented to give expression to this new phenomenon, breaks traditional categories of religious and moral analysis: the believer lives *in Christ* or *in the Spirit* by faith and not works. Besides the reliance on Pauline imagery, there are two other images for this paradoxical existence that are important for the tradition of justification: one is the parable of the Prodigal Son, who has no claim before his father, but still is accepted by grace. But just as important as the father and son are for the story, the older brother is also crucial. He is the very symbol of retributive justice, warning the father that giving back life to sinners destroys all moral conventions. For the theory of justification, this parable symbolizes the strange work of God in Christ and points to the sole basis of our standing before God. The other image is that of the good tree, which points to new life (Matt. 7:17). In this image, trees are either bad or good (note the either/or that repeatedly appears in Luther). The only way trees can produce good fruit is by being essentially good. In the context of the Sermon on the Mount in Matthew 7, with its warnings about truth and falsehood, we can assume that such goodness is derived from faithfulness to the teachings of Jesus regarding the present Rule of God. Such faithfulness comes by repentance (i.e., turning away from the entanglements of the world) and faith (i.e., loyalty in word and deed to the will of God). While the image of the good tree does not appear in John and Paul, each of these writers creates parallel images. In John we find two images that make the point: being born again, and the image of the vine and branches. In the one, life is renewed by the Spirit; in the other, life is sustained and made productive by being connected to Christ. In Paul this transformation is expressed by the new vocabulary of living by faith *in Christ*.[38]

38. With regard to the images of the tree, rebirth, and the vine/branches, we should note two things: one is that all are organic in nature, rather than mechanical, or an exchange of ideas or even influence of will. Salvation has to do with a spiritual relation *in* the Spirit of God. Just as in the Chalcedonian formula there is neither juxtaposition, cooperation, nor alternation of two independent wills and minds, so we find in all of these images a rejection of such parallelism for the unity of the believer with Christ.

What we have then is a new understanding of Christian existence, transformed by participation in the death and resurrection of Jesus. But unlike a variety of views that see movement from one life to another, the crucial aspect here is continuation of the tension of the old and new life. While one dies to sin with Christ and rises to new life with Christ, the old life of sin is still present though no longer dominant, and the new life is present though not perfected. Thus the theology of justification, in spite of celebrating the victory of Easter, still affirms our life beneath the cross. It is truly *simul justus et peccator.* On the one hand, there is the knowledge of our sinfulness, the continual orientation of repentance, and the struggle with sin. On the other hand, there are the classic marks of the new life in Christ: freedom, joy, and gratitude. If we are in Christ, then we are freed from both the power of sin and the torment of guilt. We are freed from condemnation and the judgments of the world to joyfully embrace life anew. It also means that we live in gratitude to God, accepting the life of service to others.

2. The Practice of Justification by Grace

In the ecumenical embrace since Vatican II, it has been common for Protestants to immerse themselves in traditions of spirituality drawn from early and medieval Christianity, East and West, as well as non-European churches. In many ways this has created new understanding and new bonds of fellowship. For those living in a spiritual void — be it the absence of personal prayer and reflection or a totally secular landscape — it has opened minds and hearts to traditions of art, symbols, music, and spiritual disciplines. The only disappointment in this rush to claim an eclectic mix of spiritual practices has been the failure to recognize that Protestantism does indeed have rich traditions of spirituality, though they were never named by this term until recent years. Among these multiple forms of spirituality is that stemming from the theology of justification.

There may indeed be a reason why Protestants influenced by the paradoxical affirmation of *simul justus et peccator* — be they Lutheran, Reformed, or Anabaptist — never thought of their religious life as a form of spirituality. The reason is that this tradition contains within it a suspicion regarding all religious practices. One might say that it is fundamentally a spiritual life opposed to spirituality. The reason for this is not simply the Zwinglian assault on images. Instead it stems from the general opposition to all practices as a means to generate, in and of themselves, spiritual life. Thus the spirituality of justification does not focus on disciplines, rules, habits, or set practices. Nor is it a spirituality of movement to greater degrees of perfection. To be sure, there is a movement from life dominated by sin to the new life of Christ, from the struggle of this world to the glory of heaven. Even Luther can speak of life as a struggle with progress in the warfare against sin's domination. But it is not a movement toward perfection. Indeed, his image of the church as a convalescent home shatters all of our naïve idealism about steady progress. To the extent that Protestants speak of the new life as pilgrimage, especially in the English Reformed traditions, it is more of a description of the spiritual struggle between sin and grace, disbelief and faith, doubt and confidence within the daily life of the justified sinner/believer.[39] Pilgrimage becomes not a testimony to our movement toward God or human perfection, but a metaphor of the interplay between repentance and faith. Instead of being a motion picture with beginning and end, it is a series of photographs of the believer in the various configurations of being turned to God by grace.

This highlights the point that the spirituality of justification thinks about the new life in Christ not as a conclusion to human quest, but as the interplay of remembrance and the Pauline triad of faith, hope, and love. To be a Christian is to remember one's sin and God's grace and to discern and celebrate the new life Christ gives. Both acts — remembrance and the response of faith, hope, and love — require that the focus for such spirituality is outside oneself. It has less to do with focusing on my story as with the story of Good Friday and Easter. For this reason, the primary form of individual practice is reading the Bible, whereas the primary form of communal practice is lectionary and sermon. There is never a time when we do not need to hear again what God has done and is doing in the world. Any reflection or contemplation must always begin with what is given to us in the cross and resurrection. These events break in upon us; they are not easily assimilated into our disciplines or theories of quest. These events reveal God's judgment and grace directed toward us, confounding all our spiritual plans and claims and setting before us a Word of promise. The shift from remembrance to hope becomes possible and necessary because the story inevitably contains a calling to be, to do, and to live anew in the peace of Christ. Such activity is understood as responsive, that is, being and doing made possible by the grace of God. It is for good reason that classic hymns from the traditions inspired by justification by grace engage in these two acts of remembrance and faith-hope-love. The story of cross and resurrection is retold,

---

39. Cf. the discussion of pilgrimage in Charles Hambrick Stowe, *The Practice of Piety: Puritan Devotional Disciplines in Seventeenth-Century New England* (Chapel Hill, N.C.: University of North Carolina Press, 1982), pp. 54-90.

leading to the call to respond to God. For example, in "When I Survey the Wondrous Cross" and "O Sacred Head Now Wounded," in each case the last verse concludes with the offering of love to God. In a lesser-known hymn, "O Rejoice Ye Christians Loudly," the same alternation between remembrance and hope occurs. After recounting the passion of Christ, the last verse asks:

> Lord, how shall I thank Thee rightly? I acknowledge
> that by Thee I am saved eternally.
> Let me not forget it lightly, But to Thee at all times cleave
> and my heart true peace receive.
> Joy, O Joy, beyond all gladness, Christ hath done away with sadness!
> Hence, all sorrow and repining, For the Sun of Grace is shining.

Yet another example of piety nurtured by cross and resurrection is "Fairest Lord Jesus." In most American hymnals this hymn is printed with only three or four verses, which give the impression of a rather simplistic piety. But there are more verses, including a final verse that changes the character of the entire hymn, elevating it to the level of the most radical trust in Christ the Savior:

> When I lie dying, Still on Thee relying,
> Suffer me not from Thine arms to fall:
> At my last hour Be thou my power,
> For Thou, Lord Jesus, art my All.

All of this suggests that there is within those traditions inspired by the theology of justification a certain practice of faith, life, and work. From a theological perspective we can name it a theology of the cross; from the perspective of Christian practice it is governed by total reliance on the grace of God, which frees one from condemnation and calls one to service. But such a vision is difficult to sustain. If we consider the course of the Protestant experience, where a variety of communities have sought to live within this vision, there have been serious difficulties. Here we shall note three.

a. Relying on God Alone

The genius of the theology of justification has always been the shattering of all earthly idols and the reliance on God alone. Nowhere does the temptation to divert such trust in God become more appealing than in the realm of religion itself. In Paul we find the problem appears in the religious drive to do good works (Galatians) and misunderstandings regarding the Law (Romans).

In Luther the problem takes the form of overestimating the power of the episcopacy, religious practices (indulgences and sacraments) and even the Bible. While today we might be less confident than Luther to claim one theme in the Bible to be its primary theme, the Reformers saw this as a way of reconstituting the church on its only foundation, namely, God's Word in Jesus Christ.

But as we know from Protestant history as well as contemporary struggles regarding the basis for the church, it is difficult to maintain a community that relies on God's justifying grace. Time and time again churches that claim justification by grace as their primary principle slide into a Protestant form of infallibility. On the one hand it takes the form of absolute and incontestable doctrine, on the other hand it appears in the willingness to absolutize the Bible as the infallible and/or inerrant Word of God. To be sure, the intention in both cases is noble: to maintain true faith in a world of multiple voices that affirm all the devices and desires of the human heart. But the seriousness of the danger does not justify the obvious contradiction of the very essence of the theology of justification. This must be said to both those who wish to conserve the tradition as well as those who wish to open the community of faith to new truth. We are living at a time when dogmatism of the left rivals that of the right, with each claiming holiness and truth.

For those who claim any knowledge of Paul and Luther, to adopt such dogmatism regarding doctrine or Bible, thereby closing the possibility for the Word to speak to us in new ways, or for the faithful community to relate the gospel to new knowledge, is most tragic. It has produced, in both conservative and liberal denominations, the drive to base the church on agreement regarding doctrine and right action. Such rigidity is in fact the end to the church, since it divides the church according to doctrinal, social, political, and moral preferences. The insistence for agreement, justified as the attempt to maintain the integrity of the church, represents a quest for holiness that we cannot achieve. As history shows, it can only create division and drive people (especially the children) away. Such struggles, however, will become the opportunity to hear again that trust must be directed to God alone.

b. Individualism: From Personal Decision to Isolated Persons

The Christian faith has always called people to make decisions of heart, mind, and will for God. Even when the community provides its initiating and nurturing role in baptism and fellowship, at some point the individual person is called to speak with the creed in the first person: "I believe . . ." From our vantage point, in twenty-first-century America, the personal decision has been translated into the freedom of the isolated person to believe and/or do whatever he or she chooses. One can note, for example, that since the Great Awakening of the eighteenth century and the disestablishment of religion in the new constitution, religion is judged to be a matter of individual life, subject to individual choice. One chooses to be religious and in what way according to personal preferences. The consequences of this are many, but the chief ones are: (a) that religion is thereby defined as a voluntary association of like-minded individuals; (b) that organized religion will have to persuade individuals to join, attend, give, and participate. The pervasiveness of this American way of religious life can be seen in the constant changes within the American Roman Catholic tradition, where free choice, democratization, and member preferences can no longer be ignored. By far the most destructive form of individualism is the tendency to devalue religion as the subjective activity of isolated persons. As such it is either irrelevant or divisive, since it is a violation of other persons' freedom to expect interest or agreement on such idiosyncratic experience.[40]

Much of the blame for this development has been attributed to the theology of justification, with Luther as its chief representative. Did not Luther stand alone before the Emperor claiming the right to interpret Scripture according to his conscience? Did he not give aid and comfort to humanists and northern princes seeking freedom from Rome? By translating the Bible into German, he placed in any reader's hands access to what he considered to be the final authority. He defied the authority of the church and even declared the priesthood of all believers, thereby relativizing ecclesial authority. And in spite of the inevitable exaggeration regarding his decisive conversion, does not Luther himself represent, in his personal struggle with inner demons, generations of believers that follow? In one sense, this view of Luther and his theology is so ingrained in the popular perception, as well as cultural perceptions, that it is impossible to change.[41] That Luther advocated the authority of Scripture rather than conscience, interpreted it according to a long-standing tradition reaching back to Augustine, could not envision faith without Bible and creeds, and was more medieval than modern, makes for an alternative reading of the Reformation.

But while on historical and theological grounds one might wish to defend Luther, the fact remains that Protestantism in America has reorganized, to varying degrees, its theology, worship, and ethics around the priority of the

---

40. Cf. Stephen L. Carter, *The Culture of Disbelief: How American Law and Politics Trivialize Religious Devotion* (New York: HarperCollins, 1993).

41. Cf. John Osborne's play *Luther,* and Erik Erickson, *Young Man Luther: A Study in Psychoanalysis and History* (New York: W. W. Norton, 1958).

individual. The question at this point, therefore, is whether the theology of justification can retain its integrity in the face of this pattern or will simply reinforce it. The question is complicated by the fact that even when we do not wish to reinforce individualism, the form of our practice is perceived as doing so. For example, we preach judgment and grace to individuals in the hope that they will respond with repentance and faith. In many contemporary worship discussions, the goal is for individuals to have a religious experience. Another example is that form of public religion on television and the stream of popular books by Norman Vincent Peale and Robert Schuller, which speak the language of divine help matching self-help. Here religion provides the power for self-actualization and personal problem solving. While traditional Lutherans and Calvinists may object that this does not describe their preaching and liturgy, several things need to be noted: First, before and after many members attend such traditional Protestant worship they encounter popular American religion on radio and television. Second, TV preaching, with dramatic staging and personal appeal, becomes one of the norms, if not the dominant norm, for all preaching. American religion continually demonstrates that the controversial *new measures* slowly move into the mainstream.

The concern raised here, therefore, is not to argue about cause or even whether individualism is real or perceived, but to ask: Can justification by grace be preached without reinforcing the dominant pattern of American religion? Unless we ask this question in full honesty of our complicity with the individualism of the culture, there will be little chance for an affirmative answer. To use the theology of justification as a means of proclaiming the gospel will require that we begin again with a theocentric starting point, which in biblical terms presupposes a communal and global perspective. But one cannot place such a perspective on a foundation of individualism. This would mean that worship and preaching be biblical — not in the sense of using the Bible to be the means for solving our problems or a quest for self-actualization — but the means to ask: What is God doing in the world? Why do I resist the text that is before us? It will mean that the call to individuals to repent and believe must be placed in the context of communal structures (liturgy, creed, sacraments, signs, and symbols) and include the expectation of communal participation within the congregation and in the world through public witness and service. The irony of the theology of justification is that by appealing to Scripture and the God who judges all things — including the communal structures of religion — this tradition undercuts the very communal structures that are necessary for its faith and work. Without strong communal structures — old and new — the theology of justification loses its theological and evangelical witness.

c. Claiming the Whole Gospel of Grace and Power

The great strength of the theology of justification is that it affirms the ground of our salvation in God's gracious action in Jesus Christ and calls believers to faith, hope, and love. *Sola gratia* redefines our understanding of God and functions as the great motivation for the Christian life. How ironic, then, that a tradition so founded in the life-renewing grace of God should find itself inclined to rest in that forgiving grace and be less inclined to show forth the new life. In doctrinal terms, the problem is the inability to move from justification to sanctification. To be sure, traditions taking their stand in the theology of justification have dealt with this in different ways. In the Lutheran traditions, the paradox of sin and grace allowed for the separation of Law and Gospel, State and Church. Each realm has a mandate from God, one empowered to use the sword to restrain evil, the other empowered to proclaim the gospel. Such practice could lead to quietism and complicity with the state, either by honoring its authority or because of the strong influence of a piety of self-sacrifice, modeled after Jesus. In the Reformed traditions, the theology of justification was merged with a world-transforming vision that produced the theocratic impulse as well as endless attempts at instituting the new community. This was played out in the reforms of Zurich and Geneva, the Puritan Revolution in England and the great experiments in New England, as well as endless movements and causes in the last two hundred years to transform the world.

In the last half of the twentieth century, new currents of piety and social involvement cut across old denominational labels, producing new configurations of grace and power. One is the tendency on the part of established churches to be quite comfortable with a theology of grace that repeats time and again that God loves and forgives. When Christianity is reduced to the popular slogan that "God loves you" there is an inevitable lowering of expectations regarding what God is doing in the world or how God expects us to change. Endless references to unconditional love, and a grace that knows no limits, do create a culture of contentment. Religion begins to focus more and more on what is missing in the lives of middle- and upper-class persons, namely, love and meaning. Thus the shift to a message of acceptance and encouragement, with little judgment or call to change. By contrast, the religion of power among Baptist, Pentecostal, and Holiness traditions takes a quite different approach: God expects something of us and we can expect something of God.[42] Such practices receive heavy criticism from the mainline, es-

---

42. Here it is interesting to note how the highly disciplined programs for the recovery of individuals caught in addiction, shame, or low self-esteem often rely more on the religion of

pecially when they involve material expectations or torment the sick with the burden that they have not been healed because they lack faith. In return, the religion of power accuses the religion of grace for its lack of confidence that God can change lives and the world.

If the split between the religion of grace and the religion of power suggests a simple division, the reality of religion in America is quite different. To this analysis we must add the emergence of the culture wars in the past forty years. What is unique about this phenomenon is the social activism of mainline and conservative traditions formerly known for their quietism. But while both sides now wish to apply religion to public life, they differ vehemently on what issues should be addressed, or even made the basis for membership. In some respects this means that for liberals and conservatives, sanctification or holiness (and not grace) has become the major issue facing churches and the society. The question, however, is whether broad socio-political issues such as the environment, race, war and peace, and health care are the tests of faith, or are moral norms relating to procreation, sexuality, and gender the decisive issues. The decision by some Roman Catholic bishops to use communion as a means to gain compliance on the matter of abortion is but one example. For all groups the issue is: How does a community balance the liberating declaration of grace with the call for genuine faith, hope, and love? To the extent that those inspired by the theology of justification fail to see the problem, they suffer the absence of life-giving power. To the extent that they introduce forms of practice that are so restrictive that they exclude and repress, they will destroy themselves by their lack of grace. Against both sides the gospel stands as a message of grace and power. The paradox of sin and grace was never intended to produce a paralysis, wherein the believer lives in an eternal cycle of sin and forgiveness.

---

power. It is incorrect to refer to some of these as self-help groups, since they often represent a reliance on God by people who have given up on themselves. The very structured process of some of these organizations runs parallel to the movement in the theology of justification: the admission that one has nothing or has failed; the reliance on God, commitment to a discipline in the expectation that change will occur, and loyalty to members. In many respects the difference in approach between the religion of grace and the religion of power reflects differences of class, gender, and race. One wonders whether one must have nothing or be excluded in order to call upon God in expectation. But the matter cannot be completely explained by reference to class, gender, and race. There are also crossover developments such as those of Peale and Schuller, where a conservative Reformed tradition produces a popular message aimed at living a better life for educated and economically secure people. This is a significant development in mainline churches, since it clearly moves beyond a word of grace to the word of power to change your life. It reflects the fact that all people have serious needs and all people live in a society that is in need of renewal.

3. Changes in Pauline Studies: Does Paul Support Luther?

In the last four decades a major shift has occurred in the interpretation of Romans. This new interpretation represents such a serious challenge to the traditional reading of Romans, represented by Luther, that this discussion must deal with the issues raised. The *traditional view,* which is so deeply embedded in the history and consciousness of Protestants, may be summarized as follows:[43] The Letter to the Romans is Paul's theological *magnum opus,* where the central message is justification by faith, framed in forensic language. The problem is: How can sinners, judged guilty because of their sin, but also enslaved to sin as a demonic power, stand before a righteous God? God's judgment finds expression in both wrath and the Law. Wrath signifies God's opposition to the sin and evil of the world. The Law functions in at least two ways: first, as good and given by God, the Law reveals what we ought to do and be; second, by reminding us of our failings, the Law convicts us of our sin and reveals the inadequacies of our best efforts. This second function of the Law either drives us to despair or to Christ. The general effect of all this is the trembling heart and the moral anguish of the divided self, as represented by Romans 7. In the face of such insurmountable tension and certain judgment, the righteousness of God appears in a form that we could not expect: Jesus the anointed of God assumes the role of the guilty and bears our condemnation, dying as a sinner. By participating or identifying with sinful humanity, and bearing this death, God in Christ condemns sin and overcomes death. By his resurrection, Jesus offers to sinners new life, freedom, and reconciliation with God. The gift is that sinners are declared righteous by faith, i.e., by dying and rising with Christ by faith they receive the righteousness of Christ. All this is from God, whose righteousness is revealed to be gracious and life-giving. Finally, all of this means that legalism, as our attempt to achieve salvation by good works, as demanded by the Law, is futile and condemned. The gospel therefore stands in opposition to works righteousness and the Law.

This composite summarizes the traditional reading of Romans, especially among Protestants. It appeals to Augustine, for whom grace was the resolution to intellectual and moral struggles. It obviously appeals to Luther, where the struggle between Law and gospel, with all of its anxiety and stress, usually

---

43. The *traditional* view summarized here is not simply that of Luther, but a general composite reflecting the view taken for granted among mainline Protestant interpretation at mid-twentieth century. As such it not only affected the interpretation of Paul, but was the biblical starting point for many Protestants seeking to build a systematic theology on the doctrine of justification.

overshadows Protestant theology and preaching. In a related way, Calvin's *trembling conscience* inspires a parallel development in the Reformed tradition. It should also be emphasized that the traditional view assumes that for Paul and us, the basic problem is the moral struggle with works righteousness. This aspect of the traditional view is complicated because it has too often contributed to anti-Jewish attitudes, producing a tragic history of anti-Semitism.

In essays published in 1963 and 1976, Krister Stendahl argued that justification by grace was not the central theme of Romans; instead the entire letter has to do with a defense of Paul's apostolic mission to the Gentiles.[44] The so-called *introspective conscience,* which Stendahl identifies with Luther, was judged to have nothing to do with Paul. Every major concept in Romans was reinterpreted in light of the righteousness of God revealed as salvation for both Jew and Gentile. These points became the basis for the *revised view* of Romans, which was supported by two major developments. One was the new interpretations of the Old Testament and first-century Judaism, which rejected the negative stereotypes of ancient Israel and later Judaism. The second development was the need to oppose anti-Semitism, which in the twentieth century produced the Holocaust. Taking these two together, a careful review of Christian interpretation of the Old Testament as well as pivotal sections of the New Testament, such as Romans, was required.

Here then is a summary of the *revised view:* The central message of Romans is God's plan for Jews and Gentiles, as a defense of God's righteousness and God's Law, as well as the ministry of Paul to the Gentiles. This view opposes three things: (1) It denies that moral legalism is characteristic of first-century Judaism; (2) It rejects the view that Paul in Romans was preoccupied with moral legalism; (3) It denies that Paul as a Christian displayed anxiety, inner turmoil, and excessive introspection. From a positive perspective, it affirms that the gracious action of God in creating the covenant community precedes the Law. As is the case with the concept of righteousness, the Law must be understood as relational in the context of God's covenant. Therefore the Law defines duties and obligations for staying in covenant relation with one another and with God, not for earning salvation. If the Law becomes a problem for Paul and the early Christians, it is not as a moral tyrant, but as the instrument for insisting on a distinct community, separated from

44. For the original essay, "The Apostle Paul and the Introspective Conscience of the West," and the longer essay, see Stendahl, *Paul Among Jews and Gentiles and Other Essays* (Philadelphia: Fortress, 1976). Much of what was said in these early essays was summarized in a study of Romans published in 1993 and republished two years later as *Final Account: Paul's Letter to the Romans* (Minneapolis: Fortress, 1995).

Gentiles by adherence to the Law. The technical phrase *works of the law,* it is now argued, refers not to moral achievement, but the cultic and dietary requirements that distinguish Jews from Gentiles, with the claim of special status.[45] Confronted with criticism from fellow Christians and his rejection by fellow Jews, Paul writes Romans to make the case that all — Jews and Gentiles — are justified by faith apart from compliance with such cultic regulations (e.g., circumcision). In his exposition of the meaning of Christ, Paul uses multiple images (i.e., sacrificial, liberationist, and legal) to describe the new life in Christ, all of which confirm the righteousness and faithfulness of God to Abraham, Israel, and the Gentiles.

In many respects the revised view represents gains. The positive assessment of the Old Testament and Judaism is incorporated into New Testament interpretation, setting aside many of the negative perspectives regarding Jews. The insistence that Paul not be read through modern psychological theories or even the moral struggle of Martin Luther represents a major hermeneutical shift, difficult as it may be. Finally, the revised view provides a biblical basis for thinking about Paul with social categories, rather than the highly individualized ones so familiar to Protestants. If Paul's basic message is about the plan of God for all people (Jews and Gentiles) in the economy of salvation, such a perspective may help us rethink the meaning of Christian life as a communal existence — alongside of that other community still loved by God, namely Judaism. But these positive contributions still leave us with an impossible choice between a beloved theological tradition and current biblical scholarship. To be sure, one could defend Luther's interpretation as a bold application of the idea of justification for the crisis he faced, while admitting that his interpretation was not Paul's. But that was not Luther's view, nor can one imagine it to be the view of most Lutherans and those spiritually indebted to Luther. Following Augustine, Luther thought he was reading Romans according to Paul's intention. The question becomes a simple one: Does Paul really support Luther?

The full impact of the divergence in perspective is not clear. Do the two positions in fact exclude one another or can we find common ground? It would be easy to bridge the impasse if the problem were one of emphasis. If the one view makes Romans 1–8 the core, with Romans 9–11 an afterthought, the other view makes 9–11 the core, with 1–8 a long introduction. But Romans 1–8 appears more than an introduction, and Romans 9–11 cannot simply be treated as a practical application. But overemphasis on one part will not be overcome without dealing with two broad issues. One is the acceptance of the

---

45. Cf. Dunn, pp. 334-82.

complexity of Romans as a literary work. The two views appear to assume that Paul's letter is one-dimensional, i.e., it is only about justification, or, it is only about the mission to the Gentiles. But if one takes the view that the letter is complex, rich in main argument, subarguments, admonitions, images, and ideas, then new options are before us for finding common ground. The second issue is the difference in context, i.e., the contexts of Paul, Luther, and a post-Holocaust twentieth-century world. These different contexts produce quite different interpretations of Romans, no doubt leading to charges of misinterpretation. The two points come together in a further question: How does the complexity of the letter relate to interpretations in quite different contexts?

The easiest matter to resolve may be that of the main theme. The revised view argues, on historical/critical grounds, that the theme of the letter is Paul's defense of the mission to the Gentiles. The number of scholars holding this view is so large, extending over time and place, that it appears as the current consensus. This view overturns the negative stereotypes of first-century Judaism as legalistic. In this context of late twentieth-century Jewish-Christian relations, it was a significant development to conclude that Romans is not directed against Jewish legalism or that Paul is not primarily concerned with the inner struggle of individuals seeking forgiveness. Repositioning the letter in terms of God's plan of salvation for all people (i.e., God's fidelity to Israel and the inclusion of the Gentiles) was a positive step forward. While this version of the main theme obviously requires changes in the traditional view, there is nothing in the traditional view that requires that justification by grace must be the major theme. That it has been considered to be such can be historically explained. Furthermore, the traditional view can accept the new perspective because the revised view acknowledges two important parts of Romans: first, that all have sinned; second, that justification means salvation is a gift of God offered by grace apart from the Law. This is the heart of the traditional view and becomes a basis for common ground, since the revised view emphasizes that this is precisely how salvation was always viewed in Judaism.

The real difficulties lie with three specific issues, interestingly enough, all involving the definition of sin and the way we speak about it: (1) The second use of the Law; (2) Romans 7:13-25; (3) Paul's opponents.

1. Protestants developed a shorthand to summarize the different uses of the Law: the first expresses God's will; the second convicts us of sin, driving us to Christ. Many Protestants have treated the second use as a necessary step in the movement toward justification by faith: one must first be convicted of sin and yearn for forgiveness before one can be accepted. The revised view finds no basis for this view in Romans! Instead, it views the Law as part of an

epoch in God's economy of salvation, defining obligations for membership in the covenant with Israel. It is this aspect of the Law — the cultic obligations — which now comes to an end. But more important, the revised view exposes a fundamental contradiction in the second use of the Law: justification by faith means that the Law is not a precondition prior to our acceptance by God. By insisting on the second use of the Law, one appears to want a Christian to become a spiritual Jew, i.e., enter the world of the Law in order to be convicted of sin and terrified of judgment. This criticism is valid even if one might still wish to confess that, in retrospect, the Law reveals our sin.

2. Romans 7 involves several issues that expose the wide gap between the two sides. One is the purpose of 7:13-25. In the revised view, Paul's purpose is not to expose the internal torments of a guilty conscience, caught between sin and grace. Rather it is to defend the Law and to make a point regarding the power of sin: though the will intends the good in relation to the Law, it is the power of sin that enslaves and prevents the will from doing what it in fact intends. In effect, the argument is a subpoint in the development of the main argument regarding the goodness of the Law and God's plan for Jews and Gentiles. By contrast, the traditional view saw it as the quintessential argument that validates the inability of the sinner to fulfill the Law, thereby proving that justification can only be by grace and not by works. On the surface, one could not imagine two interpretations more at odds. But one simple fact appears to be overlooked by the revised view. Even if one accepts the revised view, the fact remains that one is still left with a divided self as a fundamental aspect of Christian experience: the good will that loves God and the Law and the evil will controlled by sin. The only way to avoid this conclusion would be: (1) to deny that our will had anything to do with turning against God and the Law; (2) to affirm that our baptism in the death and resurrection of Christ conveys perfect holiness; (3) to affirm that it is all the fault of an external power that enslaves us. The first suggests a naïve innocence, the second a perfect sanctification in this life, and the third appears to open the door to cosmological dualism. Since Paul does not claim any of these options, it would appear that even on the revisionist view Paul has introduced a most powerful insight in the struggle with sin, namely, that we ourselves are of two minds.[46]

The presence of this insight in Romans 7 — not something read into it —

---

46. To make this point is not necessarily to engage in all the horrors and/or self-absorption of the "introspective conscience of the West." One can practice moral realism without the extremes the revisionist view denounces. Such realism is well illustrated in the prophets and teachings of Jesus.

points to the complexity of Paul's discourse in Romans. His analysis of sin, the Law, and the sinner includes many aspects, references, and suggestive comments. To say that one point is the primary one and another is secondary does not invalidate the claim that the second point is in the text. What it means is that the text is complex, filled with layers of meaning. But here we need to complicate the reading of a complex text even further by adding the importance of context. The revised view argues that the divided self was not the main point and therefore did not need attention or explanation in the first century. This implies that perhaps it was generally understood or accepted by the readers. But what if one lives in a world where virtually no one accepts the idea of a divided self? What if the dominant theology and piety assumes that the will is free, that we become righteous by actions, that we are responsible for doing the good, and that we shall be judged according to our works? In such a world, the shocking aspect of 7:13-25 will be both the power of sin to enslave and the fact that the will is divided and unable to do the good. That was Luther's world, and in many respects it was the world of both Karl Barth and Reinhold Niebuhr. The entire matter becomes even more complicated when the revised view takes as its primary context anti-Semitism in a post-Holocaust world.

To argue in this way does not deny the revised interpretation of Romans 7, but rather contends that the traditional view is using an insight in Paul, which does in fact support the general logic of Paul's argument for justification by grace and not works. This does not warrant dismissing the general framework of the revised view, nor does it suggest that the traditional view can simply return to business as usual. But to exclude reference to the divided self from interpretations of Romans 7 belies a one-dimensional reading of a very complex text.

Romans 7 is also a crucial battleground with respect to the assessment of Paul and the language we use to describe Christian existence. The revised view rejects the idea that Paul himself was beset by inner turmoil, thus becoming a prototype of both Augustine and Luther (though the conversion experiences of all three figures were quite different). Instead, the revised view suggests that Paul was a mature, healthy Jewish Christian, not tormented by doubt and despair, or even worried about his failings and sins.[47] This reap-

---

47. Cf. Stendahl, pp. 79-96, 7-15, and 23-28; E. P. Sanders, *Paul and Palestinian Judaism: A Comparison of Patterns of Religion* (Minneapolis: Fortress, 1977), pp. 443-47. For a commentary that utilizes this view in a consistent way, cf. Paul J. Achtemeier, "Romans," in *Interpretation: A Bible Commentary for Teaching and Preaching*, ed. James Luther Mays (Atlanta: John Knox, 1985), pp. 120-29. Following Sanders he holds that Romans 7 is not a description of inner turmoil in Paul, nor is it about the Christian life, but rather about the power of sin. To defend this

praisal of Paul parallels the broad criticism of the so-called introspective tendencies in Western Christianity. For the revised view, the description of the Christian life, from Augustine to Luther to the modern age, involves a turning of attention away from God's plan of salvation for the world toward the moral struggle within the individual.[48] The criticism carries with it an implied critique of the individualism of modern Protestantism as well as the modern propensity for psychological analysis. But while one can acknowledge the negative aspects of these tendencies, the criticism is so broad that greater clarification would be helpful. First, Paul does engage in profound insights into the human mind and heart.[49] Luther's terror may not be Paul's personal experience, but he finds his life illuminated by Paul's writing. Second, important distinctions in context as well as meaning are lost by lumping together Augustine, Luther, and the excesses of contemporary culture regarding anxiety and self-analysis.[50] It would be helpful to distinguish the introspection of moral realism, born of honesty regarding oneself and God, from whatever psychological excesses are deemed inappropriate. Greater clarity would be helpful and could possibly lead to the discovery of common ground: perhaps Paul is closer to Luther than suggested by the revised view.[51]

---

position Achtemeier offers two arguments: first, Romans 7 cannot be about inner turmoil in Christians because that would contradict Romans 6 and 8, where Paul declares that we are free from sin (Achtemeier, pp. 121-22). Second, the references to sin do not refer to moral sin in general, but opposition to Christ. It is this sin that is for Paul the primary example of wanting to do the good, but instead doing evil (Achtemeier, pp. 123-26).

48. It is interesting that Stendahl himself provides the obvious explanation for this adaptation of Paul's message: since Augustine lives in a new context where the mission to the Gentiles has in effect been completed (i.e, no one argues about admission of Gentiles into the church), Paul's letter is read as a resource for the individual's struggle to be faithful in word and deed. But having described this new context that prompts Augustine and Luther to read Romans as they do, the reader is left with the implication that such a reading is erroneous.

49. An interesting example is Paul's most popular and well-known moral admonition in 1 Corinthians 13. Paul avoids naïve sentimentality precisely because the passage exposes our deceptions regarding the purity of our love. There is a fundamental realism in Paul's description of the Christian life, caught in the dialectic of sin and grace. To exclude reference to this would impoverish our life and work.

50. Stendahl emphasizes that Paul is neither Luther nor Freud (cf. "Paul and the Introspective Conscience," p. 95). But the problem is described in such broad terms that it allows Luther to be too easily dismissed as neurotic, in need of the very psychological attention decried as excessive. By contrast, compare Oberman's thesis that Luther is not a modern but medieval man, as well as his insistence that neither Luther nor his age should be dismissed as neurotic (cf. *Luther*).

51. For two examples of writers working within the general framework that the central theme of Romans is the apostolic mission to the Gentiles, but who still discuss the tensions within the Christian life caused by sin, compare Dunn, *Romans 1–8*, pp. 396-407. In speaking of

3. In the traditional view, Paul's opponent in Romans is Jewish legalism. To some extent this negative interpretation has been overturned by the positive assessment of first-century Judaism, and of course, the major rethinking of the Old Testament in twentieth-century historical and theological work.[52] But if the opponents in Romans are not legalists, then who are they? In general, the new interpretations emphasize that the opponents are those wanting to maintain the cultic side of the Law, which sets boundaries between Jew and Gentile. This can take the form of sectarianism or simply opposition to the Christian movement in the name of adherence to the Law.[53] In the context of current Jewish-Christian relations, it may be helpful for the revised view to define the opponents in this way, in contrast to all of Judaism. But such historical judgments still leave unanswered two broad concerns. The one finds expression with questions: How did such tendencies relate to the main body of Judaism? Did they also include a quest for legal righteousness? Did they have any connection with the opponents of Paul in other settings or even the opponents of Jesus in the gospels?[54] The other concern is our concern for legalism, based on a historical view of the matter. It is frustrating in these discussions regarding Romans to find an unwillingness to speak of it. It is obviously a highly charged subject, given Jewish-Christian relations. But not discussing it creates a somewhat fragile solution. We know that legalism is an inevitable tendency (to be sure, heretical) within mono-

---

Paul's inability to do the good, Dunn can say: "By thus defining the true nature of his impotence at this point Paul avoids the mistake of allowing self-depreciation to deteriorate into self-detestation" (p. 407). See also Paul W. Meyer, "Romans," *Harper's Bible Commentary,* ed. James L. Mays (San Francisco: Harper and Row, 1988), pp. 1130-67, as well as his article on Romans 7: "The Worm at the Core of the Apple: Exegetical Reflections on Romans 7," in *The Conversation Continues: Studies in Paul and John in Honor of J. Louis Martyn,* ed. Robert T. Fortna and Beverly R. Gaventa (Nashville: Abingdon, 1990), pp. 62-84.

52. Compare in general the works previously cited by Sanders (*Paul and Palestinian Judaism*); Fitzmyer (*Paul and His Theology*); and Dunn, *The Theology of Paul the Apostle,* pp. 334-41.

53. For example, even James Dunn, a strong advocate of the revised view, is forced to admit that the question of Paul's opponents cannot be ignored (Dunn, *The Theology of Paul the Apostle,* pp. 345-82). Dunn concludes, after a lengthy historical analysis, that the problem lies with zealous, sectarian Pharisees who refuse to acknowledge that God intends to include Gentiles in the covenant. Paul's persecution of Stephen may reflect contact with this view. Applying this historical judgment to Romans, Dunn argues that *works of the law* does not refer to personal moral achievement in the traditional legalistic sense, but maintenance of those cultic and social regulations that define Jews over against Gentiles. In his commentary on Romans, Paul Achtemeier sees the problem as misguided adherence to the Law, with the inevitable result of opposition to the Christian movement (Achtemeier, pp. 121-29).

54. It is striking that Dunn does not address this question, in spite of his extensive analysis of sectarianism.

theistic religions that place such a strong emphasis on moral practice as a reflection of the divine holiness. Every branch of Christianity has struggled with both legalism and sectarianism, born of the quest for the sanctified community. Furthermore, Christian sectarian movements suggest that the cultic/social requirements are so intertwined with moral issues, that the two cannot be separated. Indeed, it is probably correct to say that cultic observances are important only because they symbolize the essential moral reality required of the faithful community.

We have then a complex problem: the debate over Paul's context (i.e., who are his opponents?) raises questions regarding our cultural context. In each case, serious issues arise: With respect to Paul's context, can the cultic and moral aspects of the Law be separated so clearly? With respect to our context, can we discuss Jewish separatism or legalism without falling into the trap of anti-Semitism? From a historical perspective, it is inevitable that we pursue these questions, given the separatist and legalistic movements in Jewish and Christian traditions. It is no more unusual to find these tendencies in first-century Judaism and Christianity than in our own time. The problem may well not be back there in the first century but in ourselves. We see this especially in those who are spiritual refugees from authoritarian and legalistic communities of faith. When persons have been hurt by repressive and unforgiving systems, they are quite sensitive to anything that hints of such practice. These reflections lead to a limited conclusion regarding Romans 7: the separation of the cultic from the moral may tend to confuse rather than help our interpretation of the first century as well as our own context.[55]

What then can we conclude from this discussion of the traditional and revised interpretations of Romans? The revisionist view makes a strong case for its version of the general theme of Romans and is on firm ground in applying new insights regarding first-century Judaism to the interpretation of Romans. It rightly exposes the weakness of the traditional view: by orchestrating justification by faith into a grand theological principle, at the expense of Romans 9–11, it slowly turned attention away from salvation as a communal event in God's plan for the world to a message of grace for individuals. Growing out of this interpretation, the traditional view directly or indirectly contributed to negative views of Judaism. While accepting these gains, I have also argued that one can still develop a theology of justification within this

---

55. A good example of speaking of the problem without making it anti-Semitic is Meyer's discussion of Romans 7. For Meyer, Romans 7 points to the general corruptibility of the religious drive to seek the good, which when subverted by the power of sin, only produces more sin and death. In this discussion Meyer comes close to the kind of tragic vision made famous by Reinhold Niebuhr.

new framework, though a serious reconsideration is needed regarding the traditional second use of the Law. The matter of Romans 7 is more complex, with gains and losses on each side. The revised view is indeed a healthy corrective to any preoccupation with introspective analysis and the modern turn toward individual salvation. That Paul in Romans is primarily concerned with a defense of God's action in Jesus Christ as a plan of salvation for Jews and Gentiles brings theology and preaching back to a theocentric focus. But to the extent that the revised view drives a wedge between the cultic and the moral, it tends to divide the understanding of sin, law, and justification in an arbitrary way.

From this perspective I believe it can be argued that *justification* is a broader and richer category for Paul than what is implied in some of the revised interpretations. While it certainly includes freedom from cultic regulations, where noncompliance excludes persons from access to God and membership in the covenant community, it also includes freedom from moral guilt, and confers standing before God. Romans presents the human condition as one tormented by many things, internal and external. While the main theme may be the mission to the Gentiles, the problem is not simply those who oppose an opening of the covenants to Gentiles, but also sin, death, and demonic powers. From his other letters we know that Paul uses the cross and the idea of justification to silence spiritual and moral pride. In 1 Corinthians Paul encounters claims to special knowledge, spirituality, and moral wisdom. In Galatians he must argue against claims to moral righteousness based on works. Given all this, it is difficult to accept the view that sin and justification in Romans should only refer to cultic requirements. Is it possible that Paul could be using justification by faith to apply to both aspects: on the one hand, as a defense against some Christians and Jews for a mission to the Gentiles, and on the other hand, as a forthright admonition to Gentiles that they enter the new covenant as sinners justified by grace? All of this is to suggest the need for a broader and more comprehensive understanding of justification by faith as it functions in Romans and elsewhere in Paul's letters.

Chapter 3   Penal Substitution

Charles Hodge

A. Introduction

Chapter Two reviewed crucial passages in Romans and presented the theory of justification by grace. Here our attention turns to the second theory that relies on the forensic language of justification, namely, penal substitution. It will be difficult for some readers to separate these two theories, since there is a point of view that assumes that justification by grace and penal substitution are one and the same. But at several crucial points, the two theories diverge. In penal substitution, the legal imagery is expanded to include: (1) the requirement of a penalty necessitated by the Law; (2) the intervention of a substitute who dies vicariously in our place; (3) a reward which allows for the salvation of humankind. The focus, therefore, is on the exchange of a penalty required by the Law and merit gained. This is a marked contrast with the theory of justification by grace, which involves the dichotomy between the justification by works and justification by grace, or to use the language of righteousness, between the righteousness that condemns and the righteousness that makes right. There is also a major shift in perspective regarding the Law. In penal substitution, there is a continuity from start to finish provided by the Law, as distributive justice, whereas in justification by grace, the emphasis is on a saving power revealed apart from the Law. In fact, in penal substitution it is the demand of legal justice that drives the entire theory. Other differences will emerge as we analyze the theory, but given these it is appropriate to separate the two theories.

It should also be noted that the theory of penal substitution usually relies heavily on the language of sacrifice, raising the question whether this theory should be treated as a subcategory of the theory of sacrifice, discussed in Chapter One. I have not done that for the following reason: the preponderance of the legal framework in penal substitution is quite different from the language of sacrifice in Old and New Testaments. As shown in Chapter One, the sacrifices for sin in the Bible were acts of purification (i.e., the removal of sin) instituted by God. They were not sacrifices offered as compensation *to* God. Thus the use of the word sacrifice in penal substitution represents a quite different development. As discussed, such a development appears in Calvin and the Roman Mass in ways that are controversial and under serious debate. This study is based on the assumption that theories must be differentiated by their basic image and internal logic, which means they should not be combined simply because a word from one theory appears in another.

B. The Theory in Outline

We can outline the theory as follows:

1. This theory begins with the reality of sin as a violation of covenant law, thereby creating separation from God and incurring the judgment of God.
2. Using the analogy of the law court, human beings are judged guilty before God and stand under the penalty of death. The crucial issue is satisfaction of God's justice.
3. But God shows love for us by sending Jesus as a substitute to die for us, thereby satisfying the demands of the Law for punishment.
4. In his death and resurrection, Jesus frees us from the penalty of the Law and offers new life to those who have faith in him as Lord and Savior.

C. The Witness of Faith: Charles Hodge on Penal Substitution

The theory of penal substitution has come under serious criticism and in many circles has often been dismissed.[1] By choosing Charles Hodge as our

---

1. The objections to the idea of satisfaction go back to Abelard's critique of Anselm's use of satisfaction in his theory of atonement (see chapter on Anselm). In our time the word satisfaction has become a lightning rod for a variety of criticisms. For a general survey of feminist and Womanist criticism, cf. L. Susan Bond, *Trouble with Jesus: Women, Christology and Preaching* (St. Louis: Chalice, 1999). For a Mennonite critique emphasizing the theme of nonviolence, cf. J. Denny Weaver, *The Nonviolent Atonement* (Grand Rapids: Eerdmans, 2001). For a critique from a Presbyterian perspective, cf. William Placher, "Christ Takes Our Place," *Interpretation* 53 (January 1999): 5-20.

case study, we have one of the strongest defenses of the theory, based on appeals to Scripture, tradition, and reason. Hodge has no interest in personal innovation but claims only to be consistent with these sources. It is not surprising that, for so many followers, such a formidable defense should provide legitimacy for this theory. Conversely, those who would reject this theory will have to deal with the biblical and theological sources used by Hodge. There is, however, one aspect of this choice that may distract from the discussion. Many Protestants in favor of the theory disagree with Hodge on the doctrine of double predestination. Since our purpose is to consider theories of atonement, this discussion will separate penal substitution from the question of predestination. While they are inseparable for Hodge, such is not the case among United Methodists, Baptists, Pietists, and other Free Church traditions. For these latter groups, penal substitution stands alone and represents their interpretation of the many biblical references to sacrifice and ransom.

In 1822 Charles Hodge began a fifty-year teaching career at Princeton Seminary. As the leading defender of conservative Reformed theology in the nineteenth century, he shaped the general theological character of the Presbyterian Church.[2] Some three thousand students and countless other clergy were influenced by his teaching and writings. In Hodge one finds a defender of orthodox Calvinism (e.g., double predestination and opposition to Darwinism). In his major work, *Systematic Theology,* Hodge weaves together three methods: (1) a reliance on Scripture as the first source for the formation of doctrine; (2) a critical appraisal of traditions, using what he determines as the standard for orthodoxy, stemming from Augustine through Calvin and the Reformed confessions; (3) an appeal to human experience, from which he derives generally accepted principles.[3] For Hodge, these three are in perfect agreement. The principles derived from rational analysis are the final confirmation of the truth of Christian doctrine.

Hodge's presentation of each doctrine includes extensive analysis and evaluation of biblical material, as well as philosophical and theological debates, past and present. This interplay of vigorous opposition to alternative positions (e.g., Roman Catholic, Lutheran, Arminian, or the radically divergent options of nineteenth-century theology) creates a multilayered presentation. In the process he demonstrates considerable knowledge of the many perspectives in biblical interpretation and theological debate in his time.

---

2. Winthrop S. Hudson, *Religion in America* (New York: Scribner's, 1965), pp. 166 and 277.

3. Cf. Charles Hodge, *Systematic Theology,* 2 vols. (New York: Scribner, Armstrong, and Co., 1871). All further references to this work are to volume 2 and will be given in parentheses within the text.

Given the extensive disagreement which he carefully notes, it is surprising that he can appeal to universally accepted conclusions. But this confidence contributes to his goal: to demonstrate the superiority of orthodox Calvinism by a carefully constructed position based on the Bible, church doctrine, and reason.

When reading Hodge's *Systematic Theology* one enters a work that is so tightly organized that several ideas emerge as the foundation for the Christology that is to follow. One is the sovereignty of God and the other is the divine justice. These principles assume the classic affirmations of Trinity and Incarnation (i.e., Nicea and Chalcedon) and shape the way God and Christ are understood in the work of salvation.

Hodge understands God to be the sovereign creator of all things. God rules over all things in such a way that nothing is contrary to God's ordaining will (p. 331). Against what he perceives to be a retreat by Lutherans, and a complete rejection by Arminians, Hodge affirms double predestination. Here we see an example of how Hodge wishes to connect a line of thought from Augustine through the Reformed confessional doctrines as fundamental for orthodoxy. His defense of double predestination is not confined to appeals to the Bible and doctrines, but also includes an example of his rational analysis of general experience. That God has ordained some to salvation and others to damnation is self-evident, since both groups exist! The assumption here, of course, is the all-encompassing Rule of God. To put it in simple terms, if it exists, it must be ordained (p. 336).

On this principle of God's sovereign rule, Hodge builds a general theory of God's plan for humankind. This plan includes four dispensations dealing with Adam, the Patriarchs, Moses, and Christ (p. 366). But while there are many dispensations, there is but one covenant uniting all things, just as there is but one plan from the beginning. This plan is revealed by Scripture as well as by general human experience of the creation, the fall, and election. The facts of history are "the interpretation of the eternal purposes of God" (p. 332). The key to this plan is the agreement between the Father and the Son for the salvation of humankind (pp. 358ff.). By mutual consent, the Son agrees to assume human nature and bear the sins of the world as a sacrifice. In turn, the Father promises to be with the Son, deliver him from death, raise him to be head of the church, and accept all those he saves. While the salvation that Christ brings is offered by faith, it is set within the larger purposes of God's double election. Thus both salvation and creation are understood in terms of the plan ordained by the sovereign Rule of God.

By itself this view of God's sovereignty could move in a variety of directions regarding atonement. But when we place alongside of it the second principle of God's justice, the direction becomes quite clear. The justice of God becomes crucial once the fall and human sin have entered the discussion. Sin violates justice and evokes the judgment and wrath of God. But ultimately the violation of sin requires that a penalty be assessed against the offender. It is at this point that Hodge introduces the concept of satisfaction as that which is necessitated by God's justice (cf. pp. 473-83). The concept is developed in several ways.

First, a variety of biblical references are reviewed for the purpose of showing that Jesus died to satisfy the justice of God. Hodge insists that Jesus' death must not be understood as the consequence of a struggle between good and evil, but as a death in our place to satisfy God's justice (pp. 473-75). Referring to the use of expiation and propitiation in the Bible and the tradition, Hodge concludes that such references mean that sin incurs the obligation to satisfy God's justice (p. 478). The requirement of blood in the Hebrew sacrificial tradition makes the same point: God must be satisfied by the death of sinners. Lest one wonder where such demands of justice leave the love of God, Hodge states quite emphatically that God must love in a manner consistent with justice (p. 479).

Second, lest there be no misunderstanding, Hodge cites the nominalist position of Duns Scotus to clarify what he means by the necessary demands of justice. According to Hodge, Scotus claims that Christ's death was not necessary but accepted by God totally according to the divine will. Hodge notes that such a view denies the force of Anselm's claim to necessity for the incarnation and the work of Christ. In effect, it could have been otherwise (pp. 486-88). For Hodge, this is unthinkable, plunging the whole passion story into arbitrariness. Against such a view, Hodge argues that Jesus' death was required. To make the point, he introduces the idea of the moral excellence of justice. Since God is just, it is the very nature of God to maintain justice and that means satisfaction is required (p. 488). There can be no pardon except "on the ground of a forensic penal satisfaction. Therefore the Apostle says (Romans iii.25), that God sent forth Christ as a propitiation through faith in his blood, in order that God might be just in justifying the ungodly" (p. 488). For Hodge, the entire biblical testimony "precludes the idea that his satisfaction was not necessary to our salvation, or that any other means could have accomplished the object. And if thus absolutely necessary, it must be that nothing else has worth enough to satisfy the demands of God's law" (p. 489).

Third, Hodge further amplifies the concept of necessity by appealing to the idea of distributive justice. The idea of proportionality between the offense and the penalty had already been introduced (p. 475), but now this idea is developed further. Distributive justice is "that form of moral excellence which demands the righteous distribution of rewards and punishments which renders it certain, under the government of God, that obedience will be rewarded and sin punished" (p. 489). Hodge refers to this as vindicatory justice, insisting that there is a world of difference between vindicatory and vindictive. Hodge's point is not to attribute vengeful motives to God, but to keep before us the matter of God's very nature. God is just and cannot cease being just. All of God's activity must therefore be in accordance with God's very nature. So he declares: "But if justice is that perfection of the divine nature which renders it necessary that the righteous be rewarded and the wicked punished, then the work of Christ must be a satisfaction of justice in that sense of the term" (p. 490).

The necessity of satisfaction, required by justice, is a principle that Hodge affirms by appeals to all of his principles of authority. His review of Old and New Testaments leads to the conclusion that expiation and propitiation by means of blood is required (pp. 475-99). He invokes the Roman, Lutheran, and Reformed traditions, which he finds all in agreement on this issue (p. 500). Even general human experience confirms the point, in that moral reason agrees that an offense requires punishment (p. 490). All of this results in what Hodge determines to be two great truths: "That God cannot pardon sin without a satisfaction to justice, and that He cannot have fellowship with the unholy" (p. 492).

It now is clear why such a view of divine justice, coupled with divine sovereignty, moves in the direction of penal substitution. With the guiding principles established, we can summarize the work of Christ. Throughout all of the discussions, there is one ultimate purpose, namely, to show how Jesus satisfies the justice of God and thereby receives authority to confer salvation to those who believe. But if there is a single theme, it finds multiple expressions as Hodge draws upon all of his sources to make the case. This allows Hodge to incorporate the variety of perspectives, with their respective titles for Jesus, as he presents Christ's saving work. He can move between the language of sacrifice, ransom, and justification, between the Bible and Chalcedon because, for him, they all point to the same conclusion: salvation gained by Christ by means of his death as a satisfaction of God's justice. Thus, there is the language of Chalcedon, where Christ is the eternal Word incarnate, the Mediator representing God and human nature. Because Jesus is human he can legitimately substitute himself for sinful humanity, which is obligated to pay the penalty; but because Jesus is God incarnate, only he can offer satisfaction of infinite value (cf. pp. 456, 465, 471, and 483). There is also the elaborate sacrificial imagery of Hebrews, wherein Jesus is the priest who offers vicarious sacrifice with his own blood (cf. pp. 498-503). Inserted within this exposition are references to ransom, which Hodge deems a variant on the theme of satisfaction (p. 518). All of these elements are gathered together within the general framework of the forensic imagery. In this light, Jesus' sacrifice becomes the substitution of himself for the guilty, as a means of bearing the penalty required by justice. Jesus dies to "satisfy the demands of the Law and justice of God, in the place of and in behalf of sinners" (p. 470). Using themes from Romans, Hodge describes Jesus as the Redeemer who frees us from the condemnation of the law, the power of sin, Satan, and all evil (pp. 517-20). In the language of justification, we are constituted righteous by the righteousness of Christ (p. 494) and become a part of the new humanity in the Body of Christ (p. 518).

D. Critical Issues in the Theory of Penal Substitution

For major sections of Protestantism, the theory of penal substitution provides the basic structure for understanding the death of Jesus. It would be fair to say that among many, it is an unshakable article of faith. To question it would probably be more unimaginable than the proposal directed toward the followers of Luther that Paul's main purpose in Romans is not justification by faith (see above). Whatever the outcome of one's evaluation of the theory, the fact is that it has provided an interpretation of the death and resurrection of Jesus in categories connected to the Bible and tradition. It has made intelligible that terrifying event of Good Friday by placing Jesus' death into a larger plan of God, leading to our salvation. In its basic form it provides a rationale and/or a principle of necessity for the events of Holy Week.

At the same time this theory has evoked the strongest resistance from within Christian communities. The theory has been criticized as representing the very antithesis of the good news. The two issues discussed in the analysis of sacrifice (Chapter One) go to the heart of the matter: one is the passivity of God, entailed in the idea that God is in need of propitiation or appeasement; the second is the isolation of the death of Jesus as an end in itself. To these we will add a third, dealing with the idea of necessity.

1. Atonement as Satisfaction of God

Penal substitution would easily slip into a variation on the theory of the demonstration of love (moral influence), if it were not for the insistence on satisfaction. In fact, someone like Hodge makes it quite clear that Jesus' death is not a display of love seeking to influence human beings (p. 497). What gives the theory its inspiration and what holds it together is the idea that sin must be punished and that such a penalty is demanded to satisfy the justice of God. Such a view is embedded in so many traditions of theology that it is difficult even to know where to begin the conversation. As with Hodge, the amount of material amassed to make the case is impressive. Nevertheless, for all of its seeming rectitude, one is left with a troubling sense that something is wrong.

a. Justice and Love

The objection to penal substitution offered here does not deny the importance of the tension between justice and love, created by sin. This issue, representing the tension between God's fidelity to the world and also God's opposition to sin and evil, is a theme running through the entire Bible. This issue is trivialized by suggesting that sin and evil can simply be ignored or forgotten. Sin violates God's intention for the world and disrupts all relations within the creation. It is, therefore, a valid theological issue and atonement theology must deal with it. The objection to penal substitution offered here, therefore, is not an attempt to eliminate the tension. The real problem with penal substitution is that it accomplishes just that: it eliminates the tension by affirming justice as the only significant and functional divine attribute.

We saw this quite clearly in the summary of Hodge's view. While there are references to love and grace pertaining to the agreement of the Father and the Son, as well as the general motive of God and Jesus in saving the world, at every point Hodge is quick to insist that love can only be in the framework of justice. The Law of distributive justice is immutable. God cannot relate to sinful humankind until God is satisfied. On these terms it is difficult to explain the creation and continuation of the covenants with Israel and the new covenant with Jesus Christ. In effect, as a theory, penal substitution fails to affirm those *theological* and *evangelical values* that are central to Christian faith. Instead of the tension of justice and love being resolved in a way that affirms God's agency and God's gracious will to save, the theory leads to the necessity of punishment according to distributive justice. We end up with the domination of a particular kind of justice over the entire theological agenda. Hodge attempts to avoid this by arguing for a difference between vindicatory and vindictive. The former upholds the requirements of God's justice whereas the latter represents vengeance and revenge. But since penal substitution does not use the concept of satisfaction as an image for the restoration of the creation, but instead for the necessity of the death of Jesus, the distinction disappears and it degenerates into vengeance. The satisfaction God demands is not obedience and holiness but the punishment of a death.

Lest this point appear to be made specifically against Hodge and not the general formulation of penal substitution, consider the fact that in general, penal substitution requires the Law to remain in full force. A death is required because of the connection between offense and punishment, drawn by analogy from legal structures. Not only does this elevate the legal doctrine of proportionality to special theological status, but it represents just the opposite of Paul's declaration in Romans that salvation is revealed apart from the Law. Instead of overturning human conceptions of proportionality and vengeance, the theory enshrines them in the interpretation of Jesus' death and resurrection.

b. The Biblical Sources and the Concept of Satisfaction

Hodge bases his claim for the necessity of satisfaction on human moral expectations, traditions, and Scripture. It is the latter that is most important, since by themselves the other two cannot provide warrant for the argument, especially if it were to be shown contrary to Scripture. When Hodge reviews Old and New Testament passages regarding sacrifice or ransom, where there is an explicit or implicit suggestion that an act of expiation or propitiation occurs, he always concludes that this is the equivalent of satisfaction, understood in legal terms. This is really the key in the entire argument. There is no question that sin offerings remove or cover sin and that the key words have come over into English as *expiate* and *propiatiate*. But what is not demonstrated is why sacrificial atonement for sin equals legal satisfaction. It will be difficult to find general support among biblical scholars that the tradition of Hebrew sacrifice involves *satisfaction of God*. The analysis of sin offerings in Chapter One made clear that: (1) the entire system of sin offerings was instituted by God for the remission of sin; (2) that the offering was to cover or remove sin; (3) that it was not directed toward God as a form of appeasement. Likewise, the examination of key passages in Romans regarding the death of Jesus (see Chapter Two) does not provide a basis for legal satisfaction. The idea of satisfaction or appeasement of God is simply not biblical.

If the issue is redefined in terms of the idea of substitution, the situation in the New Testament is complicated, but in the end leads to a similar conclusion. While there are references to Jesus dying *for us* and *in my place*, nowhere is there a fully developed idea of Jesus' death being the payment of a penalty offered to God as a requirement of divine justice. Each of these passages connects Jesus' death with sin and with our deliverance from sin. But what that connection is, and how we are delivered, constitutes the very question all atonement theories seek to answer. That the full meaning of these passages for atonement theories is not clear is illustrated by the fact that the moral influence theory (demonstration of love) uses many of the same passages but draws a radically different conclusion. What we have in penal substitution is one answer to the question of atonement, using the images of satisfaction, substitution, and legal punishment to build a case. The problem is that when the case is finally constructed, it is quite contrary to the evangelical message in the New Testament.

Without biblical support for satisfaction and substitution, understood in the full legal sense of penal substitution, one is left with an appeal to Christian traditions and general experience. But here we may find that the order has been reversed. Instead of tradition and experience finding confirmation in Scripture, it appears that Scripture has been interpreted with the lenses of traditions and experience. As Hodge notes, Roman, Lutheran, and Reformed confessions all attest to the emphasis on satisfaction. But this still leaves us with the question whether centuries of usage and interpretation of Jesus' death according to legal imagery created a theory that was imposed on Scripture itself.

c. The Use of the Trinitarian Defense

In the discussion on sacrifice in Chapter One, we noted the use of Trinitarian language as a way of defending theories. In that case as with the case before us, the issue is whether something is done to God, leaving God passive. Such a view is problematic because Scripture makes God the active subject in all of the great descriptions of saving events. To avoid such a conclusion, many appeal to the fact that the exchange is not between an active humanity and a passive God, but between the Father and Son. It is the Father who sends the Son into the world and it is the Son who offers satisfaction to the Father. Thus in both cases God is the active agent. As we argued earlier when the issue was sacrifice, the same argument applies regarding satisfaction. If the intention is simply to transfer the exchange required by distributive justice to the Father and Son, little is gained. In fact, it appears as a sort of theological sleight of hand. Why does the Father, and not the Son, need satisfaction? Does justice only belong to the Father and love only belong to the Son? Little is accomplished if we replace a human Jesus appeasing a passive God with the Trinitarian Son appeasing the Father within the Godhead.

As noted in the earlier discussion, the use of Trinitarian language could be helpful if the intention was to reveal the tension between justice and love.

This has biblical support and represents an issue at the heart of atonement theology. In this context it is legitimate to speak of God needing to be reconciled to the world, if that is understood in terms of God's unwillingness to tolerate or accept sin as a permanent state of the creation. In the discussion on sacrifice, we saw that both Aquinas and Calvin dealt with this issue and ultimately argued that Jesus' life of obedience and holiness was the true sacrifice offered to God. But such language moves us away from the ideas of appeasement of a vindictive deity.

To conclude this discussion of satisfaction, the argument made here is that while the theory of penal substitution, based on satisfaction, is in many traditions of Christian theology, preaching, and worship, it is not in the Bible. Furthermore, it is contrary to the *theological* and *evangelical* norms: It replaces the tension between justice and love with the domination of distributive justice, thereby making atonement something done to God and nullifying the central affirmation of God's gracious will to redeem the world.

2. Jesus' Death as an End in Itself

The emphasis on Jesus' death as the means of salvation is probably more controversial than matters already raised. When isolated from his life of obedience and holiness, it becomes a payment between Jesus and God, an exchange serving no purpose other than meeting the requirements of distributive justice. As such it has evoked countless protests in the name of the very justice it seeks to affirm. No matter how it is presented, it is vulnerable to the charge of divine vindictiveness and revenge. For many, the elevation of conventional views of legal justice as the standard for God's holiness and love is untenable and misrepresents the biblical affirmations of God's covenantal actions. It also recasts the gospel narratives so that everything from Jesus' announcement of the Rule of God, teachings, and mighty acts of deliverance to a new covenant community, is subordinated to the final act of death on the cross. Cross and resurrection may be the central events, but can the death of Jesus be so isolated as an end in itself?

There are also cultural factors at work in this negative reaction to the theory of penal substitution. For centuries the theory existed in the cultural context where the death penalty was standard practice for many crimes. In our time major groups in America and Europe no longer support the death penalty as an appropriate punishment for any crime. The Roman Catholic Church is officially opposed to it, as are other Christian groups. There have also been major shifts in attitudes toward the violence of war. Many no longer are willing to accept it as normal activity or as an appropriate way to resolve social-political disputes. Military interventions by the United States in Iraq and Afghanistan revived the traditional debate regarding the possibility of a just war. But what is more interesting is that few Christian groups spend much time debating the concept of just war. Their attention has turned to how they may fulfill the mandate to be peacemakers. To be sure, this may not have resulted in a decrease in war or violence, but it represents a change in the value structure of many people. The same can be said of attitudes toward violence in general, in spite of the fact that there is little decrease in various forms of violence, and the violence of terrorism has increased. Given these shifts in attitude among many religious people, the question is: How will they receive a message claiming that salvation comes to the world only by a violent death imposed by God upon an innocent person?[4]

Lest one think that this is simply a provocative and overly dramatic statement of the issue, consider the many negative implications of the very logic of the theory of penal substitution. The most disturbing ones are that justice involves the sense of proportionality and the establishment of the principle of the necessity of punishment. The former generates the cultural value that there is and ought to be a balance between what people do and what they receive. Put in simple terms, people get what they deserve. The other side of this value is that no one should get anything beyond what they deserve. But what does a person deserve? Shall it be based on some intrinsic value, or on achievement, family status, or on access to power? Taken in its traditional sense, the demand for proportionality tends to produce a social structure that not only maintains the status quo of entrenched economic and political power, but also creates a world based on the survival of the fittest. The latter value, regarding the necessity of punishment, opens the door to an endless cycle of violence, be it in the form of penalties prescribed by state systems, or punishment handed out to children and members of families. To be sure, there may not be a direct causal connection between penal substitution, with its demand for satisfaction, and a host of social policies that insist on punish-

---

4. The release of Mel Gibson's film *The Passion of the Christ* in 2004, virtually simultaneous with Lent, touched off a great debate in the popular media. The strong support for the film by conservative Catholics and Protestants makes it quite clear that a major portion of American Christianity has no problem with a view of penal substitution, where unimaginable violence is inflicted on the figure of Jesus. But one should also bear in mind that this reaction was not the only one. Jews tended to see the film as threatening, since it raised once again the outrage against Jews as Christ-killers. Nonconservative Catholics and Protestants reacted with shock and bewilderment at the violence, since it did not represent their view of Jesus or God's intention.

ment. But it would appear naïve to ignore the ways a demand for punishment as satisfaction relates to general social policy and cultural attitudes. If Jesus had to endure the penalty of death according to the Law, then it can be argued that the death penalty is justifiable.[5] Likewise, if punishment is necessary to maintain divine justice, which is at the basis of general moral order, then all violations of rules and laws need to punished. One cannot help drawing a connection between this obsession with punishment and the older brother in the parable of the Prodigal Son. This third member of the parable provides the critical edge to the story, since he represents the legal moral order which requires that people get what they deserve. Thus the parable does not simply demonstrate the most radical love by the action of the father, but it shatters conventional morality as represented by the outrage of the brother.

These concerns should not be misunderstood in either of the following ways. First, this critique of penal substitution is not an attempt to diminish the significance of the cross. The gospel message is rightly linked to Jesus' death and resurrection. What has been said is not an attempt to cleanse the passion narrative of its sorrow and blood. The issue is how such sorrow and blood shall be interpreted and what are the social consequences of such presentations in theology, sermons, and art. Second, the criticism of this theory does not mean that one is against any or all punishment for crime, discipline for misconduct, or holding persons responsible for violations of personal trust. The objection raised here is the way this theory condones retaliatory violence based on the doctrine of proportionality and the support such a view gives to cycles of blood vengeance. As was argued in Chapter One, the problem with distributive or retributive justice is that true proportionality can seldom ever occur. When the loss is monetary, compensation can approximate the loss, though never completely. When the loss is that of a life, no compensation is adequate. The idea of proportionality or satisfaction is therefore a myth, cultivated by cultural patterns to suggest that compensation can equal wrongs. Perhaps the myth of punishment has been cultivated and sanctioned as a means of ending, in a relative sense, blood vengeance. But in reality, punishment cannot satisfy — either in substance or in terms of emotions. The best that punishment can do is *appear* to demonstrate that something has

---

5. I am aware of the fact that the theory of penal substitution can motivate people in different ways in their evaluation of the death penalty. Some can argue that since Jesus has paid the price for sin, that payment is sufficient for all and therefore the death penalty is abrogated. By contrast, I have encountered just the opposite conclusion: the Law of retributive justice still stands because, if even Jesus had to die for sin, then all those convicted of murder must also die. Thus, penal substitution becomes the defender of conventional morality with its quest for rewards and punishments.

been done to make amends and/or to remove violent persons from society. It can also be admitted that there are times — notably cases of great loss of life — where even the death penalty does appear to be mandated. But we need to recognize that the demand for punishment reflects the limitations of our minds and hearts, so prone to anger and vengeance. The real question is whether the death and resurrection of Jesus should be interpreted according to worldly standards of punishment and satisfaction.

3. The Quest for Necessity

The central issue in the theory of penal substitution is the claim of a principle of necessity regarding the death of Jesus. This is created by constructing a legal argument, wherein the fact of sin requires punishment. Once that is accepted, it then follows that the punishment of a death must occur. Therefore, by interpreting Jesus' death as a substitution for sinful humanity standing under the sentence of death, we are able to understand why Jesus died. From this perspective, his death is not arbitrary, nor is it simply the consequence of his fidelity, which could be interpreted to mean that it occurred only because of the sinful action of humans. Nor is it something that happens outside of the will of God. Jesus' death is now elevated to the level of something required by God to fulfill the demands of the Law, opening the possibility of salvation. Everything depends on his blood being shed and his eventual death. In fact, it is governed by a moral necessity rooted in the very nature of divine justice. The problem with such claims is that while the conclusion appears to follow the premises, one must first accept all the premises: that sin violates the justice of God and that justice must be satisfied by a death. Since these premises in turn depend also on accepting the authority of the Bible, the number of prior assumptions begins to grow large. The notion that unbelievers or believers will accept all of these premises, before they believe in Christ, is an open question. In the case of Hodge, we saw that the whole argument rests on his assumption that every reference to sacrifice or ransom means legal satisfaction, an assumption open to dispute on biblical grounds.

An immediate response to the problems involved in the argument is to suggest that the argument for penal substitution is overextended. That is to say, in the process of moving from a creative image to the construction of comprehensive theory, the original idea has been altered. To affirm that "Christ died for me" does not necessarily imply or allow that all the details of criminal legal systems can be appropriated in the construction of the theory. The theory therefore runs the risk of bringing too much, or perhaps the wrong things, in the interpretation of Jesus' death.[6] A similar problem occurs in the theory of sacrifice, when the image of sacrifice is expanded to incorporate the general idea of a sacrifice offered to God, even though it contradicts the original use in Hebrew tradition. In the case of penal substitution, the introduction of certain aspects of the process of criminal justice tends to undercut the biblical view of God and the gospel affirmation. As argued here, the idea that God operates according to human conventions of proportionality and distributive justice, which demand satisfaction, is beyond the scope of the gospel declaration.

Why do theories run the risk of overextension in ways that they lose contact with the original and creative impulse? While there may be some truth in explaining this by saying that the error occurs in the transition from metaphor to literal use of language, by itself such an explanation does not go far enough. The idea of satisfaction required by distributive justice is an incorrect theological idea, whether it is understood metaphorically or literally. It may be more accurate to see the problem in the quest for necessity. This is precisely the added value brought to the argument by the full expansion of the legal image. All the discussions regarding law, offense, penalty, and justice are added to the original image in order to arrive at the principle of the necessity of a death. Advocates of the theory appear willing to risk overextension resulting in flawed logic for the sake of claiming necessity.

There is something disturbing about such a quest for necessity. In general, Protestants gave up on the attempt to prove the existence of God by rational necessity. Yet the quest for necessity keeps reappearing, either in claims for biblical inerrancy or infallibility, or in claims regarding blood atonement. The construction of these arguments is usually so elaborate and invested with so much value that they appear to be the Protestant version of arguments for the existence of God (or perhaps more appropriately, for the existence of

---

6. The position suggested here is that the original image or metaphor may be contradicted by assuming that everything related to its use in other contexts can be brought into the theory and made normative. The same point regarding the danger of developing an image into a theory is made by Fitzmyer and Dunn, though with slightly different language. Fitzmyer argues that the basic images are "vivid metaphors" and not theories (Joseph A. Fitzmyer, *Paul and His Theology: A Brief Sketch*, 2nd ed. [Englewood Cliffs, N.J.: Prentice Hall, 1989], p. 66). Dunn makes two important points: first, given the richness of the new life in Christ, a variety of metaphors is needed to express fully the new reality (and therefore no one image should be made dominant); second, metaphors should not be reduced to analysis or logic, lest they lose the initial point (James D. G. Dunn, *The Theology of Paul the Apostle* [Grand Rapids: Eerdmans, 1998], pp. 331-33). Such comments suggest that the value of metaphors is partly in their imprecise and fragile character. As I have argued, by extending some images into theories — for the sake of eliminating that imprecision and fragility — the original point can either be lost or destroyed.

Christ's death). One can sympathize with this quest for necessity by pointing out that it is not unique to the theory of penal substitution. As we shall see in a later chapter, Anselm attempts to establish a principle of necessity for the incarnation that is superior to reliance on metaphors and a sense of proportionality. But even in his argument, the same problem occurs: one must accept his conclusion only if one accepts certain premises that are not self-evident. In the great debates regarding the proofs for the existence of God, the so-called arguments failed because of the attempt to move from *is* to *ought*. The same may be said of theories of atonement. To find some principle established by human experience or reason that requires the death of Jesus is a precarious enterprise. If there is a reason for Christ's death, it lies in the faithfulness to God's purpose. We may even go so far as to say that it is ultimately bound up with the righteousness of God, as such finds expression in justice and love. But such a statement is quite different from any claim to necessity based on a principle of distributive justice. In the end, we must return to the Pauline admonition that we live by grace received in faith.

The theory of penal substitution presents us with a serious dilemma: on the one hand it is accepted by many traditions as the primary interpretation of the gospel of Jesus Christ; on the other hand it is perceived by others as so flawed that it converts the story of Jesus into divinely sanctioned violence. Is there any way in which this theory could be reconstructed that it might avoid the common criticisms? To answer this, let us first enumerate what appear to be its positive assumptions.

1. The theory rightly affirms that sin offends God and disrupts all human relations. It is quite appropriate to say that God is opposed to sin, or to speak of the wrath of God as the symbol of that opposition.
2. The theory is correct in assuming that the problem cannot be resolved by simply ignoring or forgetting it. Nor can appeals to the love of God resolve the matter unless one indicates, in some form or another, how sin is removed and the world is somehow in the process of being redeemed.
3. The theory is correct in confessing that, from our perspective as sinners, Jesus dies the death of a sinner and in this way does in fact *take our place*. Why he does this, however, needs to be explained without suggesting that it is compensation offered to God to enable God to redeem us.
4. Finally, the theory is correct in affirming that, from the standpoint of the history of Israel and faith in the risen Christ, there is a certain kind of necessity involved in the death of Jesus. Jesus could not do otherwise than be faithful to God; God could not do otherwise than oppose sin and seek to redeem the world.

If these four assumptions are valid starting points for reconstructing the theory, how would that process be completed? In general, one could move from these assumptions to the double affirmation: first, as Jesus dies the death of sinners but is in fact innocent, he reveals the judgment of God against sin; second, as Jesus dies in our place he reveals the obedience and fidelity that fulfill God's intention to create righteousness on earth. Taken together, this could prompt one to move the theory closer to one of the other theories, e.g., justification by grace (Luther) or the restoration of the creation as the satisfaction of God's honor (Anselm). Since the image of Christ in our place has such power to evoke repentance and commitment, the theory could be moved closer to the proclamation or demonstration of Wondrous Love (Chapter Ten). As reconstructed it would be parallel to the many theories that place the creation of holiness on earth as a requirement for atonement (e.g., compare the need for holiness in sacrifice, liberation, or even reconciliation as models for atonement in other chapters). All of this is to say that all may not be lost, if those nurtured in this theory could find new ways to give expression to the evangelical impulse that they claim is there. This undoubtedly will be controversial, because it amounts to redefining the theory to the point that it is no longer the original theory.[7] The great potential of the theory is the insistence that the cross has to do with resolving the tension of holiness and love. As discussed in other theories, this can be affirmed by using images of Christ in our place or bearing the sins of the world, without making his death compensation offered to God.

7. This is exactly what is proposed in the article by William Placher (see Note 1). In effect, Placher accepts the basic criticisms and tries to move beyond them by appealing to the central themes of other theories. Thus we find elements of justification by grace (*simul justus et peccator*), liberation (i.e., suffering that transforms the world for the sake of peace and justice), reconciliation (i.e., God reconciling by assuming the cost of love), wondrous love and sacrifice (i.e., the good news that God is with us in our suffering). Cf. pp. 13-16. Placher has basically dropped the key idea of penal substitution (i.e., a death as recompense to divine justice) and moved to an amalgam of other theories.

Theories of Atonement

B. Liberation from Sin, Death, and Demonic Powers

Chapter 4 Liberation

Irenaeus and Twentieth-Century Liberation Theology

A. Introduction

The New Testament overflows with references to two aspects of the saving work of Christ: forgiveness of sins (often described as reconciliation) and liberation. In Part One, Section A, we examined three theories that seek to interpret the meaning of Jesus in light of the affirmation that "Christ died for our sins." Now we turn to the second theme: liberation.

To understand this theme it is crucial to note the shift in the way the human condition is described. The concept of sin assumes personal responsibility for such actions. This is the case in both judgments against sin or in the laments and confessions of regret regarding sin. The call to repentance in prophets, John the Baptist, or Jesus was the call to see oneself in light of the commandments given by the God of the covenants and to turn around (metanoia), i.e., be renewed by God and to walk in God's ways. But alongside of this view of sin, there stands another equally basic human experience. This is the awareness that something has happened to us: we have lost control, we are no longer ourselves, able to choose or do the good. The instances of this phenomenon are so varied that it is very difficult to generalize. In some cases, the affliction may have come about by our own volition, thus adding an element of ironic self-deception. In other cases, the loss of control has been placed upon us by long-standing traditions or practices. The ravages of war, colonial rule, slavery, and oppressive systems based on race, gender, and class come to mind. People find themselves excluded, in poverty, without access to the means of livelihood, and exploited against their will. The one thing that connects all these experiences is the inability to emancipate themselves.

The gospels record numerous instances of people suffering from structures of exclusion and oppression: women, Samaritans, the sick in body and mind, the poor, social outcasts, and even people from the country. ("Can anything good come out of Nazareth?") What is striking about Jesus' encounter with these persons is his willingness to accept them, to invite them into table fellowship and to empower them to see the coming Reign of God. By accepting them, he liberates them from the oppressive powers that defined them as outsiders. In the case of the sick, Jesus dismisses the debate as to whether such conditions are the result of sin and proceeds to heal the person. In the case of the man possessed by demons, he appears to accept the view that this affliction is part of a larger network of demonic power, using his own power to prove that he is not in league with Satan. Other places in the New Testament speak of oppressive forces in terms of the powers of earthly rulers, of sin, death, and Satan. These trans-personal powers are described in language that takes on apocalyptic proportions. Thus the New Testament moves from the individual to the cosmic in its language of liberation from bondage.

If there is one thing that is common to centuries of use, it is that something has happened to us that we cannot control or overcome. The two great metaphors of illness or bondage can only be affirmed if one accepts this premise. Thus, for example, the dividing line between Augustine and Pelagius is precisely this point: Does Christ do something for us that we cannot do for ourselves? Modern liberalism is uncomfortable with Augustine because he refuses to endorse the position adopted centuries later by Immanuel Kant, namely, that we have it within our powers to reform ourselves. Here then is the argument in brief outline, followed by the witnesses of faith.

B. The Theory in Outline

We can briefly summarize the theory of atonement as follows:

1. Whether by voluntary action or external coercion, human beings have fallen under the control of oppressive and dehumanizing powers. These can be enumerated as sin, the law, powers and dominions of this world, demonic powers, and death. Whereas the early church employs images of bondage and enslavement, the modern age usually prefers the language of addiction, oppressive social/political forces, or ideological domination.

2. Since human beings cannot liberate themselves from this situation, Jesus Christ appears as the power of God to liberate human beings. In his crucifixion Christ identifies with us and shares our suffering; in his resurrection Christ is vindicated and made the Victor over all oppressive powers.

3. By his life, death, and resurrection, Jesus Christ inaugurates a new age and a new community of freedom, marked by inclusivity and equality, peace, and joy. The church as the Body of Christ is therefore the sign of this new age, and in its life and work it witnesses to the salvation of Christ until the final fulfillment, when all destructive powers will be overcome.

C. Witnesses of Faith: Irenaeus, Gregory of Nyssa, and Athanasius

Since the publication of Gustaf Aulén's *Christus Victor* in 1931, the name of Irenaeus has been synonymous with the theme of Christ's victory over sin and demonic powers. Yet even Aulén reminds us that this theme, so central to the New Testament, pervades the early church.[1] Irenaeus is neither the originator nor the sole advocate for describing the work of Christ in terms of liberation. As we shall see, just as important as the theme of liberation is the emphasis on Christ's representative role — a theme derived from Paul's imagery of participation. For Irenaeus, Christ recapitulates the history of the race and is the beginning of the new humanity in the Spirit. He sums up all that has gone before, but in his obedience and victory, overcomes all that was destructive of God's plan for creation.

Irenaeus was Bishop of Lyons in southern France in the latter part of the second century. He came to office after the martyrdom of his predecessor and was himself martyred in 202. It was a turbulent time within the life of the struggling church as well as the church's relation to a hostile culture. If persecution threatened the lives of the members, a wide range of religious and philosophical ideas threatened to subvert the message handed down from the apostles. Polytheism, including the many forms of Gnosticism, appeared to be an attractive alternative. Within the church the metaphysical dualism of Marcionism challenged its monotheistic faith. There also appears to be considerable speculation regarding how deities can be related to this world and human history, with claims to various epiphanies opposing the Christian claim of the Word made flesh. Irenaeus provides us with a window on such intellectual controversy in the primary work that has survived: *Against Heresies.*[2]

To counter these assaults on the integrity of the Christian message, Irenaeus presents a standard for faith, in form and substance. The faithful are

1. Cf. Gustaf Aulén, *Christus Victor,* trans. A. G. Hebert (London: S.P.C.K., 1931), pp. 32ff.

2. Cf. Irenaeus, "Against Heresies," *The Apostolic Fathers with Justin Martyr and Irenaeus,* ed. A. Cleveland Coxe, vol. 1 of The Ante-Nicene Fathers: Translations of the Writings of the Fathers down to A.D. 325, ed. Alexander Roberts and James Donaldson (New York: Scribner's, 1985), pp. 309-567. All references to Irenaeus from this work will be included in the text.

called to adhere to Scripture, tradition, and the leaders of the church for right teaching (pp. 412-17). They are also admonished to affirm one God (perhaps we can best understand this by saying *only one* God), who is the Creator and Redeemer of all things. There is but one incarnation of God, which is indeed a true incarnation of the Almighty God. In language suggestive of later creedal statements, Irenaeus declares that Jesus Christ is the only begotten Son of God and the true light (p. 329). By means of the Word all things were created (against Marcion) and this same Word was truly incarnate in the flesh (against Gnosticism) (p. 440). Jesus Christ suffered on the cross for our salvation according to the plan of God. By the bestowal of the Holy Spirit the new life of Christ is present in the world, whereby all things are gathered together in union with God (p. 330). If these statements sound quite commonplace, one must remember that Irenaeus lived prior to the Constantinian settlement as well as the great creedal affirmations of Nicea and Chalcedon. Not only is the tradition still in process of formation, but each element of this summary is seriously under attack and the outcome is still very much in doubt.

But while Irenaeus may be commended for waging the battle against opposing opinions, he is best remembered for the strong affirmation of Christ's victory over Satan. In this regard, Irenaeus takes the imagery from the New Testament (especially Paul and Mark), connects it with narratives in the Old Testament, and gathers it all together into a general view of God's plan of salvation. The story is this: Adam and Eve were beguiled by the serpent with images of immortality (p. 457). By this deception, the serpent has taken possession of them and their descendants. As a consequence they are expelled from Paradise. The language of this descent into captivity is important, since Irenaeus follows the Pauline motif of dramatic parallels between the fall and redemption. All of the details involving Adam and Eve will find positive parallels in Jesus and Mary — even to the point that both events happened on the sixth day of the week. This rhetorical device will be discussed later as we examine the kind of rationale Irenaeus and others use to explain the death and resurrection of Jesus. Here one should simply note with care the details of the fall, which will be recapitulated in the passion narrative. Most important for Irenaeus is the fact that the capture of Adam and Eve is an act of violence. Humanity belonged to God and was created for God's purpose. Satan has no right to them, and he captures them by deception and force (p. 456). While Irenaeus must affirm that God uses force to overthrow Satan, he also emphasizes that it is not an act of violence, i.e., humanity belongs to God and Christ's victory displays both justice and grace. In fact, Irenaeus prefers to speak of God's persuasion in liberating Adam and Eve.

How then does this liberation occur? Irenaeus introduces two themes that indicate a high level of theological reflection on his part beyond the mere transmission of the narrative. The first is that Adam's subjugation is so complete that he cannot liberate himself. The emphasis on captivity should not be construed to mean Adam is without responsibility, for while deceived, Adam willingly accepted the serpent's lie. But bound to sin and death in this fallen state, Adam cannot save himself. This, declares Irenaeus, can only be accomplished by the incarnate Word (p. 450). However, this incapacity of humanity is not developed in the direction of the great dilemma that characterized some forms of the legal theory of atonement (i.e., humans must do something, but only God can). Rather, this incapacity is simply stated as a given, making all the more important the Johannine affirmation of the Word made flesh. This introduces the second theme regarding the rationale for the incarnation. To Irenaeus, it was necessary for God to save humanity, lest God be conquered by the deception of the serpent (p. 455). Though long-suffering, God is invincible and will not endure forever the bondage of the creation to demonic power. It is, therefore, quite necessary or fitting for the Lord to save the lost sheep and restore humanity to the image of God.[3] What this means is that God's action is mandated by God's very nature, rather than any force or rationale outside of God. God chooses to save for the same reason God chooses to create. Both activities are expressions of God's justice and grace.

Salvation, therefore, occurs by the incarnation of the Word of God, who is truly God and the agent of creation. The Word assumes the form of human flesh, since it is humanity that is to be redeemed. Jesus Christ is made in the form of sin in order to overcome the very sin and death that have violated humanity (p. 450). Here Irenaeus draws on three biblical images: (1) Just as Jonah was engulfed in the belly of the whale, so Jesus was engulfed in sin and death, only to be released from such bondage and overcome it; (2) As the Second Adam, Jesus binds the strong man (Mark 3); (3) With Paul, Irenaeus affirms that as all die in Adam, so all are made alive in Christ. In all of these, the parallels are emphasized: as Satan captured Adam, so Jesus captures Satan. This capture of Satan brings release from the bondage to sin, death, and Satan. But the release is not only for the living, but all humanity extending back to Adam. It would not be fitting if Adam and all his descendants were not also released (p. 456). Thus Jesus sums up the whole human race and recapitulates the story of Adam with a new ending. That ending is communion or union

---

3. We should note that the use of the idea that it is *fitting* for God to redeem humanity runs through the writers of the early church. We will see it again in Athanasius (Chapter Five). It also appears in Anselm in ways that he rejects and accepts (Chapter Six).

with God by means of the Holy Spirit. Irenaeus connects the victory of Christ directly to participation in the life of the church. The link between Christ and the church is the outpouring of the Spirit. Thus for Irenaeus, Spirit and church are joined together. We have communion with Christ and the new life he brings in the Eucharist by means of the Spirit (p. 458). In a related way, Irenaeus declares that Christ is the treasure hid in Scripture (p. 496).

With this summary before us we can return to Irenaeus's contention that the means of salvation used by God was not like the violence of Satan, but a form of persuasion that was just and reasonable (p. 527). As noted before, the initial point is that it did not involve deception, nor was it unlawful, since humanity belonged to God. But it is still not clear how Christ's victory is different from the action of Satan, since it involves a binding by force of Satan, similar to Satan's binding by force of Adam. It is difficult to understand Irenaeus's point until we actually see what he means by the just and gracious persuasion of God (p. 528). It is here that he launches into the praise of Christ's suffering and the outpouring of the Spirit, actions directed not toward Satan but toward us. We are redeemed by the shedding of his own blood. His death is a soul given for our souls. We are invited into communion with God by means of the Holy Spirit. All this was from God for those who belonged to God. In effect, Irenaeus has switched the focus from the defeat of Satan to drawing all people into the life of God. One could say that the motif of demonstration of wondrous love has been incorporated into the liberation imagery.[4] Such a combination of images is not unusual and in this case it may be necessary. By itself, the liberation image draws upon the language of military power and release of captives. But that still leaves open the question of

---

4. This shift by Irenaeus undercuts the much-used distinction in technical theology between *objective* and *subjective* theories. The objective position claims that something specific must happen (outside of the human heart), such as fulfillment of the law and divine justice, or defeat of Satan and death, to be a *real* theory of atonement. It therefore classifies those theories that focus on the change of hearts and minds as *subjective,* with the implication that they are less than legitimate theories of atonement. The fact is, however, that every theory claiming that something objective happens (i.e., defeat of sin and death, satisfaction of God's justice, etc.) is still left with the question: Does this change the relation between humans and God? Put in the language of hearts and minds: Why should we love God? Therefore it is instructive that most so-called objective theories include at the end references to the demonstration of love, which is the very theory usually ignored if not held in contempt. In Irenaeus, the inclusion of wondrous love is made without any regret. Having started with the bold declaration of Christ's victory over Satan, he concludes with the praise of the self-sacrifice of Jesus for us, freely offered and confirmed by the bestowal of God's very Spirit. As noted, this move was made in spite of the fact that the logic of the persuasion of love is so very different from the logic of conquest: power and struggle.

the relation of the liberator to the captives.[5] Has one form of bondage been replaced by another, a new tyrant substituting for the old? Irenaeus appears to sense the limits of the liberation imagery, quick to deny that God's work of salvation is a new form of violence against our wills or for our destruction. To be sure, sin, death, and Satan are overcome by divine power, but humanity is invited to share the life of the true Adam who is also the Word incarnate. Christ's victory is the good news of life together in the Spirit, with one another and with God.

Every seminarian who has taken a course on the History of Doctrine remembers the story of the fish hook. The image comes, however, not from Irenaeus but from Gregory of Nyssa, two centuries later. Working within the context of Christ the liberator over the powers of Satan, Gregory affirms that God, out of the divine goodness, chooses to reclaim humanity held in bondage to Satan. The capture of humanity occurred through the deception devised by Satan, where temptation to sin concealed the fish hook of demonic power.[6] But God turned the tables on the devil. Jesus Christ is offered as a ransom for the captives, his human nature concealing his divinity. Envy and greed prompt the devil to swallow this most appealing bait, only to discover the power of Almighty God (pp. 300-301). The devil is thereby overcome and Christ in his victory offers immortality to believers, released from the power of sin and death. As with Irenaeus, this sharing of Christ's gifts takes on a sacramental form, as believers receive the new life of Christ in bread and wine (p. 320).

Finally, it is important to include Athanasius among those affirming Christ's conquest over sin and death. In Chapter Five we shall discuss Athanasius as a witness to a related theory of atonement, namely the renewal of humanity by means of the incarnation. But it is typical of writers in this time, as well as later, to include many images and theories of atonement. So with Athanasius: in the death of Christ all die so that death may be over-

---

5. This section was written in May 2003 during the time following the American military "victory" in Iraq. It was apparent that many people in Iraq were glad to see the old regime overthrown, but not at all pleased to have Americans occupying their country. That liberated people may not automatically appreciate the liberator thus appears to be quite possible, no doubt to the consternation of the liberator. From the standpoint of atonement theory, Irenaeus is correct in making the point that if God's liberation of humanity from Satan is to be effective, it must be persuasive and not against our wills.

6. Cf. Gregory of Nyssa, "An Address on Religious Instruction," trans. Cyril C. Richardson, in *Christology of the Later Fathers,* ed. Edward Rochie Hardy, vol. 3 of The Library of Christian Classics, ed. John Baillie, John T. McNeill, and Henry P. Van Dusen (Philadelphia: Westminster, 1954), p. 298. All future references to Gregory of Nyssa are from this work and will be included in the text.

come.[7] His death is the bearing of the curse laid upon all humanity, but also the way to victory. By his resurrection, death is overcome, and the knowledge of God and immortality are restored.

There are two points in Athanasius that hark back to Irenaeus: one is the frequent appeal to what is *fitting* (cf. pp. 61, 65, 67, and 80). We shall discuss this in greater detail in the later chapter, but need to note its use here as well. God is motivated by a necessity internal to God, which means that the Creator cannot allow the creation to remain in its fallen state. The second is the summing up, or inclusive nature, of Christ's work. In his death on the cross, Christ spreads out his hands, drawing all nations to God (p. 79). As with Irenaeus, Christ's death on the cross has cosmic implications extending over time and space.

D. Witnesses from Contemporary Theology

American theology at mid-twentieth century was dominated by the new developments in biblical studies, the revival of major themes from the early church and the Protestant Reformation, as well as new ecumenical initiatives between Protestants and Roman Catholics. All this was taking place amid major crises in the world: World War II, the Cold War, and the struggle for racial justice in America. Added to all this, a great deal of theological discourse was devoted to the continuing debate regarding faith and reason, set in the context of secular challenges from philosophy and the social sciences. By the 1960s it was not clear what specific direction the great revival of Protestant theology would take, though it was very difficult to imagine how it could be eclipsed. But within a decade, the social-political revolutions began to direct attention to issues of social, racial, political, and ecological justice. If there had been an overarching consensus as to theological method and agenda, suddenly it was challenged by the emergence of many new voices, which represented dramatic shifts in orientation and focus. What united them was the imagery of liberation, one of the oldest Christological themes, now applied to specific issues confronting Christians in the world. Liberation theology was suddenly a major movement, with applications and adaptations throughout the world. Its impact was immense because it challenged what appeared to be the reigning methodology for theology — Protestant and Roman Catholic — as well as the way the substance of the gospel is to be proclaimed.

---

7. Cf. Athanasius, "On the Incarnation of the Word," trans. Archibald Robertson, in Hardy, ed., *Christology of the Later Fathers,* p. 75. All future references to Athanasius are from this work and will be included in the text.

Here we shall refer to four witnesses, which reflect the development and variety of contemporary liberation theology in America. These four cases, however, cannot capture the full breadth of liberation theology in America or world Christianity. The first is the work of Jürgen Moltmann, whose *Theology of Hope* broke new ground (German edition, 1965; English edition, 1967). While Moltmann's theology arose from German Protestant theology in the context of post–World War II and the Cold War, it has had great impact in North America. The second is the liberation theology of James Cone (1969 and 1971), which focused on the issues of the oppression and liberation of black people in the United States. The third is Gustavo Gutiérrez's *Liberation Theology* (Spanish edition, 1971; English edition, 1973), a major work in Roman Catholic theology amid the struggles of church and society in Latin America. Finally, we need to include reference to the development of liberation theology among women. Given the contextual nature of liberation theology, this branch of liberation theology represents a wide range of perspectives. Since these cannot all be summarized or combined into one position, several perspectives shall be reviewed.

1. Jürgen Moltmann

Three works by Moltmann are especially relevant for our study: *Theology of Hope* (German, 1965/English, 1967), *The Crucified God* (German, 1973/English, 1974), and *The Way of Jesus Christ* (German, 1989/English, 1990).[8] The first volume introduces Moltmann's basic thesis, the second addresses the implications of cross and resurrection for thinking about God and Christ, while the third develops a broad Christology in the context of the eschatological perspective. In *Theology of Hope* Moltmann challenges Protestant theology to take up the eschatological vision announced in the New Testament. While the ultimate goal is to define the gospel as liberation, the work is just as much about the *liberation of theology.* From his perspective, Protestant theology is so caught up in methods and categories of thought which contradict the eschatological vision that the word of liberation cannot be heard. Thus the full titles of the first two books announce methodological concerns: *Theology of Hope: On the Ground and Implications of Christian Eschatology; The Crucified*

---

8. Jürgen Moltmann, *Theology of Hope: On the Ground and Implications of Christian Eschatology,* trans. James W. Leitch (New York: Harper and Row, 1967); *The Crucified God: The Cross of Christ as the Foundation and Criticism of Christian Theology,* trans. R. A. Wilson and John Bowden (New York: Harper and Row, 1974); and *The Way of Jesus Christ: Christology in Messianic Dimensions,* trans. Margaret Kohl (Minneapolis: Fortress, 1993).

God: The Cross of Christ as the Foundation and Criticism of Christian Theology.
In effect, issues of method have become issues of substance, since they govern
what is possible to think and say. As a result, all three books present the reader
with technical debates with modern theology and the interpretation of key
biblical passages. These lead to Moltmann's positive theological statements,
which often contain rich images and lyrical evangelical affirmations. The
style thus makes the point that theology itself must be liberated before it can
become a theology of liberation.

Moltmann works his way through a long list of problems that he con-
ceives to be barriers to the preaching and hearing of the liberating word. Here
is a review of the major issues.

1. In *Theology of Hope* Moltmann launches into a major attack on the recasting of Christian faith into what he calls an *epiphany religion,* i.e., the affirmation of the presence of the eternal, infinite God in the finite.[9] The problem
here is the focus on the possibility of knowing God, rather than what God is
doing in the world. So much effort is given to modern disbelief, revelation, or
the proofs for God, that little attention is given to history, the future, and
hope.[10] When the issue is framed in terms of the infinite and finite, the
knowledge of God is expressed in terms of a supra-historical presence of the
eternal. After tracking this tradition in the nineteenth and twentieth centuries, Moltmann names Karl Barth as a major example of this approach. What
disturbs Moltmann is Barth's preoccupation with the issues of time and eternity, and his juxtaposition of God's self-revelation against human experience.[11] In *The Way of Jesus Christ,* Moltmann argues that Barth's summary of
the whole gospel under the category of reconciliation fails to connect the resurrection with the new creation as an emerging possibility in history.[12] For
Moltmann, the gospel is more than the reconciliation of God and the believer, but a promise for all humanity and the creation.

A variation on the recasting of Christianity as an epiphany religion is the
reduction of the eschatological future into the sacraments as the presence of
the eternal. In Roman Catholic and the high church ecumenical consensus of
the World Council of Churches, Moltmann fears that future eschatological
expectations for the entire creation have been reduced to expectations for the
sacred moment in the faith community. The celebration of salvation for the
entire world becomes, by loss of expectation, a confinement of the gospel for

9. Moltmann, *Theology of Hope,* pp. 28-195. This is such a major debate that one really
needs to read the entire book.
10. Moltmann, *Theology of Hope,* pp. 41-44.
11. Moltmann, *Theology of Hope,* pp. 41 and 53-54.
12. Moltmann, *The Way of Jesus Christ,* pp. 230-32, 318, and 187-89.

the nurture of the believers. This charge appears quite severe. But we need to ask whether our Eucharistic celebrations do reflect an eschatological vision or a retreat from the groaning of the creation for justice and peace. But when Moltmann returns to the Eucharist in his Christology, he emphasizes both the remembrance of Christ's sufferings and liberating power as well as a communal expression of eschatological hope.[13]

2. If Moltmann finds problems with the neo-orthodoxy of Barth, he is equally disturbed by the *existentialist theology* of Rudolf Bultmann and his followers. In his view, Bultmann's translation of statements about God and public reality into statements about human existence resulted in a negative impact on the eschatological vision.[14] Instead of speaking about God, revelation was now understood as the disclosure of authentic existence. But by reducing revelation to the knowledge of the mystery of the human person, the existentialist approach lost the sense of revelation as the disclosure of judgment and hope in human time. By contrast, Moltmann argues: "That is why the revelation of God and the corresponding knowledge of God are always bound up with the recounting and recalling of history and with prophetic expectation."[15] Bultmann attempted to avoid the problems of historical criticism by translating the resurrection into an existentialist event, which creates faith in the disciples.[16] But this program of de-mythologizing the language and events of the gospels also destroys the historical and eschatological vision. For Moltmann, without the strange language of cross and resurrection as divine and human acts, the message loses the testimony to God's faithfulness and the promise of hope.[17]

3. In *The Crucified God*, Moltmann offers an extended critique of philosophical influences on theology. The thrust of the argument is that this leads to a loss of the evangelical proclamation of cross, resurrection, and eschatological vision. Two points stand out. The first is the rejection of what Moltmann calls speculative theology. This can take the form of developing a doctrine of God with classical attributes and ideas of creation and providence, *before* introducing the Trinitarian view. It can also take the form of beginning with a speculative view of the Trinity. Moltmann rejects the distinction between an immanent and economic trinity, affirming that: "We cannot say of God who he is of himself and in himself; we can only say who he is for us in the history of Christ which reaches us in our history."[18] The alternative,

---

13. Moltmann, *The Way of Jesus Christ*, pp. 204-11.
14. Moltmann, *Theology of Hope*, p. 59.
15. Moltmann, *Theology of Hope*, p. 117.
16. Moltmann, *The Way of Jesus Christ*, p. 232.
17. Moltmann, *Crucified God*, pp. 203-19.
18. Moltmann, *Crucified God*, p. 238. Cf. pp. 237-40 and 87-92.

therefore, is to begin with the cross of Jesus Christ, since it is in this event that God is disclosed to us and for us.

The second point is the rejection of divine impassibility, especially as an attempt to protect or enhance the divine sovereignty. The argument against divine impassibility constitutes the basic thesis of *The Crucified God,* which can be summarized with the twofold thesis: The cross and resurrection of Jesus Christ are the criterion for understanding God; the cross and resurrection of Jesus Christ can only be understood in terms of the revealing of the God who is Father, Son, and Holy Spirit.[19] If the story of Jesus is the criterion for thinking about God, then it means that God suffered and was crucified with Jesus. So he writes: "God not only acted in the crucifixion of Jesus or sorrowfully allowed it to happen, but was himself active with his own being in the dying Jesus and suffered with him."[20] But the thesis also requires that Jesus be understood from the standpoint of the triune God.[21] The story of Jesus, from incarnation to crucifixion, is also the story of Father, Son, and Spirit. In making this case, Moltmann appeals to the New Testament, but also to Luther, where the speculative approach of scholastic theology is rejected in favor of the theology of the cross.[22] For Moltmann, God's embrace of the world is not merely an act of sympathy for the crucified, but actual participation of the Father through the Son in the crucifixion, which also means that the Father suffers with the Son in this act of violence. The death of Jesus is not the death of God, but it is a death in God, which therefore requires a more explicit Trinitarian interpretation of the cross.[23] Put in simple terms, if God cannot suffer, God cannot love.[24]

To summarize, Moltmann's argument is that the eschatological message of hope is lost if Christology is added on to either a philosophical view of God or even a speculative doctrine of the Trinity. By contrast, he wants to force us to think of God in terms of the cross and resurrection of Christ, which in turn requires what he judges to be a Trinitarian interpretation of Jesus' passion.

4. One further revision is needed for Moltmann to arrive at a point where theology is liberated from negative restrictions. As crucial as the category history is for his entire program, nevertheless theology cannot be confined entirely to historical categories. As he argues quite forcefully, our notion of history is a modern conception, sometimes set over against science, but in most

19. Cf. Moltmann, *Crucified God,* chapters 4-6, pp. 112-290.
20. Moltmann, *Crucified God,* p. 190.
21. Moltmann, *Crucified God,* p. 204.
22. Moltmann, *Crucified God,* pp. 207-34.
23. Moltmann, *Crucified God,* pp. 207-34.
24. Moltmann, *Crucified God,* p. 222.

cases set over against nature.[25] This restricts theology and ethics to human considerations and human history, resulting in the exclusion of the rest of the created order. This reinforces the ecological crisis and disallows a positive response. Moltmann wants to speak of the entire creation (living and nonliving matter) as part of fall and redemption. From his perspective, this requires revisions in the way we think of creation and liberation. In the former case, Moltmann affirms creation as the activity of Word and Spirit; on these terms, the preservation and development of creation are a reflection of the divine Spirit as well as Word/Wisdom. In the latter case, the whole creation groans in travail — not just human beings — and longs for liberation, where violence and death will be overcome and all creation will join in glorifying God.[26] Thus, Moltmann insists that we go beyond a historical conception of things (understood as the history of humans, or even worse, understood as the sacred history of a portion of humanity).[27]

5. Running through all three volumes is the critique of Western tendencies to confine religion either to a restricted area alongside of the state or to a psychological realm within the limits of familial and social standards set by culture. Such views make it impossible for the imagination to hear the liberating Word of Christ. When the realm of religion is prescribed by state or culture, then the horizon of faith is restricted to the present, and eschatological hope for liberation from the current world of violence and death is prohibited.

Having created an open space for theology to hear a word of hope, Moltmann can then proceed to develop a Christology that embodies liberation. In method and substance, Moltmann always begins with the cross and resurrection of Jesus. The initial assault on the aforementioned problems and his own Christology flow from this starting point. If there is a progressive development, it is in his increasing reliance on messianic and apocalyptic categories. This prompts him to qualify the language of two natures as well as that of justification and sanctification, though his intent is not to reject these categories but to incorporate them into a larger eschatological perspective.[28]

---

25. Moltmann, *The Way of Jesus Christ,* pp. 234ff.

26. Cf. Moltmann, *The Way of Jesus Christ,* chapters 5 and 6, pp. 213-312.

27. Moltmann's analysis of this issue raises the question: Why has the distinction of history and nature been kept so separate in theological discussions when in fact history has been introduced into scientific analysis of the world in both geology and evolutionary biology? It should also be noted that Moltmann attributes much of the difficulty in speaking about the resurrection to the separation of human history from nature and a scientific perspective. This split is one that he seeks to overcome.

28. Moltmann states that his concern with the categories of two natures is that they try to explicate the meaning of Jesus in negative terms (i.e., each nature is not the other) and his con-

Cross and resurrection are eschatological in that they point to the promises of God and open a new horizon for our history. They are apocalyptic in that they point to God's judgment and new creation against the violence and death of this world/aeon. Moltmann uses cross and resurrection in several important ways:

First, each term is interpreted in light of the other. If the cross is the rejection and abandonment of Jesus, then we must always think of the risen Lord as the crucified and even speak of the *crucified God*. Likewise, if the resurrection refers to Jesus being raised as Lord of all things, such language must be qualified by the fact that it is the crucified who is Lord. This interchange, therefore, leads to thinking about God in terms of crucifixion and about Jesus in terms of Word and Spirit.

Second, cross and resurrection are given messianic significance through Jesus' proclamation of a new time of peace and hope, understood against the background of Old Testament prophecies and the image of the coming apocalyptic Son of Man.[29] By using Abba as a title for God and his relation with God, Jesus claims the status of Son of God. But this status is further defined by his insistence on fellowship with all kinds of people — the poor, the outcasts, women, sinners, and all who suffer. Thus when Moltmann speaks of the cross and resurrection of Jesus, these are part of a messianic and apocalyptic event.

Third, cross and resurrection, as eschatological categories, also define God. When this is done, Moltmann finds that we think of God as the God of promise, the God who is Abba, the God who is united with Jesus in cross and resurrection. In effect, Jesus' history becomes the history of God. This is the revolution in the concept of God that Moltmann has been building in the progression of volumes.[30] Jesus is understood in terms of the language of Father, Son, and Spirit, and conversely, the Trinitarian personae are understood in terms of incarnation, cross, resurrection, and final coming. The Father sends the Son, who creates the person of Christ by the power of the Spirit.[31] Moltmann explicitly combines the themes of incarnation of the Word and adoption by the Spirit. The suffering of Jesus is therefore also the suffering of God, who as Father endures the pain of the Son.[32] The resurrection is from

---

cern with Reformation categories of Prophet, Priest, and King is that they can too easily shift to a vertical emphasis, rather than the horizontal focus on the eschatological hope for the future. Cf. *The Way of Jesus Christ*, pp. 136ff.

29. Moltmann, *The Way of Jesus Christ*, pp. 2-53.

30. Moltmann, *Crucified God*, p. 153.

31. Moltmann, *Crucified God*, pp. 234, 192-234 and *The Way of Jesus Christ*, p. 71.

32. Moltmann, *The Way of Jesus Christ*, pp. 172-78.

the Father and by the power of the life-giving Spirit. The Pauline theme of the righteousness of God is revealed in God's vindication of the crucified and the liberation of the creation from violence and death.

What then is the theory of atonement that emerges from this approach? To begin, the problem is violence and death. Moltmann clearly reflects the post–World War II generation, which is overwhelmed with the powers of evil and death. Sin, forgiveness, and reconciliation are included, but in the face of global violence to humanity and nature, Moltmann wants an inclusive statement of the problem. What emerges, however, as the decisive issue is the modern protest against God based on the ever-increasing cycles of violence and death. If Christianity is to speak of God, it will have to be in relation to what he terms *protest atheism,* which curses a God who allows such suffering. At the same time, it will have to reject the neat little theism that confines religion to a message of forgiveness for the individual apart from the state of the world or its future. Without hesitation, Moltmann therefore raises the stakes of the discussion by declaring that Jesus' death is a *theodicy trial,* wherein God must give an answer for the wretchedness of the earth.[33] Moreover, Jesus' death magnifies the problem: How could one who proclaimed the promises of God and was faithful to his Abba/Father God be the subject of such violence? This is the only relevant question for those who would trust God and those who would curse God. In this framework, God must be the primary subject because the history of Jesus is also the history of God.

Moltmann emphasizes the gospel claim that in his suffering and death, Jesus the messianic Son of Man is abandoned by everyone, including God. He is God-forsaken.[34] He is, as Paul declares, delivered or given up by God. This surrender is not for the sake of appeasing or satisfying God or the Law, but demonstrating God's righteousness against sin and the powers of violence and death. Jesus is both object and subject in his suffering: the object of rejection by his enemies but the subject who chooses suffering so that he might be a brother to all those who are forsaken and left to die.[35] But every moment in his death and resurrection is also a moment in God. His suffering is also the suffering of God,[36] wherein God becomes a co-sufferer and shows compassion for those who suffer. The suffering of Jesus and God reveals solidarity *with us,* and it is vicariously *for us.* But in an attempt to go beyond the Reformation's emphasis on justification, the sufferings "are God's sufferings, fi-

---

33. Cf. Moltmann, *The Way of Jesus Christ,* pp. 171ff. and *Crucified God,* pp. 151-96.
34. Moltmann, *The Way of Jesus Christ,* pp. 171-78.
35. Moltmann, *The Way of Jesus Christ,* p. 173.
36. Moltmann, *The Way of Jesus Christ,* p. 178.

nally, because out of them the new creation of all things is born: *we come from God*."[37] So he writes:

> But if he has suffered vicariously what threatens everyone, then through his representation he liberates everyone from this threat, and throws open to them the future of the new creation. He did not suffer the sufferings of the end-time simply as a private person from Galilee, or merely as Israel's messiah, or solely as the Son of man of the nations. He also suffered as the head and Wisdom of the whole creation, and died for the new creation of all things. . . . If this death is viewed against an apocalyptic horizon, and not as something normal or natural, then the great apocalyptic dying, the death of all things, has already begun. "This world" is passing away.[38]

In his death, Christ joins all who suffer death by violence in all times and places, as well as all living things. His resurrection is the first sign of the new creation and his Lordship over the living and the dead, though what Moltmann terms the theodicy trial will only be completed eschatologically with the final defeat of death.[39]

Wanting to view Christ's liberating work from the widest perspective, Moltmann affirms that salvation includes forgiveness of sins and liberation from sin, reconciliation, new life in service, inheriting the new creation, and participation in God's justice through our action.[40] In an effort to transcend the distinction between justification and sanctification, the category *participation* becomes as important as the traditional emphasis on faith/trust. Justification alone cannot define the work of Christ, though he is less clear on how the new community in Christ shall deal with the innumerable problems involved in requiring newness of life. But it is this emphasis on participation, along with the attention given to the life-giving Spirit with the Word, which brings Moltmann back to the Eucharist. In the Lord's Supper we practice the theology of the cross: we remember and experience Jesus' self-surrender and forsakenness and receive the grace that liberates.[41] In a very rich passage, he writes:

> The remembrance of Christ's sufferings is direct and without any mediation. But the remembrance of Christ's resurrection takes place only indirectly, mediated through the remembrance of Christ's sufferings. That is

37. Moltmann, *The Way of Jesus Christ*, p. 181.
38. Moltmann, *The Way of Jesus Christ*, pp. 155 and 157.
39. Moltmann, *The Way of Jesus Christ*, pp. 169 and 183.
40. Moltmann, *The Way of Jesus Christ*, p. 189.
41. Moltmann, *The Way of Jesus Christ*, pp. 204-5.

why we cannot really speak about a *memoria resurrectionis Christi*. But the Spirit of the resurrection hope is the impelling force for the continual remembrance of Christ's sufferings "until he comes."[42]

It is appropriate to pay tribute to the initial breakthrough in the three volumes surveyed here. Moltmann sought to go beyond the Reformation categories of justification and sanctification, the two kingdom view of church and state, and even the great neo-orthodox synthesis. Moltmann redirected Protestant thought by integrating the theme of liberation with the historical and eschatological categories of the Bible. Such an approach forced us to see the discontinuity between the eschatological message of the New Testament and so much of modern theology. In this regard his work is as much a *liberation* of theology as well as a theology that thinks of God, Christ, and salvation in light of liberation.

In carrying out this approach, Moltmann affirmed what he called a *cosmic Christology*.[43] On the one hand this meant thinking about our condition and the gospel in terms of violence and death, the fall of the entire creation, and the ultimate rebirth of all things in God's new creation. On the other hand this meant going beyond so many traditional dichotomies and polarities, e.g., the separation of the so-called vertical dimension from the historical, the limitations of the language of two natures, the over-reliance on the categories of justification and sanctification. He refused to choose either the language of incarnation of the Word, or adoption by the Spirit, to define Christ. Not content with the distinction between history and nature, he explored new ways of thinking about nature, which ultimately led him to speak of the fall and rebirth of the entire creation. All of these efforts make for a very complex set of works, with many suggestive initiatives.

Given all this it is not surprising that Moltmann's works leave many questions. Several of these relate to his use of Trinitarian language. In general it is a positive step to build Trinitarian thought into every part of the theological agenda. Likewise, the attention given to the Spirit is a helpful corrective. Where this raises difficulties is in his incorporation of the history of Jesus into the history of God, understood as the relations between Father, Son, and Holy Spirit. Two problems can be mentioned. The one case involves Jesus being forsaken and suffering as a form of surrender to God. When faced with the feminist charge that this is a form of brutality against the Son by the Father, Moltmann insists that the cross is an event in the relation of the Father

42. Moltmann, *The Way of Jesus Christ*, p. 207.
43. Moltmann, *The Way of Jesus Christ*, pp. 252-62 and chapters 6 and 7, pp. 274-341.

and Son.[44] The Son freely accepts the role and the cross also involves the suffering of the Father. This use of what I have called the Trinitarian defense is somewhat out of place for a liberation theology, since he is not working in the context of an exchange between Jesus and God. His response would be stronger if he relied on the strength of the liberation theme: Jesus the Son of God accepts the role of suffering to claim solidarity with us and vicariously suffer for us, thereby leading to our liberation from violence and death. But the force of Moltmann's argument is that Jesus' death is a demonstration of God's intention to share our sufferings and liberate the creation. He emphatically declares that God is always on Jesus' side. He then continues: "So the giving up of the Son reveals the giving up of the Father. In the suffering of the Son, the pain of the Father finds a voice. The self-emptying of the Son also expresses the self-emptying of the Father."[45] What is happening here, however, is that Moltmann is joining two themes together, i.e., liberation and the demonstration of God's suffering love, expressed in the language of the internal Trinitarian relation of Father and Son. Joined together, the suffering of God and the resurrection of the Son/Jesus constitute the vindication of God to a world that has turned away from God in protest. But this does complicate the picture. The liberation perspective does not require self-surrender to God and being forsaken by God, but the demonstration of suffering love does. It is this union of two major themes that complicates the matter and makes him vulnerable to the charge of brutality against the Son. We will return to this aspect of Moltmann's thought in Chapter Ten.

The other case involves the very danger that Moltmann so boldly denounced in his analysis of theology relying on the idea of the eternal present. When Moltmann affirms that the history of Jesus is the history of God (Father, Son, and Spirit), does this not overwhelm the history of Jesus and the biblical categories he has worked so hard to place at the center of the discussion? If the cross is an event in the relation of the Father and Son and Spirit, and if it is this language that is used to defend his theology against the charge of a brutal exchange between God and Jesus, then what has happened to the history of Jesus of Nazareth? While he is not comfortable with two nature language, his idea that the Son creates the person in Jesus makes it sound like there is but one nature in Jesus.[46] Thus he is in danger of doing precisely what he accuses Barth and Bultmann of doing, namely, the elimination of history and the story of Jesus.

44. Moltmann, *The Way of Jesus Christ*, pp. 175ff.
45. Moltmann, *The Way of Jesus Christ*, p. 176.
46. Moltmann, *Crucified God*, pp. 231-34.

Finally, liberation theology sought to break out of the confines of the church set apart from the world, unable to use power, and preoccupied primarily with the doctrine of justification. Moltmann clearly seeks to break out of this impasse. Christ is the liberator who calls for new life, lived out in acts of justice, peace, and hope. But Moltmann gives little attention to the problems encountered by the impulse for new communities based on reform, holiness, and Christ-like virtue. How can we go beyond justification without falling into the legalism, self-righteousness, and divisiveness that holiness movements have engendered time and again? One could also ask, in the spirit of Reinhold Niebuhr, what limits shall be set on the drive for holiness when it takes broad political form in movements based on either political ideology or religious fundamentalism? At one point Moltmann appears to acknowledge the problem of legalism and quickly reaffirms his preference for grace,[47] but this brief comment is hardly sufficient for a work that has moved so steadily toward insisting on embodiment and practice of the new creation.

2. James Cone

In the 1960s a new set of issues relating to race, gender, war, poverty, and the environment demanded a revision of the agenda. The two books by James Cone illustrate this in dramatic ways. *Black Theology and Black Power* appeared in 1969, followed by *A Black Theology of Liberation* in 1970.[48] Each contained a bold statement of black power and black liberation, including an unyielding denunciation of the white church, its theology, and its seminaries. In the Preface to the 1986 edition of *A Black Theology of Liberation*, Cone offered reflections on the work. He acknowledges that the book was written with justifiable passion and anger, reflecting his view of theology (pp. xii-xiv). For Cone, there is no objective, general statement of the essence of Christianity (pp. 18-19). One cannot achieve objectivity by pretending to be disconnected from particular contexts. All theology arises out of a concrete situation, which involves interests, values, even the conflict of values, and most important, passion. In this sense Cone does not offer us a general theology *applied* to the black experience, but rather a *black theology* growing out of the black experience. The work was intended as a new start, based on the Bible

---

47. Moltmann, *The Way of Jesus Christ*, pp. 336-37.

48. The two works used here by James H. Cone are: *Black Theology and Black Power* (New York: Seabury, 1969) and *A Black Theology of Liberation: Twentieth Anniversary Edition* (New York: Maryknoll, 1990). The latter was originally published in 1970. All references in the text are to *A Black Theology of Liberation*.

and black experience. Using the image of old and new wineskins, this black theology cannot be contained in the old systems of white theology.

Several things follow from this perspective. First, black theology must be liberated from white theology, which he believes to be totally immersed in the system of white oppression of black people (p. 57). He concedes that his frequent references to major white theologians contradicts this, but notes that it was inevitable that he reflect the education he received. But at the same time, he wishes that he would not have used the traditional outline of topics for his writing, but let black theology be formed by black experience. Second, he is forthright about refusing to consider criticisms from white theologians, since such comments reflect the white oppressive system as well as the pretense of objective scholarship (cf. pp. xiv, 18-19). His audience for the work is black people in their struggle for liberation (p. xi).

Viewed from every angle, Cone argues that Christian theology is a theology of liberation for black people. To make the case that the biblical story has to do with liberation, Cone moves freely from Exodus to the prophets to Jesus' reading of Isaiah in Luke 4:18-19. Neo-orthodoxy had it right in emphasizing revelation as God's personal encounter with humanity, but it failed to take the next step and affirm that the substance of these encounters was God's identification with the oppressed and their liberation (p. 63). These two elements, identification with the oppressed and liberation from oppression, become the major categories for interpreting Jesus, whether it is his life, death, or resurrection (cf. pp. 37, 81, and 113). So he writes: *"The finality of Jesus lies in the totality of his existence in complete freedom as the Oppressed One who reveals through his death and resurrection that God is present in all dimensions of human liberation"* (p. 118, italics in the text).

But in what sense is this *black* theology? To make this case, Cone unites what he considers to be the fundamental characteristic of the black experience in America with what is essential to revelation. The black experience is a history of oppression, manifested in slavery, segregation, persecution, and dehumanization. The evil of racism is precisely its willingness to deny value to black people, i.e., to consider them less than human. Racism thus takes away freedom in the world, but it also threatens the spiritual identity of black people to the point that they are tempted to accept the negative status decreed by white racism. Conversely, white racism is an evil that alters the humanity of white people, in that it allows them to live in the pretense of superiority as well as engage in the multiple forms of injustice and violence against black people. To be black in America, therefore, is to be oppressed in ways where freedom and identity are always under attack.

Having described what it means to be black, Cone then proceeds to make two crucial moves. On the one hand, he argues that *black* is both the color of skin but also a symbol of certain aspects of human existence. To be black is to suffer, to be oppressed and rejected. Thus anyone who shares in these marks of human existence is *black!* In this way it is possible to say that Jesus is *black* and even to speak of God as *black,* since Scripture makes it clear that they too suffer and join with the oppressed. The universal element of Jesus' resurrection is that "all oppressed peoples become his people" (p. 3). In speaking this way, Cone connects black experience with Jesus, but also opens the door for the inclusion of all oppressed persons.

On the other hand, he argues that liberation must mean the affirmation of that which has been negated, namely, being black. This can only occur if blacks affirm an identity and freedom against the oppressive white culture. To do this, Cone affirms the sources of black theology to be black experience, black history, and black culture, along with revelation, Scripture, and tradition. It also means that the liberation of black people cannot take the form of assimilation or integration, but the freedom to determine their own identity and culture. While he displays great respect for Dr. Martin Luther King, Jr., he is in fundamental disagreement with him regarding the means to liberation. Protests and reforms do not appear effective. Thus, using a phrase that caused extensive debate as well as serious concerns, Cone stated in the earlier work: black power means *"complete emancipation of black people from white oppression by whatever means black people deem necessary."*[49] This could include economic and political strategies, but also rebellion.

If we join together these two moves, we find that *black* is now functioning in several ways: as a symbol of oppression, whether it be oppression of all people or African Americans denied humanity, but also as a symbol of the new liberation. These two uses of black allow him to unite the affirmation of Jesus as liberator and the black experience in America. Thus when Cone defines the norm for this theology, it consists in the union of the revelation of Jesus as the oppressed agent of God (i.e., being black) and the experience of black people in America. Both sources, the Bible and African American experience, lead to being black and thus substantiate for Cone *black* theology.

With this general overview in mind, we can proceed to review the traditional sequence of topics that create a theory of atonement. For Cone, human beings were created by God for freedom, which he takes to be the image of God (p. 87). Since the fall, oppressed peoples find themselves without freedom. Thus freedom comes to mean resistance against oppression, rather than what he calls middle-class self-expression. In the world of oppressed people, free-

---

49. Cone, *Black Theology and Black Power,* p. 6 (italics in the text).

dom involves the identification with other oppressed persons and the willingness to suffer (p. 97). In a parallel way, Cone approaches the concept of sin from the standpoint of social oppression. Sin must be viewed from the standpoint of the community called to be faithful to God. To sin is to fail to recognize God's action among us (p. 105). For white persons this means to support oppressive systems and specific actions. For black persons it means to refuse to be who they are in the sight of God, namely, a people created free.

In continuity with God's liberating action in Exodus and the prophets, Jesus Christ appears as the one proclaiming the Rule of God, identifying with the oppressed and suffering with them. His suffering is not passive but an act of protest (p. 81). As the Suffering Servant, Jesus is among us as the black Jesus (p. 120). He suffers death at the hands of oppressors but is vindicated by God's power in the resurrection. Thus God creates on earth a new community of liberation, where people are called to repent as their response to God and join in the community of liberation, i.e., become black as Jesus is black (pp. 123-25). Cone affirms that this salvation is the work of God and must be received as a gift. But he strongly opposes the idea of salvation as a proclamation of love, disconnected from righteousness (pp. 66ff.). Love and righteousness cannot be separated in God, in the teachings of Jesus, or in the liberated life Jesus brings. The church, as the community of liberation, displays these marks: to preach the liberation of all oppressed peoples, to share in the struggle, and to embody the new freedom of Christ (pp. 130-31).

To reread Cone, some thirty years since these books were published, inevitably draws one into reflections on the passage of these three decades. So much has happened in unforeseen ways and we have lived through so many crises that we have become accustomed to strong language. To be sure, there are still some parts of the books that shock. The appeal to use whatever means necessary to accomplish freedom and justice is still problematic, but with the passage of time it appears more hyperbolic than real. Neither Cone, nor anyone using his theology, led a violent revolution. Reading it now prompts one to see the appeal as the dramatic language needed to make a point to both blacks and whites. Likewise, the confusion created by the claim that one must be *black* in order to be Christian is largely eliminated as one reads the actual text, rather than listens to slogans. The text makes clear the multiple meanings of black. The deliberate ambiguity is parallel to the way, as we shall see, that Gutiérrez uses the word *poor.* Like Cone, he also makes claims about the need to become poor, or how Jesus became poor on our behalf. One could also find parallels in Luther, who speaks of the need for all to empty themselves before the cross of Christ before they can receive the gift of grace.

As for the other striking aspect of the work, namely, the total rejection of white society, church, and theology, there is really no way to remove the sharp edge of this judgment. To the extent that white society created the oppressive system of slavery, segregation, and systemic racism, white society must bear responsibility for it. Racism has been and continues to be the great sin of this nation. Cone has simply named it for what it is: a theological heresy, a social evil, and a tragic division within the church that claims Jesus as Lord. His books only offer a theological commentary on what has been made quite explicit in social and historical analysis, as well as honest histories of religion in America. The judgment is not muted by pointing out that Cone himself admits that he did not realize the negative aspects of sexism, and he pledges to be more conscious of the problems of black women (pp. xv-xvi). The fact is that in American society there has always been one unresolved issue: Who belongs to the community? American history records all manner of morally unacceptable responses to the question, as well as some that are acceptable and even noble. The great strength of Cone's writing is the claim that the language about God's saving presence must always incorporate within it the gift and demand for freedom and justice for all people. Whenever this gift and demand are relegated to heaven, the sanctuary, or the inner life, then the gospel loses its ability to point to the saving power of God.

There are, of course, many other issues that can be raised about Cone's writings. One general issue is whether the first part of the twenty-first century requires new strategies or emphases, in light of the changing context which Cone himself accepts as decisive for doing theology. This is an issue that falls outside of the scope of this work but is relevant to any general interpretation of Cone for today. Another issue is the tendency for liberation theologies to draw distinctions too sharply, thereby opening the door to division and excessive claims. In Christian traditions, holiness movements have often been beset by this tendency in their zeal for the new life. We shall discuss this issue in the general conclusion to this chapter, since it relates to all of the cases presented. For now, therefore, it is appropriate simply to recognize the great influence Cone has had with black and white people, inviting or forcing them to see racism for what it is, but also to see Jesus as one who is always in our midst as the crucified and risen Lord.

3. Gustavo Gutiérrez

These considerations should not make us forget, however, that we are not dealing here solely with an intellectual pursuit. Behind liberation theology are Christian communities, religious groups, and peoples, who are becoming increasingly conscious that the oppression and neglect from which they suffer are incompatible with their faith in Jesus Christ (or, speaking more generally, with their religious faith). These concrete, real-life movements are what give this theology its distinctive character; in liberation theology, faith and life are inseparable. This unity accounts for its prophetic vigor and its potentialities.[50]

GUSTAVO GUTIÉRREZ

This statement from the Introduction to the fifteenth Anniversary Edition of *A Theology of Liberation* captures the excitement and urgency of the new theology that emerged in Latin America. It reflects the impact of the landmark council at Medellín in 1968, where Latin American bishops issued a call for social justice. For Gutiérrez, this was a new historical situation, even a *kairos*. At the time, Latin America was the only area of the world where the majority of the people are Christian and poor. He considered such poverty not an accident but the result of oppressive policies. But poverty and oppression were not new. What was new was the decision of the leaders of the church to name the situation for what it was, to side with the poor, and to issue a call for justice. But even this ecclesial act reflected the fact that the poor themselves considered their state to be a contradiction of the gospel of Jesus Christ.

This seminal work by Gutiérrez is not a tract for political action or ideology, but a theology grounded in the faith of the Roman Catholic Church. In Chapter One he notes that the traditional purpose of theology is to generate wisdom and a rational understanding of the faith (p. 5). He finds that this is an acceptable starting point as long as the focus is on contemporary praxis, i.e., the situation of the people in Latin America (p. 7). This, however, is not easy to do in the context of Latin American Catholicism. Too often, theology assumed that the church was a place set apart from the world and functioned as the sole possessor of truth (p. 143). Such theology accepted the duality of sacred and secular, or two histories, leading to the emphasis on salvation outside the world or in heaven (pp. 86, 122, and 143-48). Just as disappointing, the church had allied itself with the powers of this world.

To break this focus on the church itself and/or heaven, Gutiérrez defines the task of liberation theology to be "critical reflection on Christian praxis in light of the word of God" (p. xxix). Rejecting every attempt to separate faith

---

50. Gustavo Gutiérrez, *A Theology of Liberation: History, Politics and Salvation,* trans. and ed. Sister Caridad Inda and John Eagleson, rev. ed. (New York: Maryknoll, 1988). The original English edition appeared in 1973, following the actual publication in 1971. All future references to this work will be listed in the text.

from life, church from the world, theology from the life of faith, Gutiérrez relies on the image of the hermeneutical circle. The Word of God in Jesus Christ, the reality of people in this world, and critical reflection on Christian praxis in the face of oppression — these are all moments in the theological enterprise. But within this circle, Gutiérrez distinguishes stages in theological work: the first stage is "the lived faith that finds expression in prayer and commitment" (p. xxxiv). The second stage is reflection on Christian "praxis in light of God's word" (p. xxxiv). The ultimate norms for such reflection come from the truth accepted by faith and not our praxis. But in a characteristic emphasis on faith as a living reality in the context of the church upheld by Christ and the Spirit, he goes on to say: "But the 'deposit of faith' is not a set of indifferent, catalogued truths; on the contrary, it lives in the church where it rouses Christians to commitments in accordance with God's will and also provides criteria for judging them in the light of God's word" (p. xxxiv).

This definition of theology makes it clear that Gutiérrez is unapologetic about being immersed in the world of South America. His work is not simply the left wing of modern European theology, dominated by the Enlightenment (p. xxix). Nor is it a set of political views deduced from Christian doctrines. Time and again Gutiérrez reminds us that it is reflection on the salvation of Jesus Christ tied to the poor of Latin America. While he is appreciative of Moltmann's recovery of the eschatological perspective, several critical comments create some distance between the two. Gutiérrez judges Moltmann's view to be focused too much upon the future, which leads to the inability to develop a vocabulary "sufficiently rooted in human concrete historical experience, in an oppressed and exploited present" (p. 124). At another point he turns an image used by Moltmann against him.

> Moltmann says that theological concepts "do not limp after reality. . . . They illuminate reality by displaying its future." In our approach, to reflect critically on the praxis of liberation is to "limp after" reality. The present in the praxis of liberation, in its deepest dimension, is pregnant with the future; hope must be an inherent part of our present commitment in history. Theology does not initiate this future which exists in the present. It does not create the vital attitude of hope out of nothing. Its role is more modest. It interprets and explains these as the true underpinnings of history. (p. 11)

He concludes by reminding us that he does not envision a new *theme* for theology, but a new *way of doing* theology. It is reflection that ultimately aims at transformation of the world. "Theology as critical reflection on historical praxis is a liberating theology, a theology of the liberating transformation of the history of humankind and also therefore that part of humankind — gathered into *ecclesia* — which openly confesses Christ" (p. 12).

Our summary of Gutiérrez's view of salvation will concentrate on three basic issues: sin, Christ's liberating work, and the Christian life.

a. Sin

The three-level definition of sin, introduced in the first edition (p. 25) and reaffirmed in the 1988 Introduction (p. xxxviii), becomes the framework for understanding liberation. The first level is social, economic, and political oppression, whereby people are denied the most basic elements of life. The second level is personal servitude, where the individual is prevented from reaching the freedom and maturity of the image of God. The third level is sin as the "the breaking of friendship with God and with other human beings" (p. xxxviii). The three levels are interconnected since the first and second levels could not exist without sin as a break in friendship. By joining the levels together, Gutiérrez unites the social and individual, or the secular and religious. Too often, the social forms of sin are treated as afterthoughts or applications deferred for later discussion. In this case, the three levels are seen as three manifestations of the same brokenness stemming from alienation from God and neighbor.

This approach also allows Gutiérrez to unite social and theological analysis without losing the integrity or power of either perspective. On the one hand he can engage in critical social or structural analysis of the economic and political forces that perpetuate the existing system (cf. p. xxiv and p. 13). This means that systems of domination must be exposed, that domination deliberately creates dependency, and that conflict between the rich and poor is a social fact. This analysis leads Gutiérrez to two conclusions: first, that the language of *developed* and *underdeveloped* nations conceals inequities of power and exploitation (pp. 13ff.); second, that liberating change will not occur by means of more development or even gradual reforms, especially if these are controlled by those in power (p. 32). Without being ideological, Gutiérrez insists upon radical honesty regarding the actual situation of the poor. Abstract discussions and/or pretense of innocence cannot be tolerated. This is further illustrated in his handling of the question whether the church should be involved in the social issues facing the poor. His immediate response is that the church is already involved, though on the wrong side! (Cf. pp. 63, 76, and 151.) The real question is whether the church will use its great resources and influence for change rather than maintaining the status quo.

On the other hand, his analysis of the three levels is also based on theological norms drawn from the Bible and tradition. Thus Gutiérrez evaluates the status of the poor from the standpoint of Exodus and Sinai, the prophets and Jesus' teachings. This not only frames the discussion in the language of faith, but it also connects all three levels. The economic oppression of persons is wrong because the gospel cannot tolerate the alienation of persons from one another or from God. Conflict may be a long-standing social fact, but for Christians it is a break in fraternal relations. Individuals unable to find freedom or maturity fail to achieve the fullness of the image of God. Sin is the ultimate problem because it is the rejection of the love of neighbor and of God (cf. pp. 104 and 113). By using norms from faith in this way, Gutiérrez provides a theological analysis of sin in its many forms.

b. The Liberation of Jesus Christ

The Christology presented in this work deals with traditional themes, but in a new way. The strong emphasis on liberation from social and economic oppression may cause some readers to question whether this is *really* a theory of atonement. As if mindful of such a charge, Gutiérrez writes:

> Liberation theology is thus intended as a theology of salvation. Salvation is God's unmerited action in history, which God leads beyond itself. It is God's gift of definitive life to God's children, given in a history in which we must build fellowship. Filiation and fellowship are both a grace and a task to be carried out; these two aspects must be distinguished without being separated, just as, in accordance with the faith of the church as definitively settled at the Council of Chalcedon, we distinguish in Christ a divine condition and a human condition, but we do not separate the two. (p. xxxix)

This statement combines the very traditional with the innovative. He will speak of the salvation Christ brings, but only in the context of the liberation from all forms of oppression and sin. Such an approach requires what he calls the *uncentering* of the church and its theology (p. 143). The church is neither the sole subject nor the sole realm of God's activity. For the liberation Christ brings, the field of vision is the world and human history (pp. xx and 9). As a Roman Catholic, Gutiérrez assumes the doctrines of Trinity, Incarnation, church, and sacraments. In and of themselves, these doctrines are not in question. What is at issue is how they relate to God's liberation in Jesus Christ.

To support his focus on liberation in this world, Gutiérrez emphasizes the continuity of God's saving (or liberating) activity in Israel and in Christ.

Exodus, Sinai, and the prophets are invoked in order to understand Jesus the liberator. To refer to the now famous phrase, God has always shown a "preferential option for the poor" (p. xxv). Thus when Jesus uses the prophets in denouncing oppression and announcing the coming of God's Reign, he stands in continuity with this tradition and also fulfills it (p. 90). If we affirm the traditional theme of incarnation, then this means that salvation is in the very history of the poor of Latin America. It is not confined to heaven, a sacred ecclesial realm, or an inner spiritual world, but now in this time and place (pp. 95 and 97). It will entail the advent of justice and the transformation of social systems (p. 101).

How does this occur? Gutiérrez accepts the view that Jesus dies as the result of a political trial by the Romans precisely because he threatens the oppressive structures of this world (pp. 133-34). But in his resurrection he is vindicated. God reveals the power of life in the face of death and oppression. This Paschal event, whereby Jesus passes from death to life, is foreshadowed by the Exodus, wherein Israel passes from bondage to freedom (pp. 120 and 149). Gutiérrez sees two themes regarding salvation converging in Jesus: one is the quantitative, whereby salvation is progressively revealed to more people until it is universal; the other is qualitative, whereby salvation effects the complete transformation of individuals in their movement from alienation to communion with God. Jesus as the incarnate Word represents both — the fulfillment of God's universal love for all people and the power of God in a particular saving event. As God's liberating Word, Jesus therefore liberates humankind from all three levels of oppression and sin: the oppressive social structures, the limitations on personal freedom and maturity, and sin itself. "Christ introduces us by the gift of his Spirit into communion with God and with all human beings. More precisely, it is because he introduces us into this communion, into a continuous search for its fullness, that he conquers sin — which is the negation of love — and all its consequences" (p. 103).

c. The New Life in Christ

Throughout this work, Gutiérrez maintains the basic definition of theology: to engage in critical reflection on the praxis of Christians in light of the Word of God. This means that he must guard against the "danger of oversimplifying the Gospel message and making it a 'revolutionary ideology' — which would definitively obscure reality" (p. 155). His analysis of structures of oppression is not intended to produce political ideology or to suggest that the Reign of God shall come by a temporal process (p. 103). It is precisely because the powers of oppression and sin are so great that a human revolutionary program would be a failure. Instead, his confidence in liberation lies in proclaiming the eschatological promise of God: "The Bible is the book of the Promise, the Promise made by God to human beings, the efficacious revelation of God's love and self-communication" (p. 91). This revelation is both gift and grace, received by faith, creating a new set of relations between human beings themselves and with God. The Christian life, therefore, is lived in the presence of the promise fulfilled in Christ and its actualization in our lives and throughout the world.

Gutiérrez does not provide us with a systematic outline of the Christian life. Instead he provides several glimpses of Christian life, which when taken together, convey a broader view of the church and life in Christ.

(1) The Church as a Sacrament and Sign Gutiérrez's critique of the traditional view, which made the church the center for thinking about salvation, does not prevent him from affirming the importance of the church in God's plan of salvation. Embracing what he perceives as a new ecclesiology stemming from Vatican II, he affirms the church as a visible sacrament of the plan of salvation (pp. 147ff.). This means that the church embodies the unity of God and humankind that is centered outside of itself in the world. Thus it stands as a sign or testimony of what God is doing in history. Its mission is to embody the unity of God and humankind, or as he also says, the presence of Christ and the Spirit in the liberation of humanity. The first way in which this is done is the Eucharist. Here there is the remembrance of the death and resurrection of Christ as well as the thanksgiving that by his passage from death to life, the community of faith is now passing from sin to grace (pp. 148-49). In this celebration the community receives the gifts of peace, unity, and solidarity (pp. 159-61). But in a striking move, Gutiérrez connects this unity with service. Observing that John's gospel does not record the Lord's Supper, but instead the washing of feet, Gutiérrez declares that service is thereby equated with the fellowship of the Supper. Taking it a step further, our service, worship, and fellowship are all based on the full communion of the divine personae of the Trinity (p. 151).

(2) The Witness of the Church While Gutiérrez speaks boldly of the presence of Christ's liberating work, it is apparent that we now live in a transitional time. The affirmation that Christ fulfills the promises is clearly set alongside the call to labor with Christ for the liberation of all people (cf. pp. 90-91). In this special time, where we celebrate the new communion with God and neighbor, the church is called to engage the world in a twofold witness (cf. pp. 151-53). First, the church must denounce the oppressive structures of the world and the sin that lies as the ultimate cause. This prophetic role requires that the church speak against all that dehumanizes people. Second, the church must announce the good news — the liberation of Christ and the love of God. In this act of annunciation Gutiérrez perceives the power to awaken and mobilize the consciences of people for the cause of liberation. But what shall people do? Again, Gutiérrez refuses to suggest universal answers. In general, he believes that the love of God for all people must and can be balanced by a show of preference for specific action. He is confident that the solution for specific problems lies in that situation. Every specific situation contains the problem, the announcement of the gospel with its universal demands, and the concrete situation where people are asking the question of praxis. In such situations, filled with tensions, faithful people will find a way to create just social relations and embody the unity of Christ (cf. pp. 154-60).

(3) **Poverty and Christian Witness**   Throughout the book Gutiérrez affirms God's option for the poor, but he rejects the idea that the poor have a special status because they are poor. He has no interest in elevating one class over others or making poverty a value in and of itself (p. 170). If the latter were the case, why seek liberation from it? The complexity of this issue at the social/economic level, as well as the long history of monastic poverty, draws Gutiérrez into a discussion of the meaning of poverty, with quite surprising results. To sort things out, he differentiates three types of poverty: First, material poverty constitutes a violation of the image of God in each person and of solidarity between persons. It is, he says, a scandal that must be overcome (pp. 162-65). Second, spiritual poverty is the willingness to admit that we have nothing before God. It is the opposite of pride and represents a stance of waiting for the Lord, or taking on the role of the child who is totally dependent. Third, evangelical poverty is the act of engaging in solidarity with the poor; it is a protest against oppression (pp. 171-73). Such poverty is not a higher spiritual calling or discipline. Its value is not in our detachment from material things but in the availability of the self to God and neighbor. Like spiritual poverty, it involves a willingness to be passive and receive the gift of salvation, but moves to solidarity with the poor in protest against poverty. As Christ freely assumed the role of the servant and became poor for our sake, so we are called to be open to the neighbor and await the future promised by God. This view of poverty coincides with his reflection on love made earlier in the work. Just as God's presence and love are mediated to us through Christ and other persons, so our love toward God is mediated through the love of the neighbor. In this respect, solidarity is a concrete way of living, involving a conversion to our neighbors, attention to them, work, fidelity, and prayer (pp. 114-20).

4. Feminist and Womanist Perspectives

Theological reflection growing out of the movement for the liberation of women went far beyond the quest for highly visible political and economic rights in society. It represented a thoroughgoing critique of the multiple layers of subordination of women in all aspects of society, joined with the demand for full and equal participation of women in every realm of life. But it has developed in a variety of ways. Given the contextual nature of theology, it was now possible for women to develop their own feminist liberation theologies. Thus Roman Catholic, mainline Protestant, conservative Protestant, and Jewish women began the process of thinking about their specific struggles in light of the categories of liberation. This produced even greater differentiation. For example, black women felt the need to speak for themselves, apart from the growing number of white feminists, thus creating what they called Womanist Theology. A similar development occurred among Hispanic female theologians. Women in the lesbian and gay movements also found the need to speak for themselves, but also separated along racial lines.[51] Another source of diversity was the need to address the full range of theological issues, as well as key social and economic issues relating to oppression of women. Some writers focused on the Bible and the development of Christianity in the first few centuries, others dealt with historical theology, and still others joined in the work of contemporary theology and ethics. The differences in subject and perspective thus produced greater variety in the development of feminist liberation theology.

With more and more scholars added to the enterprise over the last three decades, and with more women ordained as pastors, feminist liberation theology now represents the range of religious communities and continues to be differentiated by race, class, geography, sexual orientation, and interest. There is no one feminist liberation theology, nor do major voices expect unanimity on most issues.[52] As a result we will focus on several themes relating to atone-

---

51. Examples of these perspectives can be found in the following: for Womanist theology, cf. Audrey Lorde, *Sister Outsider: Essays and Speeches* (Freedom, Calif.: The Crossing Press, 1984), and Katie Geneva Cannon, "The Emergence of Black Feminist Consciousness," *Feminist Interpretation of the Bible*, ed. Letty M. Russell (Philadelphia: Westminster, 1985), pp. 30-40. For an overview of Hispanic liberation theology, cf. L. Susan Bond, *Trouble with Jesus: Women, Christology and Preaching* (St. Louis: Chalice Press, 1999), pp. 85-90. For lesbian writers, cf. Lorde and Carter Heyward, *Speaking of Christ: A Lesbian Feminist Voice* (New York: Pilgrim Press, 1989) and *Touching Our Strength: The Erotic as Power and the Love of God* (San Francisco: Harper and Row, 1989).

52. Cf. Letty M. Russell, *Household of Freedom: Authority in Feminist Theology* (Philadelphia: Westminster, 1987), p. 35, and "Authority and the Challenge of Feminist Interpretation," in Russell, *Feminist Interpretation*, p. 144.

ment theory. The concern is to identify how feminist theology develops a liberation Christology in ways different from male theologians, be they white, black, or Latin American. The three issues are: (a) the problem of patriarchy; (b) the authority of the Bible; and (c) salvation as liberation.

a. The Problem of Patriarchy

Feminist liberationists are united in their drive for freedom from what is usually called patriarchy. For Elisabeth Schüssler Fiorenza, patriarchy is not just

> ideological dualism or androcentric world construction in language but a social, economic and political system of graded subjugations and oppressions. . . . Patriarchy as a male pyramid specifies women's oppression in terms of the class, race, country, or religion of the men to whom they "belong." . . . In a patriarchal society or religion, all women are bound into a system of male privilege and domination.[53]

This view of patriarchy emphasizes that the subordination of women cannot be defined simply by particular acts or attitudes, but by the policies, laws, and regulations of institutional structures going back for centuries. These systems of male privilege are mandated by claims to ultimate authority and enforced by centuries of institutional practices. Writers describe the nature of this oppression in different ways, reflecting their history and social context. Serene Jones, relying on the work of Iris Young, names five forms of oppression: exploitation, marginalization, powerlessness, cultural imperialism, and violence.[54] Katie Cannon and Audrey Lorde record the oppression of black women through the successive stages of slavery, segregation, and exclusion.[55] For them, poor black women struggle against exclusion based on gender, race, and class. Along with abuse and violence, black women face the spiritual pain caused by the loss of identity and value when women are defined according to male standards.[56]

Rosemary Radford Ruether has connected oppression with specific value judgments. For example, while male and female are created equal in the image of God in Genesis 1:26, women have been subordinated in traditional the-

---

53. Elisabeth Schüssler Fiorenza, "The Will to Choose or to Reject: Continuing Our Critical Work," in Russell, *Feminist Interpretation,* p. 127.

54. Serene Jones, *Feminist Theory and Christian Theology: Cartographies of Grace* (Minneapolis: Fortress, 2000), pp. 79ff.

55. Cf. Cannon, pp. 30-40, and in general Lorde, *Sister Outsider.*

56. Lorde, p. 64.

ory and practice. In Augustine and Aquinas, women are judged to be inferior in body, mind, and will, more prone to sin. Men, by contrast, were the higher form of humanity, more capable of reason.[57] Protestants, by contrast, appealed instead to the punishment decreed by God in Genesis 3 (e.g., Luther), or simply appealed to God's ordering of society (e.g., Calvin and Barth).[58] Ruether also sees the New Testament continuing the tradition of male dominance so pervasive in the Old Testament. The emphasis on the church as the Bride of Christ reinforces those aspects of women emphasized in patriarchy, namely, passivity and receptivity.[59] A similar pattern appears in the references to the Virgin Birth in Luke and Matthew, leading to Mary as the prototype of submission. In the refusal to acknowledge the brothers and sisters of Jesus born of Mary, the tradition further elevates virginity and denigrates the natural functions of the female body.[60] Parallel to this negative evaluation of women is the removal of positive stories regarding women. Ruether refers to this as "the record of patriarchal erasure."[61] Schüssler Fiorenza laments this repression of the role of women in the early church and calls for a reconstruction of that period by means of keeping before us those texts that are androcentric and patriarchial. By going through what might be called the worst texts, one can discover something of the actual situation of women.[62]

Another approach to patriarchy argues for greater precision. In general, feminists rejected the idea of innate characteristics in each gender (known as essentialism), because this produced a view of women that omitted reason, but emphasized caring, intuition, and feelings. Serene Jones, however, proposes to reopen the discussion, since feminists inevitably do make statements about women that imply some form of essentialism. Yet she is unwilling to claim that there is such a thing as a universal desire of all men to dominate women, since that suggests the whole matter is determined by biology. Such a

57. Rosemary Radford Ruether, *Sexism and God-Talk: Toward a Feminist Theology* (Boston: Beacon, 1983), pp. 93-96.

58. Ruether, pp. 98-99.

59. Ruether, pp. 139-44.

60. While it is correct that Mary has been used, and may still be used, as a model of passivity, subordinate to the intervention of God, as well as subordinate to the risen Christ, one can also argue that at least in Luke and Matthew, Mary can be interpreted as a model of faithfulness parallel to the fidelity of Jesus in his steadfastness to the will of God. Thus in the *Magnificat*, Mary speaks for the oppressed and poor in anticipation of the redemption God will bring in Christ. Such fidelity obviously contrasts with the break in trust committed by both Adam and Eve.

61. Ruether, "Feminist Interpretation: A Method of Correlation," in Russell, *Feminist Interpretation*, p. 123.

62. Schüssler Fiorenza, pp. 133ff.

position would rule out the possibility for change or moral responsibility for patriarchy, taking attention away from the historical-social patterns of institutional life. In what she calls a stricter definition, patriarchy refers to the rule of men over women, whereby women are deprived of legal and economic rights, and are relegated to subordinate status. Such a phenomenon is not the same in all times and places, and may well not be "the 'myth of universal male domination.'"[63] Yet the historical evidence clearly suggests a worldwide pattern of oppression.

b. The Authority of the Bible

If the liberation of women entails a reconstruction of the entire social order, then one must deal with the authority of the Bible. This is especially the case since the Bible contains the defense of patriarchy.[64] As a result, feminist liberationists must determine how the Bible, and subsequent traditions, can be of support in the cause of liberation while simultaneously challenging the oppressive imagery, practices, and mandates contained in such authoritative texts. In this task, feminist theology faces a far more serious problem than the other views described above. Moltmann and Gutiérrez both presuppose the tradition and boldly use key aspects in arguing for their views. The situation is somewhat different for Cone, but the number of negative texts in the Bible dealing with persons of color is limited and the problem he faces has more to do with the way traditions have used the Bible. But the matter is significantly different for the feminist cause: The Bible and the foundational doctrines are so intertwined with patriarchy that it is not clear whether they are friend or foe. How one overcomes the oppressive traditions and language in Bible and creeds consumes far greater discussion. The now famous *hermeneutic of suspicion* represents a critical judgment against these sources of authority, given their tie to patriarchy. Unlike its counterparts, feminist liberation theology is forced to deal with a more searching reappraisal of the authority of the Bible.

How does one rebuild trust in a situation where trust has been so severely broken? As one might expect, there is a great deal of resistance to any easy embrace of the Bible. The fact that it has been used for so long to legitimate oppression of women heightens mistrust of the Bible as well as the sensitivity to particular texts. Thus a reappraisal of the Bible will be a complicated process. For example, Letty Russell argues that before we can deal with specifics

63. Jones, p. 79; cf. pp. 77-79.
64. Schüssler Fiorenza, p. 129.

in the Bible, we must recognize that traditional views of the authority of the Bible grow out of the hierarchial and patriarchial tradition that has been so oppressive of women. These views assumed that authority is fixed in text or institutions and provides mandates through a hierarchy of leaders (i.e., men), which believers must accept. This is the authority of domination and perpetuates the oppression of women and others excluded from power.[65] As an alternative, Russell endorses a view of authority emerging from the social sciences, where authority is based on the consent of those governed. Those in authority possess power not on the basis of control or domination, but by appeal to shared values (e.g., partnership and mutuality). For Russell, the Bible has authority because it relates in positive ways to women's experience and the struggle for freedom.

The move to relate the Bible with the experience of women finds repeated expression. Katie Cannon argues that black women have been empowered in the struggle for freedom and dignity by the prophetic tradition and the teachings of Jesus. The Bible is the highest authority because it inspired the black church and its members to claim their humanity in an oppressive world.[66] Margaret Farley suggests that the Bible can reveal truth if it "rings true to our deepest capacity for truth and goodness. If it contradicts this, it is not to be believed. If it falsifies this, it cannot be accepted."[67] At the top of her list of criteria is the "conviction that women are fully human and are to be valued as such."[68] For Rosemary Radford Ruether, it is not any kind of experience that is relevant to this discussion, but the experience that emerges when women become conscious of living in an oppressive, male-dominated society. She acknowledges that the ability to name experience in this way is already a sign of grace and involves a conversion, since one now views the world as well as oneself in a different way.[69] If the negative form of this experience is the naming of sexism, the positive form is the affirmation of "the full humanity of women."[70] Ruether goes on to affirm a canon within the canon, namely, the prophetic-messianic traditions. Such a canon is not a collection of texts but a self-correcting and critical perspective that "constantly reevaluates, in new contexts, what is truly the liberating Word of God, over against both the sinful deformations of contemporary society and also the limitations of past

---

65. Russell, *Feminist Interpretation,* pp. 142-46, and in general, *Household.*

66. Cannon, pp. 39-40.

67. Margaret Farley, "Feminist Consciousness and the Interpretation of Scripture," in Russell, *Feminist Interpretation,* p. 43.

68. Farley, p. 44.

69. Ruether, pp. 114-15.

70. Ruether, p. 115.

biblical traditions, which saw in part and understood in part, and whose partiality may have become a source of sinful injustice and idolatry."[71] The combination of this biblical canon with women's experience constitutes what Ruether calls a method of correlation. Instead of sanctifying the existing structures of power, it finds expression in attempts to destabilize oppressive powers.[72] Taking a similar view, Letty Russell declares:

> In spite of the patriarchal nature of the biblical texts, I myself have no intention of giving up the biblical basis of my theology. . . . The Bible has authority in my life because it makes sense of my experience and speaks to me about the meaning and purpose of my humanity in Jesus Christ.[73]

While acknowledging all of the problems in the Bible, Russell is continually drawn to "the witness of scripture to God's promise (for the mending of creation) on its way to fulfillment."[74]

A different approach is taken by Elisabeth Schüssler Fiorenza in "The Will to Choose or to Reject: Continuing Critical Work."[75] Her initial emphasis is to avoid the attempt to find a canon within the canon, since such attempts tend to extract ideas or themes out of the historical context and turn them into abstract principles that can be universally applied.[76] Such uses also encourage the notion that certain portions of the Bible are totally free from the problem of patriarchy and do not require a critical interpretation. She also argues for remembering all portions of the Bible, even the most oppressive, because they allow us to reconstruct the situation of women in the biblical period. Thus, instead of searching for a canon within the canon, or affirming some method of correlation between Bible and experience, she affirms the *women-church* as the center for interpretation. By this she means "the movement of self-identified women and women-identified men in biblical religion. . . . Its goal is not simply the 'full humanity' of women, since humanity as we know it is male defined, but women's religious self-affirmation, power and liberation from all patriarchal alienation, marginalization, and oppression."[77] In developing this hermeneutic, Schüssler Fiorenza argues that the locus of God's revelation is not the Bible, the

71. Ruether, p. 117.
72. Ruether, pp. 116-24.
73. Russell, p. 138.
74. Russell, p. 139.
75. Schüssler Fiorenza, pp. 125-36.
76. Schüssler Fiorenza, p. 131.
77. Schüssler Fiorenza, p. 126.

church traditions dominated by patriarchy, or a special canon, but the experience of women in their struggle against patriarchy.[78] While this approach sets her in opposition to both Ruether and Russell, it is important to note that Schüssler Fiorenza's development of the experience of women-church is usually tied to the interpretation (critique and reconstruction) of the Bible. What she terms the experience of *grace in our midst* occurs in both the reconstruction of women struggling in biblical stories as well as contemporary struggles for liberation. "The God of Judith as well as the God of Jesus is Emmanuel, God with us in our struggles for liberation, freedom and wholeness. The spiritual authority of women-church rests on this experience of grace in our midst."[79] It is through the critical interpretative model as well as the struggle for liberation that the Bible can become holy scripture for women.[80]

c. Salvation as Liberation

Given these views of patriarchy and authority, what then emerges in the feminist view of salvation? As is already apparent, there is a wide range of views. As we shall see, some of these views do not actually fall within the narrow definition of Christ the liberator, if one uses Irenaeus as the model. Others gravitate toward what will appear as the last form of atonement theories, namely, the demonstration of love. But since they all speak of the liberation of women from oppression, there seems to be a general acceptance of the idea that these feminist writers are doing *liberation* theology. To describe the views of salvation, I will identify two broad areas — one positive and the other critical — where there is considerable consensus, and then mention four quite different trajectories inspired by what is held in common. In this way, some of the differences between feminist liberationists and the views of Moltmann, Cone, and Gutiérrez will become evident, though this is not to suggest that these last three constitute the norm for liberation theology.

To begin with the positive, there appears to be broad agreement that salvation refers to the creation of a liberated community among women. This involves a new consciousness and protest against patriarchy *and* empowerment in the struggle for justice. It is a new community marked by inclusivity, mutuality, freedom, love, partnership, and openness. It includes opposition to all forms of oppression — racial, class, ethnic, geographic, social, eco-

---

78. Schüssler Fiorenza, pp. 128 and 135.
79. Schüssler Fiorenza, p. 129.
80. Schüssler Fiorenza, p. 135.

nomic, political, as well as gender. It is a community open to men who are willing to be liberated from patriarchy.

This positive overview is usually tied to the criticism of traditional theories of atonement, their language, and the way these theories have influenced religious life and social relations. A series of problems can be enumerated:

- The title Lord as applied to Jesus or God, as well as the imagery of Father and Son in Trinitarian and general theological discussions, is judged unacceptable. Not only is the language male, but it relates to the images of power and authority in the patriarchial family where only fathers and sons are deemed of value. The fragile character of human family life, where fathers are too often less than protective or loving, makes the use of Father as applied to God highly questionable, if not completely unacceptable.[81]

- Traditional definitions of sin tend to emphasize rebellion, self-love, and pride, which feminists judge to be characteristic of oppressive patriarchal systems. Such robust forms of sin do not characterize the poor and oppressed.[82]

- The emphasis on Jesus' suffering as willed by God, or as necessary in light of some form of retributive justice, or as somehow efficacious in the process of redemption, tends to justify and glorify suffering. For oppressed women, this has meant a legitimization of their status and reinforces their need to accept suffering.[83]

- The similar emphasis on Jesus' death as willed by God or the cause of our redemption justifies and glorifies the death of the innocent. It turns God into an abusive father and condones the sacrifice of sons and daughters in the defense of oppressive systems.[84]

---

81. Cf. Rosemary Radford Ruether, *Introducing Redemption in Christian Feminism* (Cleveland: Pilgrim Press, 1998), pp. 83-90; Sally B. Purvis, *The Power of the Cross: Foundations for a Christian Feminist Ethic of Community* (Nashville: Abingdon, 1993), pp. 21-32; and Susan Thistlethwaite, *Sex, Race, and God: Christian Feminism in Black and White* (New York: Crossroad, 1991), pp. 110ff. and 121.

82. Purvis, p. 93, and Ruether, p. 103.

83. Cf. Ruether's discussion of the criticisms developed by Joanne Carlson Brown and Rebecca Parker in Ruether, pp. 100-102, and Schüssler Fiorenza's discussion of the criticisms developed by Regula Strobel in *Jesus: Miriam's Child, Sophia's Prophet* (New York: Continuum, 1994), pp. 100ff.

84. In addition to the references in Note 76, cf. references to Delores Williams and Dorothee Soelle in Ruether, *Introducing Redemption*, pp. 102-3, as well as Ruether's own position, pp. 100-107; and Schüssler Fiorenza, *Jesus*, pp. 102-7, 127; and Rita Nakashima Brock, *Journeys by Heart: A Christology of Erotic Power* (New York: Crossroad, 1996), pp. 53-56.

- Since the suffering and death of Jesus are centered in the cross, this symbol is also the object of the criticisms just mentioned. It cannot be the central focus of the process of salvation. This leads many writers to shift the emphasis to Jesus' life and/or the resurrection.[85]

Not every feminist or Womanist writer accepts all of these concerns, or adopts the same corrective strategy. But the frequency with which these concerns are raised indicates that, in general, feminist liberation theology involves a major reformulation of the way we speak of salvation. When joined with the general positive statement noted above, the two produce several interesting trajectories.

(1) The first is that the cross must be replaced by Jesus' life, i.e., his teachings, signs, and actions. This becomes clear in Ruether, who quite clearly sets the Jesus of the synoptics over against that of traditional doctrines.[86] In clarifying what is distinctive about this Jesus, it is not that he is male, since his gender has no significance for salvation.[87] What is significant is the community he creates, the good news he brings, the resistance to oppressive powers, and above all, his kenosis of power in favor of identification with the poor.[88] What emerges is an outline for a Christology based on the prophets and the historical Jesus, interpreted through liberationist categories.[89]

(2) If the cross cannot be the focal point, then some are led to emphasize the resurrection. For example, Schüssler Fiorenza sees Jesus' death as an execution, devoid of any significance as a redemptive event. Like so many others, she sees in the extolling of the cross only abusive language, which must be rejected.[90] If there is saving significance to Jesus, therefore, it must be in the resurrection as God's vindication.[91] A similar point is made by Susan Thistlethwaite.[92] Such a Christology would emphasize the new and full life given by God to liberated women and not simply the resurrection of Jesus.

(3) A third option is to de-emphasize the person of Jesus as the single point in history through which salvation is actualized and from whom it proceeds to humanity by means of his actions upon them. Stated in the positive,

---

85. Schussler Fiorenza, *Jesus*, p. 121; Thistlethwaite, p. 108; and Ruether, *Introducing Redemption*, pp. 104-7.

86. Ruether, *Sexism*, p. 135.

87. Ruether, *Sexism*, p. 137, and *Introducing Redemption*, p. 92.

88. Ruether, *Introducing Redemption*, pp. 92-107; Schüssler Fiorenza, *Jesus*, pp. 101-27.

89. Thistlethwaite, pp. 94-96.

90. Schüssler Fiorenza, *Jesus*, pp. 102ff. and 127.

91. Schüssler Fiorenza, *Jesus*, p. 121.

92. Thistlethwaite, p. 108.

the emphasis is on the community of liberated persons, either because that is where grace is actualized or because love is relational and requires more than one person.[93] Such a Christology builds upon the traditional idea of the Body of Christ and recalls Luther's admonition to be a *Christ* to one's neighbor, though it de-emphasizes the originating agency of Jesus Christ. The result is to affirm what is happening in the struggle for liberation and/or the power of love already at work in the world.

(4) If suffering and death do not constitute a transaction securing salvation, Jesus' life and death may still be seen as the inauguration of a new community of faithfulness and love. Working along these lines, Sally Purvis wants to reclaim the cross as an expression of love.[94] L. Susan Bond develops a revision of the Christus Victor theme, where the violent overthrow of the devil is replaced by the redemptive power of love.[95]

This summary of feminist and Womanist liberation theology reveals how it challenges every aspect of the tradition. It has identified the multiple ways male privilege has controlled the church's practice and theology and has begun the process of searching for more appropriate ways to express Christian faith — in both form and substance. Following the period of biblical and Reformation studies in the twentieth century, much of its program builds on basic theological ideas of the sovereignty of God's judgment and grace, as well as the emphasis on the church as a community witnessing to justice and peace.

When the movement names contradictions between the gospel and practice, or addresses foundational issues, it opens debates that are not easily resolved. Conservative and fundamentalist traditions have clearly drawn lines between themselves and this movement. It has been relatively easy for ecumenical Protestants to support women's rights, ordination for women, and greater inclusivity in ecclesial structures. But it has been more difficult to come to terms with the many proposals for theological reformulation. By definition, feminist and Womanist liberation theology is a departure. To the extent that the options offered depart too far from what can broadly be referred to as the centrality of Scripture and Jesus Christ, the movement will encounter serious resistance. In general, the attack on patriarchy is parallel to other applications of a radical doctrine of sin, understood from a social perspective. The approaches to Scripture are so varied that each will have to be evaluated

---

93. Schüssler Fiorenza, *Jesus,* p. 121, and Russell, *Feminist Interpretation,* pp. 128-29; and Brock, pp. 65-70.

94. Cf. Purvis, chapters 4 and 5, pp. 69-100.

95. Cf. Bond, chapter 4, pp. 109-50. A similar approach appears in J. Denny Weaver, *The Nonviolent Atonement* (Grand Rapids: Eerdmans, 2001).

individually. The critique of transactional theories of atonement, requiring a death necessitated by retributive justice, is parallel to other critiques stemming from biblical studies and the primacy of God's grace (cf. Chapters One and Three). But what still needs to be determined is how far the cross can be de-emphasized or completely removed from the gospel and/or cease to function in any significant way in the story of redemption. On this even feminists do not agree and the discussion must continue.

E. Concluding Comments

The re-emergence of liberation theology must be placed in historical context. To be sure, one can point to Aulén's *Christus Victor* (1931) as a major source of inspiration. But the whole idea of Christ the victorious liberator, with its attendant images of warfare with powers and dominions, did not really break through liberal optimism until the tragic events of World War II and the Cold War. One cannot imagine the statue of St. Michael conquering Satan on the exterior of Coventry Cathedral except in this context. In many respects neo-orthodoxy laid the groundwork for liberation theologies. Its emphasis on biblical studies and traditional views of sin and salvation provided many of the elements that would be used by liberationists. It also turned attention from denominational theology, based on narrow doctrinal traditions, toward the world and the issues facing all people. In this respect it enabled new ecumenical perspectives to flourish. To the extent that it embraced transformationism, it encouraged many to take the next step toward a more public or political theology.

But while neo-orthodoxy broke with liberalism regarding the doctrine of sin and redemption, two important issues remained largely unresolved. One was the issue of power. Neo-orthodoxy was quite willing to grant to the state the right to use power — be it nonviolent or violent. This was either based on the orders of creation or something deemed a concession to the fallen state of affairs. But for many, it was not something considered acceptable to the highest Christian value, namely, self-sacrificing love. Thus, in spite of its bold affirmations of Christian realism and transformationism, neo-orthodoxy gave the next generation very mixed signals regarding political activity and the use of power. The other issue was the tendency for the distinction between justification and sanctification to become a division. Having adopted a radical view of sin, along with opposition to utopianism, it was difficult to talk about changes in the Christian life or progress toward holiness. When the 1960s presented multiple crises for the nation and churches, it became clear that the mainline Protestants were incapable of dealing with them. Like their conservative counterparts, the rank-and-file membership assumed religion had to do with the individual rather than social issues. It suddenly became apparent that the revival of Reformation theology had not prepared clergy or laity for the use of power in social settings, nor did they have a language to deal with changes in the individual or the society.[96]

Liberation theologies attracted followers because they offered a new perspective on both power and the justification/sanctification split. One could say that they took the next step. In fact, they simply stepped over these problems by introducing a new vocabulary involving the struggle between God and oppressive powers, Christ as the liberator who empowers, and the expectation that the signs of the Reign of God can and will be actualized on earth now. For this reason, all of the cases presented demonstrate that the shift to liberation theology required a critique of theological methodology as well as a reformulation of key doctrines. Likewise, in all of the cases, the appeal of liberation theology is to those who live in danger of losing hope because of oppressive forces. For them, liberation theology became a way to give expression to a new hope for the transformation of the world as well as the realization of a fuller and freer humanity.

Liberation theology helps us see why there are different theories of atonement. In the first three chapters, we examined theories relating to the forgiveness of sins. For the most part, the Western Christianity embodied in contemporary America assumes that sin relates to what individuals do in their relations with one another and with God. In spite of great exceptions in the

---

96. Many readers will take exception to this analysis, pointing to the literature of social analysis and activism in the period between 1945 and 1960. Likewise, they will point to the calls for moral reform by church leaders in the 1960s. Most important, they will point to the civil rights movement, under the leadership of Dr. Martin Luther King, Jr., as an example of a religiously inspired movement for social change. My response is simply this: the social analysis was done by individuals in the academy or church offices and never really reflected rank-and-file members. If it did, why were the churches so slow to respond to the causes? The attempts to motivate people to join in moral reforms regarding peace, civil rights, women's rights, ecology, and poverty never really worked because most Protestants had never accepted a covenant that included social justice and the transformation of society. The attempt to add moral reform on top of an individualistic religious life simply did not work. Finally, King's approach did use nonviolent coercion in the cause of social justice, but he upheld self-sacrificing love as the highest ethical norm. Whereas Reinhold Niebuhr insisted on the use of power (nonviolent and violent coercion) in the pursuit of justice, Niebuhr had always maintained the primacy of self-sacrificial love as the highest Christian value. This position was rejected by his brother, H. Richard Niebuhr, who insisted that no single value could be absolute, thereby providing a more positive approach to the use of power. In this respect, he represented the transformationism of Calvinism, a position with strong inclinations toward liberation theology.

Bible and the tradition, this focus on individual sin shifts attention away from the problem of bondage to oppressive forces. As we noted in the introduction, sins need to be forgiven, but people in bondage need to be liberated. Thus liberation theology rightly points to a distinctive form of human need and the saving power of Christ. All four of the cases reflect this convergence of human need and the power of Christ. Moltmann's work emerged in the 1960s — note that this was the close of the first generation of neo-orthodox writers and the new social crisis in the West — in the midst of the Cold War when two great views of reality were pitted against one another. Could one think about the future in any terms other than those given by current political ideology? Cone, Gutiérrez, and the feminists asked similar questions in the face of ancient forms of oppression based on race, colonial power, and gender. In every case, their theologies developed over against an old way of thinking while trying to develop a new vision, fragile and incomplete as it may be.

If the great strength of liberation theologies is the critique of injustice and a vision of freedom, all based on God's preferential option for the oppressed, herein lies its vulnerability. When the problem is defined so broadly as white people, those in power, or patriarchy, there is inevitably a loss of precision. The possibility that things are more complicated — as in the case that black women are abused by white and black men and women, or that all kinds of people engage in oppressive and abusive actions — is eliminated, but at great risk. Such qualifications do not absolve white people, dominant classes, or men from the responsibility for the kinds of oppressive systems named by liberation theologies. But they do require more precision in speaking of levels of responsibility and guilt. Likewise, some of the original themes that possessed such power (e.g., hermeneutic of suspicion or God's preferential option) too easily become slogans adopted in an uncritical manner. In liberal church structures they have tended to foster an adversarial political style that assumes either that every problem has only one solution or the tedium of political correctness.

In actuality, liberation theologies have not gone the way of a Cromwellian revolution, displaying a meteoric rise and fall. They have provided major contributions to understanding the Bible and Christian traditions. They have rightly called for a reconstitution of life in the churches and society, based on justice and freedom. But at key points the drive for sanctification has left them vulnerable to the loss of the very self-critical perspective so basic to the doctrine of justification by grace, with its dialectic of *simul justus et peccator*. For example, in spite of all his sophistication regarding theology, Moltmann has little to say regarding the danger of self-righteousness and legalism. In a related way, the feminist critique of Nicea, Chalcedon, and the symbol of the cross offers helpful correctives, but the losses can at times outweigh the gains (cf. the discussions of Nicea and Chalcedon in Chapters Five and Eleven). The tendency to view these matters always and only as symbols of oppression weakens the arguments.

There are many reasons to believe that liberation theologies will inspire a new and more promising synthesis of faith and practice. Given the tendency of Protestantism in North America to settle into the comfort of a religion of grace, based on a privatized faith and the acceptance of the world as it is, the liberation theologies have been the major voice for renewal. These new theologies sought to make the move from the grace of justification to the freedom and holiness of sanctification in actual life. They reintroduced the prospects of hope and expectation into a religious culture quite content with the present. The challenge, however, is to claim that new future in such a way that the dialectic of judgment and grace, tradition and future, realism and hope is maintained.

Theories of Atonement

C. The Purposes of God

Chapter 5   The Renewal of the Creation

Athanasius

A. Introduction

Thus far we have examined theories dealing with redemption from sin and liberation from the powers of evil. Forgiveness and freedom are two powerful marks of the new life in Christ. But what if the presence of God in Christ is not simply the means for accomplishing liberation and forgiveness, but the form of our existence in Christ? Such a question leads to another way of interpreting the meaning of Christ. It is a view of Christ as the incarnate Word who redeems the world and gathers all things together into a new spiritual reality according to the eternal plan of God.

The great exponent of such a view was Athanasius, Bishop of Alexandria in the fourth century. His view of the saving power of Christ is, of course, directly connected to the Nicene and Chalcedonian confessions. These confessions build on the work of Athanasius and establish the language and structure for thinking of God and Christ for later centuries. The presentation of Athanasius' theory of atonement shall include a discussion of the Nicene and Chalcedonian confessions, for several reasons: first, one cannot assess the Christology of Athanasius without reference to the general theological framework produced in the fourth and fifth centuries; second, the Nicene language and structure are used in some way by all atonement theories; third, these confessions have been heavily contested, as we saw in the liberationist critique of patriarchy. Such criticism calls into question both the confessions and the Christology of Athanasius. It is therefore appropriate to assess why atonement theories are so tied to these confessions.

We need to begin, however, with the New Testament, since the Nicene theology relies upon basic passages. In Colossians it is affirmed that all things were created in Christ, that God was in him for the purpose of reconciling all things to God (1:16). In Philippians we find a hymn to the Christ who empties himself of power and majesty for the sake of the redemption of the world and who is now made Lord (2:6-11). In Ephesians, all things are gathered up in Christ according to the plan of God for the fullness of time (1:10). In Romans the entire creation is groaning for the coming of new life, which God has now revealed in Christ. This redemption is not according to life in the world but in the Spirit of God, a victory that assures that nothing can separate us from God's love (Rom. 8:9-37). In John the same themes appear, only now cast in a new way: The Word is the life-giving Word, through whom all things were created. The Word becomes flesh for the redemption of the world and for the Son to make known the Father (1:1-18).

These passages from the New Testament inspire a view of atonement that is based firmly on the key image of the Word made flesh. Though Jew and Greek could see in such an image a different range of meanings, both saw in it the affirmation of God's presence in Jesus Christ. The image also raises questions: Why is God now present? What is God doing? How can God be incarnate in a human? Such questions draw us into the story of creation and fall. In this context, the image of the incarnate Word takes on power as the source of redemption. The redemption envisioned here cannot be contained in images of liberation from something, or the removal of guilt. It is the inauguration of a new spiritual existence, the new life in Christ. In this theory there really is only one actor, namely, God. It is God who creates the world, who cannot allow creation to be lost to sin and death, who sends the Son into the world so that the creation will be restored to life. As with both Paul and John, it is the presence of God, bestowing new life, that is the focal point.

B. Summary of the Theory

The basic form of this theory is quite simple, following the drama of creation, fall, and redemption.

1. By the Word, all things are created, including humankind in the divine image.
2. The glory of creation, however, has been lost in the fall. Sin and death now mark humankind. The knowledge of God has been corrupted.
3. Given the love of God, as well as the divine purpose in creation, God cannot leave the world in such a state. Moreover, the corruption of the world is so great that only God can redeem it. Therefore, God the Father sends the Son, as the incarnate Word, to renew all of creation: to restore life in

the face of death, to forgive sins by Jesus' death on the cross, and to restore the true knowledge of God. All of this constitutes the revealing of new life in the Spirit, or in Christ, or in the very life of God.

C. The Witness of Faith: Athanasius

This theory develops in the first four centuries of the church and is probably most associated with key figures of this period. In its images, language, and general orientation, it is the heart of the theology that emerged in the Nicene and Chalcedonian controversies. It would indeed be helpful for the study of these controversies, and the creeds generated from them, if this theory were kept in the forefront. The reason is quite simple. Central to these disputes was a soteriological issue: Who is Jesus, and is God truly present in him? For Athanasius, who attended the Council of Nicea in 325 and became Bishop of Alexandria in 328,[1] the entire Christian claim of salvation depended on an unqualified affirmation of the incarnate Word. To suggest that the difference between *homoousia vs. homoiousia* was a matter of the difference of one letter in the spelling of these words misses the entire point and trivializes the matter. Likewise, to suggest that the theological debate merely conceals social and political realities is to engage in a kind of reductionism where religious and philosophical ideas have no worth in and of themselves. For the defenders of the Nicene and Chalcedonian statements, the issue was one of salvation. Given the powers of sin and death, only God could save.

We begin with a work by Athanasius entitled "On the Incarnation of the Word," which summarizes his view of the history of redemption.[2] When one reads this treatise, it is clear that by the fourth century Christians have expanded the ideas of creation and fall beyond those found in Genesis 1–3. Athanasius takes such developments as a given. It is also evident that his primary audience is a Hellenistic world where death, immortality, being, and nonbeing are as important as sin, guilt, and forgiveness. For example, against Plato, Athanasius declares that God did not create the world out of pre-existing matter, even though this is suggested in Genesis. Instead, all things

---

1. Justo L. Gonzalez, *A History of Christian Thought,* rev. ed. (Nashville: Abingdon, 1987), p. 274.

2. Athanasius, "On the Incarnation of the Word, " in *Christology of the Later Fathers,* ed. Edward Rochie Hardy, trans. Archibald Robertson, vol. 3 of The Library of Christian Classics, ed. John Baillie, John T. McNeill, and Henry P. Van Dusen (Philadelphia: Westminster, 1954), pp. 55-110.

were created through the Word (pp. 56-57). The fall is now clearly seen as a pivotal transition from a state of immortality to mortality (p. 58). Although human beings were created in the image of God as a reflection of the Word, they now live in the corruption of death (p. 58). The fall brings the decline of rational existence and humans find themselves condemned to death (pp. 60-61). Though made to share in the knowledge of God, human beings turned to idols and are now subject to them (p. 67).

The drama of Christian proclamation, therefore, has to do with creation, fall, and incarnation. The story involves Adam and his descendents, sin and death, but it is really all about God. The driving force for the story is the necessity in God to renew the creation. Time and again, when Athanasius makes a point about the sorry state of things, he immediately gives voice to the inevitability of a divine response: "What was God in his goodness to do?" (p. 61). To leave the creation in ruin would be *unseemly* and *unworthy* of God. It is *fitting* for the one who created the world to redeem it.

> For if he [God] had not made them, none could impute weakness; but once he had made them, and created them out of nothing, it were most monstrous for the work to be ruined, and that before the eyes of the maker. It was, then, out of the question to leave men to the current of corruption; because this would be unseemly, and unworthy of God's goodness. (p. 61)

Athanasius admits that the incarnation is a source of scorn and ridicule (pp. 55-56). While it is appropriate to appeal to the love of God in explaining the appearance of the Word, he quickly moves to connect the redeeming Word with the creation:

> It is, then, proper for us to begin the treatment of this subject by speaking of the creation of the universe, and of God its Artificer, so that it may be duly perceived that the renewal of creation has been the work of the self-same Word that made it at the beginning. For it will appear not inconsonant for the Father to have wrought its salvation in him by whose means he made it. (p. 56)

But such a broad affirmation still leaves many questions. He goes on to reply to specific objections to such a radical solution:

- Could not repentance have sufficed in leading humankind to salvation? Repentance by itself would not change human nature from corruption to incorruption (p. 61).
- But why should the Word endure such an ignoble death? It was necessary

for death to be overcome publicly for all to see the victory of the resurrection (pp. 75-76).

• Did Jesus have to bear the curse of death? Jesus chose the cross because it would have been unfitting for him to flee (p. 76). Only on the cross, with hands spread out to all, can Jesus the Word draw all nations to God (p. 79).

• Is it not unusual for the Word to unite with a human body? No more unusual than for God to be in all things (pp. 95-96).

• Could not God have saved humankind in a nobler way, or even by fiat? Since the problems of sin and death were internal to human beings, the very creatures God wished to save, therefore the Word must become flesh.

What then is the consequence of the Word made flesh? It is important to keep in mind that Athanasius' vision of salvation is comprehensive, including reference to all of the major problems connected to the fall of Adam. Christ brings the forgiveness of sins and the healing of our minds. He notes, for example, that Jesus dies on the cross as a payment of the debt owed to God (p. 74). Since he takes our body upon himself, we are joined with him and we too die with him, thereby fulfilling the Law (p. 63). Likewise, by his presence and his teaching, he overcomes human neglect of God, thereby restoring what was originally our knowledge of God (p. 64). Since the Word enters the whole creation and all of humankind, therefore all things are filled with the knowledge of God (pp. 70-71). These affirmations are repeated several times and indicate clearly that Athanasius understands the work of Christ in broad terms. It is interesting that Athanasius readily uses several images, without extended elaboration, that go to the heart of major theories of atonement. For example, Jesus' death is viewed as a paying of a debt, as a sacrifice for us, and as a death that bears the condemnation of the Law (pp. 74-75). Later he refers to Jesus' death as a ransom for all (pp. 79 and 91). The human predicament that requires the incarnation has many dimensions: sin, loss of the knowledge of God, as well as death. But it is the latter issue — the conquest of death — that becomes the primary focal point for understanding the incarnation of the Word.

This larger theme is expounded at every turn, with several powerful illustrations. Given the reality of sin, only the Word that created humankind can restore it. Therefore the Word, as the ambassador of the Father, visits the creation (p. 62). The entrance of the Word into humanity is like a King who visits a city. The presence of the King ennobles the entire city and all of its inhabitants (pp. 63-64). If that is the case, then *much more* will the presence of the eternal Word enliven humankind.[3] Then in a reversal of the image, Athanasius suggests that the Word disguised its divinity by appearing in human form for the sake of drawing humankind to Christ and persuading them by his works (p. 70). In both cases, that of the King or the disguised Word, the Word enters all things, even our suffering and death, as all things are taken up into God. Incarnation thereby leads to resurrection and the transformation of all things by the glory of God.

The essential point in all this is the idea that the Word must take human form, suffer our condemnation and death, so that death might be conquered and we might share in this victory of the Son. There could be no victory for humans imprisoned in death if the Word had not become human and died our death. Such a death could not have occurred in secret, but must be public for all to see (p. 77). Nor could his death be of his own making, taking some easy or glorious form. He writes:

> so also the life of all, our Lord and Saviour, even Christ, did not devise a death for his own body, so as not to appear to be fearing some other death; but he accepted on the cross, and endured, a death inflicted by others, and above all by his enemies, which they thought dreadful and ignominious and not to be faced; so that, this also being destroyed, both he himself might be believed to be the life and the power of death be brought utterly to nought. So something surprising and startling has happened; for the death, which they thought to inflict as a disgrace, was actually a monument of victory against death itself. (pp. 78-79)

But having endured this death, the crucified Christ is raised as a demonstration of the power of the Word to conquer sin, death, and all demonic powers. By his being lifted up, he ". . . cleared the air of the malignity both of the devil and of demons of all kinds . . ." (p. 80). By his bodily resurrection, Christ reveals the new life for humanity (pp. 83-86). The power of the risen Christ is so great that it creates a new humanity living the transformed life. Thus, Athanasius can declare that we know Jesus was raised from the dead because his disciples do not fear death (pp. 82-83)!

When we turn our attention to Athanasius' description of the person of Christ, we find a high Christology of the Word. The common image running throughout the discussion is that of the Word in the flesh or made flesh. The

---

3. Athanasius, p. 64. One should note the similarity between Athanasius' argument about how God is constrained to renew the creation and the general argument of Anselm. But Anselm rejects the appeal to analogy or comparisons, utilized by Athanasius, in his search for rational necessity.

Word is in Jesus, dwells in Jesus, takes human form. Such an approach is typical of the traditional emphasis of Alexandria. J. N. D. Kelly describes this emphasis with the image of Word/flesh, with the weight falling on the complete union of the divine and human in Jesus Christ. By contrast, Antioch represented the emphasis on the full humanity of Jesus, which Kelly describes as a Word/man Christology.[4] Here the weight falls on Christ's participation in every aspect of our life — will, mind, and soul — thereby assuring the full redemption of our lives. There is an obvious polarity between these two approaches, with each side seeking to balance its approach to assure that the fullness of the gospel was affirmed. But each approach had a weak side: In the case of Antioch, it was the tendency to resist a full union of substance between the two natures, lest the human be denigrated. This produced questions as to whether a union was actually in effect, or whether the two natures were tied together by a unity of will. In its extreme form, which aroused suspicions, there remained a balancing of two persons in some kind of partnership or adoptionism. In the case of Alexandria, the weak side was in its preoccupation with the Word: by laying so much emphasis on the unity of humanity and divinity in one person, questions were raised whether the humanity was compromised. The more Alexandrians spoke of the humanity centered in the person of the divine Son, with the Son as the subject of all actions, the more concerns were raised. These concerns were accentuated by the extreme form of this view, known as Apollinarianism, where the divine mind replaced the human mind of Jesus. Such a view not only denied the full humanity but moved in the direction of *docetism,* which held that Jesus only appeared to be human but was in fact divine. To further complicate matters, it should be noted that both Antioch and Alexandria used many of the same images, such as the Word *dwelling in* the humanity of Jesus. This could be understood from the Antioch perspective as the Word present in the human Jesus, or it could be understood in the way Athanasius uses it, the Word made flesh. To make for more confusion, it could be taken in the sense of Apollinarianism, meaning that the Word dwells in the shell or house of humanity. Thus the overlap of key words could be a point of convergence, but too often it was and is a point of confusion.

This brief overview of the larger context is the appropriate place to mention one of the most important consequences of the Alexandrian emphasis on the complete union of divinity and humanity. This is the *communicatio idiomatum,* or exchange of properties. By this is meant that while the divinity

4. J. N. D. Kelly, *Early Christian Doctrines,* 2nd ed. (London: Adam and Charles Black, 1960), pp. 281-86; cf. pp. 291ff.

and humanity in Jesus Christ maintain in full all characteristics of each nature, the characteristics of each may be attributed to the other because both natures are united in one person. Thus it is possible to speak of the Word being conceived in Mary, being born, growing to adulthood, thirsting, suffering, and dying. In a similar way Jesus Christ as human shares the characteristics of divinity, without ceasing to be human. This idea runs through the Alexandrian tradition but appears as early as Tertullian and is later embraced by the Cappadocians.[5] It will appear in writers discussed in this work, such as Anselm, Luther, Calvin, and Moltmann.[6]

To return specifically to Athanasius, we find the person of Christ described by means of the Word made flesh. It is the Word that is active, initiating the incarnation, choosing death, and even raising the human body that dies on the cross (cf. pp. 81-85). So it is not unusual for Athanasius to conclude the main section of his treatise by saying:

> that the Saviour raised his own body and that he is the true Son of God, being from him, as from his Father, his own Word, and Wisdom, and Power, who in ages later took a body for the salvation of all, and taught the world concerning the Father, and brought death to nought, and bestowed incorruption upon all by the promise of his resurrection, having raised his own body as a first fruits of this, and having displayed it by the sign of the cross, as a monument of victory over death and its corruption. (p. 86)

Such a strong emphasis on the Son as the active agent prompts two reactions. First, those concerned about maintaining the full humanity of Jesus will wonder if Athanasius has moved too close to Apollinarianism. When he speaks of the subject of the enfleshed Word as the eternal Son, he clearly affirms the unity of the person of Christ. But is it at the expense of the humanity of Christ? Athanasius was quite aware of this danger, as well as the outrage against Apollinarius. He presided at the Council of 362 that condemned Apollinarius, a fact that is usually used to support the claim that he moved

5. Regarding Tertullian, note the comment that although Tertullian tended to keep the two natures separate, he was not opposed to ". . . using expressions like, 'God allows Himself to be born', 'the sufferings of God', 'God was truly crucified, truly died' — language which foreshadowed the 'interchange of characteristics' *(communicatio idiomatum)* which later counted as orthodox" (Kelly, p. 152). In regard to the Cappadocians, cf. Kelly, pp. 297ff.

6. While Calvin accepts the idea, he opposes "the use made of it by Lutheran advocates of the ubiquity of Christ's risen body." Cf. John Calvin, *The Institutes of the Christian Religion*, ed. John T. McNeill, trans. Ford Lewis Battles, vol. 20 of The Library of Christian Classics, ed. John Baillie, John T. McNeill, and Henry P. Van Dusen (Philadelphia: Westminster, 1960), p. 483, footnote 4.

away from his earlier position and affirmed a complete humanity in the incarnate Son. Yet Kelly is not completely convinced, finding the language of the council open to several interpretations.[7] While this matter may be difficult to resolve, what is clear in all this is that Athanasius presented a Christology that clearly tilts toward the *Word/flesh* model, perhaps even to the extreme. In this respect the later Definition of Chalcedon places a check on this aspect of Athanasius, since it insists on the full humanity and divinity of Jesus. At the same time, Chalcedon affirms the complete union of the two natures in one *hypostasis,* which seems in continuity with Athanasius.

Second, the affirmation of the Word as the active agent in the resurrection of Jesus also highlights the unique way in which Athanasius interprets his Trinitarian view of God. At first glance, it may appear surprising to us, because we are accustomed to references that simply name God as the one who raised Jesus. It may well be that a cautious or negative reaction to the idea that the Word raised the crucified Jesus reflects a latent monarchianism in us, i.e., we simply assume that God the Father did it. Put in another way, no matter how much we read that the Trinity means that all three personae are truly God, we still assume a subordinationism of the Son to the Father. To understand this usage in Athanasius, it must be remembered that Athanasius has clearly entered into a theological world where the Trinity is assumed when speaking of God. Whereas the New Testament does not differentiate Father, Son, and Spirit in the manner of the fourth century, Athanasius does. The Word is the eternal Word of God, begotten from the Father before all time. Thus, while the New Testament speaks of God raising the crucified Jesus, Athanasius assumes that it is God the Son, the eternal Word, who is victorious over death. On the cross, the Word/Son did not die, nor was the Word/Son totally confined to the humanity of Jesus. But most important in this usage is that Athanasius assumes that everything God does involves the three personae, with the active agent being the Word. All actions of God are from the Father, through the Word and in the Spirit.[8] This theme is affirmed even more strongly in the Cappadocians, where the unity of the Godhead includes the co-inherence of the three personae.[9] The personae are to be distinguished in origin and relation, but are united in essence and action. They are not separated by operation, nor does one persona act independently. What is striking about all this is that the refusal to differentiate the three personae according to action is usually attributed to Augustine, whereas here we find it clearly af-

7. Cf. Kelly, pp. 287-89.
8. Kelly, pp. 255-89.
9. Kelly, pp. 264-68.

firmed in Athanasius and the Cappadocians. From beginning to end, the story of Jesus Christ is the story of the incarnation of the Word, sent from the Father, that we might share in the very Spirit of God.

D. Athanasius and the Nicene Theology

We deliberately began with the presentation of the salvation brought by Jesus Christ to emphasize that for Athanasius the issue in the theological debates was always soteriology. It was this vision of salvation that inspired what can be called the Nicene theology of the fourth century. This position, however, did not appear in complete form in one instant. Drawing upon what it considered apostolic traditions, it found expression at Nicea in 325, but was vigorously tested in the decades following. In the initial period after 325 Athanasius emerged as the advocate for Nicea, to be joined later by the Cappadocians: Gregory of Nazianzus, Basil the Great, and Gregory of Nyssa. Their work led to the final acceptance of what we know as the Nicene Creed (Constantinopolitan) of 381. This position ultimately laid the basis for the Christological settlement at Chalcedon in 451. But time has not always dealt kindly with the Nicene theology. The Nicene Trinity is often dismissed as a theological agreement demanded by the emperor or discounted because it appears abstract and unrelated to the practice of faith. The later complaint usually includes the charge that the Nicene Trinity is an unnecessary theological construct, unrelated to the primary message of the gospel. Thus, if we assume that the Nicene Creed is absolutely essential, we can best make this case if we keep the soteriological issue before us: Do Christians really wish to affirm that God was in Christ and that the story of Jesus Christ actually reveals something about God?

Athanasius was of a mind that the gospel affirmations of forgiveness of sins, conquest of Satan and death, and restoration of the true knowledge of God are all possible only because it was truly God in Jesus Christ. For him there is, therefore, a straight line between the first apostolic message and the development of Christianity in the three centuries leading to the Nicene settlement. To speak of a settlement is somewhat precarious because the issues were not settled at the Council of Nicea in 325 and became further complicated by new Christological problems that were not resolved until Chalcedon in 451. But settlement is a useful way to speak of Nicea because the creeds of 325 and 381 sought to resolve conflicting points of view, separating the unacceptable from the acceptable. These creeds make no sense apart from the range of options competing with one another for primacy in the teaching and preaching of the churches. To affirm the final formulation (Nicene Creed) is to engage as much in a denial as an affirmation. What is denied is as important as what is affirmed. The affirmation is meaningful only in relation to the views denied and declared beyond the limits of acceptable teaching (orthodoxy). In the same way, Chalcedon extends the Nicene theology in relation to a different set of views. Here too, some were judged unacceptable and the boundaries for orthodoxy were established. It does not diminish the importance of these settlements to say that in both cases, there may be greater clarity regarding what is denied than what is affirmed. In both cases, the settlements left considerable space between the fences on all sides of orthodoxy, allowing for various interpretations within what came to be acceptable.[10]

For our purposes, we need to see the connections between the atonement theory offered by Athanasius and the Nicene and Chalcedonian settlements. In the case of Nicea, the issue was whether God was indeed present in Jesus. In the case of Chalcedon, the issue was whether Jesus Christ is truly God and truly human. Both concerns are the foundation for everything Athanasius wants to affirm about Jesus as Lord and Savior. Moreover, we need to see the essential connection between Nicea and Chalcedon. If the former affirms a view of God supporting the possibility of the incarnation of the one God, the latter affirms a view of Christ's person supporting the actuality of it. Finally, just as Nicea and Chalcedon connect to Athanasius' view of the work of Christ, the two settlements provide the foundation for all atonement theories. This becomes evident as theories make claims about God, about the humanity and divinity of Jesus, and — following John and Paul — our incorporation into new life in Christ. To put it in simple terms, if God cannot be in Jesus, how can God be in us (or, if one prefers, how can we be in God)? This is not to suggest that the settlements of Nicea and Chalcedon are perfect in every way, since the history of theology makes evident the difficulties and unresolved issues. But as a general framework for understanding God and the work of Christ, we will find again and again writers relying upon these settlements. Thus, for the sake of Athanasius and atonement theories in general, a review is in order.

One way of capturing the specific advance of the Nicene theology is to compare it with what might be called a historical view of the Trinity. By historical I mean a view that follows the sequence of events in the gospels and the Book of Acts. Such a view already appears in the New Testament, often

---

10. Re Nicea, consider the difference between East and West regarding the procession of the Spirit, leading to the final split in 1054; re Chalcedon, consider the ongoing debate between Antioch and Alexandria regarding the emphasis for thinking about the person of Christ.

encapsulated in doxological and confessional phrases: God is the Father of our Lord Jesus Christ and present among us as Holy Spirit. It is primarily confessional rather than analytic. It has little interest in explaining how all of this is possible. Rather it is content to confess the history of salvation, based on the experience of the early church. The view assumes the unity of God the Father with Jesus the Son and the Spirit, which was bestowed on Jesus and the church.

The strength of the historical view of the Trinity is that it closely follows the confessions of the New Testament. It is also easy to grasp in teaching and preaching: Christians believe in God the Father, Jesus Christ, and the Holy Spirit. But since the approach is so general, it leaves open a variety of questions and creates considerable misunderstanding. First, it is thoroughly monarchical in form, i.e., the Father is supreme, with Jesus the Son and the Spirit holding subordinate places. What exactly is the relation between the members of this Trinity? When this monarchical view carries over into later centuries in which sculpture, stained glass, and paintings become prominent means for the expression of the faith, it is often portrayed as God the Father, Jesus as the infant Son or as risen Lord, with the dove representing the Holy Spirit. In time, Mary is often present, either with the infant Jesus or being blessed by Jesus the risen Lord. Second, the relations between the three members of the confession are not clear. This is especially the case with the Spirit, which often suffers something of a demotion to a lesser rank, since the emphasis usually falls on God the Father and Jesus the Son. Third, the relation of the humanity and divinity of Jesus is left open for a variety of interpretations. Is the humanity of Jesus incorporated into the divine nature? Did the Son as second person exist before the incarnation? Most often there is a full equation of the Son with Jesus as the risen Lord, leading to the visual portrayal of God the Father and Jesus Christ. It should not surprise us that Mary should enter this family in a variety of ways. Finally, it needs to be recognized that the historical view continues to this day, quite oblivious of the Nicene theology. The best illustration is the most common definition of the Trinity for the general public: *God, Jesus, and the Spirit.* To be sure, as a definition of the Trinity this is a caricature of the original confessions of the New Testament, but it highlights the work left undone in the historical view. When placed alongside of the Nicene Creed, it is clearly not the view affirmed at Nicea.

The formation of the Nicene Trinity is indeed a complex and long story. While the initial Council of Nicea in 325 set forth a response to long-standing debates, it also appeared to precipitate even more vigorous debate, lasting until the Council of Constantinople in 381. From a theological perspective, the Nicene Trinity accomplished two things. First, it gathered in the primary affirmations of the apostolic confession, and as we shall see, resolved many of the unanswered questions noted above. But to do this, it moved away from what I have called the historical Trinity in two important respects: first, it developed a highly technical vocabulary as a prerequisite for precision in the confessions; second, it narrowed the focus of the discussion to what is strictly a view of God, rather than a loosely connected history of salvation. But while insisting on focusing on God, it incorporated into the conception of God the distinctive and personalistic language of Father, Son, and Spirit. Thus the language of the Nicene Trinity connects with the broad confessions of the New Testament even though this language is given a new and restricted meaning. So we shall see that while it *looks* like the former confessions, the Nicene Trinity cannot be understood unless we grasp the idea that it is a statement about God. As a consequence, it took two more generations after 381 to resolve the issues relating to the person of Jesus.

Second, the Nicene Trinity had to deal with challenges that were quite new, growing out of the extensive development of Christian thought in Hellenistic culture. The most significant of these challenges, from a theological point of view, were what came to be called Arianism and modalism. Arius affirmed that Jesus was Lord and Savior, but the firstborn of the creation. The rationale for this has traditionally been traced to his emphasis on the transcendence and absolute unity of God. If God is eternal and immaterial, God cannot enter the created order to assume the flesh and blood of Jesus. Justo Gonzalez suggests that the rationale may also have been to protect the humanity of Jesus and the possibility of our incorporation into the life of Jesus.[11] In either case, the result is the refusal to speak of a real incarnation of the eternal Son or Word. The line separating the eternal and temporal, infinite and finite, is not crossed. Such a view jeopardized the major parts of the Christian message. The moral realism coming from the prophets and the New Testament saw little hope for forgiveness or renewal of the human will, heart, or mind without divine intervention. The eschatological vision of the New Testament, affirming the fall of Satan and death, also was based on God's initiative in raising the crucified. In short, on the terms of Arianism, the Christian message can make no claim to an incarnate Word of God or God's presence in the life-giving power of the Spirit.

But the message is equally threatened by modalism, though in a somewhat different way. Modalism (often called Sabellianism for one of its defenders) was quite willing to affirm the incarnation of the Word and the bestowal of the Spirit. These could be described as equal with God the transcendent

---

11. Gonzalez, pp. 262-64.

one. But while modalism was willing to affirm the unity of the Father and Son, it was unwilling to affirm the distinction between the Father and the Son as having permanence. This left open the possibility that they were interchangeable, or as the label suggests, *only* modes of God rather than anything specific or permanent in God. This jeopardized the centrality of the Christian claim regarding the incarnation of the Son. From an epistemological perspective, it ultimately questions whether Father and Son are descriptive of the very essence of God. Put in another way, can we rely on these instances of divine self-disclosure if they are only temporary or passing moments in the divine life? Such caution regarding attributing something to God's being undercut the church's attempt to claim that the story of Jesus was indeed revelatory of God's very nature.

What we have, then, are two alternative interpretations of the Christian message. While different in approach, they converge in refusing to connect God the Father with the Word incarnate in a substantive way. From one side, Arianism denied the unity of God the Father with the Son in Jesus Christ, while from the other side, modalism was unwilling to declare that the language of Father, Son, and Spirit designated anything specific in God. The success of either would have substantially altered Christianity.

The history of the fourth-century debate reveals a tortured process, victories and defeats by all sides, with the outcome seriously in doubt but finally resolved with the Nicene Creed (381). Given the need for greater precision and the challenges to the apostolic faith, the Nicene settlement is a major achievement. With the seemingly simple phrase — *one nature, three personae* — the Nicene Trinity affirmed both the unity of God and the equality between the Father, Son, and Holy Spirit. The names for the three personae kept the language in continuity with earlier confessions, as well as accentuated the personal nature of God. This reinforces the equality of the personae, since the image of begetting from Father to Son rules out any mechanistic relation between them. The things that God makes out of objects are not God. Therefore, when the creeds declare that the Son is begotten and not made, the line is drawn between the Nicene position and that of Arius. The names for the three personae, rich in meaning from the New Testament and the earlier confessions, also draw into the nature of God associations with creation and redemption. If God is Father, Son, and Spirit from all eternity, then there never was a time when God was not self-giving. Whenever creation occurred, it was neither accidental nor an afterthought. In a similar way, it is not contrary to the nature of God for God to redeem the world.

But the Nicene theology created a kind of deliberate ambiguity. While the names for the personae stand in continuity with past confessions, the words

Father and Son now are invested with a new and quite technical meaning. Father and Son now refer to the relations of the first two personae in God and are not automatically identical with the previous general usage describing the relation of God and Jesus. In both creeds (325 and 381) we find the deliberate and awkward affirmation of the double begetting: The second persona is begotten from the Father before all time; now in these last days this Son comes down from heaven and is begotten of the Virgin Mary. If the second persona was Jesus, all of this would not be necessary. The full meaning of this has been completely lost in the popular current practice of assuming that the second persona is Jesus. By contrast, the creeds affirm that Jesus is not a heavenly being but one born in a specific time and place. How that incarnation of the eternal Son takes place is therefore not resolved and we are inevitably led to the Chalcedonian settlement.

If the debates regarding Trinity were highly complex, and to a great degree confused by the differences between Latin and Greek usage, the debates regarding the person of Christ were equally difficult.[12] In many respects the debate represented a reconciliation between the two contrasting positions of Antioch and Alexandria, each making an essential point and each claiming validity. But the two positions were always in jeopardy because of the extremes emerging from each, which usually went beyond the bounds of acceptability. Even when each position kept within bounds, it was easy for the other to view it with suspicion because of its wayward members. What we find, then, in the actual Definition of Chalcedon, is a highly formal balancing of what is acceptable. A large space is created for Antioch and Alexandria to coexist. What is not acceptable can be inferred by negating all the affirmations. Jesus Christ our Lord is perfect with respect to divinity and humanity (sin only excepted), joining the reality of God and humanity in one person. The two natures are not to be confused, changed, divided, or separated.[13] Concluding, the Definition de-

---

12. It is an understatement to suggest that the debates over Trinity and Christ involved a communication problem. Historians make clear that positions were constantly shifting, views were attributed to persons who did not actually hold them, some views were known only through the criticisms publicized against the views in question, and differences in nuance were often magnified far out of proportion. Added to all this was the fact that we are dealing with fourth-century forms of travel and written communication. That there was as much clarity regarding the issues and views as actually existed may indeed be a surprise. Cf. standard works such as Seeberg, Kelly, Gonzalez, and G. L. Prestige, *Fathers and Heretics* (London: S.P.C.K., 1940).

13. Cf. "The Chalcedonian Decree," in Hardy, ed., *Christology of the Later Fathers*, p. 373. The Leith edition translates the last phrase: "without contrasting them according to area or function." John H. Leith, *Creeds of the Churches: A Reader in Christian Doctrine from the Bible to the Present* (Garden City, N.Y.: Anchor, 1963), p. 36.

clares: "but rather the distinctive character of each nature being preserved, and [each] commingling in one Person and hypostasis — not divided or separated into two Persons, but one and the same Son and only-begotten God, Word, Lord Jesus Christ."[14] Both sides could read the document as justification for their respective concerns: full humanity and full divinity.[15]

But on the most difficult issue of all, namely the nature of the union, the Definition affirms that all aspects of humanity and divinity are gathered together in the one person of the Son/Lord Jesus Christ. If we understand this from the standpoint of the position of Leontius of Byzantium a century later, it is clear that this came to be understood as a union in the divine person.[16] Such a view gives justification for speaking of Jesus as the second persona incarnate, thereby assuring divine responsibility for what Jesus does, but at the same time becomes a source of concern in the modern age when interest again shifts to protecting the full humanity of Jesus.

The Chalcedonian settlement completes the theological development begun at Nicea in 325. It provides the intellectual construct for understanding the most essential Christian affirmations regarding God and humanity. On the one hand it declares that God is present in the world, in Jesus the crucified and risen Lord, and that such an act of self-giving is not the diminution of the divine nature. It is God's very nature for God to be the Father who begets the Word, the Word revealed, and the Spirit that gives life. On the other hand, the Nicene theology makes a rather significant declaration regarding human life: God can enter human life and humanity is not destroyed. This point is too often overlooked in the concern to affirm that God is truly present in Jesus. But the insistence upon the full humanity of Jesus in the union of the incarnate Word makes this additional point: Jesus, the chosen one, the anointed of God, can receive the Word, live in the Word, give himself completely to God's Rule, and be truly human. In fact, the gospel wants to make the point in even stronger terms: only by giving oneself to God and living in the will of God can humanity find its true life. As we have already noted, it is not simply the humanity of Jesus that is at stake in the debate at Chalcedon; it is also our humanity. If

14. Hardy, ed., *Christology of the Later Fathers*, p. 373.

15. Kelly observes that the Chalcedonian Definition is often seen as a victory for the West and Antioch over Alexandria, but judges this to be inaccurate, since both sides are so carefully balanced. Also, the full statement of Chalcedon bears the influence of Cyril of Alexandria as well as the emphasis on two natures from Antioch. I find this convincing. See Kelly, pp. 341-43.

16. This position is often called "enhypostatic union," i.e., the human persona is joined into the divine persona. This position runs through the history of theology and we shall see it in Anselm and Jürgen Moltmann. For the relevant text of Leontius, see Hardy, ed., *Christology of the Later Fathers*, pp. 375-77.

Jesus cannot be truly human in the union with God, how can we be truly human in union with the risen Lord?

It is hazardous to assume that all of our concerns are precisely those of the fourth century. But it is inevitable that we will understand the Chalcedonian affirmation in light of our concerns. We live in a time that is highly sensitive to issues of personal identity and freedom. Men and women have experienced a variety of infringements upon their freedom, making them extremely sensitive regarding the preservation of individual autonomy. In such a world, friendship, marriage, and children, as well as all obligations, are perceived as possible infringements upon the freedom of the self. Given this fear, certain images in the Christian message are very threatening. To deny oneself, to lose oneself for the gospel, to die to self in order to be reborn in Christ, or to live not in self-concern but in concern for Christ — all of these fundamental Christian images can be suspect. The Nicene theology is, I believe, fully aware of this tension. In the face of our caution and resistance to the loss of our freedom, the Nicene theology affirms that it is possible to lose oneself and find new life in God, not as the destruction of the self, but as its fulfillment. In this respect, the Nicene theology is faithful to the gospels and anticipates the next great advocate of this message, St. Augustine.

E. The Viability of the Nicene Theology Today

I have argued that the theological formulations represented by the Nicene and Chalcedonian settlements are absolutely essential for Christian faith. This judgment rejects the view that the Nicene theology represents a later development imposed on early Christianity by Hellenistic philosophy, or by the emperor in the fourth century for the sake of political unity. There is no doubt that Constantine had certain interests regarding unification of the empire. But such a fact cannot negate the fundamental theological differences at stake in the contending parties at Nicea and Chalcedon. Most important, the idea that Nicea and Chalcedon are foreign and inconsistent developments in the growth of Christian faith completely ignores the fact that affirmations of the presence of God in Christ and the bestowal of the Spirit are part of the earliest Christian witnesses, long before Constantine while the church was persecuted. The same can be said for the elementary affirmations of Father, Son, and Holy Spirit in what I have called the historical Trinity.

But problems remain. No matter how much one may appreciate the way Nicea and Chalcedon set limits against destructive options and give positive direction to the way Christians think about God and Christ, they present us with confessions that are less than perfect. One need only consider the way in which both the Nicene and Chalcedonian confessions present us with carefully crafted settlements, setting limits for our thinking, without resolving the tensions. This tendency toward the general, balanced formula regarding the Trinity has produced a history of extended debate. Several aspects of this debate may be noted.

First, the differences between the Nicene Trinity and what I have called the historical Trinity are still not fully resolved. A part of this unfinished work is the failure to recognize that Nicea sought to narrow the focus to a doctrine of God, rather than a discussion of the history of salvation (i.e., the relation of God to Jesus).

Second, the functional or economic view of the Trinity, which is not the same as the historical view, provides a third perspective on the Trinity. When this is added to the other two, it is clear that this central affirmation regarding God is interpreted in quite different ways. In recent decades many have been quick to seize functional language as a quick solution to the problem of masculine language for God. But the use of functional titles can also be a source of confusion. To label the three personae as Creator, Redeemer, and Sanctifier is to reduce the personae to functions and to separate them according to function. If the personae are so divided, what unites them and these functions? At its core the Trinity is about the relationships between the Father and the Son and the Holy Spirit, or if one prefers even a more general definition of the issue, about the relation of the transcendent deity to Jesus and the Spirit manifest in the church. It must also be noted that the attempt to find a functional solution to problems created by masculine language cuts us off from affirming that all of God's activities are the work of all three personae.

Third, directly related to all of these issues is the concern as to whether the final doctrine resolved the tension between unity and plurality. For example, the rejection of functionalism has always represented an emphasis on the divine unity, whereas the contrary emphasizes plurality. As we shall see in Chapter Seven, Schleiermacher felt that the issue of unity and plurality was unresolved, in spite of the fact that he considered the doctrine of the Trinity to be the summary of the two great affirmations of Christian faith: the incarnation of the Word and the bestowal of the Spirit.

Fourth, both Nicea and Chalcedon rely upon ontological categories drawn from the Greco-Roman world. But neither we nor the Bible think of God, the world, or humanity in these terms, that is, in the language of immutable substances. For example, the modern debate regarding nature and nurture in human development suggests that human beings become human, in small or large measure, in particular historical contexts. Such a view represents a significant shift in point of view from Chalcedon, and for that matter, from the rationalism of the Enlightenment. Our situation is further complicated by the fact that we may be living with such pluralism in our culture and throughout the world that there is no single ontology. When we turn to the Bible, we find there a vocabulary quite different from that of the fourth and fifth centuries. Consider, for example, the way the Bible uses the language of divine Spirit/human spirit, Word, sign and wonder, covenant and history, obedience and faith.

The differences between all of these worldviews may be acknowledged without adopting one of two problematic interpretations. One is the dichotomy between ontological and historical language, understood as the difference between Greek and Hebrew ways of thinking.[17] While this perspective can be helpful in recognizing some of the differences between Athens and Jerusalem, the distinction can be overdrawn. The Bible makes implicit and/or explicit ontological statements about reality and God, but they may be different from those presupposed by Nicea. The other pitfall is to assume that our perspective is identical with that of the Bible, or put in the reverse, that the Bible is in full agreement with the modern world against Nicea. If the biblical language is not a direct match with that of Nicea, neither is it equivalent with that of the modern world. One obvious example is the way the Bible speaks of signs and wonders. In signs and wonders, things of the creation reveal God, but God is never self-evident. The eighteenth-century attempt to turn signs and wonders into *miracles,* which are completely outside the realm of natural causation and in effect represent God breaking into the created order, may violate the Bible as much as the modern view of reality. All of this forces contemporary theology to work with quite conflicting conceptual frameworks and language systems.

If we consider the Chalcedonian formula from our complex situation, one cannot avoid some sense of discomfort with the conceptual framework. In its attempt to define the incarnation, the formula affirms the union of two absolutely different natures, without confusing them, melding them, dividing them or assigning each to separate functions. But if one begins with absolute difference, it is virtually impossible to join them together. The problem is illustrated by the Alexandrian emphasis on the primacy of the Word (or second persona). While the historical emphasis of Antioch makes it clear that

---

17. Consider the debate in biblical theology of mid-twentieth century regarding the dichotomy of ontological and historical categories (i.e., Greek versus Hebrew) as argued, for example, by Thorlief Boman. Cf. *Hebrew Thought Compared with Greek,* trans. Jules L. Moreau (London: SCM, 1960), pp. 17-183.

not everyone agreed with the views of Alexandria, nevertheless the latter position has had great influence. Its distinctiveness stands out when compared with the many forms of Christology that emerge in the modern period, emphasizing historical and eschatological categories. Yet even in a writer such as Moltmann, for whom historical and eschatological categories constitute a revolution in theological thinking, there is an unqualified affirmation of the second persona as the person of Jesus Christ. All of this forces contemporary theology to work with quite conflicting conceptual frameworks and language systems. The Bible, which is itself not monolithic, provides a range of possibilities for thinking of Christ, as do the creeds of Nicea and Chalcedon. Such variety is matched by the radical pluralism within our own cultural situation, where premodern, modern, and postmodern perspectives offer quite opposing options for theological discourse.

All of these issues have been the source of vigorous and continuing debate. They point to the paradoxical conclusion that while the Nicene theology presents us with problems regarding its language and unresolved issues, we continue to be inspired by these creedal statements. In the end, the great contribution of the Nicene theology may be precisely what appears to be its limitation. Nicea and Chalcedon appear limited by their language and the tendency to set general boundaries, without resolving once and for all the pressing questions. But their strength may well be just this ability to provide a general framework for thinking of God and Christ, which simultaneously sets limits. While the language may not be ours, we can at least comprehend the structure of the argument. It is this general framework that continues to provide positive norms for theology. As we shall see in Chapter Seven, one of the most significant attempts to develop a Christology using personal and historical categories still assumed that Chalcedon set the requirements for any revision. Thus Schleiermacher carefully developed a view of the incarnation of the Word and the bestowal of the Spirit consistent with the norms of the earlier councils. Such an effort illustrates the power of the Nicene theology to give positive direction precisely at the point where writers are compelled to overcome the limits of the specific ontological categories on which Nicea and Chalcedon are constructed. But a similar judgment can be made of most of the writers discussed in this study. The central affirmations of incarnation and Trinity underlie and affect the form and substance of atonement theology. In Calvin the biblical images of prophet, priest, and king are joined with the Nicene and Chalcedonian structure. Even in the case of a writer such as H. Richard Niebuhr, who quite intentionally wished to speak in a public language freed from the technical limitations of church doctrines, the resulting Christology ultimately relies on the doctrine of two natures. The ability of the

Nicene theology to exercise such formative power is derived from the fact that incarnation and Trinity are essential for the church's life and witness.

As serious as the issues mentioned above are for assessing the viability of the Nicene theology, the problem of masculine images may be more complex and even harder to resolve. The review of feminist and Womanist liberation theology in Chapter Four emphasized how language has played a crucial role in the subordination of women. Viewed against the background of what has been called patriarchy (i.e., the rule of men over women by means of all the structures of society, including religion), the rejection of Father/Son language by many critics is synonymous with the rejection of patriarchy. Given the controversial nature of language, can the use of Father/Son in theological language be separated from the systematic oppression of women? Such a question requires careful analysis.

Let us begin with the word *Father* as used in Scripture and the early church. Three quite different, but related, uses can be isolated. All three involve the analogical use of Father, suggesting likeness and unlikeness.[18] While God transcends human fathers in every way, and does not have the marks of their finitude or sinfulness, it is human *fatherhood* that is being transcended. The different uses, and the tendency to treat them as interchangeable, make for complications.

1. Jesus uses the word *Father* to affirm God as gracious and trustworthy. This use implies familial intimacy, generative and protective power. It includes the crucial ethical conclusion that if we are all children of God, then we are united as brothers and sisters.

2. *Father* is also used to describe the relation of God to Jesus. This is a crucial issue in the gospels, since it is not clear if Jesus is of God or Satan. In Paul, God is the Father of our Lord Jesus Christ and in John the images of Father/Son are used extensively to name the relation of God and Jesus. This use affirms that Jesus expresses the divine intentionality and is united with God in some way, though the nature of that union is not always clear (e.g., is it a unity of will, by the Spirit, or some form of sonship?).

3. In a later development, *Father* is used in a technical way within the doctrine of God. In this sense it no longer names God as in the first use, or

18. The argument that the word Father is not used analogically strains credulity. If this is the case, then why use the word at all? Why not invent a new word and define it as one pleases? God may embody the characteristics of Father perfectly and in ways that far transcend the way in which we embody them, but we are still talking about fatherhood, which we know by way of our personal and general human experience.

the relation of God to Jesus, as in the second sense, but refers to one persona within the one nature of God. This is an intra-Trinitarian use, which obviously has strong connections with the other uses, especially in relation to generativity: The Father begets the Son.

All three uses of the word *Father* are either in Scripture or early traditions and none can easily be ignored. There is often movement back and forth between the three uses, even though they are not the same. Jesus' invitation, in the synoptics, to name God as heavenly Father is not the same as the other two uses, nor are the other two uses logically entailed in the first.

Given these multiple uses, what then shall we make of the debate over the use of Father/Son language in Trinitarian language and atonement theories? There is a great deal of overstatement on both sides of this debate, which must be removed before progress can be made. First, the traditionalist claim that God is male must be rejected without qualification. Given the commandment against graven images as well as the general view of the transcendence of God in Israel, it is impossible to imagine a theological rationale for such a statement. The fact that such use has been justified by tradition cannot be grounds in support of it, since the traditions themselves are only defensible by an appeal to a masculine deity. Patriarchy was widespread in the ancient world, and even the New Testament assumes social stratification based on gender. Ancient Israel and the early church carry with them all sorts of social/political practices, such as slavery, which cannot be justified today. What is especially disappointing is that the early church sanctioned the subordination of women in spite of the radical egalitarianism contained in baptism and Eucharist.

Second, the argument that Father is the official name for God cannot be substantiated by the New Testament or the tradition. If Jesus had intended this, he would have said so and all of his disciples and followers would have followed this practice. If there is anything that comes close to a creedal affirmation of the Christian name of God, it would be "God, the Father, Son, and Holy Spirit." But to make this the new test of fidelity to Jesus Christ, in the midst of the struggle for women's equality here and around the entire world, strikes me as deliberately contentious. To insist on the use of Father in all cases of liturgy, sacraments, preaching, and teaching appears far too much like the attempt to reclaim lost status for males. But even more important, as a Protestant it strikes me as a movement toward treating this name of God the way the medieval church sought to treat the Mass, i.e., it works *ex opera operato!* The Trinity affirms the glorious gospel of Jesus Christ; it should not be an instrument of division.

Third, in spite of the reality of male domination in the first five centuries of the Christian era, I find it an overstatement to portray the Trinitarian development as *only* a conspiracy by men for further domination. Such a view is a variant on the nineteenth-century view that Nicea was *only* the means for Constantine to achieve political goals. The fact that male theologians connected the theological uses of Father with patriarchy is a word of warning. But from the standpoint of our theological work today, there are valid issues involved in all three uses of the word Father. We may want to explore alternatives, but wholesale dismissal appears inappropriate.

Fourth, the problem is not solved by a mix-and-match solution that joins personal names with functional categories as a substitute for Father, Son, and Holy Spirit. For example, one denomination uses "In the name of the triune God: the Creator, the Christ, and the Holy Spirit."[19] Such a solution is confusing and lends support for the popular but invalid view of the Trinity: God, Jesus, and the Spirit.

Once again we find ourselves in an extremely contentious situation, where the debate has become the lightning rod for larger social-political divisions. Given the historic importance of the Trinitarian formula worldwide and as a link with Christians in times past, especially in baptism, *and* the serious need to break the power of male domination in all cultures, there must be better alternatives than what have been proposed. I am unable to support the complete dismissal of the Trinitarian formula but am also repelled by the strident insistence that all Christians be compelled to use it in every time and place. In such a time it may be helpful to explore the following options.

1. We should respect the use of the traditional formula, without making it a test of fidelity to Christ; likewise, we should uphold the freedom to use nontraditional formulae.
2. We could return to variations on the doxological phrases in the New Testament that formed the historical view of the Trinity. For example, one phrase already in use is: "The grace of our Lord Jesus Christ and the love of God and the communion of the Holy Spirit. . . ."[20] Others are readily available or are easily formulated if we keep in mind that the Trinity is about the Almighty God who is present in Jesus Christ and the Spirit. To baptize someone in the name of the "God present in Jesus Christ" or "In the name of our Lord Jesus Christ" might be alternatives that express the faith of the New Testament.

19. *Book of Worship: United Church of Christ* (New York: United Church of Christ Office for Church Life and Leadership, 1986), p. 35.
20. *Book of Worship: United Church of Christ*, p. 35.

3. We could explore alternatives that attempt to express the technical meaning of the doctrine, such as "God is the Source, Word, and Spirit." But while technically defensible, such a form lacks the personal quality of the traditional language and is hardly felicitous.

4. Mindful of the impasse we face, those opposed to functional language may have to reconsider such opposition. My own view is that this would be easier to do if the substitutions were completely functional, rather than a mix-and-match combination. Thus, the alternative "God the Creator, Redeemer, and Sanctifier" seems more acceptable than "God the Creator, Christ, and Spirit." Such an option would be feasible if we also dealt in positive ways with the traditional concerns regarding functionalism.

5. Finally, it may be helpful to pull back and wait patiently in order to find still more appropriate ways to affirm our faith in the God revealed in Jesus Christ and the Spirit. Such a time could well be spent on earnest conversation, study, prayer, and repentance.

While the debate over the images of Father/Son is necessary, the unfortunate consequence of it, however, is that it has detracted attention from the fundamental connection between the saving power of Jesus Christ and the affirmations of incarnation and Trinity. While the doctrine of the Trinity is not *only* a summary, it does in fact gather up the history of salvation in its affirmations of one God, three personae. The Trinity affirms that God can only be God as the source of all that is, the Word revealed in all, and the Spirit that enlivens all. It affirms the living, personal unity of the one God. How appropriate that the Spirit has been described as the bond of love between the Father and the Son.

F. Concluding Comments

From start to finish, Athanasius is a theologian of the incarnation. Only the incarnation can account for the new life in Christ that has transformed the world. If Jesus were not the very presence of God among us, how could the bondage to sin and death be broken and how shall we explain the new spiritual life shared by the community of Christ? As we noted earlier, the controversy with the Arians and the defense of the Nicene tradition go to the heart of the gospel proclamation. It is all about the salvation present in Christ. For Athanasius, the Trinitarian formula is more than a helpful summary of Christian teaching; it is the essential affirmation that God is truly present in Word and Spirit. It is the very nature of God to be creative and redemptive. Such activities come from that one who is from all eternity Father, Son, and Holy Spirit.

For American Protestants and Roman Catholics, it is difficult to imagine an interpretation of Jesus Christ that does not focus primarily upon his death for us, which thereby leads to the forgiveness of sins. Sin, guilt, blood sacrifice, fulfillment of the law — these are images central to the worship life of many Christians. But as the Psalmist reminds us that we walk in the shadow of death, it is essential for the church to claim the message of the abundant life revealed in incarnation and fulfilled in resurrection from death. Indeed, it is surprising that this proclamation has not received more attention, given the specter of death that overshadowed the twentieth century. Perhaps the easiest way to understand Athanasius is to reflect on the division between Eastern and Western Christianity. It is in the West that the concern for sin and forgiveness takes center stage, whereas in the East, the concern for death and resurrection dominate. While the one develops in terms of moral passion, the other develops in continuity with the ontological language of Nicea and Chalcedon, where incarnation and resurrection are the primary signs for faith. But this theme is not entirely confined to the East. It appears in many Roman Catholic and Protestant traditions as a subtheme, often emerging as a major theme in high church, sacramental movements. Consider the high church liturgical traditions of the Episcopalian, Lutheran, and Reformed traditions. In a Reformed movement like John Williamson Nevin's Mercersburg theology, the affirmation of this *other* side of Christianity reappears as a witness to the incarnate Word. In such a tradition the Gospel of John receives primary attention, with its emphasis on new life and light, as well as powerful organic metaphors of vine and branches, rebirth, and living water.

Chapter 6   The Restoration of the Creation

Anselm

A. Introduction

The presentation of this theory will not follow the procedure used in other chapters, where we moved from origin to a selected case. This theory appears in the writings of Anselm of Canterbury in 1097.[1] It did not exist as a general theory prior to that time, though Anselm certainly draws upon well-known themes in Scripture and tradition. While it is sometimes merged or confused with theories of sacrifice and substitution, here we shall proceed directly to Anselm's treatise, which he described as a rational demonstration of the incarnation on conditions that precluded appeal to the received faith or Scripture.

Another reason for a change in approach is that Anselm has become the focal point for all that is wrong with atonement theories involving a transaction between Christ and God for the salvation of humankind. This of course, is not new, since the publication of *Cur Deus Homo* quickly evoked the famous rejection from Abelard in the name of the love of God.[2] The differences between Anselm and Abelard have been codified in the history of theology with the standard judgment that the former represents an *objective view* of atonement, while the latter proposes a *subjective view*. While the difference between the two theories is significant, I will argue later that the claims to ob-

---

1. Anselm, "Why God Became Man," in *A Scholastic Miscellany: Anselm to Ockham*, trans. and ed. Eugene R. Fairweather, vol. 10 of The Library of Christian Classics, ed. John Baillie, John T. McNeill, and Henry P. Van Dusen (Philadelphia: Westminster, 1956), pp. 100-183. All future references to this treatise will be included in the text, giving the book and chapter of the Fairweather edition, unless the reference includes a comment.

2. Cf. "Peter Abailard: Exposition of the Epistle to the Romans (Excerpt from the Second Book)," in Fairweather, ed., pp. 276-97.

jectivity and subjectivity are overdrawn and may well distort our understanding of these and other theories.

Since 1931 it has been difficult for Protestants to see clearly Anselm's text because of the thesis of Gustaf Aulén in *Christus Victor*.[3] Not only did Aulén lay out a grand theory for categorizing all atonement theories into three groups, but he also argued that the ransom theory running from Irenaeus through Luther was the *classic* view. This thesis included the judgment that Anselm held an incorrect view, contributing to the negative development in Protestantism of substitutionary atonement (penal substitution), with much of the blame laid on Melanchthon. Among the many charges he brought against Anselm was that of Pelagianism, since Anselm's argument requires that humankind ought to make restitution for sin.[4] It is difficult to measure the negative influence of Aulén's work, except to say that many know Anselm only through the caricature of this polemic, or the rather wooden juxtaposition of Anselm and Abelard.

In the last decade the attention given to Anselm has increased, but only for the sake of denouncing a set of negative values. These criticisms have been lodged by numerous liberation theologies (black and white, feminist and Womanist).[5] The object of protest is any theory that relies on the death of Jesus as a transaction with God for securing the salvation of humankind. Whether this is a sacrificial payment or a death incurred as punishment, in either case it is seen as making salvation depend on the principle of retributive justice. The objections to such an approach may be summarized under two general headings: First, it treats the death of Jesus as something of intrinsic value. This is problematic because it makes Jesus passive and has in fact led to the practical implication that we (especially oppressed persons) should passively accept suffering. The requirement of a death also appears as a form of abuse mandated by a Father God, again having associations with domestic violence. And obviously, it places all the attention on Jesus' death rather than placing the cross in the context of his life and resurrection. Second, as a transaction required for salvation, it makes God passive, demanding satisfaction prior to any act of forgiveness. Such an angry and vengeful God contradicts the portrayal of God in the New Testament, who assumes the initiative in the work of salvation.

3. Cf. Gustaf Aulén, *Christus Victor*, trans. A. G. Hebert (London: S.P.C.K., 1931).

4. For Aulén's basic thesis, cf. Aulén, chapters 1, 2, 5, and 8; for his charge of Pelagianism against Anselm, cf. chapter 5.

5. Cf. L. Susan Bond, *Trouble with Jesus: Women, Christology and Preaching* (St. Louis: Chalice Press, 1999), chapters 1 and 2; and J. Denny Weaver, *The Nonviolent Atonement* (Grand Rapids: Eerdmans, 2001).

This protest against a wide range of negative values is one that most Christians can accept, unless they are staunch defenders of penal substitution. I am in basic agreement with these criticisms of transaction theories and have raised these issues when dealing with the theories of sacrifice and penal substitution. But I disagree that Anselm is the origin of these negative values. Placing blame on Anselm appears to have become the conventional wisdom among many, from Aulén to liberationist writers. This I believe is unfortunate, since most of the charges do not apply and further, much could be gained by a more sympathetic reading of Anselm's text.[6]

Given this history of interpretation and the current outrage against Anselm, it seemed appropriate to acknowledge this before we begin. My purpose will be to locate Anselm's view in the spectrum of theories discussed in this work and to engage in critical analysis of it. There are indeed some problems with what he offers, but there are also some major contributions to atonement theology. But we cannot have such a discussion unless we recognize several things:

First, we need to separate different types of theories, even though they all may use the word *satisfaction*, or involve what might be called in a generic sense a *transaction*.[7] The mere use of the word satisfaction does not mean that the form and substance of theories are the same. So, for example, theories of sacrifice and penal substitution are quite different and I have treated them as such (cf. Chapters One and Three). The theory of sacrifice involves the removal of sin (purification) and does not, in its biblical form, involve a vicarious death. By contrast, penal substitution does rest entirely on the idea of vio-

6. For a positive interpretation of Anselm's treatise, compare the following: John McIntyre, *St. Anselm and His Critics* (Edinburgh: Oliver and Boyd, 1954); George Huntston Williams, *Anselm: Communion and Atonement* (St. Louis: Concordia, 1960); "Introduction to Anselm of Canterbury," in Fairweather, pp. 47-62; and R. W. Southern, *Saint Anselm: A Portrait in a Landscape* (Cambridge: Cambridge University Press, 1990).

7. J. Denny Weaver offers a good example of mixing all transaction theories together so that the concept of satisfaction denotes theories of sacrifice, penal substitution, and Anselm's theory (Weaver, pp. 16-17, 188-204). Because the theories are mixed together, Anselm is viewed as the originator of all the problems associated with the concept of satisfaction. Though Weaver's intent is to develop a nonviolent liberation theory congruent with his Mennonite perspective, from start to finish Anselm is the example of what is wrong with traditional atonement theory. This unrelenting attribution of negative values to Anselm is quite surprising since Weaver admits that Anselm's view is not really a form of penal substitution (cf. Weaver, p. 192). But having admitted this, he still lays at Anselm's door all the problems with penal substitution, especially as it arises in Protestant orthodoxy. Viewing Weaver's approach in historical context, one should note that his threefold typology of atonement theories (Christus Victor, satisfaction, and moral influence) basically follows that of Aulén.

lation of the Law, the requirement of punishment, and Christ dying and thereby paying the price for our salvation. In my judgment the negative values outlined above arise in the theory of penal substitution and not the theory of sacrifice, unless the latter has been transformed into an act of compensation, offered to appease God.

Second, Anselm's theory is not a form of penal substitution. While he uses the word satisfaction, the meaning is entirely different. There is a satisfaction required, but not the kind involved in legal theories of atonement. But if Anselm's theory is not a form of legal theory, then what is it? Some three decades ago I argued that Anselm's view was a *commercial* theory, since it relied on the image of debt.[8] This thesis was intended in part to counter the usual interpretation that assumed it was a legal theory, i.e., a variation on penal substitution. But the main purpose was to allow for a fuller examination of Anselm's argument, built about the image of something owed and the need for restitution. What Christ did, according to Anselm, has nothing to do with punishment but *restitution* of God's honor. Sin has dishonored God by breaking relation with God, corrupting the creation, and violating God's purpose for the creation. The problem is not fully comprehended by the language of guilt incurred for violation of the Law. Instead it points to the disorder of God's design for creation. Anselm struggles with the very same question posed by Athanasius: What was God to do?

But in the passage of years since that article, I no longer believe that the word *commercial* is the best way to capture Anselm's intention. Having read R. W. Southern on the meaning of honor, it now seems more accurate to describe the theory in moral language, so long as such language is broadly understood and not converted into narrow legal relations. Southern argues that honor reflects the vast set of relations, obligations, and rights stemming from the feudal worldview.[9] Honor has to do with the social bonds that hold society together in its intricate relations of authority and obligation. While the image of a king and his vassals comes immediately to mind, Anselm is far more preoccupied with the relation of the Creator to the creation. Human beings were created to love God freely and maintain the order and beauty of the creation. They were also created to overthrow the devil, but more on that later. In this broader sense, honor means more than obedience to the king and the maintenance of roles and services. It means life as a vocation of obedience, love, and service to God, in the context of the entire universe. Thus

---

8. Cf. Schmiechen, "Anselm and the Faithfulness of God," *Scottish Journal of Theology* 26 (May 1973): 151-68.

9. Cf. Southern, pp. 221-27.

honor has the quality of social relations between human beings themselves and to God, but the word also conveys a moral order and even reflects an ontological character. We were made for this purpose, as was the whole created order. It is our nature to reflect the goodness of God and to rejoice in God. By contrast, sin or dishonor means that the whole universe is out of character, threatening God's design. Understood in this way, one can understand why Southern concludes by saying that for Anselm, honor is not a private, personal feeling or attribute.[10] It has to do with the worship of God and the maintenance of right relations in the universe.[11] If Southern is correct regarding the social and moral meaning of honor, then it is inadequate to refer to Anselm's theory as a *commercial* theory. Perhaps an alternative is to view the theory as one based on *moral order*. But even this image is helpful only if it is understood as God's ordering of the creation, which includes mutual obligations derived from the interdependency of all things upon God.

Further evidence in support of the view that Anselm's theory is not a form of penal substitution is found in the very structure of the argument. Without repeating the full outline, which will be presented shortly, let us highlight the basic logic that drives the argument (I, 9-24). If sin has violated the honor of God, and if God must maintain the divine honor since it represents both God per se and God's purposes for the creation, then we are faced with an either/or: either humankind must be punished or God must save humankind. We are led to believe that either would be an equally valid way of maintaining the honor of God. But as we shall see, further reflection on God's honor leads to the conclusion that there is really only one choice: God must complete the divine purpose and save humankind. This leads to the next step: if there is to be remission for sin, there must be satisfaction. Now since the option of punishment has been ruled out and God is to pursue the only real option of completing the divine purpose, satisfaction must take the form of the restoration of the creation, which is also to say, restoring or paying back

---

10. Southern, p. 226.

11. It is most unfortunate that so many of the critics, coming from a liberationist perspective, are so intent on pressing the charge of moral legalism against Anselm that they miss the positive implications of this broad view of honor. For example, consider the case of Weaver, writing from a Mennonite perspective. Mennonite communities are witnesses to the essential character of bonds of love and service, between members and with God. It is a serious crisis within the community when one person breaks trust with another or commits a violent act against a member. The primacy of Matthew 18 means that the community must maintain on earth, in the midst of a broken world, a community of peaceful relations. From this perspective one could develop positive connections with Anselm's notion that sin has disrupted the very structure of things and placed God in a predicament: Shall punishment fall upon the world and end it all, or shall the world be restored in accordance with God's design?

the honor of God (I, 12). How such satisfaction will be accomplished will be discussed when we review the complete argument. The crucial point here is that the driving force of the argument, namely the demand for satisfaction, relates not to punishment at all, but to the restoration of the creation.

If it is correct that Anselm's argument is constructed upon the images of debt-honor which imply a moral order, then it is justifiable to distance Anselm from the legal theory of penal substitution. Furthermore, this means that whatever criticisms may or may not be lodged against such a legal theory do not apply to Anselm, unless he allows his argument to slide in that direction. There is one major area where Anselm is in danger of allowing this to happen, and we shall examine that piece of the argument with care. With these introductory comments before us we are now at the point of examining the argument itself.

B. Preliminary Considerations

Anselm's treatise on the incarnation is in the form of a dialogue between Anselm and his student, Boso. This form enables Anselm to raise issues, discuss them, evaluate alternatives, and slowly move forward. Boso does not simply play the role of the inquiring student, who asks questions to be answered by the wise teacher. Rather, Boso enters into the discussion, sometimes leading the advance to the next level. R. W. Southern points out that this is conducive to Anselm's style.[12] Instead of a clash of ideas resolved in debate, we find ideas slowly developed by discussion. But the progress is not always linear. Sometimes ideas are presented as if to telegraph what is to come later. At other times the discussion returns for a second or third reflection on a difficult matter. Some issues, such as the replacement of fallen angels, try the patience of the modern reader, though this issue does make an important point if one can stay with the line of discussion. But even Anselm admits that this may be a digression. All this makes for a complex treatise, which may indeed contribute to the possibility for misinterpretation. For example, the crucial passages regarding the death of Jesus need to be connected to passages at the very beginning, which are easily forgotten by the time one reaches the last chapters.

What all this means is that any outline of the basic argument is more of a reconstruction of the logical steps, which only roughly corresponds to the sequence in the text. Furthermore, we cannot get to the basic argument

---

12. Southern, pp. 114-15.

without dealing with a set of preliminary topics that provide the ground rules for the discussion. First and foremost is the request that Anselm reply to the charges of unbelievers that the gospel story does "God injury and insult when we assert that he descended into the womb of a woman, . . . that he bore weariness, hunger, thirst, blows and a cross and death between the thieves" (I, 3). Southern points out that the criticisms of the gospel story, involving the humiliation and crucifixion of Christ, arose not only in the universities but also in debate between Jews and Christians in London.[13] But how shall one respond? Anselm's inclination is to repeat the gospel story of Jesus' death and resurrection revealing the love of God. But that is precisely what is judged to violate the divine omnipotence and wisdom. What appears to be needed is a necessary explanation acceptable to Christians and non-Christians. This demand for necessity creates a double requirement: one is the search for a reason why God acted in the way Christians claim; the other is the demand to show that no other way was sufficient. For example, could not God have saved the world by means of angels, a sinless human, or a sheer act of will (I, 1)? Anselm finds himself faced with a dilemma regarding the incarnation that the modern world comes to face regarding the problem of evil: If God cannot use a better method, then God is not almighty; if God will not, then God is not just or wise (I, 6). With great clarity Anselm notes that the gospel is a revelation of love only if there was no other way (I, 6). Thus the challenge is accepted.

With assurances that he has not abandoned the priority of faith to understanding and the supremacy of Scripture,[14] Anselm must prepare the reader for a new way of speaking. If an argument is to be generated that does not appeal to Christ or Scripture, then a centuries-old manner of speaking must be set aside. The gospel had been transmitted by means of teaching and preaching that relied on the power of images and visual pictures. A major form of argument was the appeal to the principle of proportionality in the relations of Adam and Christ, Eve and Mary, the fruit of the tree and the tree of salvation (the cross). These comparisons generated a certain level of force, often expressed by the English words *fitting* and *proper*.[15] But through the words of

13. Southern, pp. 198ff.

14. Regarding the priority of faith to understanding, cf. Anselm, I, 1, pp. 101-2; I, 3, p. 104; and II, 15, p. 165. Regarding the primacy of Scripture, cf. Anselm, I, 2, p. 103.

15. The strong Second Adam Christology that Anselm develops is generally overlooked. Anselm draws heavily upon this tradition in arguing for the humanity of the Savior. For example, in I, 3 he points to the proportionality between Adam and Christ, Eve and Mary, the devil's conquest of humanity by the fruit of a tree, and Christ's conquest of the devil by suffering on a tree (pp. 104-5).

Boso, Anselm admits that such arguments are only pictures which do not carry the force of rational necessity (I, 4). Anselm is laying down the condition that analogical reasoning cannot attain the level of logical necessity required in this argument.

But this means that the terms of the discussion leave no room for the ransom theory of atonement. This requires careful attention, since the rejection of the ransom theory does not remove the devil from the discussion and certainly not from medieval spirituality. The devil continues to be an issue in Anselm's understanding of the fall and the work of Christ: whereas Adam was to conquer the devil, but is himself conquered and taken into bondage, it is Christ the Second Adam who finally fulfills this task. The problem with the ransom theory is the way it explains the gospel story. This theory assumed that since Adam succumbed to temptation, the devil rightfully held possession of humankind. It further implied that the deception of the incarnate Word disguised in human form was necessary because God must deal with the devil on the devil's terms. For Anselm, all this is abhorrent. God owes nothing to the devil and does not need to enter into a contest to trick the devil (I, 7). Since the devil was created by God, the devil has no right to humankind. In effect, Anselm objects to basing a rationale for the incarnation on the arbitrary relations between the devil and Adam. But as R. W. Southern points out, this changes the framework for thinking about the atonement.[16] Instead of finding the rationale in the tension between the devil and God, Anselm must now set forth a rationale in God.[17] This, of course, is exactly what Anselm wishes to do: only by appealing to the nature and activity of God will we find a necessity to meet the conditions of the argument. But if there is to be a necessity in God, shall such necessity be understood as a constraint upon God? And how shall it relate to the very mercy that the gospel proclaims? By striking out in a new direction in search of a reason in God, Anselm faces new questions that will need to be addressed along the way. But at this point we are now at the beginning of the basic argument.

16. Southern, pp. 207-12.

17. For some of Anselm's critics, the rejection of the ransom theory is only the beginning of the problems. If the devil did not cause Jesus' death, then the cause must be in God, and that makes God the vengeful and abusive Father (cf. Weaver, pp. 189, 210ff.). This interpretation misses the main point, namely, that Anselm wishes to locate the necessity of redemption in God's nature, rather than a consequence forced on God by sin. It also raises a point that could just as easily be raised against Weaver's variation on the ransom theory. If Jesus is killed by sinful humans and the forces of evil, where is God in this revised ransom theory? Did God send Jesus on this mission, knowing full well the outcome? If so, one is right back to the complicated discussion in Anselm that Jesus dies of his own free will and God willed it.

C. The Argument in Outline

In its simplest form, the argument moves through four stages and we will use this framework to summarize the argument.

1. The nature and purpose of humankind as God's creation.
2. The problem of sin.
3. The need for satisfaction and the necessity of the divine/human Son of God
4. The restoration of the creation by means of the divine/human Son of God.[18]

D. Summary of the Argument

1. The Nature and Purpose of Humankind as God's Creation

Humanity was created by God for happiness and immortality.[19] Such happiness could only be attained by obedience to the will of God. Since human beings are rational creatures possessing freedom, such obedience must take the form of free devotion wherein "every inclination of the rational creature ought to be subject to the will of God" (I, 11). All of this, however, is still not enough, since humanity was set in a universe created by God with a purpose. Humankind also bears responsibility for conquering the devil and replacing the fallen angels (I, 22). As noted above, Anselm takes us into a long discussion as to whether the number of angels was complete prior to the fall of some, thus raising the issue whether humans are to replace the fallen ones or to complete a larger number ordained by God. In the end it turns out that Anselm chooses both: humans are to restore the fallen ones and complete the number ordained by God. As this discussion concludes, Anselm draws out one aspect in anticipation of what is to come: human beings cannot replace fallen angels without being redeemed (I, 17-19). While the relevance of this

18. It is unusual that Southern's detailed outline ends with what I have designated as the third point, namely, why satisfaction is needed and why only a divine/human Son of God can effect it (cf. Southern, pp. 205-6). Thus the outline does not include what Christ actually does and how salvation is communicated to the world. But Southern does discuss in full the nature of Christ's work and its significance for the Eucharist. Perhaps his outline ends where it does because the three points do answer the question posed by the treatise, though the answer is far from complete without a discussion of what happens and how this is shared with believers.

19. Anselm, Preface, p. 100.

discussion may elude us, what is particularly important is that the issue driving Anselm's consideration of it is the necessity of God's purpose. This will be developed time and time again. It constitutes the foundation for the discussion as well as the driving force for the argument. So in this case, human beings were created by God for many purposes: to obey and love God, to conquer the devil, and complete the number of angels in heaven. To honor God is to fulfill all of these obligations that constitute humanity's role in creation as well as its relation to God. Humans are under moral obligation to maintain the conditions of the creation, and — to add aesthetics to morality — to maintain the beauty of the universe (I, 15). There is joy and beauty in all of this, not simply work!

2. The Problem of Sin

Against this vision of creation and God's purposes for humankind, Anselm turns to the nature of sin. His view of sin is quite rigorous, reflecting his monastic temperament, without being moralistic. Sin is not to give what we owe to God, i.e., "not to render his due to God" (I, 11). That is to say, it is the deliberate refusal to affirm one's place as a creature in God's design and to offer free and undivided obedience to God's will. Furthermore, by falling under the power of the devil, humankind fails to achieve one of its specific purposes, namely, the conquest of the devil. Thus we are drawn to the conclusion that sin has robbed God, and thereby incurred a debt to the justice and honor of God (I, 11).

This definition of sin raises the question how sin or anything else can dishonor an impassible God?[20] In Book I, Chapters 14-15, Anselm gives two definitions of the concept of the honor of God. As I shall argue later, the difference between these two definitions is crucial and goes to the heart of the argument. First, honor refers to God *in se*. Nothing can be added or subtracted from God's honor, which God maintains with perfect justice. If humans act against the will of God, they must either reaffirm God's will or incur the punishment of God, but they cannot escape the Rule of God, who is hon-

---

20. Those following the text closely will note that after the definition of sin, Anselm raises the question whether a compassionate God can pass over sin (Anselm, I, 12, p. 120). When this has been answered, he turns to the question of how God can be dishonored (Anselm, I, 15, p. 123). We have here an example of how the flow of the argument is not linear. The issue of compassion pertains more to the nature of satisfaction, which I think belongs logically under the third heading in our outline, whereas the issue of dishonor relates directly to the definition of sin.

ored no matter what humans do (I, 15). I will call this definition the moral sovereignty of God, since it emphasizes the unchanging essence of God. God remains sovereign in the face of human sin so that the divine honor is never impaired.

The second definition of honor is this: humans honor God by fulfilling God's design in the world. Here the word honor suggests not God per se, but the more complex relation of God and humans to God's purpose. In this light Anselm can say that the creature honors God ". . . not because it bestows something on him, but because it willingly submits itself to God's will and direction, and keeps its own place in the universe of things, and maintains the beauty of that same universe, as far as in it lies" (I, 15). In this view, what is owed God relates not simply to God's moral sovereignty, but to God's design for the creation. As such it includes several relationships: (1) humans were created as rational creatures in God's plan and also to replace the fallen angels; (2) humans were to conquer the devil and uphold the honor of God; (3) humans were created to be blessed and enjoy God forever. In a similar way, honor refers to many things: God's design for the world, humankind's intended happiness and righteousness, and the world as a realm possessing beauty and order. Honor thus involves multiple relationships between God and the divine purpose, God and humanity, and the relations between human beings themselves. Conversely, dishonor involves the violation of any and all of these relationships. In the treatise, Anselm continually points to these relationships to designate the way God is honored or dishonored.[21] I shall call the second definition of honor covenantal faithfulness. Though Anselm has set aside references to the Bible in the treatise, nevertheless this phrase expresses the second definition of honor: God's unswerving faithfulness to this purpose and the mutual obligations between God and humanity.

With these two definitions of honor before us, we must now proceed to the third step in the argument. The crucial question is: Which definition of honor is the basis for the argument?

---

21. Anselm can speak of humanity honoring God in a variety of ways, but they are parts of the same general obligation: to honor God is to fulfill God's purpose in the creation (I, 16-18, pp. 125-34), to attain to blessedness (I, 10, p. 118), to contribute to the order and beauty of the universe (I, 15, pp. 123-24), and to conquer the devil (I, 22-23, pp. 139-41). Since these activities are part of a single obligation, Anselm can say that humans cannot be blessed if they do not pay what they owe to God and restore the honor of God.

3. The Need for Satisfaction and the Necessity
of the Divine/Human Son of God

Since sin has dishonored God, the justice of God requires that what was taken away must be restored. But what would satisfy the honor of God? Up to this point Anselm has made several comments, without fully developing them. One is that satisfaction requires more than was taken away (I, 11). Another is that the Father sent the Son to die for the salvation of the world. But is such an act reasonable and necessary (I, 10)? Before Anselm can explore that question in the context of the nature of satisfaction, more work needs to be done on the necessity of satisfaction itself. Thus he returns to the question: Can God not simply set aside or pass over sin by an act of mercy, thereby restoring humankind to happiness? Several points are made against this:

- If this were done, then there would be no difference between the guilty and innocent; in effect, sin would be rewarded.
- To pass over sin would make the sinner freer than the innocent, since it would declare that the sinner can do as one pleases without being held to account.
- To resolve the problem by passing over sin suggests that God cannot achieve what God wants. This would imply that God is not just or almighty.
- Passing over sin would also suggest that sin really does not need to be removed for humans to be happy. This would contradict the nature of humankind, since happiness is derived from freedom and blessedness, both lost in the fall (I, 12-14).

These arguments make it clear that Anselm will not allow one attribute of God to be placed against another. God's mercy, justice, and holiness are one and the same, all giving substance to God's honor. As the objections suggest, God's honor has to do with the moral order, which involves humanity in the larger context of God's purpose. Anselm is hammering away at the theme that neither God nor humankind can exist without restoration.

In taking this position, Anselm explicitly rejects the nominalist option, that is, that God could do whatever God chooses, and if it is God's choice it is therefore just. On such terms, God could pass over sin and declare the antagonism between God and humankind resolved. But not so for Anselm, since it is God's nature to be just and God can only act in accordance with God's nature. There can be no solution without satisfaction, which at this stage of the argument is expressed by the two options of punishment or restoration of

God's honor (I, 13). Satisfaction is now established as an absolute require-ment.

But no sooner has this conclusion been established, when we come to the critical point in the argument. Anselm has argued that humankind has robbed God and denied its own nature. From this he has drawn the conclu-sion that satisfaction is required: punishment or restoration. But if this is a genuine either/or, why would God not take the simplest option, namely, pun-ishment? It has been clearly stated that either — punishment or restoration — satisfies God's justice/honor.[22] At this point the argument has reached a quite theoretical quality. The world did not end and, as the gospels make clear, God chose the other alternative, namely restoration. But why? Which view of honor requires the complicated solution? At last it is clear that the view of honor as covenantal faithfulness is in fact operative and driving the argument. If honor as moral sovereignty was the key to the treatise, then pun-ishment would have been quite adequate to maintain God's honor. Honor is satisfied by God's faithfulness to the purposes of creation.

Three subthemes support this conclusion. The first is the conclusion to the great digression regarding fallen angels: If God does not restore humans and in turn replace and complete the number of angels ordained, then either God cannot fulfill the divine plan or God has repented of it. But these options are impossible (I, 19; cf. II, 3-5). The second is the reintroduction of what is *fitting* for God, though at this point, fitting means necessary. It is fitting (i.e., in accordance with the divine nature) to restore humankind to happiness. The third is a surprising and dramatic move, since Anselm has observed up to this point the injunction against pictures and images. Anselm introduces the wonderful example of the pearl: What rich man, upon finding that a pearl has fallen from a special place into the mud, would not stoop to pick it up and then first clean it before returning it to its rightful place (I, 19)? So God shall take up what has been defiled and restore it. The image is irresistible, since it makes the point being made by the logical argument: restoration is necessary.

The entire matter of satisfaction has now taken a dramatic turn from any suggestion of punitive action to the restoration of the creation according to God's original design. In one sense, the rest flows easily once we have reached this point. Who can make such satisfaction in the form of restoration? Anselm earlier noted, in response to the inquiry about multiple ways of sav-

22. If the argument at this point appears to be quite theoretical, one must remember that appeals to the history of Israel or the gospels are not permitted. For Jews and Christians, history is understood as confirmation of their belief that God did not give up on the world because of sin. But in this argument, Anselm is searching for a rationale to explain why the redemption of Jesus happened the way it did.

ing the world, that the agent of salvation must be God, since humankind will serve the savior (I, 5). But now he builds toward the conclusion of the incarnation. Humans cannot make satisfaction by new acts of obedience, since they already owe such to God (I, 20). Moreover, humanity has lost its capacity to free itself from the devil and sin, since it has been conquered by the devil. Bound to the power of sin, humanity cannot escape the sin brought upon itself by its own disobedience (I, 22-24). The problem is compounded by the fact that what is owed is a price greater than the whole universe (II, 6). Thus we arrive at the now famous dictum: humanity *must* restore the honor of God, but only God *can* do this (II, 6). Therefore, it is necessary for God to become human for the restoration of the world.

4. The Restoration of the Creation by Means of the Divine/Human Son of God

In his description of the salvation accomplished by the incarnate Son, Anselm strictly follows the standard guidelines of the Chalcedonian formula: the two natures do not alternate in activity, nor can they be commingled into a third nature (II, 7). The inherited tradition of the two natures is quite compatible with Anselm's theme: humans must make restoration, but only God can. By being God and human, Jesus Christ resolves the predicament. He is the divine Son, who stands in relation to the Father and Spirit, as well as the human Jesus, the Second Adam. He is born of the virgin, assumes full humanity, and actualizes the true obedience and holiness that Adam lost. As the divine/human one, he freely accepts the life of obedience according to the will of God, offering his life to God the Father. Stated in another way, which Anselm believes is the same, the incarnate Son offers his humanity to his divinity.[23] By this act of holiness Christ conquers the power of sin and the devil, thus reversing the action of the first Adam. By his example, Christ demonstrates the true humanity for all to follow in resisting the devil and seeking holiness (II, 18; cf. II, 19). This new life embodied in Christ is, says Anselm, more wonder-

---

23. Anselm, II, 18, p. 179. Anselm's approach to the formula — one person, two natures — is to place the emphasis on the divine Son, who assumes humanity. The person of Jesus Christ is the Son incarnate. Thus he can speak of the Son (second persona) offering his life to the Father and the Spirit, and equate this statement with the Son offering his humanity to his divinity. From a modern perspective dominated by contemporary studies of the gospels, Anselm's approach does not seem to leave much room for the humanity of Jesus. Yet this approach is not unique to Anselm and reappears in our times in such writers as Jürgen Moltmann (see Chapter Four). On this matter, compare Williams, pp. 51-54.

ful than the first creation (II, 16). As such, it evokes devotion from all who see the wonder of Christ.

This brings the argument to the final stage: The Father bestows a reward upon the Son, which authorizes the Son to remit the sins of humanity. Those whom Christ chooses will be accepted by the Father (II, 19). It is as this point that Anselm connects his Christological affirmations with the spiritual and sacramental practices of the late eleventh century. The benefits of Christ are conveyed through participation in the church as the Body of Christ. On the one hand, it is available to all who follow Holy Scripture regarding how we are to attain grace and live the Christian life; on the other hand it is promised in the sacrament of the Eucharist (II, 19). By participating in the new life Christ brings, the believer encounters the mercy of God, which appeared to be lost in the requirements of justice. But it was the mercy of God as well as God's justice that redeemed the sinner. "For, indeed, what greater mercy could be imagined, than for God the Father to say to the sinner, condemned to eternal torments, and without any power of redeeming himself from them, 'Receive my only-begotten Son, and give him for yourself,' and for the Son himself to say, 'Take me, and redeem yourself'?" (II, 19).

We shall conclude this summary of Anselm's argument with a clarification regarding the meaning of necessity as it relates to the incarnation and Jesus' obedience and death. The development of Anselm's view on this issue illustrates how the movement of the treatise is not strictly linear. A point is discussed in a way we might consider quite adequate, only to be raised again later. So it is with his definition of necessity. In Book II, Chapter 5, Anselm deals with necessity and God's actions. There are, he declares, two kinds of necessity: external and internal. There can be no external necessity upon God, the Creator of all things; therefore with God necessity can only be internal, which is freely assumed. Thus, with God, what is necessary is also free and, most importantly, there is a perfect union of necessity and grace. It is both an act of grace and necessity for God to maintain the creation (57). Then in Book II, Chapter 17, he returns to the issue of necessity when speaking of the incarnation and Jesus' obedience. Here he notes that in general, "necessity is either compulsion or prevention" (II, 17). But such cannot apply to God. References to something being necessary for God (or Jesus Christ) must mean something quite different, namely, the necessity to maintain the divine nature or purposes. Thus he writes:

> Therefore, when we say that this Man who, according to the unity of his person — as has already been said — is the same as God, the Son of God, could not avoid death, or will not to die, after he was born of the Virgin, we

do not mean that in himself he was unable to preserve (or to will to preserve) his immortal life; rather, we refer to his unchangeable will, by which he freely made himself man, in order to die by persisting in the same decision, and we say that nothing can change that decision. . . . For a thing should not be said to be done or not done by necessity or inability, when neither necessity nor inability has anything to do with it, but the will alone acts. (II, 17)

From such a perspective Anselm affirms that Jesus takes up a life of obedience, leading to suffering and death, of his own free will, while at the same time judging these events to be necessary for our salvation (II, 17). This judgment in Book II, so close to the end of the treatise, relates back to a more extensive discussion of the matter quite early in the text. In this earlier section (I, 8), the formal argument has not actually begun and Anselm is free to use biblical texts. There he declares that Jesus freely suffers and dies for the salvation of the world (I, 8). An elaborate discussion follows on how such events are both the will of the Father and Son, each freely consenting to this course for the sake of the world. Since Jesus' passion and death could not have happened without the Father's consent, Anselm is willing to say that God willed it. But this willing must be understood as a divine drawing and moving, which prompts a free response from the Son. Referring to the famous verse in Philippians 2:8: "he became obedient unto death," Jesus' response becomes for Anselm the model of freely serving God. "For this is simple and true obedience, when the rational nature, not of necessity, but willingly, keeps the will that it has received from God" (I, 10).

E. Analysis of the Argument

1. The Formal Structure of the Argument

While all of the theories seek to present arguments that move consistently from premise to conclusion, Anselm's theory is unique in that it claims to show the necessity of the incarnation and death of Jesus. Unlike Hodge or Abelard, who also share his concern for a rational defense, Anselm proposes a demonstration without reference to Bible or traditional arguments. That is an ambitious claim, but also unrealized. The gap between intention and result may explain in part why the treatise has been so controversial. Two difficulties illustrate the problem — one quite simple and the other more complex.

At the outset we were told that standard methods of argument — appeals to analogies, tradition, and sacred texts — would be set aside because they cannot provide the principle of rational necessity for the incarnation. But this obscures the fact that Anselm is still arguing with an analogy. In place of an aesthetic analogy that relies on such principles as balance or appropriateness, or the image of ransom that compares the work of Christ to military conquest, he introduces the image of honor. The image relies heavily on the world of feudal relationships involving status, loyalty, obligation, and debt, caused by violations of this social order. Honor includes the place of humanity in a universal moral order, as well as the related images of debt and satisfaction when sin violates the honor of God. The concepts of debt and satisfaction possess considerable power, but at the same time they are not very precise terms. To use them as the basis for an argument claiming necessity requires that the images be tightly controlled, which is difficult to do. Perhaps the argument would be easier to understand if there was greater recognition that the entire matter was still based on an analogy. It is ironic that in spite of the stated prohibition against analogies, the argument is buttressed and enlivened at two crucial points by the wonderful analogies of the pearl (already noted) and the King (which will be discussed later).

The more complex issue follows from the fact that the argument, resting on the analogy of honor, reaches an impasse at the point of punishment or restoration. By themselves, the concepts of debt and satisfaction are incomplete and dependent upon much more general theological argumentation if they are to lead us to the advent and death of Christ. If isolated and viewed as self-sufficient, the images are capable of moving in directions that are contrary to Anselm's own general view of the atonement. In the treatise, Anselm maintains control of the images by the sheer force of his description of God and salvation. But not all of his readers have recognized that the concepts of debt and satisfaction must be interpreted against the background of other theological themes. Assuming that the images stand alone, they have used the images as weapons against Anselm. The best example of this is that of Aulén, who argued that since humanity must pay the debt, therefore the death of Jesus is something accomplished by humanity and not God. Using his own categories, Aulén refers to such a position as one of *discontinuity*, since it does not affirm that God is the author of salvation from beginning to end.[24] It may well be that

---

24. Cf. Aulén, pp. 97-98, 102, 163, and 169. It is very difficult to evaluate Aulén's rejection of Anselm. The crucial point appears to be Anselm's insistence for human participation in the restoration of the world. Yet he acknowledges the opposite interpretation of Anselm by R. Hermann, which is parallel to the position taken here. But this is simply dismissed. Like-

Anselm encourages this type of criticism by introducing the concept of debt, not as an analogy but a logical argument. But here Anselm misleads the reader. The images of debt and satisfaction are not self-sufficient principles capable of functioning by themselves. They are intelligible and useful only in a particular theological context, which Anselm must finally reveal to the reader. When this theological context is revealed, the criticism by Aulén collapses.

The interpretation of Anselm offered here proposes a mixed conclusion. The argument in quest of logical necessity fails because in the end it uses an analogy that requires appeal to the faithfulness of God. By itself the argument reached the point where satisfaction required either punishment or the restoration of humanity. But to explain why only restoration was a valid option, Anselm had to introduce a second view of God's honor, which involves God's irrevocable commitment to the divine purpose. But such an appeal relies on a theological tradition that is not self-evident. In actuality, Anselm has been hammering away at this theme from the very beginning.[25] Debt

---

wise, in general terms Aulén also affirms human participation in the salvation of the world when speaking of the Patristic period. Compare, for example, the following: "Secondly, in regarding the Atonement as God's own saving work, the Fathers do not lose sight of the fact that it is carried out in and through man. The Incarnation is the manifestation of God's goodness and the fulfillment of His saving work *in carne,* in the flesh, under the conditions of human nature" (p. 76). To be sure, it can be argued that the liberation theories, where Christ conquers Satan, do not require the participation of humanity in quite the same way as in the argument presented by Anselm. Whereas liberation theories speak of God using a human to conquer the devil, Anselm speaks of human participation as a requirement for the restoration of humanity. But there are overtones of necessity in the liberation theories, as when the appropriateness of human participation in Satan's downfall is compared to humanity's disobedience, leading to Satan's triumph. One would hardly accuse Paul of being Pelagian when he compares the agency of the two Adams — a parallelism that could not occur if Jesus were not truly human. Thus, while a difference is there, it is more of a difference in emphasis derived from the images in the theories. It certainly does not warrant Anselm's banishment from orthodoxy, which occurs in Aulén's typology. In Anselm the initiative and agency are solely with God, as Anselm assumes that the person of Jesus Christ is the Trinitarian Son. Thus when Jesus offers his life to God, it is the same as saying that the Son (Trinitarian) offers his life to the Father. One cannot help but feel that for Aulén, the issue has already been determined by the placement of the ransom view, judged as normative, over against the Latin view, judged as negative. In this respect one wonders if Aulén reflects the traditional Protestant antagonism of the early twentieth century against the Latin, medieval view. Taken in another direction, Aulén's insistence on this criticism, which governs his threefold typology of atonement theories, can also be interpreted as a Lutheran opposition to the emphasis given on sanctification rather than on justification. If this is the case, his criticism may be aimed at other branches of Protestantism and not simply Roman Catholics.

25. Cf. the following passages from Anselm: (1) "human nature was created in order that hereafter the whole man, body and soul, should enjoy a blessed immortality. It is proved that it

and satisfaction require the incarnation only on the assumption that God is in process of fulfilling a design that God cannot abandon. Moral sovereignty alone allows for the possibility of the divine wrath consuming the world. But such a catastrophe is impossible for the faithfulness of God. Thus, when faced with the question of restoration or punishment, there is really only one choice: the restoration of the world and the perfection of God's design. But while the argument fails to rise to the level of logical necessity, it presents us with a powerful witness to God's unswerving will to restore the creation. When the argument is played out, it provides us with a theory that is, to paraphrase Aulén, from start to finish the work of God. It is the Father who sends the Son, and the Son who offers his life to the Father and Spirit for the salvation of the world. Not once does Anselm suggest that Christ, acting solely as human, performs a work acceptable to God. Such an option is not possible in Anselm's Christology, where the person of the incarnate Son is the second person of the Trinity.[26]

2. The Death of Jesus: Atonement and Eucharist

The interpretation of the death of Jesus poses questions regarding the structure of the argument and the criticisms of penal substitution. Why did Jesus die and in what way is this event connected to restoring the honor of God? Anselm deals with this in many places and this causes some ambiguity as well as opening him to the charge that the death is an end in itself. In the preliminary chapters, where Anselm is still free to review and discuss Scripture (I, 9 and 10), he emphatically states that God did not

---

is necessary, this purpose for which man was made to be achieved" (Preface, p. 100). (2) "Surely we argue conclusively enough that it was fitting for God to do the things we speak of, when we say that the human race, that very precious work of his, was altogether ruined; that it was not fitting for God's plan for man to be entirely wiped out; and that this same plan could not be put into effect unless the human race were delivered by its Creator himself" (I, 4, p. 105). (3) "It is easy to see from all this that, unless God is going to complete what he began with human nature, he made so sublime a nature for so great a good all to no purpose. But if we know that God made nothing more precious than the rational nature, created to rejoice in him, it is certainly incongruous for him to let any rational nature perish altogether" (II, 4, p. 148). (4) Note especially the analogy of the lost pearl (I, 19, p. 135). (5) Other references include the following: I, 9, pp. 112-15; I, 10, pp. 115-18; I, 16-18, pp. 125-34; I, 25, pp. 144-46; II, 5, pp. 149-50; II, 16, pp. 166-72; and II, 18, pp. 176-79.

26. Williams discusses the high Christology of Anselm, reminding us that the Trinitarian Son assumes humanity, but it is always the person of the Son that is active (cf. pp. 51-54, 66-67).

compel Christ to die, when there was no sin in him, but Christ himself freely underwent death, not by yielding up his life as an act of obedience, but on account of his obedience in maintaining justice, because he so steadfastly persevered in it that he brought death on himself. (I, 9)

This appears equal to the language of our time, when we say that death was not the object of Jesus' life, but the result of his fidelity to God. But in the same chapter he extends this by saying: The Father gave to Jesus the commandment to suffer and die for the salvation of the world. A range of passages from the New Testament are discussed to support a commission to suffer and die: John 14:31; John 18:11; Philippians 2:8; Hebrews 5:8; and of course, the Gethsemane prayer. The discussion concludes: "The fact is that the Son, with the Father and the Holy Spirit, had determined to show the loftiness of his omnipotence by no other means than death" (I, 9).

When we move forward, inside the formal argument, we find that Anselm develops the importance of the death, apart from obedience. First, he states that satisfaction must be in proportion to the guilt, but then notes the fact that nothing compares to one sin (I, 20 and II, 11). Furthermore, one cannot pay the debt with obedience, because that is already owed to God (I, 20 and II, 11). Something else is required, something that no one owes, which he further describes as a price greater than the universe (II, 6). This is the death of the Son, freely offered to the Father that the world might be redeemed.

While Anselm no doubt saw all of these statements as consistent with one another, there does appear to be a progression in his view of the death of Jesus. From the standpoint of the general framework of the argument, one can say that at the outset, Jesus enters our world as the Second Adam, fulfilling the role Adam rejected, conquering sin and the devil and restoring the creation according to God's design. If one stayed with this perspective for the entire argument, the emphasis would fall upon the new life Jesus shares with believers as the restoration of the honor of God.[27] But as we just saw, as one proceeds toward the conclusion of the argument, it is the death of Jesus that becomes more central. The offering of Jesus' life was not owed to God and constitutes the ultimate gift. The gift is offered by Jesus' humanity to his divinity, or, which is the same thing for Anselm, by the Son to the Father. Since this gift is of infinite value, Jesus is rewarded with the power to save believers.

---

27. It is interesting to note that this is the view developed in the new Catholic Catechism (see Chapter One).

It is at this point that Anselm is vulnerable to the charge of making the death an end in itself, or a transaction between God and Christ for the sake of appeasing God. The problem is that it all depends on where one places the emphasis. Is Jesus offering his life of obedience, in spite of the threat of death? Or have we departed from the basic structure of the argument in such a way that the death per se is of value and required to honor God? The same ambiguity is present in the texts Anselm appeals to: "And being found in human form, he humbled himself and became obedient to the point of death — even the death on a cross. Therefore God also highly exalted him" (Phil. 2:7-9); or consider Jesus' prayer: "not my will but yours be done" (Luke 22:42). In fairness to Anselm, it must be said that the treatise never argues for a death as a required penalty or a means to appease an alienated God. There is no language of such a negative transaction. Nor is the death justified or explained by the imagery of sacrifice, though there is at least one reference to Jesus' death as a sacrifice. Instead, there is only the language of gift: the total love and devotion the Son has for the Father (II, 19). Jesus offers his life to God as a model of obedience for all people, as part of the plan to restore the world.

This issue may not find resolution simply by the treatise itself, and here we need to expand the discussion with the thesis of George H. Williams. In an essay first published in 1957 and then later in book form in 1960, Williams argued that Anselm's treatise sets forth a Christology consonant with the sacramental and spiritual life of the eleventh century.[28] In this respect, Anselm is the culmination of a long development where the emphasis shifted from baptism and Christ's defeat of death and the devil, to the Eucharist, with its emphasis on the passion of Christ, expressed in the new covenant made in his body and blood for the forgiveness of sins. Whereas the earlier theology/piety gave priority to the ransom theory and baptism as dying and rising with Christ as the means of incorporation into the church, the eleventh-century theology/piety of the West gave priority to incorporation into the church by means of the Eucharist, declaring the forgiveness of sins and calling believers to obedience. While the shift had already taken place by Anselm's time, he is the first theologian to provide a theological basis for what had become the dominant practice of faith. In this light, his rejection of the ransom theory reflects the new orientation around the mystery of Christ's presence on the altar in the Eucharist, in contrast to the victory of Christ symbolized by baptism. Finally, the treatise gives expression to the monastic ideal of obedience to the will of God. The treatise embodies the in-

---

28. Cf. Williams, pp. 5-26.

dividual quest for holiness and righteousness as a member of a Benedictine order who has forsaken the world,.

Williams's perspective helps us place the treatise in the theology of the Middle Ages and the piety underlying the Roman mass. For example, in the earlier period baptism was usually at Easter, for adults and children, as the celebration of the resurrection. Baptism was the once-and-for-all event, marking one's inclusion into the Body of Christ. Since many were baptized in groups, it had a communal character. Over time, however, baptism became disconnected from Easter and the communal initiation. In 1072 the Council of Rouen declared that children could be baptized at any time, and the Second Lateran Council of 1139 denounced anyone who refused infant baptism.[29] Parallel to this change was the new emphasis given to the forgiveness of sins in penance and Eucharist. In related writings, Anselm developed very definite ideas about how sin is forgiven: baptism washes away the stain of original or natural sin, whereas the Eucharist offers forgiveness for sins committed since baptism.[30] Unlike baptism, the Eucharist is repeated daily and nurtures the life of Christians in their struggles to be faithful to the will of God. The shift to the Eucharist reflects the general concern for righteousness in this life and the development of the penitential system involving priestly confession and remission of sins. But far more than penance, Eucharist was the primary symbol of incorporation into the Body of Christ.

If we read the treatise against the background of this new spiritual life, certain aspects of the argument take on new meaning. There are the obvious allusions to the Eucharist at the close of the argument, where we are admonished to "take" and "receive." But even more significant is the way this cultural context helps us understand Anselm's increasing emphasis on the death of Christ as the argument moves to completion. The Eucharist represents the sacrament of the new covenant, made in Christ's life broken and poured out. It involves the double movement, representative of the incarnate: Christ offers his life to God and with God offers it for the salvation of the world. The Eucharist celebrates the triumph of God in Christ over sin, death, and the devil. The central idea is that of the gift of obedience, which ultimately invites and makes possible the incorporation of humanity into a community of obedience. Here we see how Anselm's monastic mindset merges with his concern for a sacramental theology.

If one looks at the emphasis on Jesus' death outside of this sacramental

29. Williams, p. 19.
30. Williams, pp. 34-42.

context, then it can appear harsh, unnecessary, and abusive. Placed in the context of a theological commentary on the spiritual life dominated by the Eucharist, it appears more appropriate. For Anselm, the fact is that Christ died and by means of his death created a new covenant for our salvation. Recall for a moment the original objections to the Christian story, i.e., that it debases God with images of suffering that a wise and almighty God could have avoided. Anselm's response to those criticisms, finally reached in the conclusion of the treatise, is that Jesus' death was not an accident, his life was not taken from him, and most important, his life was not demanded by God to comply with penal justice. His death was a gift that he offered to God. It is the culmination of Christ's obedience and the primary symbol of the Eucharist. Thus he is both Savior but also Example for all who would seek to obey the will of God.

At this point one might say that it is *fitting* to introduce the parable of the king, who finds that all but one person has sinned against him (II, 16). This innocent man is willing to perform a service to reconcile all people to the king on a particular day. Since all in need of such reconciliation cannot be present on that day, the king grants absolution to anyone who seeks pardon through the service done on that day. In commenting on the parable, Anselm states that Christ's "death had such power that its effect reaches even to those who lived in another place or at another time" (II, 16).

To conclude: there is ample evidence in the treatise to show that Anselm has not shifted into an alternate framework involving punishment, which requires a death. When we place the discussion of Jesus' death in the context of the sacramental theology of the eleventh century, it becomes clear that Anselm is offering an interpretation of the passion of Christ that leads directly to the Eucharist. As the death is the gift of the Son to the Father and Spirit for the salvation of the world, so the Eucharist is the means whereby people in all times and places may share in Christ's salvation and begin the new life obedient to the will of God.

F. General Comments

Anselm presents us with an argument to show the reason why God became incarnate, suffered, and died. He used images of debt, satisfaction, and honor to build a rationale for restoration of God's honor. We have seen that this ultimately meant the restoration of God's purposes for the creation, or, the salvation of the world, founded on the faithfulness of God. As the argument progresses, the key event in this process of restoration becomes Jesus' obedience unto death. I have argued that there is no basis in the treatise for interpreting this as a move toward penal substitution. Instead, it is the gift the Son offers to the Father for the salvation of the world. This interpretation is supported by the general context of the eleventh century, where Anselm offers a theory of atonement that both reflects and supports what has become a reality, namely, a spiritual life where the Eucharist is central. Also, not to be forgotten is the fact that the treatise arose in response to criticism regarding the humiliation and death of Jesus. The criticism did not doubt the appropriateness of a prophet proclaiming judgment and hope, but the unseemliness of birth, passion, and death. Thus the movement of the argument to the necessity of Jesus' death reflects both the interest in the Eucharist as well as the quite specific challenge that Anselm accepted in writing the treatise.

So why defend a theory of atonement so locked into one form of medieval spirituality and a view of the Eucharist that over time proves to be problematic in the sixteenth century? The answer is simply that the conceptual framework that lies behind and informs Anselm's view offers advantages for atonement theory in general. These advantages are not the exclusive contribution of Anselm, nor does one need to argue that Anselm's theory is right and all the others are wrong. But they are emphasized and clarified by Anselm in such a way that it is justifiable to discuss them as values inhering in his understanding of the work of God in Christ. In one sense I am doing precisely what Williams saw as a major flaw in the criticisms of Anselm. Since the treatise sets such narrow boundaries according to what appears as logically necessary, interpreters have treated it as an argument apart from the eleventh century. Hence, Williams offered his corrective of recovering that historical context. Here, in an attempt to inquire what relevance Anselm provides to the twenty-first century, I will be exploring theological ideas in the treatise on the assumption that they are not bound to the spirituality of the eleventh century.[31]

1. God as the Ultimate Ground of Salvation

The fundamental value of Anselm's view is that it makes explicit the nature of God as the ultimate ground for salvation. We are counseled to think of God as the sovereign Lord who creates the world for a purpose. Because God is faith-

---

31. Williams, pp. 6-7. If Williams is to be credited for reminding us of the sacramental character of the treatise, Southern should be credited for lifting up the way the monastic vision of the Christian life bears upon the treatise.

ful to this purpose, the atonement — as the resolution of the contradictions between sin and God — occurs because of who God is. When Anselm rejected the ransom theory, which suggests that the reason for incarnation had to do with God's relation to Satan, he knew full well that this left him with the task of explaining the incarnation on the basis of God's nature and purpose. This was precisely what Anselm wanted, namely, to have us see that the incarnation of the Son arose from the very nature of God.

When we view the matter in this way, we gain a better appreciation for the differences between theories of atonement. The outline for this study differentiates theories by their concern for forgiveness of sins, liberation, the purposes of God, and reconciliation. Another way of saying that is that theories are structured by different relationships. For some, the God–humanity relation is central, for others it is the God–sin, death, and Satan relation that dominates. In the case of Anselm, it is the internal relations in God that dominate. That is, God's relation to the divine purpose, a relation in God, drives the argument. One consequence of this way of looking at theories is that they complement one another, rather than exclude, because they operate with different concerns and relations. This explains why Anselm can include in his treatise reference to the defeat of the devil and the reconciling love of God. It is also why so many great writers use more than one theory in expounding the work of Christ. It is most regrettable that theories of atonement have been treated as mutually exclusive, requiring believers to choose only one.

2. History and the Purposes of God

If one starts from the position of God's faithfulness to the divine purposes, then one has a framework for understanding particular events and the movement of history toward God's goal. We see this in Anselm's unrelenting insistence that atonement has to do with God and God's purposes. Anselm acknowledges that God is sovereign and depends on no one for existence, cannot cease to be or change. What God does is neither arbitrary nor coerced. All of this sounds quite scholastic. But he catches our attention when he affirms that whatever God does flows from the divine nature toward a purpose. Such a perspective necessitates a historical understanding of the atonement, involving a beginning and an end, with decisive events in the middle. It implies a divine freedom that brings God into the world, not away from it. To give expression to this free and necessary intervention in the suffering and violence of the world, Anselm employs the images of debt and satisfaction within a broader image of the universe as a moral order. The moral order of creation has come apart; atonement necessitates that something happen to satisfy or restore the honor of God. There shall be forgiveness, but the forgiveness of sins necessitates the restoration of our humanity and the entire world.

There are two important consequences that flow from this perspective. One is the new understanding given to the ideas of judgment and wrath. These terms raise formidable difficulties. On the one hand, they appear to suggest that God's relation to the world has been determined by God's reaction to sin, rather than God's own nature. Thus sin not only destroys the world but conquers God by turning God into a tyrant. On the other hand, words like judgment and wrath suggest a form of divine alienation from the creation. In both cases, the door is opened for portraying God as the angry, alienated deity needing appeasement or desiring vengeance. When this occurs, the inevitable reaction follows that many reject completely the concepts of judgment and wrath. But the elimination of concepts like wrath leads to an ironic twist. Wrath symbolizes the opposition of God to the suffering and evil of this world. If wrath is eliminated, what happens to the opposition between God and evil? The attempts to save God from being a vengeful tyrant by affirming unconditional love only lead to further questions about whether such a God is in fact moral.

These difficulties are avoided when we work within the framework of creation moving toward God's purpose. Here it is possible to speak of sin as the denial of God's purpose for humanity within the creation and in relation to God. Sin does in fact alienate both God and humanity. Divine judgment points to the constancy of God's will to maintain the integrity of the creation over against sin and evil. God exercises sovereignty, not in the form of withdrawal, but in terms of the faithful God who upholds the divine purpose in the face of opposition. This implies that God has a twofold relation to the world: first, relating to it as God's own creation; second, relating to it as that which exists for a purpose beyond itself. This twofold relation is illustrated by the two uses of the phrase: the goodness of the world. As God's creation, the world possesses an intrinsic goodness. But as part of the creation which is forever in process of becoming what God intends, goodness refers to the value found in actualizing what is potential or intended. If the first goodness is intrinsic, the second is derived. The first demands humility and gratitude, the second calls for responsibility.

Viewed in this way, judgment arises out of the contradiction between the world as a fallen creation and what God intends. The tension in such a statement is well expressed in the proposition that "God needs to be reconciled to the world." This does not mean God is unalterably alienated, or needs to be appeased by humanity. Like Anselm's demand for satisfaction, it reveals the fact that God will not accept the present state of the world and is only reconciled to such a world when the world conforms to its purpose. Thus we see that judgment leads us to think in historical and eschatological terms. Judgment drives toward those events wherein God is reconciled and the world is given a new future.

The second consequence derived from assuming the framework marked by God's faithfulness to the divine purpose is that it keeps before us a theocentric focus for the discussion. In traditional theology, this finds expression by speaking of the glory of God as the end of creation. Among the many things this phrase meant, it affirmed that human beings are not the chief end of creation. What this means for atonement theory is that the final end of atonement can never be equated with the world itself or the present state of the world's redemption. Is this point not what lies behind Anselm's belabored exploration regarding the replacement of fallen angels and completion of the number of angels ordained by God? There is more in God's plan than fulfilling all the desires of human beings! Creation and redemption have to do with the revealing of the glory of God — in fact, for Anselm the latter is more wonderful than the original act of God.

3. The Unity of Love and Justice

Anselm cannot conceive of any of the divine attributes contradicting one another. So it is with love and justice. Love is the creative power of God in creation and redemption, whereby God fulfills the divine goal. Love is the free expression of the divine goodness. Justice is the capacity whereby God maintains the divine integrity, as well as the integrity of the creation. At the close of the treatise Anselm reminds his student that mercy has not been lost in the demand of justice. The very justice that demands restoration of God's honor leads to the world's redemption.

Unless one begins with a view of the fundamental unity of love and justice, the two concepts soon move in opposite directions, signifying an unresolved tension in God. This happens in a variety of ways. Love can become the inclusive symbol of all the positive attributes of God, whereas justice moves in the direction of judgment, wrath, and even vengeance. On such terms, love draws God to the world, whereas justice symbolizes God's withdrawal from it. The problem with such a dichotomy is that, in general, the Bible suggests that both love and justice involve presence and distance, acceptance and opposition. Put in another way, the divine love certainly displays otherness and transcendence as much as God's justice, unless we wish to affirm that our love is identical with God's love. God's love calls into being new relationships that include new demands. Conversely, the divine justice displays the graciousness of God just as surely as does the concept of love. Anselm's insistence that justice and mercy are one is an invaluable contribution to atonement theory.[32]

32. It is difficult to understand why liberationists are so unreceptive to Anselm's insistence upon restoration (satisfaction) as essential to the redemptive process. From their perspective, liberationists are fond of insisting that the gospel cannot be limited to forgiveness, but must include new life and the works of justice and peace that flow from it. One can only attribute this rebuff of Anselm's quest for holiness to the way radically different cultures find it difficult to understand the language of each other, especially when the other is associated with long-standing traditions that have become oppressive. Anselm's connection with a medieval system that is hierarchical, and a theological tradition that has been legalistic and repressive, make it difficult for many to appreciate common bonds. This is especially the case in the interpretation of Aulén, who divides all of Christianity into positive and negative positions.

Chapter 7 Christ the Goal of Creation

Friedrich Schleiermacher

A. Introduction

The comparison of Jesus with Adam is usually designated as a Second Adam Christology. But this can be done in several ways: for Athanasius, Christ is the new Adam, whereas in Anselm, Christ is the true Adam who restores the creation. Here we shall consider Christ as the last Adam, who gathers the other meanings into the idea of the completion of the creation, the final perfection of God's purpose. To be sure, there is also the discontinuity of the fall and the wonder of redemption. But Christ is not an afterthought, nor a divine reaction to the problem of sin. From the beginning, Christ is the original goal.

The inspiration for this perspective may be traced to two themes in the New Testament. One is the emphasis on God's design, before the creation, for the redemption in Christ. (Compare the doxological passages in Eph. 1–2, Rom. 1:2, and 8:28.) While sin and death are in the picture, the emphasis is that God intended Christ not simply as a remedy for sin, but for something far greater. The second theme is the recognition of the new creation now revealed in Christ. This new reality cannot be contained in, or expressed by, the images of former times, no matter how they might be magnified. Incarnation and the presence of the Spirit create a new time, a new covenant, and a new creation. Reference could be made to all of the gospels, especially John, as well as passages like 2 Corinthians 5. When these two themes are joined, they generate the bold declaration that God has ordained from before the creation of the world the new life revealed in Christ and the Spirit. This new reality is the end or goal of God's plan.

This perspective raises in a striking way the issue of the relation of Christianity to Judaism. If the new is so different, even a qualitative difference, that it cannot be contained in the old, then one moves toward what has been called supersessionism, i.e., that Judaism is superseded by Christianity. Such a view appears to be suggested by the story of Jesus' first sign at the wedding of Cana, where the jars of purification are empty, waiting to be filled by new wine.[1] But not all parts of the New Testament share such an extreme view, as is evident from Romans 9–11. Numerous passages emphasize something quite distinctive in Jesus Christ, while still retaining a connection with Jewish traditions (e.g., new *covenant* or new *commandment*). The matter creates a serious dilemma, which can be stated in this way: How shall Christians affirm that Jesus is new, without denying God's revelation to Israel and the value of the Old Testament? In theory the easiest way of dealing with the issue is to see all of God's saving activity — from Israel to Christ — as joined together in God's single plan. What distinguishes the theory at hand is the emphasis on the unity of this plan, finally revealed in Christ.

B. The Theory in Outline

Since this theory emphasizes a single decree that includes creation and redemption, it begins with the reality of the redemption in Christ and moves backwards and forwards. Thus it joins recitation and doxology:

1. In his life, death, and resurrection, Jesus Christ reveals a new life, a new covenant, and a new creation. As the Redeemer:
   a. Jesus reveals the power of sin, death, and all demonic powers that separate us from one another and from God.
   b. Jesus reveals the power of God which transforms all things, creating new life and community in the Spirit (the forgiveness of sins and reconciliation with one another and with God). Thus he embodies the presence of God (incarnation) and generates new life by the bestowal of the Spirit.

---

1. The story of the wedding feast at Cana, with the empty jars not yet filled with new wine in John 2, is a highly charged example. This text is usually interpreted in terms of the wonder of the first sign (or miracle), Jesus' relation to his mother, or the social customs of serving the best wine first. If we interpret it according to Raymond Brown, this may well be the most severe critique of Jewish traditions in John, if not the entire New Testament. Brown places the emphasis on the fact that the jars, which normally held the water for purification, are *empty*. The contrast is not between lesser and greater, but between an end and a beginning. While other parts of the New Testament do not agree with such a sharp division, it is a serious question how the old and new are related. For Brown's view, cf. Raymond E. Brown, *The Gospel According to John (i–xii)* (Garden City, N.Y.: Doubleday, 1966), pp. 97-111.

2. Given all this (i.e., the forgiveness and reconciliation, incarnation and bestowal of the Spirit, the community of love empowered to transform the world), we are constrained to confess that the life bound by the love of Christ is the final realization of God's plan. It cannot be fully expressed either in references back to paradise (restoration) or in references to the conflict with sin. The new life in Christ is the completion of creation.

C. The Witness of Faith: Friedrich Schleiermacher

The choice of Schleiermacher was made for several reasons: first, he presents a thoroughly consistent Second Adam Christology, wherein Jesus Christ is the goal of creation; second, his Christology, set in his theological framework, has had profound influence on Protestant theology to the present day. Schleiermacher represented a bold and original response to the major intellectual movements of the Enlightenment: the rise of modern science, the critical philosophy exemplified by Kant, as well as the criticisms of religion directed toward its anti-intellectualism and sectarianism. But he has often been vilified as the source of all that is wrong with modern theology. Indeed, twentieth-century Protestant thought is marked by what Richard R. Niebuhr calls a Barthian captivity, where the bias against Schleiermacher has resulted in endless negative interpretations.[2] This discussion cannot expect to resolve the long-standing warfare. Instead, it can show how Schleiermacher's thought has been formative for later thought and may still be helpful in Christological reflection. Instead of going around him, in the fear that he is a hazard to theological health, it will be far more instructive to go through him.[3] This will, of

2. Richard R. Niebuhr, *Schleiermacher on Christ and Religion: A New Introduction* (New York: Scribner's, 1964), p. 11 and cf. the Introduction, pp. 3-17. For an example of Barth's interpretation of Schleiermacher, compare Barth, *Protestant Thought: From Rousseau to Ritschl*, trans. Brian Cozens (New York: Harper & Brothers, 1959), pp. 306-54. This is probably the harshest of Barth's criticisms, not only because of what he says but because of the patronizing way in which he claims to understand Schleiermacher's intentions and motives.

3. By formative I refer to the many ways in which Schleiermacher gives direction on issues of methodology as well as substance. This appreciation for him does not include subscribing to his specific conclusions on the full range of systematic theology. The specifics of his theology bear all the marks of this creative figure in a particular context. For example, his view on miracles is in some ways helpful, but clearly reflects a framing of the problem characteristic of the early nineteenth century. But the way he sought to affirm religion and the theological task in the face of the new science and critical philosophy is most instructive. Likewise, there are other aspects worth mentioning: that theology needs to be done in two parts rather than one,

course, be difficult to do because in language and outline, his primary work presents us with formidable challenges. But first a word about his life, which may assist us in understanding this text.

Born in 1768, the son of a Reformed pastor, Schleiermacher spent considerable time with the Pietists associated with Zinzendorf. After his theological studies at the University of Halle, he taught in an orphanage, was an assistant pastor, then a chaplain and finally a professor of theology in Berlin. Through the course of his life he wrote on a wide range of subjects, from philosophy and hermeneutics to theology. He translated Plato into German and was known for his preaching. His *Brief Outline* on the organization of theological disciplines has had wide influence. His definitive theological work, *The Christian Faith,* was published in 1820-21 and revised in 1830, the latter being the definitive text and the basis for the English translation.[4] He intended this major work for the union of Lutheran and Reformed in the Church of the Prussian Union, now known as the EKU.

Given all of these interests, Schleiermacher is indeed a complex figure and this is reflected in the different interpretations of him. One major tradition of interpretation continues to read all of his writings from the perspective of *The Speeches on Religion* of 1799, reflecting the new romanticism. The interpretation offered here relies on *The Christian Faith* as the definitive statement of Schleiermacher's theology. While there are, to be sure, important lines of continuity between the two works, *The Christian Faith* far surpasses the youthful imprecision of the *Speeches.* Most important, Schleiermacher devoted extensive time to the differentiation of methodologies involved in philosophy, science, history, and theology. By his own stated intention, *The Christian Faith* is a highly technical presentation, written for the community of faith in dialogue with traditions of the church. Focusing on this major theological work, therefore, reflects the value Schleiermacher himself gave to it. For our purposes, there are four areas that bear upon his view of the salvation brought by Jesus Christ: (1) the definition of religion; (2) God and the world; (3) the view of sin; (4) the revision of the language of Christology. These discussions will include both summary and analysis of critical issues. This will allow the reader to see how Schleiermacher builds his theology, progressing from one major point to another, as well as how I have interpreted major issues along the way.

---

or his attempt to redefine the creedal affirmations regarding Christ in the language of the modern age.

4. Friedrich Schleiermacher, *The Christian Faith,* ed. H. R. Mackintosh and J. S. Stewart (Edinburgh: T. & T. Clark, 1928). Henceforth all references to this work will be included in the text, either indicating Paragraph (Par.) or, where deemed more appropriate, page references.

1. The Definition of Religion

Schleiermacher was exposed to different approaches to religion, either by personal contact or through the great debates of his time. Seventeenth- and eighteenth-century scholasticism (Lutheran and Reformed) reinforced the idea that religion was primarily a form of knowledge. By contrast, the critical philosophy of the Enlightenment challenged any rational proof for religion. But at the same time, religion was saved either by reducing it to essential ideas or, as in the case of Kant, by finding a space for religion within the realm of morality. Taking a quite different stance, the Pietists rejected a doctrinal or philosophical approach to religion in favor of religion of the heart, with the emphasis on the practice of piety. While they appeared to converge with the liberal emphasis on love, they resisted the influences of the new science and philosophy. The new Romanticism, which figured so prominently in *The Speeches,* represented yet another approach. Here the emphasis fell upon historical and aesthetic categories, in contrast to abstract reason.

Given these approaches to religion, we are confronted with a great irony: Schleiermacher rejected all of these views of religion. Instead of embracing contemporary culture, he rejected it. The similarity of Schleiermacher to his great critic a century later is usually lost, since by then Barth saw him as part of the culture he needed to reject. But when Schleiermacher declared that religion was not a form of knowing or doing, he clearly had in mind the religious scholastics, the philosophical rationalists, the Pietists, and the cultured critics. Over against every attempt to reduce religion to something else, Schleiermacher proposed a *religious* definition of religion (cf. Pars. 3 and 4).

Schleiermacher's definition of religion consists of two parts, which can neither be separated nor merged.[5] Each represents an essential aspect of religion. The first part differentiates religion from other human phenomena such as philosophy, morality, science, or art. Such a process involves an abstract comparison of phenomena that do have some things in common.[6] His

---

5. What I have designated the first part of the definition of religion is set forth in Pars. 3 and 4; the second part is found in Pars. 5-12.

6. To understand Schleiermacher's point it is crucial to understand the nature of a generic definition. To define a large and diverse class of phenomena is an abstract, logical process, wherein one isolates what is unique to the class. But what is unique does not exist as an independent or uniform thing, common to all members of the class. It is not like the same part that is included in all automobile engines. To change the example, all mammals may have spinal columns, but not all spinal columns are the same; nor do they ever exist by themselves apart from

answer is that religion is a relation to God, given to the self by that which is outside the self. The relation is not first an idea, as an object of thought, or an act, as an expression of volition. It was crucial for Schleiermacher, though too often ignored by his critics, that what defines religion is a causal relation between the self and an Other, active upon the self. Thus religion can only be defined in terms of human receptivity. This definition is not offered as a proof for the existence of God, but as a description of what distinguishes religious experience. What should be noted, however, is that the definition always involves the polarity of the self in relation to that power acting upon it.[7] But where does that divine causality act upon human selfhood? The answer cannot be our capacities for knowing and doing, since these relations to the world involve configurations of receptivity and activity. The relation to God, by contrast, arises in moments of complete or absolute receptivity. The English translation of the technical terms, though awkward, expresses the sense

---

whole bodies. For Schleiermacher, the defining mark of religion is a relation to God, arising within self-consciousness as a sense of absolute dependence. But it is not a separate experience from the total religious experience, nor is it a common universal religious experience in the modern sense of experience. Put in another way, the defining element of religion as religion is different in different religions; the relation to God is not interchangeable. In his inclusion of Schleiermacher into his experiential-expressive category, I think George Lindbeck misses this point (cf. *The Nature of Doctrine: Religion and Theology in a Postliberal Age* (Philadelphia: Westminster, 1984).

7. In this sense the standard Barthian criticism that Schleiermacher has reduced theology to anthropology misses the mark, since by definition religion always involves that which is over against us. Lindbeck adopts the Barthian criticism by judging Schleiermacher to be the originator of his second category for classifying all theology, namely, the experiential-expressive (the first being the cognitive and the third being the cultural-linguistic). One problem with his system of classification is that at times he treats the three categories as mutually exclusive, whereas at other times the experiential-expressive and cultural-linguistic represent a dialectic of inward experience and outward culture (Lindbeck, pp. 33-35). Such ambivalence undercuts the argument, since the one side of the argument leads to the rejection of the experiential-expressive, while the other side retains it in some larger synthesis. Further confusion is introduced by lumping together into the experiential-expressive category radically different positions. For example, inner subjective experience is placed side by side with the affirmation of a universal common experience, which becomes actualized in different religions. It is difficult to imagine how an inner subjective experience can be universal (cf. Lindbeck, pp. 21-47). Completely ignored by Lindbeck's analysis is that Schleiermacher sets Par. 15 in juxtaposition to Par. 19. The former affirms that doctrines "are accounts of religious affections set forth in speech," while Par. 19 balances this with: "Dogmatic Theology is the science which systematizes the doctrine prevalent in a Christian Church at a given time." If Par. 15 appears to open the door to the experiential-expressive interpretation, Par. 19 comes quite close to Lindbeck's cultural-linguistic perspective. For Schleiermacher, the religious consciousness always presupposes the relations of the self to other persons, culture, and the world.

of this: it is the *non-self-caused* element, a *having by some means come to be* (Par. 4.1). Thus the relation to God can only be located in the most primary form of being, the immediate self-consciousness, or feeling. In its total receptivity, the self is determined by an Other. Thus feelings or affections describe the states of the soul or heart.

In this first part of the definition of religion Schleiermacher made two major and interrelated points: religion has to do with something outside the self that determines the self; this determination of the self occurs at the most essential level of selfhood. Taken together, this means that being in relation to God is direct or immediate; it is not an idea originating in the process of logical reflection, nor is it an act that becomes the object of our will. Herein lies Schleiermacher's defense against all reductions of religion to knowledge (be it ideas or doctrines discovered or organized by reason) or doing (be it moral principles or the practices of communal life).[8] But the positive side of this definition is that religion is self-involving and determines the shape and substance of the self. As we shall see in a moment, it can only arise in and through language, practices, and all manner of cultural symbols and expressions. But what distinguishes it as religious is the way the self is determined by a relation to God.

---

8. Schleiermacher's attempt to define the feeling of absolute dependence as a determination of feeling apart from knowing and doing has received serious criticism from the perspective that affirms the social-cultural context of all human experience. Cf. the comprehensive discussion of this issue by Wayne Proudfoot, who argues that there can be no religious experience prior to the influence of language, tradition, and culture. Cf. Wayne Proudfoot, *Religious Experience* (Berkeley: University of California Press, 1985), chapter 1, pp. 1-40, especially pp. 31-37. If this is correct, Schleiermacher's position would have to be revised to take into account the way all consciousness is formed by language and traditions. But in fact, Schleiermacher may have already done this in a manner Proudfoot considers to be an inconsistency. The crucial issue is what is meant by the appeal to a pre-reflective moment of consciousness. Proudfoot rightly notes that since Schleiermacher insists that the feeling of absolute dependence requires a correlate of the Whence (or God), such a religious experience cannot be prior to language and thought (Proudfoot, p. 32). One could grant this without losing the main purpose of Schleiermacher's description of religion, which is to bar the door against rationalism, which bases religion on a series of logical steps. For Enlightenment culture, the standard for thinking was critical reason as well as scientific inquiry regarding the world. In both cases such thought would make God an object for human analysis. In affirming that the relation to God is given immediately, Schleiermacher sought to deny that the relation to God was constructed by human reason. But it presupposes consciousness of self and the world, as well as the ability to differentiate one's affectional responses through language and culture. Since it occurs within a person, it only exists with co-determinations of the consciousness of self, community, and the world. One consequence of Proudfoot's analysis is the clear recognition that Schleiermacher is not affirming an indescribable subjective feeling unrelated to the development of consciousness in the individual.

The second part of the definition pertains to the social/historical character of religion, which provides the means to differentiate one religion from another.[9] The relation to God only exists in conjunction with one's relation to the world, in all of its social and historical determinations. It is always and only formed by particular communities in time and space. As in *The Speeches,* so in *The Christian Faith,* Schleiermacher argues against defining religion solely by the relation to God in the immediate self-consciousness. The feeling of absolute dependence is not a universal datum of human experience, constant and unchangeable, to which is added particular historical elements. The historical and social aspects of a particular religion are not merely accidental forms. This is the rationalist position, that religion can be defined by an abstract essence, extracted from particular manifestations. It is precisely what he rejected, even though his view is repeatedly interpreted in these terms.[10]

What we have then is religion defined by a double relation: to God and to a community. If one asks: "What is Christianity?" Schleiermacher's answer is: To be a Christian is to be in relation with God through the transforming power of Jesus Christ, mediated through the community's life, practice, work, and faith.[11] Such an answer is both simple and complex, carefully avoiding the major options that violate the integrity of religion. Rationalism and morality shun the emphasis on heart in the first part of the definition, as well as the emphasis on the historical community as the mediator of faith in the second part. By contrast, Schleiermacher holds the two together, refusing to reduce religion to ideas or action abstracted from historical communities. At the same time, his rejection of anti-intellectualism requires that he hold heart, mind, and will together. As we shall see, there is no doubt that Schleiermacher did this in ways quite typical of the modern age.

---

9. Cf. Pars. 5-10, especially the Postscript to Par. 6.

10. As we have noted, Lindbeck attributes to Schleiermacher the idea that religion is based upon a universal, common religious experience. But in many respects Lindbeck's major concern appears to be his opposition to the idea of the unity of all religions, which he finds in theologians such as Rahner and Lonergan, but reads back into Schleiermacher (cf. Lindbeck, chapters 2 and 3, pp. 30-72). Schleiermacher's rejection of this idea is unyielding. He states emphatically that there is no such thing as a universal religious experience prior to identifiable religions. He denies natural religion and religion in general (cf. Postscript, Par. 6). As if anticipating Lindbeck's argument that similar words mean something quite different in different religions, Schleiermacher declares that the feeling of absolute dependence is itself different in different religions (cf. Par. 5.4).

11. I have rephrased the famous thesis of Par. 11 to emphasize the way it combines the two parts of Schleiermacher's definition of Christian religion (cf. p. 52).

2. God and the World

What is seldom recognized is that the definition of religion discloses Schleiermacher's fundamental vision of God: the sovereign power who is totally active and impassible. It was for this reason that he argued that the sense of being in relation to God cannot be explained by a relation to the world. Our relations with the world always involve activity and passivity, whereas only our relation to God involves absolute dependence. As Schleiermacher develops the doctrine of God, it is clear that he is neither a pantheist nor a deist. If the former merges God and the world, the latter so separates them that God is either removed forever or must find a way to break into the course of human history or the system of nature (which is exactly what the modern idea of miracle implies). God is eternal but the world is temporal. Eternity is not simply more time, but qualitatively different from time, since finitude implies a changing natural order. The temporal is the realm of the reciprocity between passivity and activity (p. 201). By contrast, God's omnipotence means that God is totally active, eternal power (p. 204). But having distinguished God from the world, the two are not separated. The world consists of a universal system of nature totally dependent on God (pp. 170-73). Such a view is consistent with piety, because it is by means of such a system that the divine preservation guides the world (p. 174). From this perspective, we may speak of God's eternal and omnipotent will manifest in the created order. Eternity and time are not absolutely separated, since time reflects the eternal decree of God. This also means that there is but one eternal decree, gathering everything together in the eternal purpose of God.

This view of God has major consequences for every part of his theology, but especially the Christological discussion. First, like Calvin, Schleiermacher admitted no distinction between cause and permit (pp. 325-26). If God is active in all things, and all things reflect the divine will, then God cannot be excluded or excused from some events. This judgment will obviously create difficulties for the doctrine of sin. Second, we cannot speak of something *absolutely supernatural* or *absolutely suprarational*, since such could neither appear in the natural world nor be comprehended by human rationality (Par. 13). Likewise, since the natural order is upheld by divine providence, it makes no sense to speak of it as absolutely natural. By contrast, it is appropriate to speak of a supernatural origin of Christianity, since it could not have occurred by a natural process, given the reality of sin (p. 67). But even here, the eternal and temporal cannot be absolutely separated: the coming of Jesus is eternal because it is grounded in God's decree, but it is temporal because it became actual in the finite realm (p. 401). Third, Schleiermacher rejects the concept of miracle for two reasons: (a) It violates the concept of the world as a universal system of nature, thus pitting religion against the new science. (b) More important is a theological argument: Given one divine decree, there is no need for a miraculous intervention, since everything needed for redemption is already contained in the one decree (pp. 179-81). Fourth, it follows that creation and redemption are joined together in God's one decree, though not merged in any such way as to deny sin or the need of redemption. Jesus Christ does not take us back to a former paradise, or elevate us to a higher realm, but is the completion of creation. In this sense, he is truly the Second Adam, the Mediator of the new reality that completes God's original design.

Schleiermacher is usually criticized for allowing the definition of religion and the methodology of *The Christian Faith* to determine the substantive doctrines. My conclusion has been just the reverse: it is his doctrine of God that determines his view of religion and methodology.[12] What has been presented thus far illustrates how this is the case. This leads to two comments: One is that Schleiermacher does indeed stand apart from much of contemporary theology in his adherence to divine impassibility and a single decree. Such a commitment places certain constraints on the view of sin and redemption. The other is again the ironic note: instead of finding Schleiermacher to be, as twentieth-century critics claimed, the one who reduced theology to anthropology, we find a theology governed by the doctrine of God. He may well have had more in common with Calvin than the later liberalism of the nineteenth century.

3. The Doctrine of Sin

While Schleiermacher rejected any speculative basis for theology, we are allowed to posit an original perfection and the fall as inferences from our formation in Christ, who makes us aware of sin and the possibility of redemption (cf. Pars. 60 and 61). If one did not draw these inferences, then one would be forced either to deny the goodness of creation or the reality of redemption. Yet such an original perfection is not to be identified with a nature or a power in humanity, or located in a specific time or place (pp. 241-44). The exposition of sin, however, is far more complicated, not because of liberal optimism,

---

12. This judgment was the basic conclusion of my doctoral dissertation. Cf. "The Divine Love: The Doctrine of God and Theological Method in Friedrich Schleiermacher's *The Christian Faith*" (unpublished Ph.D. dissertation, Harvard University).

but the very doctrine of God that we have just described. How shall we describe sin as an act of human freedom against God, if for God there is only activity without passivity? Schleiermacher's answer is to weave together two themes: sin is an act of human freedom *and* sin is ordained by God. Only by affirming both does he deem it possible to avoid both Pelagianism and Manichaeism, since the former denies the reality of sin and the latter places it completely outside the realm of God's power.

a. Sin as an Act of Human Freedom

Schleiermacher connects traditional images of sin with his own language of the religious self-consciousness. With Paul, he can speak of sin arising out of the tension of the flesh and spirit.[13] Humanity has turned from its Creator and become absorbed in self-centeredness. Preferring to refer to Christ rather than the Law, he can say that sin desires what Christ condemns. But in his own language, sin reflects the disparity between our consciousness of God and our self-consciousness. The God-consciousness has become so deranged that sin must be seen as a corruption of it (Par. 68). In either vocabulary, sin must be judged to be the action of human freedom: human beings are responsible for their action and are justifiably guilty and in need of redemption (p. 262).

Since the first turning from God, however, sin refers not only to actual sins but to original sin. Here Schleiermacher emphasizes social-historical categories to describe the meaning of this traditional concept, without appealing to the sexual transmission of sin. Original sin presupposes the corporate life of humankind, involving an "interdependence of all places and all times" (p. 288). As a result, the relation with God is arrested and the consciousness of God has been vitiated, disjoined, and obstructed (pp. 278 and 308). Schleiermacher cannot accept the ideas of the loss of freedom and total depravity, because they suggest a change in human nature. But there is no possibility of escaping from sin by means of human powers. Imprisoned by this environment of self-centeredness, human sinfulness constantly expresses itself in actual sin. But the hopelessness of sin points to the need for redemption, which is only achieved in Jesus Christ (cf. Pars. 70 and 71).

13. The contrast of flesh and spirit needs to be interpreted in the Pauline sense, and not as a dichotomy of body versus spirit. On this Schleiermacher is quite clear. The problem of sin is not our physical bodies subverting our spiritual longings. The tension he has in mind is not between physical existence and mind/spirit, but between the self open to the will of God in contrast to the self following the dictates of the world. So he speaks of the God-consciousness being subverted by relations to the world. Schleiermacher's interpretation parallels the Augustinian theme of sin as that act where the creation is substituted for God.

b. Sin as Ordained by God

If there is no distinction between cause and permit, or if God does not allow human revolt as an exception to the divine causality that creates and preserves the world, then the origin and actuality of sin must somehow be within the divine causality. Schleiermacher sees no way around this sobering conclusion without minimizing either sin or God's sovereignty. God's governance does not involve reciprocity between God and humankind, with God having to respond to unforeseen human actions. This leaves Schleiermacher no choice but to understand sin as connected with the goodness of humanity, as an incapacity for good. He will even go so far as to say that the "gradual and imperfect unfolding of the power of the God-consciousness is one of the necessary conditions of the human state of existence" (p. 338). But even this must be understood from the view that sin exists along with the good and has been ordained by God only in view of redemption, since "from the beginning everything has been set in relation to His (Christ's) appearing" (p. 328).

There is one significant qualification that Schleiermacher does offer, as if mindful that he has pushed his point too far. Though sin is ordained by God along with grace, God is not the author of sin and grace in the same way: "in the case of sin there is lacking that specific divine impartation which gives to every approach to salvation the character of grace" (p. 327). This qualification appears to be offered not simply to make room for human freedom, but again to defend against Manichaeism, which sees sin as a foreign intrusion and ultimately leads to the despair of any redemption (p. 330). But how does human freedom relate to this divine causality? The two relate not as alternating agents, or by matter of degree. Human freedom stands under and is grounded in the divine causality, so that there is always a mutual interpenetration of the two in every human act. Sin is a turning from God, a free act that incurs guilt and an act grounded in God's ordination, a part of human existence only in relation to the movement towards redemption. One final point: if sin exists only in relation to God's ordination, then moral evil is related to the human capacity to do the good and can only exist in relation to the divine causality (p. 351). Things in themselves are not evil, but become so through sin (pp. 315-18). Thus for Schleiermacher, Christ's redemption relates to the realm of human beings, sin, and moral evil, not to the realm of nature as ordained by God (p. 180).

4. A New Language for Christology

The Christology of *The Christian Faith* represents a bold and creative attempt to uphold the central affirmations of the creeds while at the same time translating them into a new language. This was not the first or last time this happened. The Enlightenment had already produced descriptions of Jesus without the language of John, Paul, and the creeds. These invariably presented Jesus as the teacher of religious and moral ideas, over against the divine/human figure presented in creeds and doctrines. Schleiermacher rejected these attempts. He sought to affirm continuity with the Christological norms of the past. For example, in the Introduction he indicated that theology must avoid the natural heresies of Pelagianism and Manichaeism (one denying the need for a Redeemer and the other implying the impossibility of redemption) as well as Ebionitism and Docetism (one implying that Jesus was only human and the other that Jesus was only divine) (cf. Par. 22). Likewise, he completely rejected the notion that Jesus did not intend to found a church.

But one might ask, with words from the Gerhardt hymn: "What language shall I borrow" to describe Jesus the Redeemer? Schleiermacher assumed that the incarnation could only be described in language consistent with *our* understanding of God's activity in the world as well as our view of humanity. But this posed a serious problem: the language of *nature, person, and the divine/human union* relies on categories that are either foreign to us or extremely imprecise. Here we may quickly record his concerns in Pars. 95-96:

- How can the same category (i.e., nature) be used of both God and humanity?
- How can one person have two natures, without mixing them into a third entity, or violating their true union?
- The word person is used equivocally: first regarding three Trinitarian personae and then regarding the person of Jesus Christ. If this is not the case, then either there would be three personalities in God or Jesus ceases to be human.
- The name Jesus Christ sometimes is used to refer to the second person of the Trinity and at other times to the historical Jesus, providing additional confusion.

Given the imprecision in language, Schleiermacher saw endless debate without any resolution. But just as important, these categories appear foreign to contemporary use, which relies on new ways of describing God and human life. Thus, his conclusion was to replace the language of *nature* and *person* with that of God's activity, the religious self-consciousness and the consciousness of God. Such a revision would make the language of Christology consistent with the language of God's agency upon human beings in the broader scope of divine providence.

While Schleiermacher was intent on introducing a new vocabulary, the structure of his Christology followed familiar patterns. We may speak of Christ's person and work by virtue of the salvation present in the Christian community. Thus his work constitutes the new creation over against sin and points to the unique dignity of his person. Jesus is the Redeemer because what he does is not common to all human activity. The work and person thus become indistinguishable, since it is by his person that he affects the disciples gathered around him and through them new believers. He can be the Redeemer only if the new life is communicated through him. He is the new creation in his person, thereby representing a new beginning over against sinful humanity. The Redeemer cannot be explained by his environment or by any sort of evolutionary process, but only as the new activity of God which completes the creation.

In developing this Christology, the basic movement is by inference from the reality of redemption to the dignity of Christ, and from the dignity of Christ to the special activity of God. But while developing this theme and introducing his new vocabulary, Schleiermacher includes critical reflections on the tradition. In these comments he proves to be both innovative and conservative. First, Schleiermacher rejects *both* the Virgin Birth and Adoptionism. This is surprising because they are usually presented as alternatives. Adoptionism is unacceptable because the dignity of Christ must be internal to his whole life since birth, but also be a part of God's eternal decree. The insistence on the Virgin Birth to guarantee the sinlessness of Jesus is inadequate, since the elimination of a human father still leaves a human mother affected by sinful humanity — leading to the additional claim of Mary's immaculate conception. But this only adds further complications and diverts attention from the fact that Jesus' perfection is unrelated to the means of physical procreation. Then in an even more surprising move, Schleiermacher insists that Jesus the Redeemer can only be explained by virtue of a new originating act by God. Thus while the Virgin Birth is judged superfluous, the idea of a supernatural conception is affirmed (p. 405).

How then can the presence of God in Christ be described if the language of Nicea and Chalcedon is set aside? Schleiermacher's technical language for expressing this is that Jesus possesses an absolute potency of God-consciousness, though he also uses a simpler formula that has strong ties to the New Testament: *God is in him.* In Par. 93 Schleiermacher uses the term

Ideal, meaning that Jesus was the true human, freed from sin — a point repeatedly affirmed by the creeds. From his birth, his whole life is formed by the activity of God upon him, leading to his dignity and sinless perfection. But the more Schleiermacher speaks of the dignity of Jesus as the true human, the more he insists that this could only have occurred by God's initiative, as we have seen in his revised reading of the Virgin Birth.

In Par. 97, Schleiermacher introduces his formula for describing the incarnation, but the matter is complicated. The Paragraph heading states that in the act of union, the divine alone was "active or self-imparting, and the human alone passive or in process of being assumed; but during the state of union every activity was a common activity of both natures." Thus the act and state of union involve different God/human relations. But this is immediately qualified by the additional canon that in both origin and state of union, both relationships apply: God takes the initiative in contrast to Jesus' passivity, but all activities of Christ are the common activity of both natures. It would appear that while each part of the original formula is valid, each needs to be qualified by the additional canon. For example, with respect to the act of union, the incarnation must result from the initiative of God, but Jesus' humanity cannot be absolutely passive since this would tilt too far toward Apollinarianism, or worse, Docetism. This, however, creates an acute problem, since God is pure activity and cannot be acted upon by the human. Schleiermacher's solution is to affirm that in the act of union, the human is active by means of a person-forming activity.[14] A similar double affirmation must exist regarding the state of union. In Jesus' life, every moment must be seen as proceeding from "the being of God in Christ," while at the same time every activity represents the common activity of both (Par. 94). One application of this canon is instructive, namely, the sympathy of Christ for humanity. Since sympathy is an affection prompted by action upon the self, how shall we explain Christ's sympathy? Schleiermacher's answer is that Jesus' sympathy is ultimately motivated by "the reconciling being of God in Christ." Jesus is aroused to compassion, not simply by the plight of humans, but by the divine love in him which continually gives direction (p. 407). To conclude, the formula of Par. 97 and the additional canon provide the means to affirm the initiative of God as well as the true union of the divine and human. "What comes into existence through the being of God in Christ is all

14. Schleiermacher rejects the tradition stemming from Alexandria, which sees the second person of the Trinity as the person of Jesus, taking human form but placing the emphasis on the divine person. This is unacceptable for Schleiermacher because humanity cannot exist apart from human consciousness. The union of God and Jesus must include human consciousness (cf. Par. 97).

perfectly human, and in its totality constitutes a unity, the unity of a natural life-story, in which everything that emerges is purely human . . . so that every moment also reveals the divine in Christ as that which conditions it" (p. 409).

D. Jesus Christ as Redeemer

The discussion of Jesus Christ, justification, sanctification, and the church extends over several hundred pages. They invariably involve the alternation of his new language and outline with detailed analysis of traditional doctrines. Since *The Christian Faith* was intended for the union of Lutheran and Reformed traditions, Schleiermacher was extremely careful to show the continuity between his positions and what had gone before him. As a result, the discussion is long, with considerable repetition. Instead of tracking this complicated discussion through its many stages, I will first present his position so that it can stand by itself, and then summarize the dialogue with traditions, indicating where he rejects, retains, or revises certain themes.

As a theologian of the incarnation, Schleiermacher affirms that the very life of Christ is a divine intervention in the course of history. Given the corporate life of sin, Jesus Christ cannot be the result of a natural progression of humankind. He is the Redeemer because he inaugurates the new creation, which overcomes the corporate life of sin. But viewed in the larger context, the title Redeemer must be qualified. The reason has to do with how creation relates to redemption: (1) Is redemption the restoration of the creation, each being two parts of one decree or derived from separate decrees? (2) Is redemption entirely separate from creation, being an elevation to a new state of being? (3) Is redemption the completion of creation, with both included in one decree? Schleiermacher chooses the last option. God's eternal decree can only be directed toward a positive goal, whereas redemption implies only the removal of sin. It is the new community of Christ that is the final goal of creation. Thus Christ is more appropriately called the Second Adam, the Mediator of the completion of creation (Par. 89).

As the Mediator and Redeemer, Christ incorporates believers into fellowship with him and thereby into communion with God. This incorporation includes redemption, as sharing the power of Christ's consciousness of God *and* reconciliation, as sharing the fellowship of his blessedness (cf. Pars. 100 and 101). The former accentuates the moral character of Christian faith, since it produces the awareness of sin while the latter affirms the new life of forgiveness. While the two are distinct, they are interdependent. Reconciliation or forgiveness cannot occur without the former. In both activities Jesus exercises his *person and world-forming power,* drawing persons into fellowship by his persuasive influence. At this point Schleiermacher connects the act of union and state of union with Christ to his earlier discussion regarding God's presence in Jesus. The same double relation shall apply: the initiative will always lie with Christ, but all activities must represent the union of Christ and the believer. This parallel will be extended yet again in speaking of the incarnation of the Spirit in the church.

What we have, then, is a view of the work of Christ heavily dependent upon the organic images drawn from John (e.g., new birth, living water, bread of life, vine and branches) and Paul (e.g., the Body of Christ). Christ draws persons into a new community where Christ empowers each person to participate in the Kingdom of God. Jesus accomplishes this through the power of his whole life, which is to say, *the power of God in him.* Moreover, Jesus' intent is not to gather isolated individuals, but a new community. The church comes into being through the direct spiritual influence of Christ. By continuing to draw persons into the new community, the church extends the power of Christ through history. Thus Schleiermacher can affirm that there is no salvation outside the church. The presence of Christ in the church is further affirmed by the bestowal of the Holy Spirit, which is described as the union of God with believers — parallel to the union of God with Christ and Christ's union with the believer in justification and sanctification (cf. Par. 123).

Once this general perspective has been established, Schleiermacher expands on it by using the traditional categories of prophet, priest, and king (Pars. 102-5). He embarks upon this course for several reasons: to show the difference and harmony of the Old and New Testaments, to maintain continuity with the history of doctrine, and most important, to make clear the way salvation is communicated to us.

The *prophetic* office consists of Christ's teaching, prophecy, and miracles. All three are the outward expression of his relation to God (pp. 443-45). But Schleiermacher de-emphasizes the miracles, partly to avoid the usual debate over them, but primarily to keep the focus on the power of Jesus' person. His teaching and prophecy are so complete that Jesus brings an end to prophecy, miracles, and teaching, i.e., there can be no advance beyond the knowledge of God given by him. Schleiermacher also rejects the distinction between the teaching of Jesus and teachings about Christ, since this divides his person, bound up with God revealed in him, from ideas derived from him (pp. 444-45).

The *priestly* office consists of the fulfillment of the Law, Christ's atoning death, and his intercession with the Father on our behalf. Schleiermacher uses the distinction between active and passive obedience (or suffering), but is quick to stipulate that the two cannot be separated, since actions upon him produced reactions always consistent with his own commitment to the divine will.

The active obedience refers to the way the sinless Christ represents us before God, which is comparable to the role of the high priest before God on behalf of the sinful people (p. 454). As we are incorporated into Christ, God sees us in Christ and thereby we are declared righteous, which is the meaning of imputed righteousness.

The passive obedience refers to Christ's suffering on our behalf (p. 457). Just as membership in a community always involves sharing in and bearing the sufferings of others, such is the case with Christ, though he chooses fellowship with sinners and freely bears their guilt and sufferings. Christ's identification with us culminates in his death on the cross. Since we are set free from sin and punishment by the sufferings of the cross, the cross is a revelation of self-denying love. It rightly confirms the holiness and blessedness of Jesus and reveals "the way in which God was in Him to reconcile the world to Himself" (p. 458). Schleiermacher summarizes the meaning of the active and passive obedience by pointing to the centrality of Christ: God sees us in Christ and we see God in Christ. So he writes:

> And just as the active obedience of Christ has its properly high-priestly value chiefly in the fact that God regards us in Christ as partners in his obedience, so the high-priestly value of His passive obedience consists chiefly in this, that we see God in Christ, and envisage Christ as the most immediate partaker in the eternal love which sent Him forth and fitted Him for His task. (p. 459)

From this priestly role of Christ, several related points follow. While Christ means an end to all priesthood, his priestly ministry now passes to the church: as Christ suffered, so we are called to share in the sufferings of the world; as Christ supports our prayers before the Father for us, so the church is called to intercede for the world with God.

In his office as *King*, Christ's authority extends over the community of faith, not the world, which remains under the rule of God the Father. This allows Schleiermacher to affirm the distinction between church and state, as well as several important points: Christ's rule is over the community of the church, not isolated individuals, and he possesses all the church needs for its spiritual life. As the church extends the redemption of Christ in the world, there can be no question that Christ intended to found the church (p. 467).

If what has been presented reveals how Schleiermacher adopted and revised traditional doctrines, we may now list what he clearly rejected. Ever mindful of the sensitive nature of these matters, on more than one occasion Schleiermacher shifts from criticism to reinterpretation, so that the emphasis will fall on what is gained, rather than what is lost.

With respect to Christ's active obedience, three problems are noted: (1) Christ's obedience was not offered to the Law as an external demand but to the will of God. (2) His obedience was not offered *in our place,* either as a substitute for our obligation or because it possessed such extraordinary value that it compensates for our failure. (3) Nor can it be *for our advantage,* in the sense that in and of itself it changes our relation to God. Christ's power arises from his relation to God, and our redemption arises only through fellowship with him (pp. 455-57).

With respect to Christ's passive obedience, two ideas are rejected: (1) There can be no place for a *wounds theology,* which focuses on the details of Christ's suffering. Such a practice incorrectly identifies the value of Christ's death with the suffering itself rather than Christ's fellowship with us and his commitment to God. (2) Also rejected is the long-standing view that the suffering of Christ is an exchange required by divine justice (pp. 459ff.). Schleiermacher opposes this in part because it assumes that the divine nature in Christ suffered, generating a value exceeding the burden of sin. God cannot suffer, nor does God demand to be satisfied by punishment (pp. 459-60). But then Schleiermacher shifts from straightforward denial to positive reinterpretation. Christ did in fact make satisfaction for us, in the sense that he brings redemption and is the source of our new life (p. 461). His death is vicarious, but not in ways often claimed: it does not relieve us from the acknowledgment of sin or our obligation to pursue the spiritual life, nor did his taking our place mean that we could have done what he did. But it is vicarious in his sympathy for our sin and his bearing of the suffering that rightfully should have fallen on others. In this regard, Schleiermacher again notes that those in Christ are called upon to share in the fellowship of his suffering. Finally, in an irenic effort to find common ground with traditionalists, Schleiermacher proposes that we may indeed call Christ our *suffering representative.* By this he means that he represents us before God, who sees us in Christ, and that his sympathy with us leads us to a fuller awareness of our sin (pp. 661-62).

Included in the redemptive work of Christ is the creation of the church. On the one hand, the church is grounded in the one decree of God, which is revealed in the divine causality at work from creation and preservation to redemption. The doctrine of election points to the fact that the new life in Christ — the Kingdom of grace — is ultimately grounded in a divine good pleasure (p. 556).[15] On the other hand, the church can only be explained as a community of the Spirit of Christ, i.e., Spirit of God or Holy Spirit (cf. Pars. 121-25). The bestowal of the Spirit upon the church is both Christ's gift to the church and the union of God with the believers in a new vital unity. It is the continued presence of Christ, which allows the church to witness to Christ and participate in fellowship with him. As the community of Christ, it witnesses to the Kingdom of God until that Kingdom and the world are one.

However one assesses Schleiermacher's Christology, it is helpful to observe his own assessment. He saw it standing between two unacceptable approaches: the *magical* and the *empirical* (pp. 428-38). On the one hand, the *magical* disconnects claims to spiritual power from the community or even fellowship with Christ. Miracles as isolated supernatural events, the Bible as a self-evident book, even the death of Jesus as efficacious in and of itself or somehow accruing salvation for others — all these things strike Schleiermacher as a magical move away from actual fellowship with Christ in the church. On the other hand, the *empirical* employs only natural categories and can even dispense with Jesus. Religion as ideas, or as practices that generate progress toward perfection based on human capabilities, becomes the standard. Against these two options, Schleiermacher judged his approach to be the *mystical:* the redeeming power of God is disclosed in Jesus Christ and continues through the community of Christ and the Spirit. The personal, social, and historical language introduced by Schleiermacher was not intended to reduce theology to anthropology, but to emphasize how it is that God is present to us. The spiritual relation to God in Christ is mediated to us by participation in the life of the redeemed community of Christ. It possesses the same twofold structure described in the formula for Christ's person. It cannot be verified in any worldly way but it can be confessed.

E. God Is Love

The reader who persists to the very end of *The Christian Faith* does indeed find a reward. There we find that it is love (and wisdom) that defines God. If so many earlier sections were dominated by highly technical language and Schleiermacher's caution regarding anthropomorphic usage, at this point

---

15. It is not surprising, given Schleiermacher's emphasis on the one decree and absolute causality, that he would affirm predestination. But no effort is made to resolve the question why some appear to be included in the new life in Christ and others not included. Either we must take comfort in the grace that stands at the beginning or await the final ending to discover the answer to such questions (cf. Par. 120).

there is an abundance of personal images: love and wisdom, self-imparting and self-communication, the union of God in Christ and the Spirit with the church, the world as a work of art. These images emphasize the personal nature of God and reveal why Schleiermacher placed so much weight on these two attributes. Love and wisdom name the character of that divine causality that has been described in each stage of the system. The Whence — that indeterminate but fearsome power described as the correlate to the feeling of absolute dependence — is now named by the redemption in Jesus Christ. The divine causality — that overwhelming activity flowing from the one decree — is now named as the power active in love and wisdom, which moves all things toward the Kingdom of God.

To understand how Schleiermacher can arrive at such a conclusion, we need only be reminded that his theology as a whole represents the interaction of confessions regarding God and Christ. It is not until the end that the two reach their ultimate union in the final affirmation regarding God. To trace this movement, let us first review the two major themes.

1. God as Absolute Causality

Throughout *The Christian Faith*, Schleiermacher describes God as absolute causality, in which there is no passivity. This view of God underlies the entire theology and is decisive at major points. We encounter it initially in the definition of religion. The sense of being in relation to God and not some part of or even the entire world rests on the claim that we are never absolutely dependent on the world. In our relations to the world we always retain an element of freedom. When we conceive the world, we find that it consists of a network of absolute dependence upon something other than itself. It is because God is active upon the self and the world that we are conscious of the determination of the self by that which is over against us. But this underlying view of God was also determinative for understanding God's redemptive activity. Schleiermacher had no patience with the anthropomorphic biblical narratives that describe action and reaction between God and humanity. Nor could he conceive of a reaction to sin as separate from the original decree, lest such a distinction imply that God's plans have been altered or that Jesus Christ appears only as a response to human sin, but not intended before the creation of the earth. Thus, while holiness and justice are indeed attributes that describe the essence of God, in his final judgment they are subordinated as preparations of the work of love. Likewise, such an overwhelming sovereignty of God created problems for the definition of sin itself. While he affirms the reality of sin, which corrupts humanity, it is difficult to speak of sin in the language of rebellion and warfare. In the conclusion we shall return to some of the difficulties created by this view of God. Here the point is to emphasize how the view of God's absolute causality is crucial for the entire theology.

2. The Redemption Brought by Jesus Christ

The second element that shapes this theology is the redemption brought by Jesus Christ. Schleiermacher's theology is customarily described as Christocentric, given the central place accorded to Christ. Richard R. Niebuhr has argued with good reason that it is more appropriate to speak of this theology as Christomorphic, i.e., everything is shaped or determined by the redemption of Jesus Christ.[16] Such a statement, however, is itself quite complex. On the one hand, it contains the recognition that while Christ re-forms our relation to God, the relation to God — however deformed or incoherent — is not totally equal to our relation to Christ. No matter how much we elevate Christ with titles such as Mediator and Redeemer, Christ still points to God. This perspective is built into *The Christian Faith* by the insistence on doing theology in two parts: what is presupposed by and what is determined by Christian consciousness. The distinction is difficult and allows for endless misinterpretations. Yet it makes an essential point, which is also conveyed by the outline of Calvin's *Institutes*. The doctrine of God and the doctrine of Christ are logically distinct, even though as Christians we may not remember a time when they were separated. But on the other hand, the Christomorphic concept affirms the transformation of our relation to God (or the Other, however else conceived) by the redemption of Jesus Christ. The movement of theology cannot be an uninterrupted progress from creation to Christ, but must include the tension between sin and the new life Christ brings.

The tension expressed in this Christomorphic approach is illustrated by Schleiermacher's ambivalence regarding the appropriate title for Jesus. If theology is the unfolding of the completion of creation in Jesus Christ, then the appropriate title would be *Mediator*. But if theology must deal with the tension of sin and grace, then the title of *Redeemer* comes to the foreground. On principle, Schleiermacher acknowledges that Mediator is the preferred and more appropriate title in light of God's single decree. But in actual fact, the organization of the theology reflects the importance of Christ the Redeemer. Christ is the completion of creation, but in the face of sin and evil. The cross does have an essen-

---

16. Niebuhr, pp. 21-228.

tial place in Schleiermacher's theology; it is not all about Christmas. Jesus is the last and new Adam (the Mediator), but also the true Adam (the Redeemer).

3. Naming God

The tension between the two themes of God as absolute causality and the redemption of Jesus Christ is also reflected in the way Schleiermacher speaks of God. It is not resolved until the final discussion of the divine love. Before we consider this, we need to clarify how and where he speaks of attributes of God.

There are eight attributes developed throughout the parts of the system: In Part I, four are presupposed by the consciousness of sin and grace (eternity, omnipresence, omnipotence, and omniscience). In Part II, two relate to the consciousness of sin (holiness and justice) and two to the consciousness of grace (love and wisdom). The status of these attributes has been complicated by Par. 50, where Schleiermacher stated that attributes do not refer to anything special in God but to our relation to God. On the surface, this appears to contradict the declaration that "God is love" and places all of the attributes into a provisional status. But if we read the explanatory sections, as well as other relevant sections throughout the work, this was not his intent. He did not wish to say that we only know the relations between God and us or that we do not know God's essence. Rather his intention was twofold: First, divine attributes are not separate or distinct aspects of God. If they were, we would rightfully ask how they relate to one another. The attributes are not separate parts of God; God is one and all attributes describe the one essence of God (cf. Par. 50). Second, Schleiermacher's entire theology was constructed in opposition to what he called a speculative approach, i.e., the claim to speak of God apart from God's relation to us. Speculation assumes we can describe the inner life of God as observers, or by means of natural theology delineate the difference between God's inner life and God in relation, between God hidden and revealed (Par. 50.1-2). His preference would have been not to speak of attributes at all, since here again a distinction is implied between essence and attributes. Nevertheless, he declares that the attributes describe the divine causality acting upon us and as such describe the essence of God (cf. Par. 51.2).

Where things get complicated is in Schleiermacher's claim that *only* love expresses the essence of God (Par. 167.1).[17] Having worked so hard to clarify

---

17. It should be noted that seven of the eight attributes are introduced in Paragraphs with the language: "God is. . . ." Only in the case of wisdom does Schleiermacher refrain from saying "God is wise." His reason is that wisdom is basically an aspect of love.

the nature of the attributes and to develop them throughout the system, on what basis can he now distinguish them? The long and complicated answer is that as he concludes the work, he now wishes to prioritize the attributes on the basis of distinctions suggested earlier: (1) Those attributes presupposed by sin and grace are basically adjectival in nature, qualifying the divine causality. Since they are indeterminate regarding the character of God, they are subordinated to love. (2) Holiness and justice describe the divine causality in relation to sin and evil, but the real goal of the decree is the completion of creation in Christ. Therefore, holiness and justice are judged to be preparatory states of the divine love and must be merged into the work of love (Par. 167.2). (3) Wisdom is "the art (so to speak) of realizing the divine love perfectly" (p. 727). Wisdom is so closely integrated into love that the two are merged. Now if we pressed these distinctions, we would end up with three classes of attributes. Such a situation, however, would only bring us back to the problem of different types, either implying divisions in God or opening the way for a speculative commentary on the inner life of God. Thus Schleiermacher stays with the formal structure of the system, wherein there are eight attributes that express the divine essence, while at the same time affirming that love (joined with wisdom) is the attribute that reveals the character of God.[18]

But the short answer to the primacy of love is the Christomorphic character of Schleiermacher's theology. The redemption in Christ is the pivot (i.e., *Angelpunkt,* or crucial point or hinge) in the divine government of the world (Par. 165.1). Everything in the one decree, from creation to preservation, moves toward this point. At the center is the self-communication of God in the union with Christ and with the church through the Spirit. Love, says Schleiermacher, is the will "to unite self with neighbour and to will to be in neighbour" (Par. 165.1). There is, therefore, no other way to conceive of God's underlying disposition than by the word *love.*

This leads Schleiermacher to define love and wisdom so that the latter is virtually incorporated into the concept of love as an interrelated aspect of God's governance of the world. If love names the divine self-imparting revealed in redemption, wisdom "orders and determines the world" (Par. 168). It is wisdom that prepares for and perfects the self-communication of God in Christ and the Spirit. But Schleiermacher objects to any interpretation of wisdom as the means toward love as the end. The human use of *means* and *ends*

---

18. It can be argued that Schleiermacher could have avoided the confusion created by his differentiation of the eight attributes by simply holding that love (with wisdom) is the key to understanding all, and therefore the primary way to define God. Thus I believe the matter was complicated by his intention to differentiate them, after having established through a very lengthy process, that all eight are valid and in fact do describe the divine essence.

allows for trial and error, as well as the means to be merely utilitarian devices, discarded once the end is achieved. Nor is he satisfied with the concept of governance, since here again we encounter a word that implies the interaction of opposing factions. Against these images, Schleiermacher introduces the aesthetic image of a *work of art* to explain the work of wisdom. Just as a work of art possesses beauty by the unity of form and design, so in God's wisdom there is a perfect unity of means and ends, whereby everything reflects the goal of love and contributes to its realization. It is love, then, that is the final word to be offered in describing that divine causality active in the redemption of Christ. Love stands as the motivating force behind the one decree for creation and redemption, behind the incarnation of God in Christ and the Spirit in the church. If love propels the forward movement of redemption through history, wisdom assures that all things work together toward the Kingdom of God. The section closes with a sentence filled with eschatological tension and hope: "Hence the world can be viewed as a perfect revelation of divine wisdom only in proportion as the Holy Spirit makes itself felt through the Christian Church as the ultimate world-shaping power" (Par. 169.3).

F. Concluding Comments

Schleiermacher presents us with a unique theory of atonement: It is a Second Adam Christology, based on the incarnation, which sees Christ as the completion of the creation according to the single decree of God. The tension between sin and grace is included — indeed, it provides the very structure for Part II of *The Christian Faith* — but the primary image of redemption is the new life brought by Christ and now shared through the bestowal of the Spirit in the community of Christ.

This approach is crucial for discussions of atonement because it gathers together so many traditions and currents of thought into a coherent systematic theology, which reformulates them for a new time and place. What does he gather together? If one reads the entire work, including the notes and references, it is clear that Schleiermacher took quite seriously his task of presenting a theology for Lutheran and Reformed churches. His treatment of Nicea and Chalcedon was based on careful examination of this tradition and it was clearly his intention of affirming the substance of each, even though he treated Nicea as an unfinished summary. He relied heavily on Paul, though of course his Christology is marked primarily by Johannine images. The influence of Pietism upon him appears in his definition of religion, where he avoids the scholastic and philosophical tendency toward the religion of ideas, but instead gives emphasis to the community in the redemption that Christ brings. And of course, he reflects the concerns of the modern age, with its new philosophy and science. He could not accept the possibility that faith would require a retreat from the quest for knowledge of this world.

But if he gathers together all of these elements, *The Christian Faith* is marked by his ability to synthesize them in his attempt to reformulate a theology of the person and work of Christ. This effort displayed several characteristics. First, he sought to translate the fundamental affirmations of Chalcedon into the personal, historical, and social categories of his time. Second, he developed a Christology of the incarnation, with the emphasis on the power of God working in and through the whole life of Jesus Christ. In this way he sought to overturn the magical and transactional views of Jesus. Third, by placing the emphasis on the power of God in Jesus and the new community of Christ's Spirit, he presented a Christology that he believed was intellectually defensible. This was supported by his view of religion, which sought to avoid the dangers of reductionism and anti-intellectualism.

Given the scope of his attempt at theological retrieval and reformulation, it is no wonder that his work is controversial and interpreted in a variety of ways. He is scorned as the modern liberal who rejected miracles, but at the same time as someone still caught up in fidelity to Chalcedon. Just when one thinks one has found a view of religion that opens new possibilities, one runs into a view of God who rules by one divine decree. Yet his Calvinism is tempered by his pietist reliance on the spiritual life of the community. His Christology relies on the Gospel of John rather than the synoptics, though there are important references to the Kingdom of God. He has been denounced as reducing all of theology to anthropology, but his Christocentrism dominated theology for nearly two centuries — even that of his major critics. When one takes all of this into account, one can begin to understand the judgment that his Christology is crucial for our discussion. In what follows I shall comment on four specific issues that illustrate the creative but problematic nature of Schleiermacher's reformulation.

1. The Freedom and the Risk of New Language

At two major points in his theology, Schleiermacher introduced new language: first in the definition of religion and then in the definition of the person and work of Christ. Both cases displayed great freedom in opening new ways for thinking about these subjects, while both were filled with considerable risks.

In the case of the definition of religion, Schleiermacher employed the language of his analysis of human selfhood, involving the polar elements of activity and receptivity, freedom and dependence, as well as the forms of consciousness (thinking, doing, and feeling). Such language seemed appropriate to his time, but also allowed him to avoid the reduction of religion to something else. The result was a religious definition of religion, i.e., the sense of being in relation to the sovereign God who is always active upon us. There is no doubt, however, that such language poses difficulties. On the one hand, it has been so heavily criticized and misunderstood that it is difficult to employ without some revision. After reading Athanasius, Luther, Calvin, and twentieth-century neo-orthodoxy, it is always a bit jarring to have faith described as a form of religious self-consciousness or consciousness of God. To have Jesus' divinity translated into the idea of the absolute potency of God-consciousness does not satisfy many readers today. The long list of reductionist critiques of religion makes one uneasy with language that is so technical as well as inward, or if one prefers, psychological. On the other hand, though we may agree with Schleiermacher's general methodological point that religion is not a form of philosophy or science, seldom is it carried through an entire theology with such consistency. Schleiermacher wanted to keep the critical point before us: namely, that faith is in fact a relation to God formed by Jesus Christ, but not a form of objectively verifiable knowledge. He refused to confine this point to the Introduction, while then proceeding to speak of the knowledge of God, divine attributes, the authority of the Bible, miracles and the supernatural, or the divinity of Christ, as if all these are given to us in some worldly, objective way. But his insistence on making this point has repeatedly brought down on him the criticism of subjectivism. If there were a way to prove God, or to avoid this vulnerability by a rhetorical *tour de force* of claiming that the subject of theology is God, one could understand the criticism. Perhaps our discomfort with Schleiermacher is that we resent the way in which he exposes the vulnerability of all religious language and ultimately faith itself. Religion is not a branch of philosophy, history, or morality. It is something that only the religious can confess. This attempt at understanding his intention, however, does not remove the awkwardness or the risks of this vocabulary.

In the other case, Schleiermacher set aside the fourth-century language of *nature, persona,* and the *union of natures,* in favor of a combination of personal/ historical and technical language to formulate the person and work of Christ. Oddly enough, he continued to speak of the divine and human *nature* of Christ, probably to show the parallel between the tradition and his language. This also illustrates how difficult it is to set aside the structure of the fourth-century debate. But many will not be impressed with the language of *consciousness of God,* or *absolute potency of God-consciousness.* In his defense one can ask: How else shall we describe God's presence in a person, if not by a divine agency upon the self or one's whole consciousness being determined by God's action upon us? Schleiermacher did try to connect his technical vocabulary with more traditional language when he equated the absolute potency of God-consciousness of Jesus with "God was in him." But part of the problem is that we live on the other side of the great revival of biblical studies in the twentieth century, which reintroduced biblical language. In some respects the biblical language is closer to us (e.g., covenant, prophetic witness, and Reign of God), but in other cases it is not (e.g., apocalyptic and eschatological images). Our attachment with this biblical language may be what causes us to shun his technical language of human consciousness, especially since even he never intended it to be used in preaching or liturgy (cf. Par. 15-17). While he may have been correct in naming the problematic nature of the fourth-century language, his own vocabulary is so tied to his time that it has now become foreign to us. Such a judgment still allows us to respect his intention, namely, to give expression to God's activity in Christ in a new way. One thing is clear: he sought to capture the basic structure of biblical and patristic thinking. For example, in John 17 we find the imagery of the Father sending the Son, the Son gathering disciples and then sending the disciples into the world, so that the love of the Father to the Son shall be revealed. This progression appears in Schleiermacher's Christology: Jesus Christ, the Redeemer by the power of God in him, gathers disciples (i.e., engages in person-forming activity), and then sends them forth, endowed with his Spirit to transform the world as a community of faith.

2. The Modern Worldview

Schleiermacher reflects the sensitivities of the modern age, wishing to understand reality with scientific, social, and historical categories. It is evident that he did not want to become embroiled in a debate over miracles. His emphasis on incarnation and Jesus' power to form persons enabled him to do this. But this approach also prevented him from speaking of what the gospels refer to as signs and wonders. Most important, since he held that the redemptive power of Christ was present in his life, he did not see the resurrection as the basis for claiming that Jesus is the Christ.[19] Moreover, he confined the power

---

19. This statement does not mean that Schleiermacher rejected the resurrection. To the contrary, his whole theology is founded on the redemption brought by Jesus Christ, who bestows the Spirit upon the faith community and continues to exert person-forming power

of Christ to the personal/historical dimension of human existence rather than the entire world of nature. On these points, we find a serious gulf between his position and much of contemporary biblical and theological work. Serious questions have been raised whether the entire modern worldview, and even the conception of history, are too confining.[20] We are willing to ask whether the so-called scientific worldview is itself a philosophical construct that is far too restrictive. In a postmodern worldview, it is far more difficult to say what can or cannot happen. But more important, in a world overwhelmed by demonic powers, physical and spiritual illness, and the power of death, a broader understanding of the redemption brought by Christ is required. This may well explain why the biblical imagery — even though it defies attempts at explanation from the standpoint of modernity — is so attractive and important for so much of theological work in the past sixty years.

3. The Divine Impassibility

In the twentieth century there was a general movement away from the idea of divine impassibility and in many cases, a radical affirmation that God suffers with and for the world. This represents a serious departure from Schleiermacher's perspective and for many makes his theology hard to embrace. The problems this view creates for the understanding of sin have already been noted, as well as the view of holiness and justice. Schleiermacher's merger of holiness and love suggests that the tension between them over sin in God has already been resolved, as God wills the redemption in Christ. This may be preferable to approaches that try to resolve the tension by means of an exchange or payment of a penalty, or even preferable over views that simply deny the tension. But the question can rightly be asked: Could this theology be revised so as to incorporate divine suffering? Such a move would require extensive alteration to the phenomenology of religion in the Introduction, since we have seen that it rests on the assumption that we have no freedom

---

through the church. But like his approach to the divine attributes and the doctrine of the Trinity, he insisted that doctrines must relate directly to the consciousness of grace present in the Christian community. On this basis, there is no way to discuss resurrection and ascension as historical events. He did say, however, that the claim of the resurrection does enter his system through the doctrine of Scripture, i.e., one must either accept or reject the witness of the disciples (cf. Par. 99).

20. Compare the earlier discussion of Moltmann's critique of the category of history, as well as the analysis in Richard R. Niebuhr, *Resurrection and Historical Reason* (New York: Scribner, 1957).

over against God. It would also require a thorough revision of most doctrines, since his view of God's absolute causality influences every part of the system. There is no doubt that the Christology could be reconstructed, since this in fact has happened in various views of redemption mediated through a historical community. But Schleiermacher displays all the strengths and weaknesses of a theology constructed on the basis of an absolutely sovereign divine will.

4. Christology and Trinity

The point has been made several times that Schleiermacher's Christology relies on the Gospel of John, with its themes of incarnation, spiritual power, and life transmitted to believers by means of spiritual union.[21] But here a crucial distinction needs to be made. Schleiermacher does not develop a *Christology of the Word.* He is Johannine through and through, but he does not begin by first positing the eternal Word. We can make this point by reference to the Nicene theologians. Those writers interpreted Jesus by reference to the Word of God being in him. In the face of the Arian challenge, they then argued that the Word is equal to the Father, true light from true light, unbegotten and not made. But Schleiermacher could not endorse this approach for two reasons: First, the Christian consciousness is only aware of the redemption that Christ brings. It can legitimately infer, according to his method, that this could only happen because of the presence of God in him. But that was as far as he could go. On his terms, we have no way of speaking of an eternal Word separate from God the Father before creation and redemption, or of determining the relation of Father, Son, and Holy Spirit in God. Second, he considered that a Christology of the Word — as represented by the tradition of Alexandria — invariably moved in the direction of the Word dominating the union with Jesus. As we saw in the discussion of Athanasius, the Alexandrians quite willingly equated the second person of the Trinity with the person of Jesus, thereby threatening his full humanity. Schleiermacher made the decision to develop Christology outside of the context of the Trinity primarily because of this Christological problem. From his view, the *enhypostatic* union tilted too far toward the absorption of Jesus' humanity into the person of the Word.

21. It is worth noting that there are over 130 references to John's gospel in *The Christian Faith,* far exceeding those to all of the synoptic gospels. Yet the number of references to the entire Pauline corpus exceeds those to John.

This leads directly to his treatment of the doctrine of the Trinity, in the Conclusion of the theology. What he considered to be the positive intent of this doctrine (namely, the union of God in Christ and the church through the Spirit) had already been affirmed in earlier sections (cf. Pars. 93-98 and 121-23). Thus the doctrine of the Trinity summarizes the heart of the Christian faith, i.e., "the coping-stone of Christian doctrine . . ." (p. 739). But he could not say more about this doctrine, nor utilize it in the formation of the system, for several reasons. First, as just noted, doctrines must be directly inferred from the Christian religious consciousness. Whereas the affirmation of God in Christ was a direct inference, he found no basis for speaking of the three personae, their relation to one another, or to the one nature of God.[22] Second, he saw no way to resolve the problem of unity and plurality in the Trinitarian doctrine, which has resulted in a continual imbalance one way or the other. He was especially opposed to assigning functions to each person. Third, since the Reformers did not subject the doctrine to serious consideration, it must be considered unsettled and waiting for future revision. A fourth reason may be added, as noted above, namely, that the Trinitarian language pushed Christological reflection toward the supremacy of the divine over the human in Jesus.

For anyone who considers the doctrine of the Trinity as an essential affirmation of faith, this treatment is very disappointing, especially in light of the fact that the basic affirmations regarding the Trinity are so crucial to his theology: on the one hand, there is the twofold union of God with Christ and God in the Spirit with the church; on the other hand, the elements of ultimacy, relationality, and intentionality are either implied or present in his discussion of the divine attributes. This is especially the case with respect to love and wisdom. But true to his methodology, he insisted that we have no basis for stepping outside of our perspective as recipients of grace to discuss the intra-Trinitarian relations of the three personae. He granted that Christians could make the initial inference that God was in Christ, thereby agreeing fully with Athanasius. But his concerns about what he considered unsettled matters ultimately prevented him from a fuller embrace, even though the doctrine was given a place of pre-eminence in the Conclusion.

22. Schleiermacher argued that the prologue in John does not lead directly to Nicea, since both sides in that debate appealed to the same texts in John. Furthermore, he considered the debates leading to Nicea to arise because the Word had been "eternalized and made antecedent to the union" of God in Christ. In effect, the position he is taking is that one can avoid such debates by limiting the affirmation to "God in Christ" and not positing an eternal Word, which must then be related to God the Father and the Spirit with the elaborate construct of the final doctrine (Par. 170.2).

Theories of Atonement

D. Reconciliation

Chapter 8 Christ the Way to the
Knowledge of God

H. Richard Niebuhr

> *It may well be that the meaning of the cross must become apparent
> to our time in new situations somewhat as the meaning of the
> spherical nature of the earth has become apparent in a new way to
> us in recent years.*[1]

H. RICHARD NIEBUHR

A. General Background

While it can be said that every atonement theory tells us something about
God, the theory we shall now discuss makes the restoration of the knowledge
of God the central theme. To understand this theory, we need to recall the pe-
culiar way the Bible approaches what we in our time call the knowledge of
God.

In the traditions of the Patriarchs, Exodus, and Prophets, the encounter
with God reveals something about God. What was hard to grasp, then as now,
was that such knowledge involved a double discovery regarding God and ourselves. The encounter with God always reveals a God who stands over against
our preferred views and personal longings for the sacred. Such a revelation —
of who God is and who God is not — ultimately shatters as well as creates a
knowledge of God. In a parallel way, the discovery of who and what God intends us to be stands over against our preferred assumptions regarding ourselves. This tension, no less traumatic than the first, again shatters and creates
a new image of ourselves in the very image of the Creator. Such a knowledge
of God needs further analysis.

---

1. H. Richard Niebuhr, "War as Crucifixion," *The Christian Century* 60 (April 28, 1943): 314.

First, to be in the presence of God is to encounter one who is sovereign. God is free and uncontrollable. While God's mercy and goodness are trustworthy, God's ways are unpredictable, especially in relation to the devices and desires of humankind. The mysterious encounter of Moses makes the point. Moses' request for the name of God is well understood against the background of ancient religious practices to influence and control sacred power. But we should not imagine that the twenty-first century has less interest in such human desire to control life-giving power. The key for such control is access to the very name of God. Moses' request is covered with presumed innocence — it is only so that people will know who it is that has sent me. But God will not be cornered. The request is refused because God will be God and Moses must accept his role as one sent. The name given is both evasive and revealing. Moses can name God and call upon God, but Moses cannot control or manipulate God. Every generation after Moses will discover the tensions involved in this sovereign God.

Second, the tensions of God's name are continually described by the dynamic of holiness and love. To know God is to be in the presence of holiness and love. Both attributes set God apart from humankind. We willingly grant that there is a gap between God's holiness and ours, but compliment ourselves by assuming perfect continuity between God's love and our own. But if our holiness is flawed, no less is our love. The divine love terrifies us as much as the divine holiness and the history of Israel can well be read as a commentary on the relation of holiness and love. Let us remember that Israel never separated the two or affirmed only one, though it was often tempted to do so. Thus Israel's history reveals the working out of all the tensions between holiness and love. The sorrowful and tragic story of the Golden Calf in Exodus makes the point.

Third, to know the sovereign God is to know God's promises and live in the expectation of their fulfillment. For Israel, God is known in this world (understood as creation) and in the ambiguous and tragic events of human life. The key categories for knowing God are covenantal promises, Torah and the land, justice and mercy, hearing and remembering.

If faith in God in ancient Israel can be characterized in this way, then our use of the word knowledge needs to be carefully defined. In spite of current debates regarding postmodernism, our culture still links knowledge with scientific and/or philosophical paradigms that value a critical, independent reason, seeking objective truth. This enterprise is viewed primarily as a cognitive act, which is best achieved when one separates it from personal or cultural values. The history of such a view reveals a great divide between the quest for knowledge, so conceived, and religious commitments. A quite different view is presented in the biblical perspective. In the Bible, knowledge of God involves more than cognitive recognition of clear and distinct ideas. Nor is it best grasped by stepping outside of time and space in search of a neutral and objective point of view. It is not descriptive knowledge that can be filed away as facts, nor is it practical in the sense that it will allow us to use and control things. It is a highly moral knowledge that confronts and challenges existing ideas of God and ourselves. In the language of our time we would speak of such knowledge as *self-involving* and *relational*. The former refers to the way this knowledge makes claims on our minds and hearts, on how we value ourselves and express ourselves in acts of will. The latter refers to the relational character of our existence: the self in relation to God, oneself, other people, and the world. The true knowledge of God orders all of these relations for life in community. To know God is to be faithful to God and one another. How apt that in Deuteronomy, faithfulness to God is to remember who God is and what God has done, as well as to love God and neighbor. By contrast, sin is to fail to remember.

The highly moral and personal character of this knowledge requires that it be freely internalized. The moral behavior commanded by the Law is to be the free expression of hearts and minds. Thus, what is required of us is not only specific behavior, but to love God with our hearts, minds, and strength and to find joy in God. The positive expectation underlies the harshness of the prophets. Their rage is not only directed at immoral behavior, but at the pretense of true piety. For Isaiah, in the Day of the Lord, God will see not as we see things but see into the hearts and minds of people. There shall be no security in pretense and concealment. For Jeremiah, the covenant is to be written on our hearts. To know God is to do certain things, but also to be faithful in the depth of ourselves.

The fact that this knowledge of God entails fidelity to God leads to an inevitable crisis, given human mistrust and disobedience. Those given the knowledge of God prove to be unfaithful, from the profound stories in Genesis 3–11 to those of national catastrophe in the Book of Judges. In utter frustration Isaiah laments that ox and ass know their master, but Israel will not acknowledge the very source of its life. Or to go back to the very inception of Israel's formation at Sinai, no sooner is the covenant sealed than Israel forsakes Yahweh for the worship of tangible idols. In all of these examples, it becomes evident that what is crucial for the biblical tradition is not the knowledge of the existence of God as a cognitive fact (compared, for example, to knowing that New York is a city on the east coast of the United States), but fidelity to the God of the promises.[2]

---

2. The attempts to interpret the Sinai event in terms contrary to covenant fidelity have undermined the essential message of the Mosaic covenant. For example, the philosophical reading

The crisis created by human infidelity follows a familiar schema: God is known and commitments are made; there is a break in fidelity by human beings; a time of judgment occurs; the covenant is restored through human repentance and divine forgiveness. This cycle is repeated so often that in the Book of Judges it becomes an editorial outline for telling the story of each generation. The prophets utilize their own form of it to remind Israel of promises, infidelity, and idolatry, followed by judgment and a call to repentance. In this cycle of covenant making, breaking, and renewal, we see why the restoration of the true knowledge of God involves atonement. The absence of the knowledge of God is never a faultless situation wherein one can claim innocence. The absence of true knowledge is not ignorance but idolatry and infidelity — as becomes evident in Israel's history. Therefore finding the true knowledge of God always requires the recognition that we have turned from God. The situation is a highly charged moral one. To make matters worse, not only are we comfortable in our state of loss, but even when we become conscious of such loss, we are unable to recover the true knowledge of God. What is needed, therefore, is not mere instruction but the restoration of our relation with God. This is more than an intellectual discovery; it is an act of spiritual transformation.

When we turn to the New Testament it should not surprise us that Jesus appears in Mark as the prophet of the coming Rule of God. Knowledge is central, but it is the knowledge unique to the covenant tradition of Moses and the prophets. In a first-century world of broken covenants, multiple interpretations of traditions, and foreign oppression, Jesus proclaims the pres-

---

of Exodus, as a revelation of the existence of God as the Highest Being ("I Am Who I Am"), and thereby the starting point for philosophical reflections, diverts attention from the covenant and the new relationship between God and Israel. Such an interpretation moves the discussion of the knowledge of God to the realm of God's existence. In the modern age discussions about the knowledge of God become involved in questions regarding essence and existence and whether the ideal can be known in the realm of existence. A somewhat unexpected example of this misconstrual appears in Schoenberg's opera *Moses and Aaron*. In a complete rewriting of the story, Aaron becomes the spokesman for popular religion seeking tangible signs and symbols, while Moses appears as the austere advocate of a God who cannot be known by things of this world. Completely lost is the theme of God's fidelity in making the covenant or the call for Israel to be faithful. Yet another reinterpretation, on the popular level — but no less influential in shaping the religious mind of Americans — is Cecil B. DeMille's stylized epic *The Ten Commandments*. In this film the narrator makes clear that the basic theme for the Exodus drama is the freedom of the Israelites from bondage in Egypt and the promise of the land. In a culture that values freedom and considers the land a part of its chosen destiny, the story of the formation of Israel as a covenant people is transmuted into another sanction for the popular American dream.

ence of God with the twofold demand so unique to older covenants: repent and believe. This knowledge of God places us in right relation with God and neighbor. It is made possible, against worldly skepticism and fear, only by the intervention of the ever-present and amazing grace of God. It continually upsets things by calling men and women to a new vocation to love and serve.

There are many descriptive and honorific titles, as well as metaphorical images, assigned to Jesus in the NT that link him with the true knowledge of God. Initially the title of "teacher" introduces this general theme. The importance of this teacher is foreshadowed in the Lucan and Matthean birth narratives, with hymns of expectation and thanksgiving. The mouth of the speechless is opened and the aged finally see the revealing of God's mercy. Even the story of the boy Jesus instructing the elders in the temple anticipates what is to come. The synoptic gospels draw lines of contact between Jesus and Moses (e.g., forty days in the wilderness, the transfiguration), and make his role as teacher one of the dominant images (Sermon on the Mount and the parables).

But as helpful as the title "teacher" is in locating Jesus in relation to his counterparts and the tradition, the title "teacher" moves to the background as the story progresses toward Holy Week. In the post-resurrection world of the early church, it is seldom used as a primary title for Jesus. The reason for this is that, by itself, the title "teacher" does not carry the heavier meanings contained in the story of redemption and salvation. While students may love their teachers and be indebted for new insight, seldom does the student-teacher relation lead to the kind of spiritual transformation contained in the cross and resurrection. For this reason, other titles appear in the attempt to describe Jesus. One is of course "prophet," though it does not become common in confessional statements in the New Testament or the early church. In most instances it appears in the form of questions as to who Jesus is, or in comparisons. The use of "Son of God" and "Son of Man" moves the attempt to describe Jesus to an even higher level, though there is no consensus as to what either of these titles means. But whatever the outcome of that debate, both terms are suggestive of our theme: Jesus is associated with the knowledge of God. For example, if the title "Son of Man" is in fact an apocalyptic image of a heavenly figure, then it does have implications for a revealing of God. When we turn to the most prized honorific title assigned to Jesus in the early church, namely "Lord," such a title conveys implications for the true knowledge of God. If Jesus is Lord, then our knowledge of God is reconfigured by what Jesus said and what happened in cross and resurrection.

There are also a host of metaphorical images that are central to the theme of the restoration of the knowledge of God. Some of the most important represent the Johannine vision of Jesus. Jesus is the Word: the Word present at creation, the Word present in all things, the Word rejected by the world, and the Word made flesh. Jesus is the Light that shines in the darkness of the world and which the world can never extinguish. Jesus is the Way — to God and to our selves. Jesus is the Truth that shall set us free. Such truth is not the sort of encyclopedic knowledge that leads to analysis and control of the world, but the truth about life-giving relations with God, our selves, and others. In all of these titles and images, Jesus is described as the one who changes the way we know God, and in so knowing God also come to love God and one another.

B. The Theory in Outline

1. The problem is that the true knowledge of God, revealed in the creation, has been lost because of human sin. Forsaking the true God, humankind has substituted the creation for the Creator. As a consequence, humankind is now characterized by idolatry and unable to discern the truth regarding God or its own life.

2. Jesus appears as the agent of God, revealing the truth about both God and humanity. He announces the Rule of God and gathers a new covenant community that embodies life-giving knowledge. Entrance into the new community, however, can only occur through repentance, wherein one forsakes the idols of the world and false trust in things of this world, including oneself.

3. Jesus is rejected by the world in its resistance to God. In his suffering and death, Jesus remains faithful to God and dies for the sake of God's Rule.

4. Jesus is raised by God as a demonstration of judgment against the false wisdom and power of the world and a validation of Jesus as the chosen one of God. In this double act of judgment and grace, the true knowledge of God is revealed. The gospel proclamation that Jesus is Lord is therefore a call to turn from the idols of the world and from a false confidence in things or self, and trust in God.

5. The church is therefore constituted as the community of good news, forsaking confidence in things of this world and relying solely on the knowledge of God as gracious Father. However, the Christian life will be defined as a continual process of conversion, wherein all of our intellectual and moral claims are subject to the judgment of God and we ourselves are continually renewed by the true Word.

C. The Witness of Faith: H. Richard Niebuhr

> This conversion and permanent revolution of our human religion through Jesus Christ is what we mean by revelation.[3]

In American theology of the twentieth century, the theme of Christ the way to the true knowledge of God is best represented in the writings of H. Richard Niebuhr. He was born in 1894, the son of a pastor of the Evangelical Synod of North America, consisting of German immigrants from the Church of the Prussian Union. If his brother Reinhold Niebuhr lived in the realm of Paul and Luther, where everything was understood in polarities and dualities (sin and grace, law and gospel, Christ and Satan, love and justice), H. Richard Niebuhr lived in the tradition of the prophets and Calvin, where everything stands under the one sovereign God. In such a world, knowing God is crucial, but it is always tied to the ambiguities of human love and hate, strength and weakness. Life is therefore ultimately defined in terms of trusting and obeying this sovereign God in times when God appears absent or present, terrifying or gracious. Given the fact that human life is viewed as coming to terms with God's sovereignty, Niebuhr redefined ethics as responding to the gracious and sovereign will of God. For example, consider the title of his book on ethics: *The Responsible Self.*

Three works stand together as Niebuhr's reflection on the meaning of Christ: *The Meaning of Revelation* (1941), *Faith on Earth* (1989), and *Radical Monotheism and Western Culture* (1960).[4] While the second was published long after his death in 1962, the essays come from the 1940s and 1950s (*FOE*, p. xi). Some of the essays added to the major essay in *Radical Monotheism* also come from earlier years. Add to this the fact that *The Meaning of Revelation* announces most of the themes taken up in the later two works. Thus it can be said that these three works stand together as Niebuhr's continuing reflection over some twenty years on the subject of faith, revelation, and Christ.

It is very difficult to describe the progression of thought in these three

---

3. H. Richard Niebuhr, *The Meaning of Revelation* (New York: Macmillan, 1941), p. 191. Henceforth all references to this work will be given in the text and designated by the symbol *MR*.

4. Reference to the first of these is given in Note 3; the other two are: H. Richard Niebuhr, *Faith on Earth: An Inquiry into the Structure of Human Faith*, ed. Richard R. Niebuhr (New Haven: Yale University Press, 1989); and H. Richard Niebuhr, *Radical Monotheism and Western Culture with Supplementary Essays* (New York: Harper and Brothers, 1960). Henceforth references to *Faith on Earth* will be given in the text and designated by the symbol *FOE* and those to *Radical Monotheism* will be designated by the symbol *RM*.

works. It obviously is not the case that they move from preliminary to final formulations. *The Meaning of Revelation,* published in 1941, foreshadows many developments in Protestant theology over the next thirty years. There are passages in *Faith on Earth* that are far more probing in the examination of Christ and his reform of our faith than the later essays in *Radical Monotheism.* One can only imagine that Niebuhr lived with all of these themes for several decades and was continually rethinking the issues. The fact that the essays in *Faith on Earth* did not reach publication by his own hand testifies to this ongoing process that could never be completed.

On first reading one notes the distinctive style and approach to the subject. Niebuhr did not adopt one of the standard approaches of systematic theology. Nor did he explicitly use traditional categories. For example, he seldom uses the language of the two natures of Christ, or standard theological headings such as Creation, Sin, Redemption, or Church. Distracted by the absence of these touchstones, some readers have failed to persist in reading, missing the fact that Niebuhr ultimately moves along lines parallel to the creedal affirmations. My assessment is that Niebuhr was trying to find an appropriate way to speak of God in a world where so many traditional options had been called into question. He obviously could not pretend to write as an objective observer about God, as if God were given to our apprehension as objects of this world. Likewise he clearly refused to treat theology as a series of ideas or doctrines that contain God, and that, if only expounded properly, would produce faith. While it is commonplace to say that God cannot be contained in theology or doctrines, Niebuhr took this so seriously that it prevented him from seeing the traditional theological agenda as the natural starting point for reflection. But if there was no objective point of departure, or a prescribed method given by church doctrine, how then could one engage in theological reflection? Niebuhr sought an answer by examining the life of faith as one seeking to be faithful. That the three works considered here retrace many of the same questions and return time and again to the same issues, suggests that the task was always a process that was never quite completed. So he sought to speak of faith in all of its expressions, religious and nonreligious, speaking as a person seeking faith immersed in communities of faith.

At the same time he could not retreat into the security or privacy of the believing community, especially if that meant confinement to private language. It was important to be in conversation with other faith communities as well as those claiming no faith. This meant that in the examination of faith, he needed to speak in a public way, using language not dominated by doctrinal or even religious usage. It also made it possible, for writer and reader, to enter into reflection on issues fully open to love and fear, belief and unbelief.

Time and again the discussions occur in that strange place where we are try-ing to discover something about God that will be truly faithful to God and ourselves. Paul's fear and trembling are the background for many of these dis-cussions. If it were not the case, then the process would simply be transmit-ting information or clarifying the meaning of statements within the life of the religious community. While these are important tasks, they do not always get close to the matter of faith. The move toward a public language, therefore, was Niebuhr's attempt to place the conversation in the tension of belief and unbelief, trust and mistrust. If he sought clarity regarding faith, it was as much for those inside the community of faith as for those outside it. Thus he wove together two approaches: one speaking out of faith, the other searching for faith in an unbelieving world.

At times Niebuhr engages in descriptive analysis of the religious life, in order to establish his basic understanding of faith. In *Radical Monotheism*, this approach is very abstract in an attempt to develop a general phenomen-ology of faith. For example, the phrase *center of value* is used instead of God, so that faith may be viewed in the broadest terms. The same approach ap-pears in Chapter 4, "The Structure of Faith," in *Faith on Earth*, where he lays out his analysis of faith as a defining mark of human existence.

At other times, he makes it emphatically clear that if he is to speak of faith in Christ, it can only be of the living Christ known to a person, in the context of the community of faith that has nurtured such a person (cf. *FOE*, pp. 86-97). This Christ of faith is not an idea contained in doctrines, nor is he a historical fact, though all of these are related. This judgment, while at times difficult to comprehend, stems from his view that faith, as the quintessential act of persons, is a living relation with other persons and that one who is truly Person. To affirm God known in Christ is to recognize that God cannot be contained in ideas, formulas, propositions, or doctrines. This is based in part on his understanding of God's sovereignty, but also in part on his conviction that our faith is always broken and perverted. There could be no resting place in the face of the demand for continual *metanoia*.

Since Niebuhr repeats discussions of his basic analysis of faith in all three works, let us begin with what is perhaps the clearest presentation, in *Radical Monotheism*. There he proposes to speak of faith, rather than religion. In the modern world, religion has been pushed into a particular sector, often privat-ized by believers or ignored by public intellectual discourse. If religion is marked by creeds, doctrines, hymns, prayers, and practices known to ecclesial bodies, faith is a more basic human activity that appears nearly everywhere. His definition of faith has two parts: trust and loyalty. Trust is the passive side of faith, evoked from us by that which proves trustworthy. We cannot create or pretend to have trust; it emerges through time and experience. Loyalty is the active side of faith, the act of pledging the self in response to a call or cause (*RM*, pp. 16-23).

To open the analysis to the widest possible application, Niebuhr describes the object of faith as a *center of value* (*RM*, pp. 18ff.) Such a center of faith could be oneself, one's family, one's group, class, race, nation, religion, or God. The advantage of such an abstract definition of faith allows Niebuhr to argue that faith appears in every realm of human experience: religion, politics, family, economics, science, class and racial struggles, and obviously in war, where trust and loyalty are raised to the highest levels. While he is hesitant to claim that everyone has faith, he notes that he has yet to meet someone void of trust or loyalty (*RM*, p. 22).

There is an important epistemological point that needs to be added before proceeding. It stands behind Niebuhr's claim that trust and loyalty are essential marks of human life, but also places him in the tradition that runs back through the Reformers, Augustine, and the Bible. In all three works cited here, Niebuhr goes to great length to reject the split between faith and reason (cf. chapters 1 and 3, *MR*, pp. 1-42 and 91-137; chapters 1-3, *FOE*, pp. 1-42; *RM*, pp. 11-16). There is no human rationality independent of trust and loyalty. Reason always exists side by side as well as in an elaborate network of engagements of trust and loyalty. We did not come to reason in isolation from a familial or social world of trust and loyalty. Moreover, in our acts of trust and loyalty we reason for and against certain things. Our reason is always tied to our love, bound up with our total existence in time and place. And of course, this means that it bears both the responsibility for, and the consequences of, our self-centered trust and our perverse loyalties. The other side of this relation of reason to trust and loyalty is that in our faithfulness to centers of value, we employ reason for and against certain things. Wherever trust and loyalty find expression in social, political, or religious forms, more than likely such forms will display the work of human reason. This complicated relation of faith and reason therefore shapes the way Niebuhr will speak of the knowledge of God. One cannot approach the subject claiming some kind of neutrality or objectivity. One can engage in vigorous critical reflection on faith, but such reflection must be moral as well as intellectual reflection. In the end, the journey toward the knowledge of God will eventually move more and more toward the language of renewal, reform, and reconstruction.

Let us then return to the analysis of faith. Having defined faith so broadly, Niebuhr introduces a threefold distinction for differentiating faith (cf. *RM*, pp. 24-37):

1. *Polytheism* or pluralism recognizes many centers of value. It accepts the

fact that trust and loyalty are distributed between many centers, producing inevitable disagreements, tensions, and conflicts. While those in the West associate religious polytheism with premodern cultures, Niebuhr uses this type to interpret the tensions of modern life, where multiple centers of value (the state, politics, economics, professions, corporations, family, race, gender) force people to choose between conflicting loyalties.

2. *Henotheism* (literally, one god) is the attempt to make one of the many centers of value in the world into an absolute. It recognizes that others exist, but demands trust and loyalty for only one. For example, nationalism admits there are other nations, but requires absolute loyalty to one nation and denies that other nations have any claim on one's loyalty. Given the conflict and loss of life due to nationalism, racism, sexism, classism, and other ideologies, Niebuhr viewed henotheism as the greatest threat to monotheism in the modern age. Henotheism always produces conflict because it is by nature divisive and oppressive. It continually strives to make one among many the sole center of value. In biblical terms, this is the idolatry of claiming something in this world as ultimate.

3. If polytheism accepts many parts of our existence as having relative value, and if henotheism tries to absolutize one part against all the rest, *monotheism* is the attempt to see all things unified in one center of value. But to do this, two elements must be joined together. On the one hand, God must be affirmed as the source of all that is; on the other hand, all that is, as well as the source of all being and power, must be affirmed as good. It is the union of the one source with goodness that makes monotheism a radical form of faith. To again revert to more familiar biblical language, radical monotheism is the affirmation that the Creator is the Redeemer, i.e., that power and goodness are united in one God.

By stating the matter in this way, Niebuhr is basically arguing that if we cannot be monotheists, then we will at least be dualists. We will inevitably be concerned about power and, more than likely, also about goodness. Such an evaluation of human faith, Niebuhr believed, is born out by human experience: if God is the source of all that is, but is not good, we will hate God and seek goodness somewhere else. Conversely, if God is good, but powerless, we will gladly relate to God but be required to find ways to deal with what is powerful. All of this may seem quite elementary. Yet it is the consistency with which Niebuhr presses his point that allows the radical character of such monotheism to emerge. Radical monotheism can accept nothing less than the affirmation that every part of creation is of value, while also denying that any part can ever claim to be the absolute center of value. Genuine faith can only be placed in the one and true center of value by giving up all of the false loyalties — a process that inevitably will involve a revolution in our trust and loyalty.

This definition of radical monotheism, in contrast to polytheism and henotheism, lays the basis for the discussion of revelation. Niebuhr affirms that revelation is any event where faith in the one God becomes incarnate. Using the example of Moses, Niebuhr suggests that revelation embodies three characteristics: (a) God is revealed as the source of all that is; (b) God as the source of all is revealed as good; (c) human beings are called to choose God's cause as their own. The encounter of Moses is thus explicated in terms of power, goodness, and cause (*RM*, pp. 42-43). Before leaving this example, we should note how it illustrates what was said earlier about Niebuhr's hesitation in equating faith or God with doctrines. He will provide a quite formal definition of revelation (i.e., the incarnation of faith in the one God) and even go so far as to give three characteristics. But instead of then defining the one God or the revelation, he moves immediately to an example, which is a narrative of personal encounter between one person (faithful and yet highly cautious) and the powerful and holy God who announces a cause. The same approach repeatedly occurs in the other writings. Just when the reader is ready for the definitive statement that will summarize everything, Niebuhr gives an example, which is quite specific and personal.

A parallel analysis to this approach to revelation appears in *Faith on Earth*, where Niebuhr portrays human life as a fiducial process (*FOE*, cf. pp. 43-62). To be personal or a person is to engage in trust and loyalty between oneself, others, and a cause. To the extent that we seek a transcendent Person who is trustworthy, or a transcendent cause, faith becomes explicitly religious. But this does not lead to a natural theology or general concept of God. If there is, for Niebuhr, a natural state of religion or faith it is not the positive idea of a god but the sense of disappointment, disbelief, and distrust (*FOE*, p. 67). Our experience of trust will always be mixed with instances of broken trust and the discovery that our trust and loyalty have been misplaced. Thus, turning the tables on those who seek some primordial, positive definition of God as the natural basis for religion, Niebuhr suggests that if there is a natural religion it is the recognition that God is our enemy (*FOE*, p. 72). It is precisely at this point that Niebuhr introduces our encounter with Jesus Christ. Set against the background of the quest for that which is trustworthy in a world of broken trust, Niebuhr offers a view of Christ so profound and comprehensive that it constitutes a general theory of atonement.

In language consistent with orthodoxy, Niebuhr has described the human condition with the same realism as Paul, Augustine, or Calvin. "When we contemplate our human history, this network of interpersonal relations, it is not difficult to describe it as the history of treason. . . . There is no area of human conduct — not economics, not religion, not the family — which is free from the wreckage of broken words" (*FOE,* p. 81). Such realism means, however, that human faith is perverted, but not eliminated or totally destroyed (*FOE,* p. 78). Most importantly, Niebuhr believed that the starting point for thinking about Christ is not the fall but the persistent hope of salvation in the midst of the brokenness of life. Even in the face of the worst, our distrust presupposes a prior state of trust (*FOE,* p. 78).

In such a world where hope struggles with deception, we hear the story of Jesus: his loyalty to God, the betrayal by those threatened by him, and God's vindication of the forsaken one. Every story in the passion narrative leading to the events of death and resurrection reveals the key elements of trust and fidelity. But while the narrative has a large cast, it is Jesus and God who are at the center. First, there is the trust and loyalty of Jesus to God. By these acts he confirms that he is anointed of God. Among the many human figures, Jesus appears as the truly human. Second, there is the trust and loyalty of God to Jesus, whereby Jesus is called, baptized, anointed, and sent as God's messenger. In the end, it is God who raises the crucified to be Lord. Though betrayed and abandoned by his disciples, God keeps the promise (*FOE,* p. 97). By these events, but more importantly, by his relation to us as risen Lord, Jesus is revealed to possess the twofold status affirmed in the tradition of Chalcedon. Closing the reflection, Niebuhr himself claims the titles "Father" and "Son" as the final affirmations of God and Jesus: In the resurrection God is revealed as the faithful and trustworthy Father; Jesus is bestowed with power confirming his Sonship.

> The resurrection of Jesus Christ from the dead, the establishment of Jesus Christ in power, is at one and the same time the demonstration of the power of goodness and the goodness of power. But the demonstration remains a demonstration of a God who is both Father and Son, not of a Father who is identical with the Son or of a Son identical with the Father. When Jesus Christ is made known as Lord it is to the glory of God the Father. And the Absolute is made known as Father in his glorification of the Son. (*FOE,* pp. 100-101)

D. Commentary and Summary

There is a sense in which Niebuhr's general approach, as well as his style, is uniquely twentieth-century American. His own life reflected the many transitions from a tightly connected ethnic and religious culture in the Midwest to the pluralism of modern America. The radical pluralism of mid-twentieth century, with Protestant, Catholic, and Jewish traditions interacting with one another, characterized the religious culture of his time. Moreover, in a culture marked by freedom rather than tradition, such pluralism had the opportunity to create all manner of new and strange expressions of religion. Parallel to these developments was the rise of modern secularity, with its multiple criticisms of religion. These quite diverse issues always seem to be present as the context for his discussions. He is cautious about grand generalizations or claims for the justification of religion, quite willing to admit that he speaks out of a confessional position. The modern critical outlook was accepted as a given. But while he could never abandon the faith community that had nurtured him, neither could he retreat into the security of its traditional methodology and doctrinal formulations. A denominational or sectarian option was simply not possible for him. So he took up the questions of faith, God, and Christ, in a time of continual world crisis: two world wars, depression, the atomic bomb, the cold war, the racial crisis in America, and finally Viet Nam. The writings examined here suggest that his theological reflection was his way of gathering together all of these things. As a result, his writing bears several distinguishable marks.

First, while his writings do not include what we would call personal stories, they are highly personal in that they are about our life in faith. The use of the first person plural *(we* and *our)* dominates these works. They often read as the personal narrative of a pilgrim, or as a collective autobiography for the faith community. This is said mindful of the fact that at times the subject is quite abstract and difficult, especially for the first-time reader. But no matter how technical or abstract, one is always reminded that the subject is being discussed from a personal point of view.

Second, gathering all of the parts of our lives together was for Niebuhr essential to the life of every person and a decisive mark of faith. As he noted in *Radical Monotheism,* if we cannot integrate the parts of our lives, be they broken or neatly compartmentalized, then we suffer the pain of a divided self. This internal quest for unity is parallel to the attempt to find unity outside of ourselves, be it with other persons, the larger social order, and the cosmos, however these might be defined. The chief consequence of monotheistic faith is the ability to affirm unity outside of oneself, which ultimately offers the possibility of a unified selfhood (*RM,* pp. 30-31, 44-48). For Niebuhr, all of this affirms the connections between individual identity, faith, and God. When these connections are broken, there is the possibility of a shattering of our internal and external worlds.

Such an approach has decisive implications for theological reflection. What it means is that the fundamental issue in the question of the knowledge of God is really the issue of reconciliation. Given the multiple relations involved, reconciliation will have multiple levels of meaning. There is the reconciliation of the parts of an individual life, of one person to another, and of groups of persons. Niebuhr describes all of these moments of human life as marked by brokenness, mistrust, and betrayal. There is also the reconciliation of human beings to God. On the human side, this relation is marked by suspicion, anger, and fear. Such is the case because human life is filled with such a range of experiences that it is not self-evident that all of life is either from one source or that all is good. God too often appears either absent or hostile to our wants and needs. Finally, there is the reconciliation of God to us, since God also has been betrayed by the idolatry and mistrust of the world. Mindful of the deliberate turning away from God, we can only wonder what God's response will be.

Third, to speak of the knowledge of God will be a process of gathering all things together. We cannot approach the knowledge of God simply as a handed-down set of ideas or doctrines, with helpful explanations. It will involve the destruction and reconstruction of our faith in our time. This will happen because we are drawn into an analysis of our history as faithful and faithless persons. But even more important, for Christians the process will be governed by the encounter with the life, death, and resurrection of Jesus. This encounter cannot be reduced to the historical record or the life of the faith community, as indispensable as these are for the formation of faith. The data of history or the bonds of the community cannot by themselves generate true faith. Faith will ultimately be incarnate only in the personal encounter with the risen Christ, who shows the way to the God who is trustworthy.

Finally, all of this illuminates the choice of language used to describe the encounter with Jesus Christ and God. To the consternation of many readers, Niebuhr refuses to organize the material by the standard categories, or use the language of creedal formulations, such as the two natures of Christ. In the powerful opening of *Radical Monotheism*, Niebuhr declares that he wishes to speak of faith rather than religion. Other examples could be given. On the one hand, this choice of framing standard issues in nontraditional or public language reflects Niebuhr's intention to speak to those outside of, or alienated from, Christian faith. For him the modern context requires such a choice. But on the other hand, the choice is a way of affirming that doubt and alienation are also in the believing Christian. Niebuhr writes for the unbeliever and those in the faithful community who still engage in the struggle for faith. He also writes for himself.

We have emphasized that Niebuhr's writing is marked by a highly personal and public language; nevertheless his discussions are parallel to the traditional theological discussions. The doctrines of creation, fall, sin, and redemption shine through the language of the text. Thus, when he speaks of Jesus Christ the Way, it becomes apparent that Jesus is our Way to God and God's Way to us. The affirmation of the two natures of Christ is indeed present. Likewise, when he draws things to a conclusion, having explored a variety of contemporary images for God, the language of Father and Son appears. Even the main theme of reconciliation brings us back to one of the central affirmations of the Bible and the tradition. All of these examples reveal that while Niebuhr appears to avoid traditional language, in actual fact he works through issues in such a way that we are reconciled to the faithful language of previous generations.

It is appropriate to conclude, as our attempt to gather things together, by referring again to Jesus the Way to the knowledge of God. As we have stated, the way is not simple or straightforward, complicated as it is by our anger and mistrust of God. To know God also means to discover the way in which God is opposed to the idolatry and disorder of the world. Thus our Way to God and God's Way to us will involve the judgment against our false acts of trust and loyalty. When our sacred ideas and practices are shattered, we feel forsaken and God appears as our enemy. This breaking of the idols is the inevitable consequence of our propensity to invest ultimate trust and loyalty in things of this world. But Jesus is the Way not only in resisting false faith, but as our companion (*FOE*, p. 89) in the struggle for a more truthful faith. He is also the demonstration of a grace that invites us into relation with the one who is trustworthy and ultimately revealed as Father. Christian faith continually witnesses to the fact that in the encounter with Jesus' cross and resurrection, our defiance and suspicion are overcome and we receive a Word of grace. The Way to the knowledge of God, therefore, takes the form of judgment, but ultimately of grace, a shattering of our world of faith as well as its reconstruction in ways that defy our claims to justice or grace.[5] It is not the imparting of information but the reconciliation of human faith with the God who is faithful.

---

5. For a profound and courageous affirmation of the cross and the grace of God, set against all attempts to claim justice by all sides in World War II, see "War as Crucifixion," pp. 313-15.

Chapter 9 Christ the Reconciler

1 Corinthians 1–2

A. Introduction

This theory proclaims the saving power of the cross as reconciliation in the face of spiritual or ideological warfare. This is significant for two reasons: First, given the tendency to relate saving power to individual life and its problems, the Christian message is seldom so explicitly defined in terms of the social dimension (liberation and the attack on idols in the previous chapter being notable exceptions). Second, while the New Testament names a variety of disputes that involve the social dimension, these are usually treated indirectly as variations on the religious dispute over the Law. For example, disputes over circumcision, ethnicity/race, gender, or social status (i.e., poverty or slavery) are often treated as another form of one side's claiming righteousness based on works. By first comparing them to the tyranny of the law, one can then also appeal to Christ, who frees us from such tyranny. Things change, however, in the theory at hand. From the outset, the problem is social conflict so infectious that it produces spiritual warfare. Likewise, the answer is not an application of the gospel by extension, but an interpretation of the cross that goes directly to the heart of all spiritual or ideological conflict.

The source of this theory is also our case study. In 1 Corinthians 1–2, Paul deals directly with the problem of spiritual conflict. To be sure, there are other places where Paul affirms the unity of Christians over against the great divisions (social status, ethnicity, race, and gender). What is so unique about 1 Corinthians 1–2 is that Paul does not first equate ideology with something that is already problematic (e.g., legalism, ethnic or gender divisions). Here there is no "since this is like that . . . ," but instead an unrelenting denunciation of spiritual warfare in the name of the cross of Jesus. It is the thesis of this chapter, therefore, that in 1 Corinthians 1–2 we have a theology of the cross that is: (1) a distinctive theory of atonement, not like Paul's other approaches; (2) a theory of atonement that is different from all of the others considered in this study. To demonstrate both parts of this thesis we shall turn directly to the outline of the argument and then an analysis of the theory, based on 1 Corinthians 1–2.

B. Outline of the Theory

1. Human beings invariably are divided by claims to moral, intellectual, and spiritual power. These claims become the basis for social conflict and violent warfare.
2. Jesus, the Christ of God, is crucified by those in authority, making claims to wisdom and power, revealing the disorder of the world and its alienation from God.
3. Since Jesus is the Christ, whom God raised to be Lord, therefore the cross is a judgment against the world's claims to wisdom and power.
4. The gospel declares that whereas the world's claims to wisdom and power invariably lead to unhappiness and death, God's wisdom and power are given to all as a gift, received by faith.

C. The Witness of Faith: Paul's Theology of the Cross in 1 Corinthians 1–2

The letters of Paul provide Christians with a unique form of theological discourse. While they contain broad theological affirmations and at times rise to lofty heights (e.g., Rom. 8:31-39, 1 Cor. 13, and Philippians 2), they repeatedly present discussions of quite specific problems and disagreements. There is no indication that Paul intended these quarrels to be publicized and we can only imagine the humiliation felt by these congregations to discover that for nearly twenty centuries they are remembered for their spiritual and moral faults. History, no doubt, would have forgotten these disputes if not for the fact that Paul elevates the terms of the discussions above the specific personalities and details to the level of general affirmation with universal application. So a dispute regarding eating questionable meat leads to the conclusion that something may be lawful but not helpful, that concern for the weaker brother takes precedence over individual freedom. The debate over circumcision for Gentiles leads to affirmations regarding what is needed for entrance into the church. An extremely nasty and complicated church fight in Corinth leads to profound reflections on the cross. These specific problems, with their solutions, have come to function as landmark decisions. When Christians argue, it is quite common for them to say that the current issue is so *like* one of Paul's problems that therefore Paul's solution applies.[1]

We only know about Paul's relation to Corinth through 1 and 2 Corinthians and the Book of Acts.[2] The first indication of problems, relayed by Chloe's people, is a marvelous understatement (1 Cor. 1:11). But the magnitude of the quarrels emerges in the letter: various factions claim wisdom and authority; there are conflicts over marriage and sexual practices, even involving the civil courts; the practice of eating meat consecrated to idols has become divisive; and some have uttered the charge: "Jesus be cursed!" (1 Cor. 12:3). Extensive study has sought to analyze the nature and source of the conflicting views. It appears to involve the claim that Christianity is a new form of knowledge or wisdom that elevates the recipient to a higher spiritual state, free from the restrictions of earthly life, be it tradition, rules, or even concern for physical life. Such spiritual freedom sets the earth and our fleshly bodies against the Spirit. But such spiritual freedom moves in conflicting directions. Some are libertarian while others assume superior knowledge. Others affirm the exalted Christ but disdain any reference to the historical Jesus, who suffered death. The cursing of Jesus probably reflects this later view.[3] The origin of these claims to new spiritual life is complicated by the general appeals to knowledge and power in Hellenistic culture and early Christianity. Paul him-

---

1. One can draw a helpful parallel between the way Paul's settlements of disputed issues function for Christians and the way decisions of the United States Supreme Court function in courts of law. It is characteristic of the court that it will not debate a general issue unless it arises in connection with a specific case, fraught with a complicated history and details. But once decided, the decision becomes a point of reference for dealing with all other cases that can be shown to be *like* the original case. If this is established, then the ruling also applies. So for centuries Christians have compared new problems to the dispute over circumcision and meat offered to idols, as well as legalistic and libertarian tendencies.

2. Scholars disagree on the chronology of Paul's life. The dates used here are from W. G. Kummel, *Introduction to the New Testament*, rev. ed. (London: SCM Press, 1966). For our purposes it is helpful to bear in mind that Paul was active in founding the church in Corinth around 49-52 C.E. Several years later he received word of problems from Chloe's people (1 Cor. 1:11). When a delegation visits Paul requesting assistance, Paul writes what we now have as 1 Corinthians around 54/55 C.E. Some believe that Paul made an earlier trip to Corinth, which resulted in failure, and wrote a letter that is now lost. Cf. C. K. Barrett, *A Commentary on the First Epistle to the Corinthians*, 2nd ed. (London: Adam and Charles Black, 1971), pp. 1-7.

3. For an explanation of this strange remark see Walter Schmithals, *Gnosticism in Corinth* (Nashville: Abingdon, 1971), pp. 125-36, and Birger A. Pearson, *The Pneumatikos-Psychikos Terminology in I Corinthians* (Missoula, Mont.: Scholars Press, 1973), pp. 23-33.

self had brought to Corinth a message of freedom from the Law and a new knowledge of God in Jesus Christ. Some of the Corinthians obviously felt they were being faithful to Paul, since Paul had asserted that Jesus Christ is the "wisdom of God" (1 Cor. 1:24), which bestows upon the believer a new spiritual life, indicative of a new age. Thus the words knowledge and wisdom could reflect genuine Christian faith or its very antithesis.

D. The Structure of the Argument in 1 Corinthians 1–2

Paul's response to these reports produces a letter that quickly shifts from greetings to a complicated argument involving intricate contrasts and serious conclusions that threaten the readers. To understand all this we need to analyze with care the structure of the argument. The place to start is to ask: Why introduce the cross into conflict involving quarrels, claims, and questionable moral practices? Would it not be more effective to admonish them, send Timothy, and warn them that Paul himself will visit? In other words, tell them to stop what they are doing and warn them of penalties! No doubt Paul did not do this because he had already tried it. But here I would propose that the reason is more complex. The reason lies in the nature of Paul's ultimate goal and the way all of us must travel to reach it.

Paul's goal for the Corinthians reflects his understanding of the cross, but also his understanding of human nature. Elsewhere in his writings Paul proves to be a most perceptive analyst of how and why human beings think, love, and act. These assumptions are now brought to bear upon the Corinthian problem. Paul assumes that human actions proceed out of the person, whether we wish to speak of mind and heart, or self-consciousness or one's being. Actions reflect the way we perceive the world and God, the commitments of mind and heart, our identity and worth. Applied to Corinth, such analysis suggests that the quarrels arise out of the way these people perceive the world and God, their identity as well as how they give themselves worth. The quarrels are not accidental or insignificant. The quarrels affirm and defend the claims that members make about what they value, including their own personal identity and worth. It is important for them to do what they do because their actions grow out of their sense of being. This means that if one wishes to change their actions (i.e., stop the quarreling), one must change their hearts and minds (or being). But if this is the ultimate goal, it requires a specific strategy to achieve it.

We are now coming close to why Paul introduces the cross instead of rebuking his readers for their inappropriate actions. What follows is the complex argument regarding wisdom and power. This argument constitutes a rhetorical trap. Paul creates a situation that ultimately undercuts the basis for all the claims. The best way to understand this is to ask the question that is implied in the argument: Who killed Jesus? The answer one would expect Christians then and now to give is Jewish and Roman leaders. This, however, is not the answer Paul's argument aims to produce. Paul's answer is: Jesus was crucified by persons making claims to wisdom and power. It is this answer, in the context of the importance of the claims being made at Corinth, that drives the argument. Here then is the argument.

In 1 Corinthians 1–2 Paul interprets the cross as a conflict between the world and God over wisdom and power. In the first stage, Jesus is crucified by the wisdom and power of the world. In his rejection, suffering, and death he becomes foolishness and weakness. The world appears victorious in its affirmation of worldly wisdom and power. But the gospel story does not leave it there. In the second stage, God raises Jesus to be Lord, thereby overcoming the world's wisdom and power in the victory of the crucified. This represents a turning of the tables, the ultimate transvaluation of values. God's weakness has now become power and God's foolishness has become wisdom. At this point, Paul can spring the trap. Since he knows that these frail Christians do in fact believe that the crucified is their Lord and Savior, he can draw them into the judgment of the cross. *If Jesus is the Christ, then something is ultimately wrong with the world's wisdom and power.* To put it in simple terms, the world promised happiness but produced anger and division; it promised life but only produced the death of the innocent. In the crucifixion and resurrection of Jesus, the world is revealed as being unable to know or achieve those things that make for life, justice, and peace.

It may well be that Paul sees the connection between the story of Jesus' crucifixion and the conflict in Corinth because of his own conversion experience. All three stories involve claims to wisdom and power, leading to negative results. In the passion narrative, Jesus is rejected by those seeking to preserve religious and political traditions, with the result being a crucifixion. In the case of Corinth, rival factions compete for authority and special status, with the result being division and spiritual warfare. Paul's story contains direct parallels with both conflicts as well as the resolution proclaimed in 1 Corinthians 1–2. Paul had lived a life in radical obedience to the Law. He had actively opposed the Christians, "breathing threats and murder against the disciples" (Acts 9:1). He refers to his own zeal in confronting Christians (Acts 22:3), helping to send some to prison and giving consent to the death of others, including that of Stephen. His conversion contained a direct challenge to his claim to knowledge and righteousness. "Why are you persecuting me?" a voice asks him. He suddenly finds himself in the wrong, having lost his claim to wisdom and power. He is overwhelmed by light — the very symbol of knowledge — and then struck blind. Before he can see in a new way, he must lose his sight. When sight is regained, it is the basis for a new knowledge as well as a new identity. The point is that before Paul ever writes to the Corinthians about the strange wisdom of God in the cross, he has already experienced it in his own life. How different 2 Corinthians 4:6 reads if we understand it against the background of Paul's conversion: "For it is the God who said, 'Let light shine out of darkness,' who has shone in our hearts to give the light of the knowledge of the glory of God in the face of Christ." However, before that light can shine, God must make "foolish the wisdom of the world" (1 Cor. 1:20).

The first consequence, therefore, of the wisdom and power of the cross is the judgment against all claims used to define our identity and worth. When such claims to worldly wisdom and power — be they ultimate or penultimate — are used to define our identity and worth, they inevitably turn us from God who is our true source of life. In this respect they become idolatrous. Since idolatry is by nature divisive, they also separate us from those who do not share in the claims made or who are deliberately excluded from the claims to saving power and wisdom. Thus the cross must first appear as the strange wisdom and power of God that shatters our claims.

If Paul appears to be engaging in deconstruction (i.e., a rejection of all systems and structures because of their corruptibility), we need to remember that he stands in a long tradition. In the Mosaic covenant, God will not be contained in human forms (be it magic or religious traditions). The prophets make it quite clear that there is a difference between the ways of God and humans. Likewise, Jesus certainly displayed the ability to discern the way religious and political institutions lose sight of their original intent and become ends in themselves. What Paul demonstrates to the Corinthians is that if the world, in its power and wisdom, does not know God and the messengers of God, then there is something wrong with the world. The sign of this error is the crucifixion of Jesus, but also the crucifixion of the innocent in every time and place. That the innocent (i.e., the poor, the victims of religious and racial hatred, the peoples living under tyrannical systems) should suffer and die by deliberate design or benign neglect reveals the moral evil present in the world.

The application of this radical judgment against the world is unrelenting and total. 1 Corinthians 1:26-29 is unmercifully blunt:

> For consider your call, brethren: not many of you were wise according to worldly standards, not many were powerful, not many were of noble birth;

but God chose what is foolish in the world to shame the wise; God chose what is weak in the world to shame the strong; God chose what is low and despised in the world, even things that are not, to bring to nothing things that are, so that no human being might boast in the presence of God.

Whatever their claims, in fact they do not amount to much. In the new covenant community, no one may assert higher status or special privilege based on human claims. Paul is proposing that Christians live without claims. But even more, he is denouncing every act of claiming as a form of violence (crucifixion) against one's brother or sister. Since these are brothers and sisters in Christ, the violence is also against Christ.

This brings us to the second consequence of believing that Jesus the crucified is the Lord. If the cross destroys all ultimate claims as a basis for identity and worth, it simultaneously reveals that saving power and wisdom are gifts of grace. This affirmation of salvation as a gift is fundamental to all of Paul's writing. Whether we speak of salvation as forgiveness, access to God, freedom from destructive powers, reunion with other persons, or saving power and wisdom, salvation is not a human achievement or a reward conferred on those with special status. It is a gift. This was central to Paul's own conversion experience and became the governing image for interpreting the gospel. From the human side, just as the only valid response to the judgment of the cross is repentance, so the only valid response to the gift is trust of the heart or faith. Those who receive this gift are reborn in Christ; they live in Christ and in the Spirit. This new being in Christ therefore becomes the basis for a new way of acting contrary to the divisive claims and self-centeredness of the world. As they have been given a new identity and worth, so they may now share the gifts of the Spirit: faith, hope, and love.

E. Christ the Reconciler as a Theory of Atonement

A theory of atonement is an interpretation of the life, death, and resurrection of Jesus as saving power. It utilizes one or more images related to a central issue, either in God or the human condition, to create a comprehensive view of the salvation accomplished by Jesus Christ. The purpose of this section will be to show how 1 Corinthians 1–2 fulfills this definition of a theory of atonement. In the process it shall also be shown that the theme of Christ the reconciler is distinct from other atonement themes in Paul (e.g., sacrifice, justification, or liberation) and in general, other theories considered in this study.

Thus far I have argued that 1 Corinthians 1–2 presents an example of the clash of certain ideas. These ideas are somewhat different from those at the center of debate in Romans or Galatians, which involve debates regarding God's fundamental purposes for Jews and Gentiles, the role of the Law, and the problem of legalism. In Corinth, claims to wisdom and power are set forth, drawing on a mixture of sources: Paul's own preaching of a secret wisdom (1 Cor. 2:7), other preachers, other religious ideas in Hellenistic culture, and what was perceived to be inspiration of the Spirit. The point is that 1 Corinthians is not just another version of Romans and Galatians, but breaks new ground because the central issue is a different kind of religious debate. It can best be called spiritual or ideological conflict, since it is much closer to broad conflicts in our day than the more narrow debates over the Law or circumcision.

The problem at Corinth is division based on claims of superior wisdom and power. These claims constitute the basis for exclusion and inclusion as well as the freedom to violate trust. It is not surprising that such claims produce boasting and quarrels, but as argued above, such actions reflect the deeper issue: the claims are made in the illusion that we ourselves have access to saving wisdom and power. By means of our accumulation of knowledge and power and through our achievements, we give ourselves identity and worth. Speaking in quite abstract terms, Paul sees this as the strategy of the *world:* continual self-assertion in the search for self-sufficiency, followed by relentless defensiveness to assure that what we claim is in fact true. Such a strategy produces a way of being in the world, protected by claims of virtue, unwilling to see how it inevitably produces the crucifixion of the innocent.

If then the problem is the alienation caused by spiritual warfare with its attendant claims, how is the cross of Christ the instrument of salvation? The answer must be given in stages, since one question invariably leads to another as we are drawn deeper into an understanding of God's foolishness and weakness in Christ.

1. God uses the cross to shatter the false claims of the world. To understand this we must consider the way we claim too much for our knowledge and ability to create just systems. Overcommitted to claims, our causes become crusades and our moral standards become oppressive. As Reinhold Niebuhr never tired of pointing out, there never has been a war where the participants did not claim that it was fought in self-defense or in defense of universal values. Religion is not exempt in this drive to invest claims with too much authority. In fact, it is tempted all the more precisely because it holds its claims as sacred, justified by appeals to God. This is the truly frightening thing about the crucifixion. Jesus was rejected and put to death by institutional authorities (religious and governmental) committed to maintaining honored traditions. These were the values that undergirded the current order.

Conversely, Jesus was not killed by thieves and gangsters, terrorists, or even random violence. He was put to death in accordance with claims on which the world relies for its survival. The judgment that falls upon the world, therefore, is the judgment upon the evil we do when intending good. The sign of this judgment is the death of the innocent — in Jesus or wherever the innocent suffer and die or the righteous die in fidelity to God. Crucifixion functions here as a specific event in the story of Jesus, but also as a general symbol that exposes the failure and idolatry of the world's claims. In practical terms, an idol is that which cannot produce what it promises. When the crucifixion of the innocent reveals the ignorance and impotence of the world regarding the things that make for life, then such crucifixion shatters the world's wisdom and power.

2. God uses the cross to create a new way of being on earth. The antagonist here is the world's wisdom and power, not the covenants of Israel. Those covenants already represent a community of faith and love, which according to Paul, God has not abandoned. The argument here is not with Israel but with the general human tendency to construct its own value systems, which inevitably produce spiritual warfare. It is not enough, however, for the cross to shatter the spiritual claims of the world. There must be an alternative to such worldly systems, a new community that actually represents a new form of being. We must keep in mind that the problem in this theory is not the broken relation between God and the individual, but the alienation between warring factions. Moreover, if the cross is to create such a community, it must draw people into it. Even those whose worldly security has been shattered must be drawn to Christ. Why? For two reasons: First, though they may have lost all, they are still tempted to try again to find their security in new claims by the wisdom and power of the world. In this world, one false ideology quickly replaces another. Second, if they have indeed suffered the loss of faith and hope, they are tempted by despair and cynicism. Having one's idols exposed for what they are does not necessarily lead to trust in God.

3. The question then is: How does God use the cross to create a new way of being on earth? Let us first recognize that such language, like that in 1 Corinthians 1–2, uses a theological shorthand in speaking of *using* the cross, or the cross as the *means* of salvation. Such shorthand requires qualification. First, Jesus is not *used* by God in a utilitarian way, to make a point and then be discarded. The tradition wisely reminds us that *what* Jesus does expresses his person. The means of salvation is Jesus himself and the way he embodies the new reality of reconciliation. Second, the cross has to be placed in the context of the whole gospel story of Jesus' life, death, and resurrection. The cross by itself is not a magical transformation of the world. It is significant because it

is the cross of Jesus who proclaimed the coming Rule of God and was invested with additional meaning because of the resurrection. The ability to interpret the cross as possessing the saving power of God is only possible from this larger perspective. Thus, while the cross obviously refers to Jesus' crucifixion, its ultimate significance is derived from his life and resurrection.

4. Having placed the cross in the larger context of Jesus' life and resurrection, the question then becomes: How does God create a new way of being on earth in this Jesus, crucified and raised from the dead? There are two ways this question might be answered. When we are asked this question, we inevitably turn to the gospels and name key teachings, parables, and events that point to the formation of a new community. By contrast, Paul says very little about the ministry of Jesus. We assume that Paul learned about that period, either by oral tradition or through collections of sayings, parables, and events. Even prior to his conversion, he probably knew something about the Christian movement, if only as motivation and justification for his opposition. Paul's answer to the question relies almost entirely on the resurrection and the bestowal of the Spirit. Therefore, we shall outline both ways of answering the question — one from the standpoint of Paul and one from the standpoint of Mark. By doing this we shall avoid reading the gospel material into Paul, or Paul into the gospel material. Though the approaches are different, I believe they are consistent with each other.

For Paul, the new way of being on earth comes about because of the resurrection of Jesus, the crucified, and the bestowal of the Spirit. Consider these passages that point to this new creation: (1) the righteousness of God is revealed in Jesus, the crucified, declaring our standing before God (i.e., justification) by grace. (2) In Christ we die with him and rise with him to new life. (3) We are called to have the mind of Christ (Phil. 2). (4) In Christ and in the Spirit we are free from every form of bondage, to love and serve God and neighbor. (5) In Christ we consider no one from a human point of view, but have become ambassadors for Christ, in whom God was reconciling the world to God (2 Cor. 5). All of these passages point to the way Paul sees God creating a new form of being on earth — in fact, the language of new being, new creation, new age is Paul's invention to give expression to the new life set against the old life.

By contrast, the Gospel of Mark delights in portraying people attracted and amazed by Jesus, though they do not know who he is. Baptized by John, Jesus declares the fulfillment of time in the coming of God's Rule. He displays the power of God to attract followers, cast out demons, teach, reinterpret the Scriptures, and gather a community that breaks with the present social and religious conventions. In a world of massive social disorder and political repression through military force, Jesus actualizes mercy and justice for the poor and outcasts. There is liberation from lifelong illness and confinement. Persons enduring the burden of shame receive forgiveness of sins. Old ideas that exclude and repress are set aside by a higher truth. Persons who had settled into the routine of life receive a call (i.e., a vocation). A circle of friendship and acceptance is formed that sets aside the rebuke and disgrace of current conventions. Eyes are turned from the overwhelming sense of a world dominated by demons to the discovery that the world is the creation of a sovereign God. After a triumphal entry into Jerusalem and the events leading to his arrest and trial, Jesus is crucified but raised on the third day.

Here we have two different answers to how God is working in Jesus' life, death, and resurrection. If Mark attempts to provide glimpses of Jesus' life prior to cross and resurrection, Paul is quite content to make his case entirely on the basis of the new life generated by resurrection and bestowal of the Spirit. With both in mind, we may attempt to create a general answer to the original question: How is God creating on earth a community of reconciliation?

In Christ, God is creating a new way of being, a new community of reconciliation:

- by resisting and overcoming the wisdom and power of the world with God's saving power;
- by drawing people into the community of reconciliation, whereby they are enabled to be agents of reconciliation and practice faith, hope, and love.

This reconciling work occurs in the life, death, and resurrection of Jesus. Each of these interprets and reinterprets the other. For example, the Lord's Supper presupposes teachings and events that precede it in time, but in retrospect takes on new meaning because of the death and resurrection of Jesus.

This reconciling work is also the work of God and may therefore be understood as the presence of God in all of the events.

This summary requires several clarifications. First, the reference to *saving power* is an attempt to emphasize the life-giving and life-transforming agency of God in Christ without evoking the complications caused by many of the standard words. If we say, for example, that God reconciles by *sacrificial love,* that immediately raises the question whether we are absolutizing sacrifice and suffering as ends in themselves. Use of the word *love* too easily pits love against justice, or grace against holiness and righteousness. The phrase *saving power* is Pauline and points to the unity of love and holiness, in the way in which Paul uses the word *righteousness.*

Second, in speaking of the cross, we need to be clear what is meant by the traditional symbols of Christ *suffering for us, bearing our sins,* and *taking away the sins of the world,* lest we become lost in ideas quite contrary to the gospel. The cross reconciles not by magic, nor because it exemplifies self-sacrifice for others, however noble that might be. Rather, in this view, the cross expresses saving power because by means of it Jesus resists and overcomes the world. His suffering and death are consequences of his fidelity to the Reign of God. Against the ever-present concern for self and the fear of death, Jesus commits his life to God. It is this fidelity and witness to God that generates a community of reconciliation. Moreover, he reconciles because he *overcomes* the violence of the world by refusing to respond in kind. By his resistance he breaks the cycle of violence. It could have been different. Like all who suffer for righteousness' sake, Jesus earned the right to demand vengeance, but he refused, knowing that such an act would only continue the cycle of blood vengeance and claims to power. Such a demonstration of saving power in Jesus points to the saving power in God. It is not only Jesus who bears and overcomes the sins of the world, it is also God. When we speak of Christ taking away our sins, where are they taken? Where can we hide sins from God? Where can we put them that they will no longer cause anger and division, remind us of former wrongs, or inspire a desire for retaliation? In this interpretation of the cross, the answer is clear: in bearing the sins of the world, God takes them into the divine life and overcomes them. In Jesus the crucified and risen Lord, God wills to reconcile human beings with one another and with God. The circle of blood vengeance is ended because God bears all the anger and violence of the world, but will not perpetuate it. This is the saving power of the cross.

Third, if the cross reveals a saving power that overcomes the spiritual warfare of the world in order to reconcile, then all language for God must be reconsidered. No longer can we think of love and justice as polar opposites, of righteousness as something that requires vengeance, of sacrifice and power as mutually exclusive. Paul's wordplay on weakness and strength, foolishness and wisdom, requires such a reconsideration. Christ in his life, cross, and resurrection reveals a God who will not condemn the world to destruction, or perpetuate the warfare of the world. In Christ the warfare ends in a revealing of grace and holiness on earth.

5. The goal of the saving power of God in Christ is reconciliation: the uniting of persons with one another and with God. But all talk of reconciliation requires that one specify what is the basis of union for alienated parties.

The basis of union cannot be the worldly claims that posed barriers to union in the first place, no matter how they might be revised or modified. To be reconciled means that we are no longer defined by the old divisions, but by a new reality. Likewise it must be absolutely clear that the new basis of union is not our *agreement* or fulfillment of specified standards of achievement.[4] Nor is it, in an act of naïveté, pretending that there are no divisions or that there are no wounds that divide us. All of these approaches to union deny the fact that the reconciliation of Christ requires repentance and the willingness to set aside our preferred claims as a basis of union. To say that reconciliation is a gift according to the strange wisdom and power of God is to affirm that it depends entirely on God's will to unite us by grace. It is the union of those who, in spite of their disagreements and history as enemies, are brought together by the cross of Christ. It is the crucified and risen Christ who binds us together in the household of God. Such a definition of reconciliation has far-reaching consequences for the doctrine of the church, which will be explored in a later chapter. Here we need only point to the fact that this view requires that the church be defined as God's gift to a warring world and that the symbols of our life together must be baptism (i.e., prevenient grace) and the Lord's table (i.e., the new covenant in his life, death, and resurrection).

F. Summary

This analysis of the theology of the cross, based on 1 Corinthians 1–2, supports the double thesis of the chapter: that the view of Christ the reconciler in this passage is different from Paul's other interpretations of the cross and that, when fully developed, it stands as a distinctive theory of atonement. What we have is a view of Christ as the one who reconciles those caught up in spiritual warfare with one another and with God. No other theory of atonement is as explicit as this regarding the issue of the spiritual warfare among opposing groups, which results in endless cycles of conflict and violence. While I believe this to be a faithful reading of Paul's text, it can also be said that our interest in such an interpretation reflects the fact that we have en-

---

4. We are living at a time when the church is being destroyed by the assumption that it is founded on our agreements. From both right and left there flow demands that to be a member, one must agree with doctrines and moral norms, or oppose each side's list of evils. What this has done is substitute our claims to righteousness for the righteousness of Christ as the basis for the church. As I read Paul, the integrity and unity of the church is in Christ, and we who are at war with one another are invited to his table where there is a new way of being at peace with one another.

dured a century of ideological warfare based on economic, social, political, racial, and gender claims to wisdom and power. If Luther asked, in an age dominated by sin and guilt, How might we find a gracious God, we in our time have asked, Who will deliver us from these divisions and violence?

The image of Christ the reconciler combines the realism regarding sin as spiritual warfare with the affirmation of God's saving work in Jesus Christ. In the cross God shatters the claims of this world and offers in their place a new community in the peace of Christ. One cannot enter this peace without repentance and the willingness to give up the endless cycle of assertion and defensiveness. But in the peace of Christ all sides are given a new identity as sons and daughters in the household of God. Such a theory has powerful implications for the practice of peacemaking. While most Protestants and Catholics have not become pacifist on principle, they appear to accept the calling announced in 2 Corinthians: to be ambassadors for Christ and agents of reconciliation. There is indeed a strategy for peace in this theory, but only if the move toward strategy retains the proclamation of judgment and grace revealed in the cross. It is first and foremost a theology of good news.

One thing that stands out in this view of atonement is the clarity regarding the meaning of Jesus' suffering and death. Jesus suffers and dies as a consequence of his fidelity to God and because of the violence of the world. This death has saving power because in Jesus Christ, God suffers the hostility and violence of the world and overcomes it. As I have argued, the violence of the world is not taken away, but taken into God, that the world might see what it has become and that the violence might come to an end. How appropriate that it is in the Corinthian letters, just when Paul is speaking of God's reconciling act in Christ and our ministry of reconciliation, that Paul should interject the line: "For our sake he made him to be sin who knew no sin, so that in him we might become the righteousness of God" (2 Cor. 5:21). Here is a verse that is usually seized as evidence for some kind of substitutionary atonement, with the issue defined as individual sin against God's laws. But in fact, it comes in the context of Paul's extended assault on the spiritual warfare at Corinth. Jesus dies the death reserved for sinners, which is always the case of the innocent and righteous caught in the warfare of this world. He did this for our sake, not as an offering to God. Its purpose was that in him we might be righteous, that is, be at peace with one another and with God. So it is in this view of atonement: God in Christ receives (i.e., bears) the violence of the world and offers in its place the peace of Christ.

It is precisely because this view of atonement is so strong on the divine act of reconciliation, received only as a gift, that it is so difficult to accept. There are many questions and concerns as to how this gift relates to the need for actual new life on the part of all parties, following abuse and violence. It is not an easily resolved issue, since Christians have explored a wide range of solutions as to how reconciliation and liberation, justification, and sanctification should be related. For now, however, it is enough to present this view as a comprehensive and valid theory of atonement.

G. Comment and Conclusion

There are several critical issues that arise from this theory of reconciliation. The first has to do with the judgment that we are to live without ultimate claims. To put the matter directly to Paul, if the Corinthians are to give up their claims to knowledge and power, how is it that Paul is allowed to make his claim? The fact is that he does make one claim, which he believes takes precedence over all others. The same may be said for this theory in general. If all worldly claims are shattered, why is it that the claim of the cross as the saving power of God should still stand? The question discerns rightly that at least one claim is still being made. The response to the question may take two directions. One is to say with Paul that our encounter with Christ gives us confidence that this one claim is indeed a saving claim rather than a destructive one. While one may truly believe this, in a contested situation all sides may usually make the same claim. The other response is to test the insistence on this one claim by its consequences. Does it in fact produce unity and peace, or simply the perpetuation of the old divisions? In the current climate, where there is a temptation to reduce whatever is said to the perceived self-interests of the speaker, it is very difficult to know whether a claim represents the claim of Christ or special interests. Given our frailty and the limitations imposed by context, it may well be both. But if there is any hope of stepping out of these factional standoffs, it can only be by discerning again the saving power of Christ, who offers a basis of union quite different from what disputing members have to offer.

The second issue relates to the impact of making no claims upon the individual's sense of self-worth. If we return to 1 Corinthians 1–2, Paul has stripped the Corinthians of their claims. Persons living with a sense of self-worth and confidence are suddenly left without status. For many in our times, imbued with perspectives drawn from the social sciences, Paul appears to be advocating a kind of psychic self-destruction. Others will simply take this reading of Paul as confirmation that Pauline Christianity is indeed negative and repressive. These charges involve a profound misreading of Paul. The issue is not about what we today would call positive human development, i.e., the ability to affirm oneself in and among other persons, based on self-confidence and self-esteem. Intellectual development, emotional stability, and practical competence are all aspects of normal human development. The claims this theology of the cross calls into question are those that elevate one person or group over another, that place self or group interest above the common good. Such tendencies are encouraged by a society that expects individuals to create their identity and worth by their achievements and possessions. Such a process is marked by endless competition and conflict. When this process results in ultimate claims regarding ourselves and other people, they divide us from one another and from God. Here we are reminded of the way Paul concludes the argument in 1 Corinthians 1 with the ban on boasting. The practice of boasting separates one person from another, elevating the one and diminishing the other. So it is with claims: they reflect the desire to elevate oneself or a group over another and thereby transform the relations with others. Boasting divides and threatens. God's gift unites and liberates. It is in this sense that there can be no ultimate claim except that of God, no boasting except that of God's gift in Jesus Christ.

Third, a far more difficult issue involves the relation of reconciliation to liberation. Are those to be reconciled required to change or make some movement toward sanctification or holiness, however those terms may be defined? The theory at hand has affirmed a radical view of God's saving power or grace as the basis of union between contending factions. It has argued that the only way to break out of the cycle of competing claims is to affirm an alternative that rests entirely in God's gift. But are there any expectations placed on the parties when they come to the peace of Christ? Such a question implies qualifications and preconditions that threaten to destroy the very nature of the gift. But, say critics, if one does not set expectations, how else could we reconcile oppressors with oppressed, those who have offended with those who have suffered offense? It is not surprising to find advocates of liberation (i.e., holiness) insisting that we cannot be reconciled with persons unless they cease certain practices. Carried to its logical conclusion, such an insistence moves toward setting doctrinal or moral requirements for admission to the peace of Christ.

When one considers this problem it is easy to see that the vision of reconciliation, derived from the cross as a judgment against claims and as a gift of unity in Christ, quite easily unravels. The problem is not simply the insistence by some on what they consider to be appropriate standards. It is also the perennial problem of how justification and sanctification are to be related. In the broadest terms, it poses the following dilemma: On the one hand, if holiness is a requirement, there probably will not be any reconciliation, since one or both parties will probably not satisfy the other. On the other hand, if both parties are allowed to come to the table before any movement toward holiness, then reconciliation becomes a sham, covering up and even perpetuating the existing injustices. Either the demand for liberation nullifies reconciliation, or reconciliation appears to postpone liberation.

Whether we speak of domestic disputes, church fights, or social conflicts, there is no simple formula for resolving this dilemma. Indeed, Christian churches have given a full range of answers as to how reconciliation and liberation (or justification and sanctification) relate to one another. While there is a continual affirmation that they must be held together, how that is to be done can only be resolved in the practice of repentance and the hard work involved in the peace of Christ (i.e., listening, prayer, reading of Scripture, discussion, sacramental worship, and life together). The need for repentance (giving up one's claims) suggests that it is hard to imagine how groups can be reconciled if one group has no comprehension of the spiritual or physical violence done to another. The peace of Christ is not meant to perpetuate suffering and warfare. At the same time, the insistence on imposing standards for entrance to the table, in the name of holiness and the integrity of the church, too easily perpetuates the warfare. In a time when social, political, and coercive solutions have failed to bring peace, the peace of Christ may be the only alternative. But there is no doubt that living in the peace of Christ is not easy. It requires a willingness to set aside one's claims and join Christ in resisting and overcoming the ways of the world with saving power. Here, of course, Christians have for centuries engaged in vigorous debate as to whether such fidelity to Christ involves noncoercive or coercive, nonviolent or violent strategies. While that debate cannot be resolved here, we need to at least acknowledge major developments that have changed the traditional debate. For example, the theology and practice of Dr. Martin Luther King, Jr., embodied a theology of reconciliation and had great impact on American churches. The same can be said for the peace movement and the work of traditional peace churches. It is now common to find Christians from many traditions searching for ways to make peace as an alternative to power politics. There are also powerful examples coming from the reconciliation process in South Africa, where opposing parties were brought together in the face of a long history of oppression and suffering. These developments provide glimpses of reconciliation on earth, based not upon human claims, but as the gift of God.

Chapter 10   The Wondrous Love of God

Peter Abelard, John Wesley, and Jürgen Moltmann

A. Introduction

The final image in our outline is the *wondrous love* of God. This image appears in all interpretations of the death and resurrection of Jesus in some way, either combined with other images or as a conclusion. Its great strength has to do with why God redeems the world and what God intends for redeemed humanity. When it appears as a freestanding interpretation of Jesus, it constitutes a simple and direct appeal to the love of God.

Love as the motivation for God's activity is central to the entire Bible. This needs to be kept in mind as we move to interpret Jesus from the standpoint of wondrous love. In the Old Testament, creation and redemption are repeatedly understood as the outpouring of love, grace, and mercy. Likewise, Jesus' commandment of love as our response to God relies on the teachings of Israel. Therefore we need to guard against the idea that the demonstration of the wondrous love of God is new to the gospels. We dare not make the proclamation of God's love a cause for antagonism toward Judaism.

With this caution in mind, let us consider the ways the New Testament uses wondrous love as a decisive image for thinking about Jesus. In the synoptic gospels, a variety of texts can be enumerated: First, in his teachings about the Rule of God, Jesus repeatedly points to the unmerited grace of God. So the parables of grace point to the immeasurable love of God: for example, the prodigal son, the lost coin, the rain that falls on the good and evil, the king who sends his son as an emissary. Second, the Sermon on the Mount assumes a new situation grounded in God's gracious action, which makes possible new relations between humans and a new relation to God. The great commandment lifts up this new set of relations between God and neighbor. Likewise, Jesus' Gethsemane prayer, which reveals Jesus' obedience and faithfulness to God, needs to be included. In this prayer Jesus points to no other reason for his action other than his love and fidelity to the will of God. His petition to God from the cross in Luke 23:34 ("Father, forgive them; for they know not what they do") also suggests the power of love to overcome the violence done to him. In the Johannine literature several texts have been used extensively in the theology of wondrous love. John 3:16, 1 John 3:16-17, and 4:13-19 are key texts. But John 17 is just as important: the ever-flowing love from the Father to the Son, from the Son to the disciples, and from the disciples to the world, constitutes a vision of redemption. It culminates in the restoration of the knowledge of God, but also enables the world to love God. Finally, there are many references in the Pauline corpus that support the theme of wondrous love. In addition to the numerous doxological statements, Ephesians 1 and 2 and Philippians 2:6-11 provide vivid testimonies to the love of God. Romans 5:8 declares: "But God shows his love for us in that while we were yet sinners Christ died for us."

There are, of course, many other passages one could cite, but quantity is not the issue. The passages already mentioned are so central to the New Testament that they cannot be dismissed as being secondary or irrelevant. When these passages are used to formulate a general theory of atonement, two things need to be remembered. The first is that one must be careful not to argue from these passages to the conclusion that wondrous love is the only valid theory. The New Testament is quite willing to combine wondrous love as an interpretative image with other images (e.g., Romans). The second point is that as a distinctive theory of atonement, wondrous love does in fact take very seriously the cross and resurrection. Something does actually happen: Jesus Christ demonstrates in his life, death, and resurrection the wondrous love of God. The standard charge that this theory is only subjective, and lacks objectivity, misses the mark. There is no doubt that part of its strength is the power to motivate sinners in turning to God and believing the gospel. This aspect has usually been called the subjective side of atonement. But its strength is also found in the revealing of God's love in Jesus, who inaugurates a new covenant, a new community, and a new age. In this respect, this theory can claim the same kind of objectivity as any other theory. Love is demonstrated in these events, and our relation to God has been changed by them.

If this is the case, why then has this view of atonement been so heavily criticized and belittled?[1] In general, the negative reactions are directed more toward revisions of this theory, which reduce the gospel of wondrous love to

---

1. Cf. Aulén's treatment of Abelard in *Christus Victor*, trans. A. G. Hebert (London: S.P.C.K., 1931). The threefold typology of Aulén (i.e., Classic, Latin, and Subjective) has unfortunately become the standard way for understanding all atonement theories.

teachings by Jesus or about Jesus. Thus Jesus either is the great teacher who advocates love or the exemplar of love in his life and suffering. This study has not included the theme of Jesus as *moral teacher* or *example* precisely because such an approach does not seek to interpret the death and resurrection of Jesus as having saving significance. Jesus' teachings about love stand by themselves and have significance to the extent that they persuade us to take up the commandment of love. In this sense, the criticisms of such an approach are correct: in theories of Jesus as teacher there tends to be no crisis created by sin or redeeming value attached to his obedience, suffering, death, and resurrection. But I consider such theories of Jesus as teacher and exemplar to be quite different from the theory of wondrous love outlined here.

B. The Theory in Outline

The outline of this theory in its basic form is simply this:

1. God created the world in love and for love. The image of God constituted a relation of love and obedience toward God.
2. Sin constitutes a break in the relation with God, caused by pride and self-centeredness. It has alienated human beings from God as well as from one another.
3. Jesus Christ appears in the world as the Son of God to reveal the eternal love of God in human form. By his life of obedience and love, his suffering and death, the wondrous love of God is demonstrated.
4. In his resurrection God vindicates the crucified and makes him Lord, thereby establishing a new community of love for the sake of the world's redemption.

C. Witnesses of Faith

To understand this interpretation of Jesus Christ, as well as its potential for multiple applications, we shall examine three cases. The first is obvious, since the name of Abelard is virtually synonymous with the theme of wondrous love.[2] Writing a generation after Anselm, Abelard's view constitutes a baseline for this view, which appears again and again in later centuries.

2. Cf. "Peter Abailard: Exposition of the Epistle to the Romans (An Excerpt from the Second Book)," in *A Scholastic Miscellany: Anselm to Ockham*, ed. and trans. Eugene R. Fairweather,

The second is a variation, illustrating how the theme of wondrous love can be combined with other views. Since it speaks so strongly to the issue of God's underlying motivation for redemption, it helps place other views in a broader framework. But it also is added to many views as the bridge from God's action to our response: as Christ demonstrates such wondrous love, so we ought to love God. A good example of such a combination is found in the sermons, writings, and hymns of John and Charles Wesley. In these two figures we find the theme of wondrous love added to other atonement theories (e.g., sacrifice, substitution, and the ransom/conquest theory). Since they rely on several theories, they avoid the standard criticisms leveled against Abelard.

The third case is another variation, which extends the theme almost to the point of a complete revision. In its basic form, wondrous love affirms that God bridges the chasm separating God from sinful humanity. Though humanity is justifiably guilty, God unilaterally reveals a love that draws humanity back to God. The parable of the prodigal son stands as the great witness to such love. But in this variation, the conditions of the two parties are reversed. Humanity may be sinful, caught in a terrible network of strife and evil, but it is humanity that is alienated from the God who has created and allowed the terrors of life to prevail. The focus thus shifts from the divine rage against sin to the human rage against the God, who appears to stand idle as millions are slaughtered. Therefore, in this variation, the demonstration of love is God's participation in the suffering and death of the world, in order to vindicate God. Since we have already noted this theme in the writings of Jürgen Moltmann, we shall briefly summarize it here to illustrate the point. But the theme appears in many voices raised in the last two centuries, expressing the protest of suffering humanity against God.

1. Abelard: The Liberty of Love

Two things are usually said of Abelard: that he loved Heloise and that he objected to Anselm's argument by appealing to the love of God.[3] While both are

---

vol. 10 of The Library of Christian Classics, ed. John Baillie, John T. McNeill, and Henry P. Van Dusen (Philadelphia: Westminster, 1956), pp. 276-97.

3. Compare standard works on the history of Christian doctrine or church history: Justo Gonzalez, *A History of Christian Thought*, 3 vols., rev. ed. (Nashville: Abingdon, 1970); Williston Walker, *A History of the Christian Church* (New York: Scribner's, 1918); Reinhold Seeberg, *Text-Book of the History of Doctrines*, trans. Charles E. Hay (Grand Rapids: Baker, 1958), as well as the introductory comments in Fairweather, *Scholastic Miscellany* and comments in R. W. Southern, *Saint Anselm: A Portrait in a Landscape* (Cambridge: Cambridge University Press, 1990).

true, our concern is with the latter. In Chapter Five we saw that Anselm rejected earlier forms of argumentation (such as the ransom theory) in search of a new rationale for the incarnation. An elaborate argument was developed to show how the incarnation is required to restore the purposes of God. The argument involved the satisfaction of God's honor, based on God's justice and design for the creation. But as was argued in the earlier chapter, the argument is complicated by the fact that Anselm does not reveal all of his theological assumptions, seeking to find a principle of rational necessity that mandates the incarnation. It is precisely because the argument moves so close to the edge of a transaction between Christ and the justice of God that it arouses criticism. Such criticism was not long in coming in the person of Abelard.

Abelard's style is brief and precise. His writing is like a thunderbolt directed at two positions. The first is the ransom theory. Here one must remember that for both Anselm and Abelard, this argument included the idea that the devil had rightfully gained authority over humanity, obligating both God and humanity. Abelard undercuts the logic of this argument by appealing to the sovereignty of God.[4] First, if we are saved by eternal election, the devil's deception of Adam cannot alter this decree. Second, the devil can have authority over humanity only by permission of God, who has every right to remove it. Therefore, if God gave the devil permission to hold and/or torture humanity, God can remove it. Third, since the devil is guilty of disobedience against God, the devil loses all authority over humanity. Moreover, it is humanity that has a claim on the devil because of the latter's deception. Fourth, in a telling denunciation of the devil, Abelard holds that the devil has no rights over humanity because the devil could not grant the immortality that was promised: thus the devil is a liar. Abelard's conclusion is this: if the incarnation is not required by obligations to the devil, then it must be an act of grace. Furthermore, if it is an act of grace, then it is by grace that sins are forgiven and humanity is freed from the torment of the devil.

Abelard now turns his criticism to any transactional view that relies on payments to retributive justice. The question is: If the network of obligations and rights between the devil, humanity, and God is undercut, and if God can free us from the devil and our sins by God's free and gracious appearance, what necessity is there to require Jesus' life of suffering, humiliation, and death? In several steps Abelard dismantles the transactional view.[5] First, if the cumulative sins of humankind since Adam's fall constitute a great obligation, still greater is the burden humankind bears for having crucified the Son of

4. Cf. Abelard, pp. 280-81.
5. Cf. Abelard, pp. 281-83.

God. How can Jesus' death reconcile us for past sins, when his death is in fact the worst of all sins? Who or what shall compensate for such an offense? Second, it would have been far simpler for God to forgive the former sins and avoid the insurmountable burden of the crucifixion. Third, it is difficult to conceive how we are made righteous by the death of the innocent Jesus. If such a death is in fact a ransom or price, it could only be paid to God (since it is God who gave us to the devil). But how can God be both the one who determines the price required *and* the one who receives the price? For Abelard, it is cruel and wicked to demand the death of an innocent person as a price for anything! Such a view would suggest either that God is pleased by the suffering of the innocent, or that God considers the death of the Son as an acceptable means to reconciliation. Abelard's conclusion is that the idea of redemption by means of a death of one who is innocent is unacceptable.

The only acceptable explanation for the life, death, and resurrection of Jesus, according to Abelard, is the simplest and most straightforward proclamation of God's love.[6] God became human, endured suffering and death, because of God's love. By this demonstration of love, we are freed from the slavery to sin and offered by faith the liberty of the children of God. Indeed, Christ demonstrates the liberty of love to evoke our love toward God (Rom. 5:5-8). Here Abelard emphasizes the difference between the hope for something unrealized and the actual reality: because the love of God is actual in Jesus crucified and raised from the dead, we love God all the more. Likewise, love draws us into a new relation to God that casts out fear. We are therefore motivated to live and act out of love. All of this is captured in a brief declaration:

> he [Christ] has more fully bound us to himself by love; with the result that our hearts should be enkindled by such a gift of divine grace, and true charity should not now shrink from enduring anything for him. . . . So does he bear witness that he came for the express purpose of spreading this true liberty of love amongst men.[7]

Three things stand out in Abelard's position. The first is that he does in fact think of Christ in terms of the history of salvation.[8] The gospel is not a disembodied idea or principle to be grasped by the mind. Sin as disobedience came into the world through Adam, leaving humanity in bondage to sin and the devil. The old covenants represent a dispensation of the law, based on works. But in the new dispensation of grace, both Jew and Gentile are judged

6. Abelard, pp. 283-84.
7. Abelard, pp. 283-84.
8. Abelard, pp. 276-80.

to be without merit before God. Jesus Christ is, therefore, a decisive point in the history of salvation, inaugurating a new time of salvation by grace, claimed by faith. Abelard includes multiple references to Romans 5:5-8 and 8:35-38, John 3:16 and 15:13, as well as 1 John 4:19. Therefore, the charge against Abelard that atonement has been reduced to an idea, or that nothing happens, really does not apply. Something does happen that changes the course of history: the love of God is revealed for Jew and Gentile in Jesus Christ. This demonstration of love is an objective event. The theory is not completely reduced to the subjective response of humanity.

The second is that Abelard brings to his interpretation of Scripture a certain singleness of mind. When he refers to righteousness or justification, he makes it clear that he understands these words to mean love. Likewise, to claim that we are saved by the blood of Jesus, or his death, means that salvation is a gift of grace. At every point, incarnation and crucifixion demonstrate love.[9] By translating key concepts into love, Abelard eliminates the need to resolve any tension between holiness and love, or the complications involved in images of sacrifice or ransom. John 3:16 and 1 John 4:19, as well as Romans 5:5-8 and 8:35-38, are the interpretative lens for understanding the entire New Testament.

The third distinctive thing about Abelard's position is the continuity from start to finish in his interpretation of Jesus Christ. It begins with love, as the underlying motivation for incarnation and crucifixion, and concludes with the love evoked within the hearts of faithful people as they receive the redemption of Christ. Everything God does in Christ involves the demonstration of love for the sake of reconciling the world to God; everything expected of humanity is already revealed in Christ, namely, the liberty of love.

What we have then in Abelard is a *tour de force* regarding the issue of the reconciliation of God and humanity. It is the love of God — as the divine intention and as the human response made possible by the intervention of Christ — that underlies our reconciliation with God. In one sense, Abelard anticipates Occam's razor, which requires that one choose the simple answer rather than the complex. It is as if Abelard is saying: If in the end, the complicated relations and tensions of holiness and love are ultimately resolved into love, why not just say so? Abelard thereby undercuts any theory based on a transaction between humanity and God (or the Son and the Father) that requires punishment or ransom as payment to God (or to the Father). Such theories end up with God doing precisely what God demands, as well as having God appeased by the suffering and death of the in-

9. Abelard, pp. 278-79.

nocent. In either case, God is compromised. Against such theories, Abelard stands as the great witness to the love of God revealed in Christ, designed to evoke love from us.

It is difficult to question a position so tightly constructed, especially if we are asking about God's motivation and what is the appropriate human response. This may well explain why some form of *wondrous love* appears in virtually all Christological formulations, even though other atonement motifs may constitute the primary focus. At some point, one must ask why God is doing whatever happens in Christ and what shall be our response. To be sure, God may have more than one reason for redeeming the world in Christ. But even if this is the case, love must be included.

If one is to question Abelard's position, it is precisely at the point of his single-mindedness. The problem is not that he is wrong, or that his position must be completely set aside, but rather that it fails to see other issues involved in God's redemption of the world. There is no doubt that Abelard undercuts a transactional view such as that of penal substitution, as well as that aspect of the ransom theory that suggests God owes something to the devil. But if my interpretation of Anselm is correct, then Abelard's attack misses the mark regarding Anselm's basic theme. This is the case because Anselm's view is not a transactional theory of a price paid to justice, but a view founded on God's faithfulness in restoring the creation. Indeed, from this perspective Abelard has the distinction of being the first person to misunderstand Anselm! The other theories in this study are vulnerable to Abelard's attack only if one accepts his contention that there are no issues other than the demonstration of love. The survey of these theories does, I believe, make the case that there are indeed other issues, which simply cannot be reduced to the demonstration of love. In Abelard's argument, the decisive issue is the reduction of all key words (e.g., *righteousness* and *justification*) to the word *love*. This assumes that there is only one issue in thinking about God and Christ. But consider, for example, several alternate ways of speaking of God and Christ, which are not necessarily implied in the word *love*.

The Bible presents a long tradition of speaking of God in terms of multiple attributes: holiness, justice, righteousness, mercy, faithfulness, and love. This practice arises out of the fact that these terms do not mean exactly the same thing in God or in God's relation to the world. The biblical record also provides numerous examples in which God's justice and love are in tension, requiring some kind of resolution. To eliminate all that is involved in the intricate relations of holiness and love runs the danger of reducing everything to one moral value. This is especially dangerous when that value (i.e., love) is so easily corrupted by the human capacity to define it according to its interests.

By interpreting Jesus Christ solely by means of the concept of love, Abelard leaves little room for discussing God's opposition to sin, death, and evil. The same can be said of those two words that are always problematic but necessary in atonement theology: *judgment* and *wrath.*

Finally, the central value in Abelard's understanding of God, Christ, and atonement (namely, *love*) is a word filled with a wide range of meanings and subject to misunderstanding. In the modern age the word is too easily interpreted only as forgiveness and unconditional love, rather than renewal and sanctification. Abelard may avoid the trajectory that ends up with cheap grace, since he does speak of liberation from sin and the devil, making possible the new life and the liberty of love. But from our vantage point, one can make the case that the concept of love needs to be protected or balanced by other concepts central to the redemption in Jesus Christ.

To say all this does not, as already suggested, mean that Abelard's view is completely wrong. Rather it emphasizes the problems that occur from such single-mindedness.

Finally, it is appropriate to mention the oft-made distinction between objective and subjective theories of atonement. Theories are said to be objective if something happens in a decisive way to change the relation of sinful humanity to God. One can think of the claim in the Letter to the Hebrews that Christ's sacrifice is once and for all, or the claim of substitutionary atonement that Christ's death removes the judgment of God. Subjective views, by contrast, are supposed to place emphasis on a change in human beings. The problem with this distinction is that it is a false dichotomy. In the case of so-called objective theories, does salvation occur if no one responds by faith in Christ? The prospect of the divine justice being satisfied, without any new community on earth believing or praising God, borders on the absurd. Furthermore, the more one emphasizes a change in God apart from any change in the world, the more one moves toward the appeasement of an alienated God, with the emphasis on the death of Jesus as a value in and of itself. It was to avoid this problem that, in theories of sacrifice and restoration, the emphasis was ultimately placed on Jesus' obedience and the creation of a new community of obedience in the world. Such obedience did not change God, but resulted from God's will to change the world. The distinction between objective and subjective is also called into question by the fact that virtually every theory must deal with the so-called subjective issue. This explains why so many writers, while beginning with one of the other theories, end up appealing to some aspect of the wondrous love of God as the basis for a human response. The reason is simple, though often ignored. Whatever God does in Christ (e.g., forgive sins, conquer the devil, complete the creation) still begs for an answer to the questions: Why does God do this and why should we respond? For Abelard, the answer to these questions is the main theme of the argument.

If it is correct to minimize the distinction between objective and subjective theories, one can still ask whether Abelard incorporates both elements. This is especially important since he has been dismissed for so long as holding a subjective view.[10] Abelard's text makes it clear that while love is the ground for reconciliation, the death and resurrection of Jesus are decisive as a demonstration of the divine love. The reality of the gift far exceeds our hope. Moreover, the dispensation of the law has been replaced by the dispensation of grace. The world is changed because the liberty of love casts out fear. The point is that in all these ways, Abelard has far more to say about Jesus Christ than reducing the gospel to a postcard of heavenly love. His view may need to be enriched by other themes, as suggested above, but it is stronger than is usually imagined.

2. John Wesley: Love of God, from Beginning to End

The names of John Wesley and Charles Wesley are rightly connected to the eighteenth-century revivals of Protestant religion in Great Britain and the American colonies. Their influence on the form and substance of American religion was tremendous and continues to this day. John Wesley was a creative and powerful preacher and leader. He was also a gifted theologian, committing to paper his sermons and essays, as well as long and detailed examinations of the doctrines of original sin and predestination. Constantly attacked from many sides, he was able to withstand the pressures from strict Calvinists and Anglicans, as well as walk a narrow path between reform movements of a more legalistic and libertarian perspective. His genius was the ability to set forth a vision of the Christian life that embraced elements of the tradition in a new way.[11] Thus he resolutely affirmed original sin and the prior graciousness of God at every stage of salvation, but rejected predestination in favor of a free response to the gospel and was constrained on scriptural grounds to af-

---

10. Cf. again Aulén, pp. 160-76.

11. Cf. Albert C. Outler, ed., *John Wesley* (New York: Oxford University Press, 1964), pp. iv and 119-22 as well as Colin W. Williams, *John Wesley's Theology Today* (Nashville: Abingdon, 1960) and Thomas C. Oden, *John Wesley's Scriptural Christianity: A Plain Exposition of His Teaching on Christian Doctrine* (Grand Rapids: Zondervan, 1994).

firm the possibility of Christian perfection. The Methodist movement, however, did not simply consist of a new theological formula. It was given birth and nurtured by great preaching and the hymns that he and his brother wrote. Blessed with long life and great energy, he endured the hardships of constant travel, including several trips to the colonies, for the sake of proclaiming the new life in Christ.

Wesley was ordained in the Church of England, taught at Oxford, had served a parish and participated in a mission to the colony of Georgia. He was active in spiritual renewal groups, especially influenced by the Moravians, and experienced a conversion in 1738. As most commentators affirm, the general framework of his theology was quite orthodox, with innovations coming in the area of the way believers enter into the new life of Christ. He stood within the traditions of Nicea and Chalcedon, assuming Trinity and Incarnation as points of departure.[12] He interpreted the image of God in relational terms, rather than as a capacity such as reason. This relation, which included the love of God, constituted our original righteousness and was the basis for a holy and happy life.[13] The fall, however, constituted the break in this relation to God. Wesley describes this original act with all of the key words: it is an act of *disobedience,* the *misuse* of the creation, or the *heart turned in on itself.*[14] In all these ways, sin alters the human condition. As a result, humanity becomes captive to the deceptions of the heart as represented by pride and sensuality. Though once free to love God and do the good, humanity now loses this gift and is unable to accomplish the good or achieve any merit before God.[15] Fallen humanity can only be described as alienated from God, helpless, and bound over to the power of death. Since this constitutes a universal state of corruption, there is no basis of hope within humanity.[16]

In his approach to atonement theories, Wesley embraces several perspectives. Whenever he deals directly with the issue of salvation by the death and resurrection of Christ, he combines images of sacrifice and satisfaction, with occasional references to ransom. But the theme of wondrous love provides a broad framework for understanding God's intention in salvation and in the development of Wesley's distinctive view of sanctification. This becomes especially apparent in the Wesleyan hymns, where the death of Christ, which

12. Oden, pp. 177 and 184; Williams, pp. 89-97.

13. Williams, p. 48; Oden, p. 135; Outler, pp. 198ff.

14. Outler, p. 199; Williams, pp. 49-50.

15. Oden, pp. 134, 149, 153-54; Williams, p. 44.

16. Williams, pp. 47-48; Oden, pp. 134, 159; *A Compend of Wesley's Theology,* ed. Robert W. Burtner and Robert E. Chiles (New York: Abingdon, 1954), p. 78.

merits our salvation, is framed by the general affirmations of grace and love. Our discussion will follow this development.

The first thing to recognize, therefore, is that Wesley weaves together images of sacrifice, satisfaction, and ransom. This is done primarily by appeals to Scripture, rather than a tightly constructed rational argument, as appears a century later in Charles Hodge. Wesley's approach appears to be aimed more at proclamation rather than a tight doctrinal statement. The basic issue is that sin has offended God, leaving humanity under the judgment and wrath of God.[17] He has no hesitation in speaking of the anger of God against sin.[18] Such a barrier between God and humanity requires priestly mediation, which Wesley describes in several ways: Christ offers satisfaction to the Father; his death is also a sacrifice and ransom.[19] In explaining this Wesley refers to the active obedience offered to God and passive obedience as bearing the punishment intended for us. Jesus thus makes satisfaction for sin and in his person is the representative human, the true Second Adam — even our second Parent.[20] In doing this Jesus institutes a new order or covenant of grace, in contrast to the order of works, which includes our dying and rising with Christ. In sermons and essays, Wesley draws on all of these themes, displaying little interest in critical questions regarding the exchange between Christ and God. It may well be that the sharp edges of sacrificial or substitutionary atonement are softened by Wesley's appeal to the wondrous love of God as the overarching framework of atonement. What is most clear is that the images of sacrifice and substitution are invoked to magnify how God in Christ offers salvation to sinful humanity.

The doctrines of justification and sanctification constitute the core of the "Scripture Way of Salvation." Quite adept at quotable phrases, Wesley declares that "the one implies what God *does for* us through his Son; the other, what he *works in* us by his Spirit."[21] Following the Reformers' emphasis on *sola gratia*, Wesley declares that justification is totally dependent on the merits of Christ and his righteousness. Since we have no righteousness, it must be a forensic declaration, whereby Christ's righteousness is imputed to us.[22] The primary meaning of justification is forgiveness or pardon. Such pardon takes away our guilt and fear of punishment. As justification depends solely on God's grace and love, the only condition is faith.[23]

---

17. Williams, pp. 80-81.

18. Burtner and Chiles, p. 78.

19. Outler, pp. 124 and 200; Burtner and Chiles, p. 78; Oden, p. 187; Williams, p. 88.

20. Williams, pp. 73-76; Burtner and Chiles, p. 78.

21. Outler, p. 201.

22. Oden, pp. 184 and 198; Williams, p. 100.

23. Williams, p. 70; Burtner and Chiles, pp. 140-64; Oden, pp. 192-93; Outler, p. 125.

At this point a reference to one of the critical issues is appropriate. As already suggested, Wesley broke with the Reformers on the matter of predestination, insisting that faith must be the free act of the believer, even though it was in response to grace and enabled by grace. Furthermore, Wesley liked clarity and order, a preference that surfaces in his penchant for definable stages. Such elaboration of the meaning of repentance or the work of grace was not new, being quite common in Augustine and the Middle Ages. The question, then, is whether this emphasis on the stages of grace and human activity implies leanings toward a Pelagian perspective.[24] For example, Wesley distinguishes stages of grace leading to justifying faith: preventing grace is the initial awareness of sin; convincing grace is the conviction that we are sinners and in need of repentance; saving grace is the trust of the heart in the grace of Christ.[25] Tied in with these stages of grace was the question whether repentance was a condition of justification. On this matter, Wesley could not imagine faith without repentance and the fruits of repentance. Thus at times he appears to affirm the necessity of repentance. But also mindful of what is at stake here in the battle with those claiming a human action as the ground of justification, Wesley categorically affirms that the sole basis for justification is faith.[26] So he writes:

> repentance, and fruits meet for repentance, are, in some sense, necessary to justification. But they are not necessary in the *same sense* with faith, nor in the *same degree*. Not in the *same degree;* for those fruits are necessary *conditionally;* if there be time and opportunity for them. Otherwise a man may be justified without them, . . . but he cannot be justified without faith; this is impossible. . . . It remains, that faith is the only condition which is *immediately* and *proximately* necessary to justification.[27]

While the many references to stages of repentance may be confusing, in the end Wesley's position is clearly that of *sola gratia.* Wesley sees no human activity that is not prompted or enabled by grace. As Colin Williams argues, it is not the natural will but the will empowered by grace that turns to God.[28]

If justification and sanctification are logically separable, they are not in the temporal process. Saving grace which bestows pardon on the basis of the merits of Christ brings the gift of the Spirit, with new birth and change of

24. Williams, p. 61.
25. Burtner and Chiles, p. 155.
26. Burtner and Chiles, pp. 158-59; Outler, p. 125.
27. Burtner and Chiles, p. 156.
28. Williams, p. 72.

heart.[29] This inward work of the Spirit, or conversion, involves many things: spiritual power to overcome the power of sin, the restoration of freedom to love God and neighbor, and the restoration of the image of God. At this point Wesley moves beyond both Luther and Calvin.[30] For Wesley, faith relates not simply to justification, but also to sanctification. It is by sanctification faith that we open ourselves to the grace of God.[31] In one of his more dramatic statements of what God intends, Wesley writes:

> 'But what is that faith whereby we are sanctified, — saved from sin, and perfected in love?' It is a divine evidence and conviction, first, that God hath promised it in the holy Scriptures. . . . It is a divine evidence and conviction, secondly, that what God hath promised He is able to perform. . . . It is thirdly, a divine evidence and conviction that He is able and willing to do it now. And why not?[32]

The "why not?" is more than rhetorical hyperbole. Wesley bases his optimism not on human powers but God's power in Christ and the Spirit. If Pelagius reasoned that what God commands must be possible, Wesley reasoned that if God is at work in us, then new life must be possible.[33]

Three issues demanded clarification by Wesley and his interpreters. One was whether the assurance of forgiveness was a necessary sign of true faith. Outler notes that early on Wesley wanted to make it such, but then backed off because of the possible legalism involved.[34] Wesley's intention was that it is the Spirit that provides assurance, though it cannot be made into a test. A second issue was whether conversion was instantaneous or gradual. Here also Wesley gave support for both positions, but again refused to insist on one pattern of spiritual change for all persons. Since the change was the work of the Spirit, and not us, Wesley could not foreclose the possibility of radical change. Finally, what did he mean by perfection? On this issue Wesley was caught between his confidence in the power of the Spirit and moral realism.[35] So, on the one hand, he readily admitted that Christian perfection does not eliminate ignorance, temptation, or mistakes. But on the other hand, he firmly believed that we may expect gradual growth toward perfection. In an attempt to narrow

---

29. Oden, pp. 198, 243, 247; Williams, p. 199.
30. Williams, p. 100.
31. Outler, pp. 278-80; Burtner and Chiles, pp. 159-60.
32. Burtner and Chiles, p. 159.
33. Oden, p. 248.
34. Outler, p. 209; cf. Williams, pp. 103-12.
35. Oden, p. 321; Burtner and Chiles, p. 182; Outler, p. 274.

the scope of the issue, he stated that those who are converted and filled with the Spirit are free from deliberate (i.e., willful) sins.[36] This, however, may cause as much confusion as clarity. In the end, Wesley conceded that the Christian is not free from sin and that repentance is still needed. But such qualifications did not dampen his confidence that by the Spirit the love of God is poured into our hearts and we are enabled to love God and neighbor in new ways. Grace may not be irresistible, but the promise of God must be taken so seriously that gradual growth in grace is an expectation.[37]

Wesley's handling of these three difficult issues is in many ways symbolic of the middle ground he sought to occupy. Whereas he clearly moved beyond Luther and Calvin, he was not willing to endorse claims to sinless perfection, utopianism, and antinomian spirituality. The opposing answers to the three issues — that the marks of assurance can be a test, that sanctification should be instantaneous, and that full perfection is possible in this life, lead to positions Wesley himself did not support. That his position is a delicate balancing of all of these variables may well explain why holiness and perfectionist movements were inspired by his preaching in his time as well as in generations that followed.

We have now reached the point where the importance of the theme of *wondrous love* for Wesley's theology may be made clear. At the outset I suggested that Wesley used the theme of wondrous love as the overarching motif for understanding the more specific atonement themes of sacrifice and substitution. Wondrous love reveals in the most dramatic way what motivates God in the redemption of the world (cf. John 3:16). But there is a second vital connection. Wondrous love allows for perfect continuity from God's intention and action to the work of the Spirit in the believers and their response to God. The love of God, revealed in Jesus Christ and shared with the disciples, is now poured into our hearts by the Spirit, producing the fruit of the Spirit in works of love. The argument here is not that this is the only way one can get to Wesley's doctrine of sanctification.[38] Rather it is that the theme of won-

---

36. Oden, p. 324.

37. Oden, p. 338; Burtner and Chiles, p. 174; Williams, p. 115; Outler, p. 281.

38. It is conceivable that one could reach the optimism of Wesley's view of sanctification by means of a liberationist emphasis on freedom from sin, or an incarnational approach joined with sacramental unity with Christ, or even extending Paul's emphasis on life in the Spirit. Likewise, the juxtaposition of images of sacrifice and substitution with wondrous love, leading to radical expectations for the Christian life had already appeared in Anabaptist and pietist movements. This does not minimize Wesley's achievement, since in many respects he stands closer to Lutheran and Calvinist traditions and for this reason his use of wondrous love is especially important.

drous love provides a direct bridge from other images of atonement to sanctification as growing in grace.

This transition from images of sacrifice, substitution, and ransom to wondrous love is dramatically portrayed in the hymns of John and Charles Wesley. The hymns, however, do more than simply illustrate the point, in the manner of the proverbial sermonic illustration. Rather, the hymns embody the form and substance of the Wesleyan movement and certainly rival the preaching in affecting minds and hearts. The first thing to be emphasized, therefore, is that in their hymns the themes of sacrifice, substitution, and ransom are merged with that of wondrous love. Wondrous love does not eradicate or minimize these images, but assumes them and builds on them. In hymns such as "Lo! He Comes with Clouds Descending," or "Come, Thou Long-Expected Jesus," or even "Hark, the Herald Angels Sing," we see images of incarnation, suffering for us, ransom, and deliverance. In their hymns there is no hesitation to describe in vivid detail the suffering of Jesus for our behalf.

> And can it be that I should gain
>   An interest in the Saviour's blood?
> Died he for me, who caused his pain?
>   For me, who him to death pursued? . . .
>
> He left his Father's throne above —
>   So free, so infinite in grace —
> Emptied himself of all but love,
>   And bled for Adam's helpless race.
> 'Tis mercy all, immense and free;
>   For, O my God, it found out me.[39]

A similar theme appears in the lines: "O for a heart to praise my God, A heart from sin set free; A heart that always feels thy blood So freely spilt for me."[40] In "Jesus Comes with All His Grace" we find the work of Christ described: "He hath our salvation wrought, He our captive souls hath bought, He hath reconciled to God, He hath washed us in his blood."[41] In another hymn, Jesus is portrayed as:

> O thou eternal Victim, slain
> A sacrifice for guilty man,

39. H. A. Hodges and A. M. Allchin, *A Rapture of Praise: Hymns of John and Charles Wesley* (London: Hodder and Stoughton, 1966), p. 97.
40. Hodges and Allchin, p. 115.
41. Hodges and Allchin, pp. 123-24.

> By the eternal Spirit made
> An offering in the sinner's stead,
> Our everlasting Priest art thou,
> And plead'st Thy death for sinners now.[42]

What we have, then, in these hymns and others, is a dramatic lifting up of the themes of sacrifice, substitutionary death, and ransom. In fact, ransom and liberation may receive more attention in the hymns than in John Wesley's writings. So, for example, compare the great Easter hymn "Christ the Lord Is Risen Today."

The second thing the Wesley hymns reveal is that it is wondrous love that most often provides the overarching theme and the transition from the cross to sanctification. Time and again, grace and love are portrayed as the motivation for God in redeeming the world in Christ. Consider hymns such as "Stupendous Height of Heavenly Love," or "Love Divine, All Loves Excelling," or "Jesu, Lover of My Soul," or "God of Unexampled Grace." What stands out in these hymns is the way they easily make the transition from God's eternal love as the motivating force behind our redemption, to the love poured in our hearts evoking from us love of God and neighbor. In "Love Divine, All Loves Excelling" we find the words: "Thee we would be always blessing, Serve thee as thy hosts above, Pray, and praise thee, without ceasing, Glory in thy perfect love." The final verse opens: "Finish then thy new creation, pure and spotless let us be."[43] The hymn "Sons of God, Triumphant Rise" concludes with the verses:

> Grace our every thought controls,
> Heaven is opened in our souls,
> Everlasting life is won,
> Glory is on earth begun.
>
> Christ in us; in him we see
> Fulness of the Deity.
> Beam of the Eternal Beam;
> Life divine we taste in him!
>
> Him we only taste below;
> Mightier joys ordained to know,
> Him when fully ours we prove,
> Ours the heaven of perfect love![44]

42. Hodges and Allchin, p. 140.
43. Hodges and Allchin, p. 120.
44. Hodges and Allchin, p. 156.

What the hymns make clear is that there is, for John Wesley, a continuous line from John 3:16 to the doctrine of sanctification. His optimism was based not on confidence in human possibilities but God's promise in Christ and the bestowal of the Spirit.[45]

Wesley provides an excellent example of how wondrous love can be combined with other theories, used primarily as the overarching theme connecting God's love and the love perfected in believers. In this respect he is not alone and he would no doubt find nothing unusual in blending these images into one general view. His primary theological achievement, however, was his ability to unite in a coherent way many elements that have so often proven to be divisive. On the one hand, he joins a most realistic doctrine of sin with very traditional images of atonement, but without relying upon the doctrine of predestination. In his advocacy of a divine grace that precedes and surrounds all human activity, he anticipates much of the theology in the next two centuries that joins together human freedom and God's sovereignty without the contentious idea of predestination. On the other hand, he is unrelenting in his insistence that Christ and the Spirit mean the promise of new life and freedom from sin, while refusing to endorse either legalism or perfectionism. In this respect Wesley has been underestimated by Lutheran and Calvinist traditions. To the extent that these traditions resist the language of sanctification for fear of legalism or utopianism, Wesley offers a counter voice faithful to the New Testament. His confidence may also anticipate the twentieth-century liberationists, who base the hope of new life on God's eschatological promise.

3. Jürgen Moltmann: The Suffering of Love

The third variation on wondrous love to be considered has a long history but emerges in the twentieth century as a significant Christological development. In what I have called the basic form of *wondrous love*, it is God who has been offended and humanity is estranged from God as the guilty party. Nevertheless, God wills to be reconciled and bridges the gulf in the demonstration of love in Jesus Christ. But in this third variation, the tables are turned. It is humanity that is offended and estranged from God by virtue of the immeasurable sufferings of the world. The logic that appeared in Anselm, but was made popular by Hume, now takes the form of moral outrage: either God wants to prevent suffering, but cannot and therefore is powerless, or God can, but does

---

45. Burtner and Chiles, pp. 188-202.

not and therefore is not good. Jürgen Moltmann refers to this human cry against God as *protest atheism,* and one can easily cite many examples. But the moral outrage extends beyond atheists, since it torments believers as well. In fact, the Christological development considered here may speak more to the unrest within the Christian community than outside of it. For this reason I think it more appropriate to see this development as believers' outrage, rather than a form of atheism. The modern world of holocausts and tragedy has left us tormented, angry, and alienated from God.[46]

As a response to this estrangement from God, wondrous love offers a Christological appeal: In the face of the world of suffering and death, God is incarnate in Jesus Christ, lives among us, suffers and dies with us, for the purpose of reconciling us to God. All the New Testament texts regarding wondrous love can be invoked to support this application, especially Philippians 2, John 3:16, and Romans 5:8. God appears as co-suffering with us and for us, enduring all that has befallen us.

It is helpful to place such an appeal within broader trends since the Reformation. In the sixteenth century, the doctrine of predestination was strongly defended by both Luther and Calvin. It was indeed a statement about God and God's relation to the world. We see this played out in Calvin and later in Schleiermacher. But predestination was also a defensive doctrine, i.e., it functioned as a defense against certain dangers or threats. One was Pelagianism, which wanted to base salvation upon some form of human activity. Against this, predestination denied absolutely any basis for salvation within the human and answered the question of assurance by pointing to the eternal decree of God. A second danger was the anxiety created by the sufferings of this world. Against such torment, predestination affirmed that everything was ordered by the wise and gracious will of our loving Father — even though such a will was often unknown. This use of the doctrine of predestination has always been controversial, since it quite deliberately makes God the cause of all that happens, but appeals to the hidden counsels of God which will ultimately be revealed at the end times. Perhaps the best way to understand this use of predestination in a writer such as Calvin is to see the pastoral context: If Calvin were faced with comforting the mourners of someone who died a tragic death, Calvin sees three options: chance, the devil, and God. If one interprets the death by means of chance or the devil, then the

---

46. One might note the acceptance of this idea by referring to the UCC funeral service. There the pastor announces that we have gathered here to worship, share our grief, and to "release our anger" (Book of Worship: United Church of Christ [New York: United Church of Christ Office for Church Life and Leadership, 1986], p. 372). When theological concepts become institutionalized in liturgies they have indeed achieved a level of acceptability.

world has either gone mad or is demonic. Thus, while Calvin makes no specific claim as to why the person died, he would prefer to see it in the context of the total plan of God, revealed in Israel and Jesus Christ.

The modern age, however, has not been receptive to the doctrine of predestination. In certain parts of Protestantism it has been openly rejected (e.g., Wesleyanism and liberal traditions) and in other parts it has simply been quietly revised and reinterpreted to signify God's general sovereignty. In effect, most have given up the attempt to defend predestination or to explain how human freedom is real in the face of such an absolute causality. But what happens, then, to the defensive uses of the doctrine of predestination? In the case of Pelagianism, modern theology has found quite acceptable ways to hold the line and affirm the priority of grace (cf. the writings of Reinhold Niebuhr and H. Richard Niebuhr). But the case of suffering becomes a more serious problem: If we can no longer appeal to the ordaining will of God which governs all things, how then shall one respond to the torments of doubt and anger in the face of the world's suffering? It is at this point that we see the significance of the Christological development now considered. As the doctrine of predestination declines and there is less resolve to appeal to the hidden decree (or decrees) of God, attention shifts to a Christological solution. Jesus, the presence of God among us and our brother, represents the co-suffering of God with us and for us. To be sure, this affirmation is not new. One could recall that famous incident in Luther's development. When he was tormented by doubt and his own unworthiness, his teacher Staupitz comforted him not by appealing to the doctrine of predestination but to Jesus on the cross. It is this theology of the cross that emerges again in the twentieth century as a response to the doubt and torment of believers trying to find meaning and hope in a world gone mad.[47]

In Chapter Four we reviewed the theology of Jürgen Moltmann, where the co-suffering of God emerges as a major theme in response to what he calls *protest atheism.* For Moltmann, theology must be redefined by the cross and resurrection: Jesus is always the crucified, forsaken, and rejected; the crucified is always the incarnate Son who is raised as Lord. Using the technical language of the Trinity, Moltmann boldly speaks of the incarnation of the Son, who lives among us. Since his suffering is the suffering of God, Moltmann can speak of the crucified God. While redemption relates to the reality of sin,

47. While I recognize that Luther affirms the doctrine of predestination, I have always thought that his position was more defensive (i.e., a means to ward off certain dangers) than truly operational. The center of his theology is the theology of the cross and the promise of the Word offered to the trust of faith. In this sense, the doctrine of predestination is not operational, though it is formally affirmed.

Moltmann wishes to envision redemption on a cosmic scale. God chooses the life of suffering and death to overcome all the demonic powers of this world: sin, moral evil, and death. The resurrection of Jesus is the first sign of the new creation, and we are called to participate in a new community of justice and peace.

Moltmann is an excellent example of the shift to a Christological answer to the problems of suffering and moral evil in the world. In the face of our anger toward God, Jesus represents God's participation in our suffering and death. It is ultimately an appeal to the wondrous love of God for the sake of reconciling us (i.e., those who are alienated from the Creator) to God. While most may not have actually read Moltmann, consider the number of times preachers have made this shift in sermons. When faced with the tragedies of life, attention turns to Jesus our co-sufferer and the demonstration of the love of God, with a final reference to Romans 8.

While I have classified this approach with wondrous love, there are parallels with other theories. For example, some might see in this theology a strange reversal of the logic of penal substitution. Instead of portraying Jesus' death as a price paid to the justice of God, in this case Jesus' death is offered to propitiate estranged humanity. Or, one might compare the shedding of blood in sacrificial theories with Jesus' act of self-sacrifice in this theory. Such parallels, however, obscure the real differences between the views. Any suggestion that Jesus' death is some kind of reparation proves indefensible, for how can his death equal the death of all innocent persons? Jesus' death may reconcile us to God, but not in the same way that sacrificial offerings remove or cover sin in the theory of sacrifice.

The real power of the theme of God's co-suffering is the affirmation of presence or participation in our life. In this sense the theme relies on the traditional notion of Jesus' passive obedience as sympathy and solidarity *with us.* At the center of this solidarity with us is the cross, i.e., the shedding of blood by the incarnate God. Here we must note the power of voluntary sacrifice for others. In other chapters we have noted the concerns regarding the isolation of Jesus' suffering as an end in itself as well as the graphic portrayal of pain and blood. These criticisms, however, too easily overlook the many levels of meaning — rational and nonrational — tied to the shedding of blood. As the old gospel hymn affirms, there is "power in the blood." Blood is the symbol of life. The shedding of blood for someone attracts attention, i.e., causes us to stop doing what we are doing and look. It makes sacred the places where life is poured out for others. All of this is caught up in Romans 5:8 and John 15:13: "No one has greater love than this, to lay down one's life for one's friends." It is very difficult to explain how or why these images of co-suffering have such power. On an intellectual or moral level we rightly resist the attempt to reduce it to some kind of balance of payments, lest it become a grotesque statement of blood vengeance, with humanity demanding the death of the innocent Jesus. But the fact is that when life is given in ways to sustain or save other life, it can be rightly called a gift. For a world where suffering appears to be endless, in this theory the cross again becomes a symbol of a gift of love.

Part Two   **Conclusion**

Chapter 11

Jesus Christ the
Saving Power of God

*What then shall we say to this? If God is for us, who is against us?
He who did not spare his own Son but gave him up for us all, will he
not also give us all things with him?*

ROMANS 8:31-32

A. Introduction: One, Three, or Many Theories

The first purpose of this study has been to demonstrate that there are many
theories of atonement. This thesis contradicts two conventional views: either there is only one general theory or there are three. When everything is
lumped together in one general theory, one can be overwhelmed with problems. This may well be the reason why so many have given up trying to
make sense of atonement. Consider the essay by William Placher in 1999,
where he acknowledges that *the atonement* presents us with puzzles and dilemmas.[1] Placher reviews and accepts basic criticisms of atonement in general, without indicating that he is actually describing the theory of penal
substitution. He then attempts to retrieve the traditional idea of Christ *in
our place.* But to do this, Placher moves completely out of the logic of penal
substitution and introduces key elements from at least five other theories:
sacrifice, justification by grace, liberation, reconciliation, and wondrous
love as co-suffering. While all of the elements introduced are positive ones,
the reader is never informed that the traditional theory of penal substitution has in fact been rejected on biblical and theological grounds, or that
the solution is a composite of other views. In effect, from start to finish we

---

1. William Placher, "Christ Takes Our Place," *Interpretation* 53 (January 1999): 5-20.

are left with the idea that there really is only one general theory. Whereas the article begins with the problems associated with one theory, the solution appears to be the refinement of one general theory that is a composite of many theories.

The other conventional view, originally set forth by Gustaf Aulén, is that everything can be neatly packaged into three theories: Christus Victor, a general transactional view, and the liberal affirmation of love.[2] To arrive at three theories, important distinctions are judged irrelevant. In the first category, liberation is combined with justification by grace; in the second, sacrifice, satisfaction, and penal substitution are merged. To this day one finds in print and public statements the assumption that atonement comes in three types. Aulén's view has exercised a sort of theological imperialism over atonement discussions. To reduce all atonement theories to three is a major reconstruction of historical theology. But in fact, the end result is not really three bona fide theories, but one: after the second and third theories are judged to be inadequate we are left with one valid theory, which runs from the New Testament through Irenaeus to Luther![3]

Against these two approaches I have argued that the New Testament and the traditions present us with multiple theories of atonement. I also proposed that a theory of atonement consists of a basic image, developed into a comprehensive interpretation of the life, death, and resurrection of Jesus as the saving power of God. There are many images in the Scripture and traditions that do not have the ability to move from a striking insight to a comprehensive interpretation. To do that, a theory must be able to correlate the saving power of Christ with a specific human need, placing both elements into a larger theological context. The theories presented here fulfill this requirement. Each begins with a specific image in order to portray an aspect of the human condition redeemed by Christ. While I have made it clear that the theory of penal substitution is problematic and in need of serious revision, all the theories point to the different ways Christian communities have perceived human need and the fullness of Christ. Since they cannot be easily combined or reduced to one another, it must be concluded that there is great

---

2. Cf. Gustaf Aulén, *Christus Victor,* trans. A. G. Hebert (London: S.P.C.K., 1931).

3. The popularity of the threefold schema for atonement theology was illustrated in the debate over Gibson's *The Passion of the Christ.* In newsmagazines and television interviews, the general public was informed that there are three theories. Recent publications still rely upon Aulén's outline. For example, J. Denny Weaver follows the schema, with a heavy and continuous critique of transactional views. His view is especially unusual because he uses Anselm as a symbol of all that is wrong with transactional views, even though he admits that it is not really Anselm's view. Cf. Weaver, *The Nonviolent Atonement* (Grand Rapids: Eerdmans, 2001), p. 192.

variety and richness in the interpretation of Jesus' life, death, and resurrection as saving power.

It was also proposed that a theory, as a comprehensive interpretation, must possess three values: symbolic, evangelical, and theological. First, each employs a basic image that possesses *symbolic* value, i.e., the ability to capture the imagination of listeners when used to interpret Jesus. Such an image, however, must also have *evangelical* value: the ability to correlate a specific human need with the saving power of God in a given cultural context. This is one reason why there are many theories, with countless variations. Likewise, it reveals why all people are not drawn to every theory. For example, preaching Christ as liberator assumes people have a sense of being bound or oppressed. Or again, Luther's message of grace presupposes a culture where there is a sense of sin and guilt, and both are understood theologically. Our problem is not, I believe, that people do not find themselves under judgment or suffer from self-condemnation, but rather that guilt and condemnation are understood in a nonreligious way and the solutions are sought in a variety of therapeutic strategies. This leads to the *theological* value: the ability to interpret theologically both the problem and Jesus in a manner consistent with the church's understanding of God current at the time. This includes what is presupposed about God from the Old Testament (e.g., that God is one, revealed in holiness and love, has made covenants with Israel). It also includes the central affirmations of the New Testament (e.g., the coming of the Rule of God, the new covenant, the presence of God in Christ, and the bestowal of the Spirit). Without theological value, theories lose their credibility. In the cases of Marcion and Arius, what was affirmed of God and Christ violated the community's perception of what was presupposed or affirmed about God.

Having presented this variety of perspectives, we are now in the position to inquire what can be learned about these theories and atonement theology in general. To do this we will: analyze the structure of atonement theories, develop a framework for assessment, and reflect on the relation between the theories.

B. The Structure of Theories of Atonement

Before considering common elements, it may be helpful to ask: If the theories are so different, how can they have common elements? The answer is that while each of the theories has a distinctive image and theme, using quite different biblical texts, all are forced to operate in quite prescribed circumstances. This can be seen in two ways: First, all of the theories are post-resurrection interpretations of events that have already occurred. It is a given that Jesus gathered disciples, taught, healed, created a new covenant, was crucified and raised from the dead. For the theories, the fact is that he did die a horrible death and was then raised from the dead. Thus it is already a given that the salvation we now experience has come about by some means in and through these events. While the theories are required to operate with a completed narrative, nevertheless they are driven to ask — after the fact — why these events happened. To the extent that they try to take up a position prior to the events, thus stepping out of our post-Easter viewpoint, their actual location is obscured. This is especially the case when theories take up a position prior to Jesus and assume that every logical option is a possibility. But no matter how much theories try to tell a story as if the outcome is unknown, the fact is that they are forced to operate from a vantage point of living after the decisive events of Holy Week. The actual narrative therefore becomes a framework or structure for atonement theories.

Second, the theories display a continual attempt to find connections in three significant directions: (1) between Jesus and God; (2) between Jesus and the known world of Jewish Scripture and religious practices; (3) between Jesus and the disciples' experience with Jesus before Good Friday. The crucifixion and resurrection are displays of power which, in and of themselves, are unintelligible. The meaning of neither event is self-evident, as demonstrated by the fear and confusion among the disciples following each event. Both events terrify and attract. In this sense they require connections with God as the one who sent Jesus and the disciples' relation to Jesus before and after the resurrection. Thus all of the theories reveal an intentional search for connections to make intelligible the events of cross and resurrection. In saying this I am assuming that it is appropriate and inevitable for theories to connect Jesus' death to God. All of the theories assume that God was involved in some way, for if this were not the case, then Jesus' death is either an accident or simply the result of sinful people. The issue, however, is in the way God is related to Jesus and the particular events of Holy Week. As we have seen in the theories, there is a great difference between interpreting the cross in light of God's purposes and Jesus' fidelity to God, in contrast to making the death of Jesus a requirement by God.

Taken together, these two aspects set certain limits for the theories and thereby become the basis for commonalities. The events in the story of Jesus are given and the search for connections follows definite patterns. Taken as a group, the theories display a common narrative structure regarding participants, themes, and logic. By logic I mean the driving force that moves the theory from one point to another. In Anselm and Hodge we found writers seeking a rational necessity to drive the argument, which threatens the narrative structure of the gospel story. But in most theories the driving force arises from the interaction of the participants. In this respect, most bear the marks of a drama or story, with characters, events, conflict, and a final resolution. Given this narrative character, most of the common elements they share are relational, as for example God's relation to the world, humanity, and Christ. In other cases they involve the internal relations within God, as when it is said that God can only act in accordance with the divine nature, which is holy. Still again, they may involve the relation of one form of brokenness to the saving power of Christ. Sometimes these relational components appear as presuppositions, at other times as the driving force that moves the story (or argument) forward. Here then are five common elements.

1. A Defining Image: Problem and Resolution

The proposal that theories are a comprehensive interpretation of Jesus, based on an image, highlights the fact that each theory concentrates on a specific theme. By announcing the theme, the image thereby sets it apart from other themes. Thus sin is distinguished as a theme from death or demonic powers. But the image also reveals the particular way the theory views the problem of sin, in contrast to other ways. For example, our study has shown that sin has been treated in four quite different ways when approached with the images of sacrifice, justification by grace, penal substitution, and honor (i.e., Anselm's view). Thus the image names the general issue, but also the specific way the theory will speak of the saving power of Christ. The point can be further illustrated by the multiple ways the problem of bondage to demonic powers can be resolved: the image of the fish hook suggests that God tricks the devil; Christus Victor suggests a display of power that defeats the devil; still others propose nonviolent images suggesting the power of love to overcome demonic powers. From these examples we note that the image gives the theory a certain character and tone by the language, practices, and logic connected to the image. To return to images for dealing with sin, the image of sacrifice draws us into a very different world of ideas than that of justification by grace or penal substitution.

The image, then, provides structure for the theory in several ways: it divides and even subdivides the field of options open to Christian teaching and preaching; it gives us a specific theme involving a problem waiting to be resolved; it allows the theory to draw upon practices, language, and logic connected to the image. It is quite possible that in this latter respect an image will create problems if everything connected with it is included in the theory.

2. God's Opposition to Sin, Evil, and Demonic Powers

When Jesus first appears in the Gospel of Mark, a series of events occur in rapid succession (Mark 1:1-15):

- John the Baptist appears in the wilderness and is interpreted with reference to Isaiah's command: "Prepare the way of the Lord, make his paths straight."
- Jesus receives the baptism for the remission of sins from John the Baptist.
- The Spirit descends upon him with a public blessing.
- The Spirit drives Jesus into the wilderness where he is tempted by Satan.
- Following John's arrest, Jesus proclaims good news: "The time is fulfilled, and the kingdom of God has come near. Repent, and believe in the good news."

In a manner so typical of Mark, the passage overflows with words, acts, and signs, all pointing to the tension between God and moral evil. The stage is set for a great struggle that will be described in different ways throughout the other gospels and the entire New Testament. But the drama is not new to the story of Jesus and his followers. It appears in the earliest passages of the Old Testament, whether one goes to the foundational events of the Exodus or the accounts of creation and patriarchs in Genesis. The Almighty God is holy, and this combination of sovereign power and holiness sets God over against human beings. God cannot be deceived; from this God there is no hiding; even the conspiracies of the nations are to no avail against the holy one. But lest we think of holiness only as that which differentiates God from humanity, we need to remember that the holy God bestows holiness or goodness upon the world. In all of God's actions there is a will to affirm goodness. What God creates is declared good. God calls people and creates covenants with the expectation that God's people will be holy as God is holy.

This recitation of themes from the Bible points to the opposition between the holy God and a sinful world. But here we should note that in the New Testament the problem facing humanity is not only sin, but Satan, demonic powers, and death. This array of hostile forces presupposes what we would call ontological assumptions regarding the difference between God and the fallen world, though the Bible never discusses these ontological matters apart from the overriding moral perspective.[4] God is always the holy one in acts of creation and redemption, who calls and expects the chosen ones to be holy. This drive for goodness sets in motion the tension between God and sin, demonic powers, and death. In one sense, all atonement theories arise as reflections on how this fundamental contradiction is resolved. To the extent that sin, demonic powers, or death as a tyrant are nonexistent, then there really is no need for atonement. The same conclusion may be reached if the problems are resolved by human agency of mind or will.

The concepts of judgment and wrath play an important role in describing the tension between God and sin. To the extent that they express God's unalterable opposition to sin and moral evil, they are positive affirmations of the holiness of God. But they can also be problematic, for the very same reason. They can suggest that sin has changed both God and God's relation to the world. Shall the final result of sin be, in addition to the disorder of the creation, that it has alienated God from God's own creation? If so, how shall this tension be resolved? Three responses to the concepts of judgment and wrath can be observed in the theories reviewed:

The first general response is to accept without flinching that there is a break in the relation between God and humanity, which can only be overcome by compensation offered to God. In what I consider an unacceptable variation on the theory of sacrifice, this response makes Jesus' suffering and death an offering to God. In penal substitution, it appears as Jesus paying the penalty demanded by retributive justice. Both views suggest that holiness, defined as retributive justice, is the decisive factor. This then leads to the unfortunate consequences: a passive God waiting to be appeased and the death of Jesus as having intrinsic value. Such an outcome violates both the evangelical and theological values arising from the Bible and at work in most theories (cf. Chapters One and Three).

Here a final word regarding what I have called the *Trinitarian defense* is in

---

4. One is reminded of the long debate on the question whether ontological or historical/moral categories are predominant in the Bible. The attempt by Thomists to introduce a fully developed ontology, by means of the name of God in Exodus 3:14, is hazardous, given the linguistic analysis of the Hebrew text. On the other hand, there are obvious ontological implications in such language as *Creator, Almighty,* or the affirmation that God's love *endures forever.* Here the point is that in general, the God of the Bible is always the holy one. For example, even in the creation story found in Genesis 1, dry land comes into being by the restriction of the waters of chaos, and each day's activity is pronounced good. In a different context, Second Isaiah gives us a profound theology by equating the Creator with the Redeemer, thereby allowing each title to be partially defined by the other. As a consequence, Israel is assured that ultimate power is trustworthy because the Creator is the Redeemer and conversely, that the promise of redemption is feasible because the Redeemer is the Creator.

order. It is often argued that since it is God the Father who sends God the Son, and it is God the Son who makes the offering to God the Father, therefore God is not passive but still retains the initiative for the redemption of the world. But the attempt to transfer the tension between God and the world to relations within the Trinitarian personae is hazardous. Is the tension between wrath and grace solely within the Father? Or is it between the Father and the Son, with only the Father being repelled by sin while the Son acts to appease or satisfy the Father? But if the Father needs to be reconciled, why does not the Son? Is justice the attribute of the Father and love the attribute of the Son? If one replies that the Father possesses both justice and love, since it is the Father who sends the Son, then one has already affirmed a resolution of justice and love in the Father as a presupposition for sending the Son. These lines of argument inevitably reflect a divided deity, with the Son appeasing the Father. As a consequence, I am drawn to the conclusion that the Trinitarian defense fails to save transactional views from the unacceptable consequences named above. The same conclusion applies to the attempts to transfer the division of justice and love to Jesus Christ and Mary, with Mary being the one to receive our appeals and approach the throne of Christ.[5]

A second response is to reject the way the problem is framed. In Schleiermacher, we saw the refusal to consider God as being subjected to such alteration. If God is absolute causality and impassible, he could not accept an interaction between God and sinful humanity, as suggested by images of anger and wrath. But this made it difficult to understand God's opposition to sin and moral evil, resulting in a strange disjuncture. On the one hand Schleiermacher clearly affirmed Christ as the Redeemer and rejected any view of salvation as a capacity inherent in human beings; but on the other hand he was prevented from using interactive language (such as political) to describe sin and God's opposition to it.

Anselm would share Schleiermacher's concern for God's sovereignty, but finds a way to speak of judgment and wrath without implying an alternation in God. For Anselm, God possesses the source of God's own existence and God's nature does not change. But within this all-encompassing sovereignty, God relates to the world in light of the divine nature and the divine purpose. This means that God upholds the divine integrity in opposition to sin, but also responds to the world in accordance with the divine purpose, which includes redemption. From this perspective, the idea of divine impassibility is

---

5. This discussion needs to be correlated with Luther's attack on the sixteenth-century Roman Mass, where he argued that it had become a work rendered unto God for our benefit (cf. Chapter One).

qualified: while God's nature cannot change, God is responsive to the world in light of God's faithfulness to the divine purpose. But for Anselm, God is not passive in the way that we are passive. Activity upon us can cause us to change our intentions or provoke us to action contrary to our true interest. To deny that God is affected in this way does not rule out the possibility of the interaction between God and the world implied by judgment. Judgment, as a divine response to the world, points to the constancy of God's nature and God's faithfulness to the divine purpose for the restoration of the world.

Another example of refusing to accept the implied gulf between God and sinners is Abelard's *tour de force*. In this case, the major attributes of God are redefined as aspects of love. Having rejected any view involving transactions between humanity and God, Abelard appeals directly to this love as the motivation and cause for salvation. While such a view has the advantage of rejecting any transaction to appease an angry God, it ultimately reframes the whole issue of atonement. If the opposition between God and sin is completely removed, then there is little room for proclamation of the cross as judgment against sin and evil. In its modern formulations, which move beyond Abelard, the demonstration of love has been transformed into an unqualified declaration of love. But as we shall see shortly, strange things happen when love is disconnected from its relation with justice and holiness.

A third response accepts the language of judgment and wrath, but avoids the problems associated with transactional settlements described in the first response. The key here is the unity of justice and love, rather than their separation. This, however, requires a critique of traditional uses of the words. When love and justice are separated in God, they become competing attributes in God. On these terms, love signifies the way God relates to the world and forgives sinful humanity; justice points to the way God is distinguished from the world (wholly other or free) and opposed to sin and evil. How the love and justice are related is never clear. While there are specific biblical texts that suggest such a bipolar message, a more comprehensive view of the Bible suggests a unified view. Both love and justice possess characteristics of immanence and transcendence, life-giving presence and opposition. The divine love certainly displays the otherness of God just as much as God's justice — unless one wishes to defend the optimistic view that human love is identical with God's love. God's love calls into being new relationships that include new demands. In a similar way, the divine justice displays the graciousness of God just as surely as does the concept of love. The holy God who creates the world and calls it good calls Moses for the redemption of Israel. In the New Testament the classic example is Paul's assertion that the righteousness of God — not love, mercy, or grace — is displayed in Jesus Christ. Paul's choice of words represents a resolution to the question of how love and justice are related. It is an answer that insults our pride and wisdom, since we assume that holiness and righteousness lead to the punishment of the wicked. But if we accept Paul's solution, henceforth the justice of God no longer stands for the condemnation of the world but the life-giving power that opposes all that destroys life and wills to make all things new. From Paul's perspective, love and justice are united in the righteousness revealed in the cross.

But while the unity of love and justice are so central to atonement theology, in practice the separation is quite common. Justice becomes revenge and love is declared to be absolutely unconditional. On these terms, justice is upheld when the guilty are punished and the practice of religion is defined in terms of an impersonal legalism and works-righteousness. While the phrase *unconditional love* points to the gracious acceptance of God, in contrast to the endless demands of judgmental systems, it leaves open the entire concern for change, renewal, or call to discipleship. Moltmann's long and insightful critique of Christianity as an epiphany religion of the eternal present points to the problem of love separated from justice. Thus even the proclamation of the love of God offers the greatest danger, especially when love is made an end in itself. When this happens, our view of God is restricted to gracious self-giving at the expense of holiness. Thus we glorify Christ's crucifixion rather than his life, obedience, and preaching of the Rule of God. There is great irony in the criticism against the concepts of judgment and wrath based on the absoluteness of love: it runs the risk of reducing God to silence in the face of the unspeakable suffering and violence of this world. It makes little sense to try to uphold the love of God by making God irrelevant to the majority of people. This suggests that love, as the proclamation of God suffering for us, must be taken up into a broader framework whereby God wills the restoration of the creation.

3. The Purposes of God

A third component is the rich and varied tradition regarding the purposes of God. Both Israel and the church read history from the standpoint of the decisive events in the middle. Israel understands the purposes of God from the standpoint of the covenants and the conquest of the land. The early church interprets the beginning and end of time from the standpoint of the glory of God revealed in Jesus Christ. In both cases, faith is formed in relation to God's purposes. Creation and redemption reveal God's glory and yet are open to the future of a new humanity and a new creation.

This emphasis on the purposes of God provides structure to atonement theories in the following way. From God's side, the problem created by sin and evil is not only a break of trust or a challenge to God's authority. It is the deliberate subversion of God's purposes. The created order now stands opposed to the revealing of God's glory. This creates a twofold relation between God and the world: opposition to sin and faithfulness to the divine purposes for creation. Time and again we encounter variations on the words of Athanasius: "what was God to do?"[6] In Anselm the fidelity of God to the creation finds expression in the parable of the man who will not allow the pearl to remain in the mud. Such a line of thinking, of course, harks back to numerous biblical images, where God will not remain silent or inactive in the face of the need of people and the violations of the divine purpose.

The introduction of the purposes of God has momentous consequences for altering the framework for theology and preaching. When the purposes of God are left out, we have basically a theological framework of two points: the relation between God and believers. In American religion this has led to the question: Does God love me? The conservative answer is "Yes, if. . . ." God's love is conditional, depending on adherence to doctrines and practices of churches. But this attempt to control and channel grace usually provokes great protest in the name of God's sovereignty. By contrast, the liberal answer is a resolute "Yes!" with an affirmation of God's unconditional love. But since there is no expectation to participate in the community of faith or to place oneself at the disposal of God's purposes, then faith becomes a matter between the individual and God. (It is quite possible for the liberal answer to revert to the form of the conservative answer, by insisting that God's love is conditional upon adopting the alternative liberal agenda.) While there may be some overstatement in this caricature, it does point to two consequences when religion is conceived strictly in terms of the question: Does God love me? One answer amounts to dispensing tickets to heaven; the other sends postcards announcing the love of God. But note the change when the purposes of God are introduced. Now there are three points for the theological framework: God, the world, and God's purposes. In this framework the question becomes: What is God doing in the world and how can I/we participate in that purpose for the glory of God? This is a radically different approach to the gospel and provides a broader vision for understanding the work of Christ. Theories that empha-

---

6. Athanasius, "On the Incarnation of the Word, " in *Christology of the Later Fathers*, ed. Edward Rochie Hardy, trans. Archibald Robertson, vol. 3 of The Library of Christian Classics, ed. John Baillie, John T. McNeill, and Henry P. Van Dusen (Philadelphia: Westminster, 1954), p. 67.

size this approach turn our attention to a historical and/or eschatological vision that generates hope for the revealing of the glory of God.

4. Persons in Community

Participation in the covenant community is essential to atonement theories. While this relates to the previous point, it needs to be emphasized for several reasons. First, atonement theories have a conscious evangelical goal: to draw persons to faith in Christ. Such faith has traditionally involved the dialectic of the individual before God and in community. On the one hand, faith is an intensely personal act, involving repentance, conversion, being baptized, or claiming one's baptism from infancy. On the other hand, one was baptized into the covenant community where faith was nurtured and the Spirit gave new life. In our modern context, where religion is disestablished and Christianity splintered, we *hear* the language of faith, repentance, and conversion primarily, and too often only, from the perspective of the individual. It is difficult for us to imagine that prior to this cultural setting, the personal faith of the individual was always in the context of the community. But this way of thinking of persons in community is severely threatened by a modern world that has separated the individual and his/her religion from social structures. For example, in contemporary America it is assumed that religion is a matter of individual choice, based on personal interest and need. In this struggle between a communal and individualistic interpretation of Christianity, atonement theories have been pressed into service on behalf of the modern perspective. But did Luther intend the preaching of justification by grace, received by faith, to introduce an individualized approach? Or is that the way we appropriate it? Or consider the uses of substitutionary atonement: Is the watchword "Christ in *my* place" or "Christ in *our* place"? In our situation it is an uphill climb to interpret atonement theories in communal terms, be it the collective form of sin or the collective form of redemption. How one chooses to affirm the communal dimension gives structure to the theories in our time.

Second, atonement theories have much to say about who belongs to the community. When Moses does battle with the followers of Aaron over the golden calf, the issue is both the bloody struggle between two factions but also who belongs and on what terms. The New Testament is filled with disturbances and divisions over who belongs. Shall outcasts and public sinners, women and children, Samaritans, rich and poor, slave and free, only the wise and powerful, Jews and Gentiles belong? What is the basis for the participation of these varying people at the table of the Lord? These questions continue to divide churches today and it is necessary to see that theories provide answers quite different from the ones prescribed by a divided culture.

Finally, atonement theories contain explicit or implicit signals as to how we receive the benefits of Christ. Here we need to make a distinction between the way a theory describes *what* Christ does and *how* Christ's work is appropriated across time and space. It will be argued, here and in the last chapter, that the way Christ's benefits are communicated can be decisive in the formation of Christian communities. For example, if Christ is described as Lord and Life-giver who overcomes death, it is not surprising to find that baptism and Lord's Supper become the means for our dying to the old world and rising to new life (baptism), as well as participating in the new life of Christ on a continuing basis (Eucharist). Such connections can be found in Irenaeus and Athanasius. Likewise, a similar connection appears in Anselm between Christ's restoration of the purpose of creation and participation in the Eucharist. But consider the shift that occurs when Luther defines the gospel as the Word of promise, received by trust of the heart. The change in describing what Christ does changes how it shall be communicated to us. Contained in this shift are the seeds for new forms of the community: the vernacular Bible, the sermon (vs. the homily), a new hymnody and catechism. The final chapter shall explore the relationship between atonement theories and the creation of different forms of the church. Here it is sufficient to note that the ability of theories to form the community is yet another aspect of their structure.

5. *God as the Primary Subject*

The final structural component is that these theories are about God. Lest this sound like stating the obvious, there are choices. The primary subject could be some part of the problem (e.g., sin, demonic powers, human alienation, or spiritual warfare). The primary subject could be Jesus Christ, since theories are interpretations of his story. But as central as Christ is to each theory, Christ receives meaning or value only because of his relation to God. What God is doing in and through him is always the real subject matter. Atonement theories are theological in that they place the story of Jesus in the context of God's nature, purpose, and action. It is in this sense that God is the primary subject, both as the main character in the story as well as the main theme.

Paul demonstrates this point in his great exclamation: "What then shall we say to this? If God is for us, who is against us? He who did not spare his own Son but gave him up for us all, will he not also give us all things with him?" (Rom. 8:31-32). Because God is the primary subject, it follows that it is God who takes the initiative and is the primary agent in atonement theories. God cannot be passive or the object of propitiation. This point is the foundation for the gospel. It is supported even by statements that appear to focus attention on Jesus Christ. Take, for example, the idea that Jesus does something for us that we cannot do for ourselves. This idea is extremely helpful in breaking the hold of naïve optimism regarding salvation. But the idea actually points to the agency of God whose saving power is revealed in Christ. Jesus possesses saving power only by the agency of God.

The fact that atonement theories may place emphasis on God's justice or holiness on earth does not necessarily mean that God has become the object of atonement. Leaving aside the case of penal substitution, we have seen that in most theories there is more than one reason for the advent of Christ. The forgiveness of sins is of course always before us, but the completion or restoration of God's design for the world is also included in God's activity. From God's perspective, the two are the same: to save humankind is also to restore God's design. The same can be said for fulfilling the holiness of God (and removing the wrath of God). God's opposition to sin and demonic powers will not end until God creates on earth the new creation in Christ and the Spirit. A completely different picture is portrayed when the requirements of God are converted into things that humanity must do to or for God as a passive object. This, I have argued, is to subvert the evangelical and theological values of the gospel.

To summarize this section on the structure of theories of atonement: atonement theories possess a general structure because they include, in varying ways, five components: a defining image; God's opposition to sin, death, and demonic powers; the divine purposes; persons in the covenant community; and God as the primary subject. In each theory these components interact and affect each other in different ways, thereby giving a theory its distinctive character. Nevertheless, it is possible to see continuities regarding these issues. One thing becomes quite clear: when these components are missing or subverted, then atonement theology collapses. Without the divine opposition to sin and moral evil, or some sense of being estranged or bound by spiritual powers, there is no need for atonement. Those who are innocent or who have sufficient power to reform themselves are immune to the proclamation of the cross. In similar ways, if there is not an urgency derived from the purposes of God directed toward a final revealing of God's glory, or a longing for the healing of human community, there is little interest in atonement. Without the purposes of God, the story of Jesus no longer points to an eschatological vision, but is reduced to helpful ideas for individuals seeking self-realization in a world where they already have almost everything.

C. Analysis and Assessment

What are we to make of this breadth of vision regarding the saving power of Christ, where ten theories claim to be viable interpretations of Jesus Christ? Is it possible to develop some standard for evaluation? Several theories have often been the object of criticism (e.g., Anselm, penal substitution, Abelard). But are all theories subject to criticism or capable of misuse? These concerns prompt further analysis and assessment. The question is: How shall we assess them regarding form and substance? I propose that we develop norms out of the analysis of structure in the preceding section. In arguing that these were essential components of atonement theology, we have already implied their normative character. Before proceeding, however, we need to clarify the relation between these five components of structure with the three values identified at the beginning of the study: the symbolic, evangelical, and theological values. Perhaps the simplest way to express the difference is this: the three values were developed *going into the study;* the structural analysis was developed *coming out of the study,* after the analysis of ten theories. At the outset the three values were stated in broad terms and functioned as working assumptions regarding viable theories. When ten theories had been outlined in detail, with extended case studies, it was then possible to develop the analysis of structural elements. In effect, this chapter represents final reflections on the way traveled. But as we now shift to the five components from the structural analysis for assessment, I believe it will become apparent that they incorporate the symbolic, evangelical, and theological values. Finally, it should be mentioned that the discussion will not review all ten theories in light of the five points. Such an approach would state the obvious. Instead I shall concentrate on specific ways these five points help us assess atonement theories, past and present.

1. From Image to Theory

Theories may be assessed by their ability to develop a basic image into a comprehensive interpretation of Jesus Christ. This requires: (1) that the image be capable of correlating a specific problem with saving power; (2) that it be developed in a comprehensive way; (3) that the theory display precision in language.

From the standpoint of form, all ten theories qualify as theories of atonement. A specific theme is introduced by means of an image and developed to show how some aspect of saving power liberates or reconciles humanity with God, with one another, and with God's purposes for creation. But with respect to substance, the history of interpretation regarding these ten theories reveals considerable debate. Much of this criticism relates not to the original image per se, but to the way it is developed. For example, most Christians can relate to the image of Christ in our place, if this affirms that the innocent Christ died the death of sinners for us. Likewise, the idea of satisfaction can make a crucial point when it refers to the necessity to restore the order of the universe (cf. Anselm, Chapter Six). But when substitution or satisfaction is interpreted in terms of a narrow view of retributive justice, then these images violate other theological standards.

To understand the different ways the theories interpret the saving power of Jesus Christ, I have classified the theories into four groups, based on the central issue or theme contained in each: (1) The Forgiveness of Sins; (2) Liberation; (3) The Purposes of God; (4) Reconciliation. There are, of course, other ways to organize them. Since the two categories of reconciliation and liberation are so basic to the New Testament, it would be possible to use but two categories. Likewise, on the surface it might appear natural to combine the first and fourth group (forgiveness of sins and reconciliation). While such alternative schema may have some merit, I think the four categories are justified. In each the general theme is quite distinct and not reducible to any of the others.

Such a perspective considers it a great blessing that Christians, in different times and places, should encounter Christ the Savior in various ways. The New Testament, with four gospels and other materials, demonstrates this. It is no wonder that the church of the first five centuries did not seek to reach creedal agreement regarding the work of Christ. Our time has heightened the sense of the variety within the Body of Christ, within and between denominations here and worldwide. To be sure, some resist this, still claiming supremacy for their traditions. But if one is inclined to consider ecumenism a gift of God, then it is imperative that we recognize the many theories that point to the fullness of Christ. The older and polemical approach to this subject, which assumes that the favorite interpretation of one's own tradition is the only valid one, will not stand the scrutiny of historical or theological study.

More attention, however, must be given to the need for precision in the use of basic images, language, and logic. This is difficult to achieve, given the tendency to mix the theories together and use key words in different ways. This is especially characteristic of the primary speech used in preaching, hymns, and confessions. But it complicates the task of theology, which requires a level of precision for analysis and assessment.[7] Lack of precision in the use of the basic images or key words leads to great misunderstanding. For example, consider the different uses of the word *sacrifice* uncovered in this study:

1. Sacrifice can refer to sin offerings in ancient Israel dealing with *purification* and the *removal of sin,* instituted by God but definitely not offered to God. This use is unknown to most Christians. However, there is a strong connection between the idea of removal of sin in the Jewish rituals of purification and strategies for healing interpersonal conflicts in our culture. When, for example, we seek healing by using spatial imagery (move on, get past it, let go of it), such language is suggestive of the removal of sin in ancient Judaism.

2. The New Testament merges several ideas into a new use of sacrifice: (a) the Paschal sacrifice of the Exodus, which was not an offering for sin; (b) the Suffering Servant of Isaiah; (c) Jesus' suffering and death on the cross. All of these come together in the words of institution in the Eucharist and in the proclamation of John the Baptist: "Behold the Lamb of God who takes away the sin of the world" (John 1:29). In this use, Jesus gives his life for the salvation of the world.

3. A general use of sacrifice is found in common experience: the giving of time, effort, funds, or life to enhance or save the life of another (e.g., the sacrifices of parents, or the sacrifice of those who die in battle). In this common use, something is done for another, but not necessarily to someone. That is, the emphasis is on something done for us. For example, it is quite natural to say that people died on D-Day for us, but quite unnatural to say that they gave their lives to the Germans.

4. Finally, there is what I have argued is the invalid use: sacrifice as a meritorious act that provides relief, compensation, or reparations to an offended God, thereby enabling God to set aside anger or wrath and extend

---

7. In Chapter Six we noted the confusion that arises from failing to differentiate the theories: Aulén attacks what he calls the Latin theory, which is a mixture of Anselm, penal substitution, and sacrificial ideas found in the medieval mass. Weaver admits that Anselm does not really advocate a transactional view, but includes him in his assault on such views. In this chapter reference was made to William Placher, who rejects all the things wrong with traditional atonement theology when in fact his critique is aimed at penal substitution. He then constructs an alternative made up of elements from several theories.

forgiveness to sinners. As argued in Chapter One, there is no basis for this idea in the New Testament.

Given these many uses of the word *sacrifice,* the word itself can hardly identify the specific content of a theory. Three positive uses, which often converge, and one most unfortunate use create the potential for poor communication at the least, but also the possibility of gross distortion of the gospel. When one or more of these positive uses slide into the fourth, then the use of sacrifice merges with substitutionary atonement, creating a transaction for the purpose of changing God.

A similar situation of multiple uses exists with the word *satisfaction:*

1. Satisfaction could mean something that is necessary to do to or for God, prior to any action by God. Thus, the accomplishment of satisfaction allows or causes God's subsequent action. The obvious example is substitutionary atonement.
2. But satisfaction could mean the completion of something that is necessary, but as an end result of God's own activity. In this case, what is necessary is the goal toward which God's action is directed. God is not satisfied until the divine purpose is accomplished, which simultaneously resolves the tensions within God. Such use of satisfaction might appear in all of the theories, with the exception of wondrous love. Thus it can be said that God needs to be reconciled to the world (i.e., God requires the redemption of the world), or God needs to complete what God has begun.

With both sacrifice and satisfaction, great caution is needed in using the words or interpreting texts. This suggests several things: First, the mere use of a word like sacrifice or satisfaction does not necessarily tell us in what direction a theory is moving. Second, we will have to look beyond the mere use of a key word to the theory as a whole in order to determine its meaning and viability. Precision in language will be helpful, but the total scope of a theory must be considered. Finally, if key words can be used in positive and negative ways, then any theory is open to subversion against its evangelical intent and/ or loyalty to central theological norms.

2. God's Opposition to Sin, Death, and Demonic Powers

To be a comprehensive interpretation of Jesus Christ, theories must show the correlation between a problem and saving power.

1. From a formal perspective, the statement of the problem provides structure for theories: something has gone amiss and is opposed by God.[8] If there is nothing amiss, there can hardly be a theory of atonement. Since the problem is named in radically different ways, we have reason for multiple theories. From a systematic perspective, this range of interpretations may function as a general view of the fall. The more we explore the full range of the world's fallenness (sin, moral evil, sickness and death, and demonic powers), the more we find that the saving power in Jesus Christ takes many forms. In this respect, the patterns of spirituality among Roman Catholics, Protestants (including Free Church and Anabaptists), and Orthodoxy represent a far greater range than in any one group.

In the theories considered here the problem has been named as sin, death, demonic powers, and the obstruction of divine purposes. Within these categories further distinctions have been made. Liberationists are quick to point out that the sins of pride and power, so strongly identified in Augustine and Luther, are not the only forms of sin. Oppressed peoples as victims do not embody the sins of pride and idolatry, though they may be tempted by sins of passivity. Others remind us that there is a significant difference between guilt caused by our actions and shame caused by a state of being. If the one seeks forgiveness, the other hopes for liberation. The word death may refer to the loss of life, but it can also create such fear that it dominates the lives of the living. Moltmann insisted on expanding the idea of the fall by referring to illness and disease as forms of the corruptibility of the physical world in need of redemption. Demonic powers may refer to the devil and evil spirits, or transpersonal powers that corrupt individuals and society. In our time the many forms of social, political, economic, and racial ideology have been described as demonic powers that infect individuals and societies. References to spiritual warfare and culture wars are commonplace as descriptions of social conflict. With respect to the loss of freedom by individuals, words like *com-*

---

8. Some writers would be uncomfortable with making this concept a norm, lest it suggest that sin is the dominant factor in the story, rather than God's will. This concern finds expression in two ways: First, it appears in the view that the history of the covenants is founded on the eternal decrees of God and is not simply a reaction to sin. This line of thinking resists the implication that the incarnation would not have occurred if sin had not happened. From this perspective, Jesus Christ is the Last Adam who inaugurates the completion of humanity, rather than the Second or True Adam, who takes us back to, or restores, the original Paradise. Schleiermacher is probably the clearest and strongest advocate for such a position among those reviewed. Second, the concern is the framework for atonement theories that place attention on God's goal. In this case, attention focuses more on God's will to fulfill God's purpose, rather than simply on the forgiveness of sins. For someone like Anselm, the framework is distorted if atonement is viewed only from the standpoint of God's opposition to sin.

pulsive behavior and *addiction* are frequently used. Finally, some theories take the most fundamental issue to be the disruption of God's purposes for creation. Such a view presupposes all of the problems already named, but focuses attention on this ultimate theological concern. What we have, then, is a broad range of ideas that Christians use to describe the fall or the problem.

The statement of the problem also points to a particular aspect of saving power. Theories can be rather single-minded in their focus on one issue. Theories dealing with forgiveness of sins speak with great power about the torment of guilt and estrangement from God. If not connected with other motifs, they may miss the needs of many people, such as those suffering from shame caused by social or physical status. It is also possible for traditions to become preoccupied with the sinful acts of individuals. Walter Rauschenbusch, Reinhold Niebuhr, and the liberationists have all tried to expand the highly individualized notion of sin to include social forms. But if theories in their logical form are single-minded, very often writers are more inclusive. So Athanasius does not only refer to victory over death but also to forgiveness of sins, and Luther sees Christ waging war with death, the devil, and demonic powers as well as speaking a word of forgiveness. The fact that theories are structured by a particular form of the problem and its resolution becomes a strong argument for teaching and preaching many theories of atonement.

2. The interaction between the problem and God's response also provides energy for theories, i.e., the force or logic that drives the theory. Consider the simple phrases in Exodus 3:7-8: "I have seen the affliction of my people . . . and have heard their cry. . . . I know their sufferings . . . and I have come down." God's opposition generates the categories that become so decisive for biblical faith: for example, call, promise, historical remembrance, cross and resurrection, hope, the glory of God, and the final goal. By contrast, theories lose their ability to witness to saving power when the statement of the problem and God's opposition are unclear. The theory of wondrous love has a more complicated history on this point. I have argued that in fact Abelard assumes a traditional view of sin and affirms Jesus Christ as the Savior who creates a new community as part of God's history of salvation. Nevertheless, his view has been connected to so many other views that offer a quite weak view of sin and see Jesus primarily as the teacher of love. It is against this view that the criticisms have been rightly directed.

To adopt this norm, however, we must discern how it may be faithfully applied to the life and work of churches today. American religion is constantly tempted to dilute the way the problem is defined. The most common form of this is by trivializing the gospel. The serious life-and-death issues are replaced by those small, individual irritations or the social taboos of a given culture.[9] But if American religion trivializes the problem, it also tempts us with the illusion of innocence. Ideas regarding the corruption of reason and will, of excessive self-love, of pretensions to power and goodness, are all quickly discounted by a society confident in its ability to find meaning and fulfillment in worldly knowledge and achievement. In the face of world conflicts and pressing national interests, there is little room for introspection, self-doubt, or the admission of culpability. Those who claim innocence or who have sufficient power to reform themselves are immune to the proclamation of the cross. Without the divine opposition to sin and moral evil, or some sense of being estranged or bound by spiritual powers, there is no need for atonement. In similar ways, if there is not an urgency derived from the purposes of God directed toward a final revealing of God's glory, or a longing for the healing of human community, there is little interest in atonement. The story of Jesus no longer points to an eschatological vision, but is reduced to helpful ideas for individuals seeking self-realization in a world where they already have almost everything.

3. The Purposes of God

Theories must place the problem and its resolution in the larger context of God's purposes.

This norm requires a shift in perspective. Human needs and interests are relevant but are not the only issue and certainly not the ultimate issue. The three theories of Athanasius, Anselm, and Schleiermacher are especially strong on this point. But they are not alone. In our time liberation theology has capitalized on the historical perspective of biblical studies and placed new emphasis on an eschatological vision. Likewise, the other theories are careful to place the saving power of God in the context of God's purposes.

The danger the churches face stems not from one of these theories, but the way any and all are subverted by the egocentric perspective of American religion. This takes acute form in the functionalism that dominates our culture. Functionalism means that religion and its institutions are defined primarily by their utility, i.e., they have to do with *doing* rather than *being*. In the

---

9. I once heard a preacher illustrate temptation (in a sermon on the three temptations of Christ) with reference to delicious food! Of all the temptations facing individuals and our society, the only one lifted up was an obsession with a high-calorie food. One is reminded of Ignazio Silone's novel *Bread and Wine,* dealing with faithfulness in the face of the horrors of Mussolini's rule over Italy. In such a situation, a priest writes an essay on the dangers of immodesty in dress. There appears no end to the domestication of sin.

language of popular religion, it means: What will it do for me? In American religion, religion exists as a way of meeting human needs. These needs can range from monetary to health needs, as well as personal needs for happiness, success, and personal fulfillment. There appears little concern for sorting out what ostensibly are genuine human needs from those derived from a culture dedicated to happiness and material success. The church growth movements have institutionalized this shift in focus, making the cross and resurrection the means for personal happiness and self-fulfillment.[10] The paradox of Jesus' call to lose oneself in service of God and God's Rule is completely destroyed. The broader vision of God's purposes is replaced by the preoccupation with human interests and then coupled with a highly individualized view of sin. The groundwork is laid for a privatized religion that has lost any sense of judgment or salvation for the world.

4. Persons in Community

Theories must be assessed by their affirmations regarding the community of Christ: (1) the call to participate in Christ's community; (2) the witness to the grace of God; (3) the ability to generate and sustain specific forms of communal life.

---

10. In America, user-friendly forms of Christianity abound. In spite of criticism, the organizers of these movements seem to grow in popularity and financial support. Norman Vincent Peale was followed by Robert Schuller, who not only created his own cathedral, but effectively promotes his message on television. (Schuller also produced his own version of the King James Bible known as the *Possibility Thinkers Bible*, where verses Schuller believes are suggestive of personal growth are highlighted in blue. What is and is not selected reveals a unique set of principles for interpretation.) The Willow Creek phenomenon has spawned countless imitations and adaptations in conservative and mainline denominations, as churches rush to increase membership. While these movements differ in many ways, they stand over against traditional Protestantism in the rejection of traditional doctrine and liturgical forms, the inventive use of electronic media, and extremely well-organized promotional systems. The common thread is the promotion of religion as something that will solve problems and improve the lives of individuals. In this sense they promote a functional view of religion, with God as the Almighty Technique. For example, the highly successful publications of Rick Warren appear to place the emphasis on God's purposes. But the question remains whether churches and individuals are being asked to give their lives to God's purpose, or is God's purpose simply another technique to enhance our quest for meaning and success (cf. *The Purpose-Driven Church: Growth Without Compromising Your Message and Mission* [Grand Rapids: Zondervan, 1995]). Mainline and conservative Protestant churches need to bear in mind that many of their members have already heard representatives of user-friendly religion on television before coming to church on Sunday morning.

Participation in Christ's Community

The great American heresy is that one can be Christian without belonging to a community of believers bound by Christ. None of the theories considered here proposes this, but each can be revised and/or degenerate into a rationale for individualized religion. If we are to make any progress in restoring the connection between faith in Christ and fellowship with other believers, we must make the connection in the most basic form of preaching and teaching, namely atonement theories. Just as one cannot add on a social ethic to the piety of individualized religion, so one cannot add the bonds of community to isolated believers. Atonement theology must connect the cross of Christ with the Body of Christ.

A Community Witnessing to the Grace of God

The church is called to witness to the grace of God in Jesus Christ as a message of hope for the entire world. In general, all of the theories affirm Christ as Lord and Savior.[11] Such confessions, however, create a continuing struggle, which can be described in terms of the dialectic between exclusivity and inclusivity. If saving power is revealed in Jesus Christ and the new life he brings, then Jesus and the new spiritual life are decisive and must be the standard for participation in the community. How one defines Jesus Christ and this new life varies in the New Testament and in Christian communities in every time and place. But it still can be said that virtually all Christians have some point where the line is drawn for inclusion into the community, be it a primal confession, doctrinal statements, or ethical behavior.[12] The most liberal Christian on doctrinal matters is quite often dogmatic regarding social issues. In these ways the confession of Christ contains the impulse to exclude. But at the same time, the confession of Christ is one of *sola gratia* and the judgment of God against all claims to intellectual or moral self-righteousness.

---

11. As discussed in Chapter Four, feminist theology would qualify this statement in a variety of ways, from completely rejecting it to more moderate revisions, often rejecting the idea that suffering and death can be redemptive.

12. There was a time when many dealt with the problem of unity and diversity with the words: "In essentials unity, in nonessentials liberty, and in all things charity." But in our time, many press for making everything an essential, e.g., authority of bishops, relations to the modern world, as well as opposition to abortion and homosexuality. Communities have become quite absolutist in their insistence for agreement, moving more and more toward the position that the church is based on our agreement. It is at this point that Paul's affirmation of living without claims, except Christ, may be the word of judgment and hope emerging from the theories.

The New Testament repeatedly provides instances of radical inclusivity. Compare, for example, Jesus' acceptance of the poor, common working people, public sinners, Samaritans, women, and children. In the early church this openness is extended, after great debate, to Gentiles. Likewise, there is an unusual egalitarianism based on the presence of Christ in the Lord's Supper and the bestowal of the Spirit. To be sure, this rule of equality was violated, in spirit and in practice, by the subordination of women and the continuation of slavery. But at least in principle, the confession of Christ clearly contained, at the earliest stage, a radical inclusivity.

These two quite opposite impulses create a level of tension and instability in the process of forming Christian communities. How does one confess Jesus is Lord and Savior (which implies limits) when that confession is itself a word of grace and a rebuke against all self-righteousness? There is no doubt that the early church struggled at great length regarding this issue. For example, the gospels and letters contain a variety of mandates for the new community. But against the tendency to define the community according to unyielding requirements we have the affirmation of grace in parables and broad confessions (cf. Galatians and 1 Corinthians). But does the affirmation of grace as the sole basis for membership mean that those who lean toward an ordered life with rules and regulations are excluded? Or are we to be gracious to them as God has been gracious to us? In other words, can a community of grace exclude those who are ungracious? The other major example emerging in the New Testament is the relation of Christians and Jews. If Jesus is Lord and Savior, what shall the new Christian community make of its Jewish heritage? The confession of Jesus Christ has led to the rejection of the Jews, as passages in John illustrate. Individual lines from Paul can also be used to argue for the absolute requirement of faith in Jesus for salvation. But in Romans 9–11 Paul affirms that God has not rejected the Jews. The church's rejection of Marcion also stands against a complete separation, which included the retention of Jewish scriptures.

The theories considered in this study incorporate the two impulses in various ways and have produced a variety of configurations and endless debate. If theories are used in support of *either* inclusivity *or* exclusivity, the results have proven to be both indefensible and destructive for creating community. When the emphasis falls only on inclusivity, there is usually a loss of continuity with normative traditions. If every idea or practice is acceptable, it is difficult to know what the confession of Jesus Christ means, which in turn undercuts the importance of the confession itself. In America, where the chief value is liberty, religion falls into the domain of individual freedom. As such, people decide the form and substance of religion according to their individual reason and interests. This does indeed create challenges for churches where there is a desire to affirm biblical and orthodox traditions. By contrast, when the emphasis falls on exclusivity, communities are in danger of claiming to be the sole possessors of truth and salvation, while everyone else is excluded. Such a premise has too often led to division and spiritual warfare, as well as violence. For example, this has produced tragic results regarding the Jews in the West. Shall this be extended to the nominal Christians within the West and all other religions? It is very disturbing that theories of grace and mercy, of God's suffering for sinners, and the liberation of oppressed people should become the basis for more division, hatred, and violence.

But if the two impulses are not to be separated, what is the alternative to thinking of Christ and the church with only one of these categories? The answer may be not in particular texts in the New Testament, but in the New Testament as a whole, where the two impulses are held together in creative tension. Such a dialectical solution would require affirming the value of each, in spite of the tensions and apparent inconsistencies. A spiritual life seeking to incorporate both inclusivity and exclusivity is difficult and certainly confusing, forever requiring new configurations and decisions for new issues. It cannot be codified in an absolute formula. But several suggestions may be helpful.

The first is the need to recognize the dialectical character of the confession that Jesus is Lord, i.e., the crucified one who reveals the judgment and grace of God is now the sign of saving power. The fullness of that confession cannot be contained in either impulse by itself, but each needs to limit and renew the other. From a historical perspective, Protestants and Catholics have struggled with both impulses. Each has elements that represent the best and worst of inclusivity and exclusivity. But in their traditional relation to one another, they may represent something of the very dialectic in the confession that Christ is Lord. If Protestants have traditionally upheld the judgment of God against all attempts to control grace, by contrast Catholics have traditionally upheld the affirmation that grace is indeed a reality in the Body of Christ on earth. There are elements of inclusivity and exclusivity in each tradition, but worked out in radically different ways. A more careful examination of these matters could lead to greater clarity regarding faithful witness.

The second is to keep before us that salvation is a gift of God and not our personal achievement. Atonement theories do not suggest that the church is for the personal benefit of those who were or are now included, but a missionary community called to witness to God's saving power. Paul and Luther take great comfort and joy in this casting aside of every human confidence and trusting in God alone. Contained in this reliance on God is a willingness, as expressed in Jesus' teachings and his actions, to disregard one's own interests — even one's own salvation — in service to the will of God. As Philippians 2 proclaims, Christians should have the mind of Christ, who emptied himself for the sake of service to God. For those who have come to know the grace of Christ and the new life in the Spirit, it is self-evident that saving power is found in the many and varied forms of Christian community. It does make a difference to confess the name of God and embody on earth the peace of Christ. From the Christian perspective, those who have no knowledge of God in Christ have not known this saving power. We can share the good news with them and regret what appears to be their loss. But we need to avoid making our faith in Christ (and their lack of faith in Christ) into the decisive issue. That is to say, the Christian life — faith in Christ and its practices of new life — are not the price we pay for salvation, but our grateful response to what God has done in Christ. I cannot help but hear the voice of the older brother, from the parable of the prodigal son, in the relentless insistence that one cannot be saved if one does not believe in Jesus Christ. Do we need to ask whether such insistence arises from our need to justify our decision for Christ? Like the brother, it is quite tempting to wonder why we should practice the way of discipleship if a spiritual reward is not the result for us alone. But if we follow the brother's line of thinking, then faith and practice are the work or sacrifice we make to guarantee our place with Jesus in eternity.[13] At the end of this argument we find a self-righteous legalism and the denial of both the grace and justice of God. If we, by contrast, rely upon the free and gracious will of God to save, then it is conceivable that we can disconnect the affirmation of the centrality of Christ from the exclusivist conclusion. To disconnect them would not mean less confidence in the saving power of Christ, but rather a testimony to Christ in our lives and the sovereignty of God to judge and save. For those who have known Christ, that knowledge is a foretaste of what God has promised and does not need the added claim that they alone are saved. For those who have not known Christ, we would do well to commend them to the very grace and mercy so richly lavished on us.

---

13. Looking at Protestant piety, as it appears in mainline and conservative traditions, one wonders whether the dominant emphasis has been shaped by a variation on Hellenistic mystery religions: the key appears to be the assurance of eternal life with Jesus, freed from the world. Those traditions that engage in millennial speculations cast this message in dramatic, apocalyptic terms.

Since this aspect of atonement theories will be discussed in the next chapter, I will defer a fuller discussion to that place. It should be noted here that the theories suggest multiple ways in which the benefits of Christ may be communicated to believers across time and space. This flies in the face of denominational insistence on the absolute rectitude of one method of communication, or one form of the church. Just as this study has moved to the recognition of multiple theories of atonement, we shall see that there are indeed multiple ways of forming communities of Christ.

5. God's Initiative

Theories must be assessed by their ability to affirm God as the primary subject, rather than the object.

The rationale for such a norm has been amply provided throughout this study. Such a norm means the rejection of any theory that makes God the object of action by Jesus Christ or humanity in general. In the discussion regarding the defining image, the need for precision was illustrated by reference to the way the concepts of sacrifice and satisfaction can be turned into compensation to God. But any theory can be subverted by a move in such a direction. Since it is not sufficient simply to ban words like satisfaction, or substitution, it is more helpful to find a precise formulation for this norm. The following criteria may be used to assess theories:

1. God is the primary subject when Jesus is seen as part of God's initiative for the sake of changing the world (i.e., restoring the creation, reconciliation, or liberation).
2. God becomes an object when Jesus performs a meritorious act in order to offer compensation to God to change God (i.e., either remove wrath, motivate God to forgive us, or resolve tensions within God).

The critical issue is not whether Jesus acts as the representative human (e.g., Second Adam) or as the incarnate Word, but whether Jesus' action is a form of compensation directed to God. The second proposition undermines any theory of atonement by nullifying God as the subject in redeeming the world. As argued above, even the attempt to elevate this compensation into the life of the triune God by having the Son offer the meritorious act to the Father still does not overcome the damage done. On these terms, atonement still involves reparations to the injured justice of God, rather than the restoration of the creation so that it might fulfill God's goal of holiness on earth. The test, then, is to search any teaching, sermon, or hymn to determine what is happening in Jesus' life, death, and resurrection. What is the relation of Jesus' death to God? When Jesus' death becomes an end in itself, then God is probably the object, in marked contrast to theories that speak of his death as a demonstration of holiness and love on earth.

D. The Theories in Relation to One Another

If the ten theories demonstrate different aspects of the saving power of Jesus Christ, then it is possible to view them as parts of a larger whole. Assuming that the problems with substitutionary atonement could be resolved by serious revision, then all represent valuable interpretations of Jesus Christ, which should not be ranked in some kind of hierarchy. Little is to be gained by trying to suggest that some theories have temporal or logical priority, if in fact each points to a form of saving power. They complement each other because they speak to different issues and in so doing reveal the fullness of Christ.

One conclusion to be drawn from this judgment is that the church, as well as the spiritual life of individuals, needs this variety in order to comprehend fully the nature of sin and grace. Once one becomes immersed in the power of these witnesses to faith, it is quite impossible to return to that single-mindedness that characterizes so many traditions and/or writers. When saving power takes the form of forgiveness of sins, it is different from that saving power that liberates people from death and demonic powers. How wonderful that some theories speak a word of grace to personal guilt and despair, while others expose our social idols and spiritual warfare. One might even hazard the suggestion that if the theories do indeed point to the fullness of Christ, then our liturgies as well as our preaching need to be reconsidered in light of this range of ideas. The traditional liturgies for the Eucharist, in spite of numerous revisions and attempts at a broader perspective, still tend to focus on the forgiveness of sins as the primary problem. Furthermore, if it is correct that most participants will hear the word of forgiveness spoken to individuals, then we have a liturgy that is quite limited in the sense that this essential form of saving power is but one aspect of the fullness of Christ.

While the theories complement one another, they also stand in tension with each other, expose the omissions, and inspire criticisms of one another.

Wondrous love stands alone by interpreting the story of Jesus solely by reference to love — a fact the nine counterparts have not always accepted kindly. When wondrous love takes the form of God seeking to overcome the moral protest of humanity against God, we have a dramatic shift in emphasis. The same can be said of all of the liberationists, who shift the emphasis from forgiveness of sins to release from oppressive forces and death. If many of the other theories affirmed obedience, suffering, and self-sacrifice, liberationists have affirmed saving power as resistance, self-affirmation, and freedom.

A long-standing tension continues to separate those theories that cluster around images of forgiveness/reconciliation in contrast to images of liberation/holiness. This takes many forms, but two require discussion. In the first form, the tension is the separation of justification and sanctification. In theory most writers affirm the unity of the two and affirm both as marks of the Christian life. But in practice different traditions have gravitated toward one or the other side, producing what I call the religion of grace and the religion of power. The religion of grace focuses on God's acceptance of sinners by unconditional love; the religion of power focuses on how God is changing things now. The former is so mindful of the pervasiveness of sin that it is forever cautious about perfectionist and utopian dreams. What results, however, is a rhythm of confession of sin and forgiveness that produces a stalemate. From one perspective, it may be called cheap grace, from another it is a kind of paralysis of the spirit, mindful of sin but unable or unwilling to risk a move toward sanctification. By contrast, the religion of power expects something of God and declares that God expects something of us — now! There are obviously high correlations with the religion of power and the powerless.[14] Its proponents see the religion of grace as far too comfortable and allied with the status quo. These two forms of religion based on grace and power illustrate the unresolved tensions between and within theories of atonement. Between theories the tensions find expression when justification by grace is set against the power of the Spirit for sanctification (e.g., between Luther and Wesley). But the tensions may well be within theories. It is striking to discover that substitutionary atonement is widely used by traditional Lutherans and Calvinists on the one hand, but on the other hand by Free Church traditions, Holiness groups, and Anabaptists. In the next chapter we shall explore how traditions can draw radically different consequences from the same theory.

The second form of this tension is the opposition of reconciliation and

---

14. There are, however, important exceptions. For example, both Peale and Schuller offer power to middle- and upper-class persons, even though they already possess a great deal and have great access to the powers of this world.

liberation. Each offers a powerful witness to saving power. In the case of reconciliation, there is the divine initiative that creates the peace of Christ as a pure gift, given in the face of all our hostility and warfare. It is a word of judgment against our willful rebellion from God and our arrogance in claiming that we possess the basis for union. The affirmation of reconciliation requires that we acknowledge that the sole basis for the church, our standing before God and with one another, is the grace of God in the cross of Christ. Its caution regarding reforms and revolutions, rules and plans, is born of the sorrow such ventures create. As such, reconciliation is a powerful testimony to the gospel and, in the face of our perennial desire to base the church on our agreement, is always a word of judgment and hope. In the case of liberation, there is the divine initiative that sides with the oppressed and liberates individuals and communities for life together in justice and peace. Here too is a word of judgment against the willful oppression of other persons and the hypocrisy of those in power. Saving grace, however, takes the form of empowerment and liberation over against fear, despair, and passivity. Its willingness to risk action for change is born, not out of optimism in human potential or designs, but out of the eschatological vision revealed in Jesus Christ, which empowers persons to act for justice and peace. As such, liberation is also a powerful testimony to the gospel and a protest against the lack of hope and action in churches too comfortable with the status quo.

This opposition between these two views is not easy to overcome. As much as one may find comfort in the proclamation of grace as a pure gift, or see it as the only alternative to endless conflict, the concerns for justice and holiness always remain. Can we be reconciled to persons who persist in breaking trust or committing acts of violence? Does not justification by grace at some point and in some way require newness of life? From the other side, while there may be the acceptance of an end to physical violence as a requirement for reconciliation, there persists a weariness regarding the imposition of moral, social, and doctrinal standards as a basis for union. The religious zeal for righteousness is far too often a problem rather than the solution.

When one reviews the history of this debate and reflects on the great variety of ways Christians have sought to resolve it, one must face the fact that no Christian group has solved the problem of perfect justice and holiness on earth. The problem has not been lack of trying. No doubt there are still some options to be tried, but the history of the church teaches us a great deal about the limits and possibilities of sanctification. For this reason I shall not pretend to have discovered a new way to resolve the tensions between grace and holiness. I can only offer several comments to encourage further discussion.

First, the current ecumenical sharing of faith and work, along with the lively mix of old and new theological perspectives (i.e., liberal and conservative, Protestant and Catholic and Orthodox), create a hopeful situation. The combination of biblical studies, ecumenical partnerships, and new perspectives (e.g., liberationist and feminist) allows us to think in new ways. It is a very unsettling time for those who wish to remain in the confines of traditional denominational ways of thinking. But for those who consider all these developments as part of God's providence, it is an exciting time. For example, liberation theology has caused us to shift our view from the past to the future. It has offered new ways of thinking about saving power, thereby allowing us to rethink the relation of love and justice with regard to theology and ethics. Another example is the way we are able to think anew about the relation of being and doing. Paul makes it clear that the indicative always precedes the imperative: the new being in Christ must be the basis for our identity and worth. But he also is just as clear that the new being necessitates a new doing. What is needed, however, is not another formula as to how being and doing relate, but hard work in prayer and worship, witness and fellowship, among Christians across traditional boundaries.

Second, while there is great cause to be hopeful, a certain caution is in order. If it is the case that the traditions present us with only imperfect solutions, then perhaps we need to plan for failure. We need to explore what went right and wrong about the many great movements and experiments of Christian life. Of particular interest might be the exploration of the way traditions have institutionalized responses to failure. For example, the liturgical confession of sin and the Roman Catholic sacrament of penance recognize that the baptized Christian still sins. Among Mennonites, Matthew 18 is a determinative text for the community since it requires that members be reconciled before they come to the Lord's Table. Here too there is an assumption that sin still persists even in the beloved community. The Lutheran caution regarding utopian dreams and the Calvinist appeal to the sovereignty of God presuppose the persistence of self-deception and the abuse of power — even among those authorized to rule church and state. The liberationist use of a hermeneutic of suspicion — if it is practiced among the faithful as well as against oppressors — also suggests the persistence of sin. The point is that Christians have been quite inventive in recognizing the limits of their holiness as well as courageous in pursuing it. A careful review of these institutionalized responses to failure might examine whether any of these practices are time bound, or whether some are more appropriate for certain settings. Such discussions need not conclude with the acceptance of failure, but might give new direction for the movement from grace to holiness.

Finally, attempts to embody grace *and* power will have a greater opportunity for progress if they begin with repentance and humility at the foot of the cross. Christian traditions have used the failures of others to wound one another and find self-assurance. The language and logic of the debate between grace and power are well known. One side claims Paul, Augustine, Luther, Calvin, and Reinhold Niebuhr, while the other claims Paul, Anselm, Calvin, the Anabaptists, Wesley, and liberationists. But even such an alignment may offer opportunities for mediation. If Paul inspires both traditions, so does Calvin, as well as Reinhold Niebuhr in his insistence on an ethic of love and justice. The liberation theology of Gutiérrez is so firmly rooted in the affirmations of Incarnation, Trinity, and sacraments that many can find common ground in his work. But perhaps all of these sources might be viewed in new ways if we approached them with greater confidence in our unity in Christ. That unity in Christ is not monolithic, as the ten theories make evident. Learning to live with the tensions between the theories may be part of the discipline of the peace of Christ. Hence a postscript: while there is much to mandate continuous exploration of ways grace and power may come together, perhaps they should always stand in tension. Given the reality of sin, the efforts toward holiness — no matter how well intentioned and Spirit filled — stand in need of grace; given the reality of sin, our willingness to find repose in grace — no matter how well intentioned and Spirit filled — requires the mandate to awaken and become children of light.

The differences and tensions between the theories inevitably lead to alternations in the interest paid to each one. The rise of liberation theology testifies to this alternation of interest, born of changes in the life and work of faith communities. One would expect the theories pertaining to social issues to receive more attention (e.g., theories regarding idols and reconciliation in the face of spiritual warfare). But more interest appears to be turning to the combination of liberation with wondrous love in the advocacy of Christ and the church as a nonviolent movement for peace. Another development has been the new attention given to Christ *in our place*. While some feminists reject the idea of suffering as redemptive, many others are drawn to the image of sacrifice because of its prevalence in human experience. The emphasis on God's suffering to win back alienated humanity develops this theme in new ways. The traditional Protestant emphasis on justification by grace is always a powerful theme, though this religious message may be eclipsed in a secular culture, where forms of therapy and self-help claim to provide a word of assurance and acceptance. One is reminded again that the theories make no sense outside of a theological context.

E. The Saving Power of Jesus Christ

Recent decades have seen considerable warfare between liberal and conservative Protestants on theological and social issues. Parallel to this has been a serious decline in membership and influence by the so-called mainline traditions. Conservatives have claimed that these changes are the result of their liberal tendencies. But it is more accurate to see these changes among liberal and/or ecumenical traditions as resulting from a lack of confidence. At the heart of this uncertainty have been caution and confusion regarding Jesus Christ. It is difficult to have confidence if one does not know what to proclaim regarding Christ. Thus at the heart of the churches' struggle to find their identity and mission are the Christological questions posed by the life, death, and resurrection of Jesus. When ordained and lay leaders are not clear about atonement, there can be no confidence regarding vocation, ministry, or the future of the church.

It is not necessary to review the reasons why ecumenical Protestantism fell on hard times between the 1960s and the present. Whether these churches were overwhelmed by new and critical theological issues or preoccupied with social issues is part of the ongoing debate about their viability. The thesis proposed here is that enthusiasm and confidence for the churches' mission stem from clarity regarding the meaning of Jesus Christ. This is the case because Jesus Christ means salvation. When all the other reasons for being religious and joining churches fail (e.g., personal enrichment, social status, guidance for children, or even fear), one must ask whether the churches have anything to say about the saving power of Jesus Christ. Luther declared that the gospel was the true treasure of the church, and he was right. The cross and resurrection of Christ are the church's only foundation. Its daily life requires clarity and commitment regarding the good news. This then is the only justification for this exploration of the theories of atonement. Each theory stands, like John the Baptist in the painting of the crucifixion scene on the Isenheim Altar, pointing to Jesus Christ.

But what is that good news, that priceless treasure which the church requires in order to be the church? Having argued against reducing the fullness of Christ to one general theory, it would be contrary to the entire study to suggest now that it can all be summarized in one statement. It is appropriate, however, to give several affirmations regarding the life, death, and resurrection of Jesus Christ that grow directly out of the structural analysis. With only several exceptions, these can be found in all of the theories, where they possess somewhat distinctive formulation. They run through the theories as common threads and constitute a foundation for atonement theology.

1. Jesus' life, cross, and resurrection mean a judgment of God against the world. This affirmation expresses the opposition of God to sin, death, and demonic powers. It draws upon the long history in the Bible and traditions, which utilize images of judgment and wrath as expressions for God's refusal to accept the fallenness of the world. It is not necessary to give examples from all of the theories, but references may be made to the theories of sacrifice, justification, Christ in our place, Anselm's emphasis on restoration, the breaking of this world's idols, or the judgment against the wisdom and power of the world (1 Cor. 1–2). By his actions and teachings, Jesus embodies the Rule of God and thereby creates a crisis. He stands against all that denies the just and gracious rule of God, even in those moments where his acts of grace confound the wisdom of the world. It is this theme of judgment that sets the stage for atonement theories. The tension between God's goodness and the sin of the world reaches its culmination in Jesus' rejection and death. The resolution is revealed in God's vindication of the crucified at Easter, but awaits its complete manifestation in the final revealing of God's glory.

2. Jesus actualizes the new being for humanity and the world according to God's purposes. In his faithfulness to God, Jesus represents the true humanity, whether the emphasis is placed on a restoration of the first Adam, the introduction of a new Adam, or the last Adam as the completion of God's plan. The judgment of God is taken away by God's intervention, wherein holiness is revealed in Jesus and the community he creates. Every theory affirms this, in its own language, as the revealing of God's righteousness, holiness, love, and grace. It is God's will in Jesus Christ to give life in the face of sin and death. It is precisely at this point that Jesus' suffering and death enter the story as the consequences of his holiness and faithfulness. His suffering and death have a purpose in that they attest to his willingness to lose all for the Rule of God, to engage the powers of evil in combat, or as a testimony of God's will to redeem the world. Such statements reject any idea of his suffering and death as ends in themselves or as compensation to God. One can rule out the negative transactional views and still affirm the power of the cross because it points to the fidelity of both Jesus and God. It is the ultimate form of fidelity and self-giving, and it always points in two directions: it reveals the demonic and idolatrous character of sin and evil *and* it points to the holiness that gives life.

All theories face the serious temptation of turning Jesus' suffering and death into ends in themselves or as compensation to an offended deity. But while such negative developments must be resisted, it diminishes atonement theology to suggest that death cannot have redemptive value. The proclamation of the church can and must proclaim the cross of Jesus for two reasons.

The first reason relates to the way Christians think of salvation. Salvation has to do with forgiveness of sin, liberation from sin, death, and demonic powers, and our reconciliation with one another and with God. Sin is a break in relation with God and neighbor, creating separation and alienation. Death is the ultimate form of separation, which threatens to control our lives. Consider what human beings do in order to avoid the fear of death as well as its reality. The life of Jesus, therefore, is the place of conflict between God and sin, between life and death. This must be said of his whole life. Even in the birth narratives we are confronted, not with sweetness and quiet, but terrifying stories of life and death. But as much as his whole life represents the point of conflict, even more so do his passion and death on the cross. It is quite appropriate and inevitable that the cross should come to represent Jesus' fidelity in the struggle between life and death. Thus, if the proclamation of salvation does not include the cross, then it is in danger of telling a story of salvation without judgment or struggle. This is not an idle fear, since examples abound of Jesus being reduced to teachings of love, or the entire gospel being translated into ideas of happiness or universal truth. But the story of Jesus cannot be separated from his life of fidelity (with its resultant suffering). This is, as Bonhoeffer reminded us, the visible witness to the cost of salvation.

The second reason why the church must proclaim the cross has to do with the power of life given for others. Acts of self-sacrifice are powerful because they are expressive of the intentions, and ultimately the character, of the person performing the action. They are also powerful because they have the capacity to draw the recipients to the person, creating a bond of obligation. One reason they possess such power is that they draw upon the general fascination humans have with any struggle for life in the face of death, or with blood itself. To be sure, part of this fascination with blood arises out of the association with danger. Such interest is easily manipulated by the media, the arts, and even religious practices and preaching. Yet in spite of such abuses, we need to acknowledge that the association also grows out of a natural concern for life and the fear of death. Such fascination with blood is heightened in the case of persons who give their lives for others. History is filled with examples of military valor and noble sacrifice. Parallel to such public examples are the many instances of self-sacrifice within family histories. In all of these cases, it is quite common for acts of self-sacrifice to reveal positive intentions and generate a sense of obligation. All of this is part of the great impact self-sacrifice has upon us.

St. Paul captures something of the wonder of such actions when he observes: "Indeed, rarely will anyone die for a righteous person — though perhaps for a good person someone might actually dare to die" (Rom. 5:7). But in this case, Paul's point is not to extol heroic activity, but to point to the self-giving of Jesus Christ as a demonstration of the love of Christ. This demonstration of love and fidelity to us and to God is forever tied to that self-giving of his very life. There is no doubt that the isolation of suffering and death as ends in themselves, or the separation of Good Friday from his entire life and his resurrection, leads to distortions. But such misinterpretations do not nullify the fact that Jesus' love and fidelity are forever tied to his suffering and death. He did not die by accident, nor was his death a mere historical detail that can be glossed over. As one faithful to the Rule of God, he is the recipient of the hostility of the world. He takes into his life the consequences of sin, does not respond in kind, and remains faithful. By bearing this suffering and death, he overcomes the power of suffering and death to control us or turn us from God. Such affirmations are captured in two great symbols of Christ's fidelity and self-giving. In John we have the symbol of the Lamb of God who takes away the sin of the world. By his life he bears and removes all that separates us from God. In Paul we have the symbol of the power of the cross, whereby Christ bears the rejection of the world. In his suffering and death he appears as weakness and foolishness to the world, but in his resurrection he becomes the power of salvation. In both of these symbols, what Jesus does is tied to his suffering and death, but it is also tied to God. It is not simply Jesus who is suffering and dying for us, but God. Thus the suffering and death of Jesus reveal something of Jesus' intentionality (e.g., Phil. 2), but also the character and intentionality of God. It is in this sense that one can say: if the proclamation of Christ is not connected with his cross, then the gospel loses its power to reveal the saving power of Jesus Christ.

3. The final affirmation has to do with Jesus' participation in our life. The gospels make clear from beginning to end that Jesus was one of us, identified with us, and took part in our life. To be sure, he participated in the joy and goodness of human life. But it should not surprise us that what stands out, in retrospect, is his willingness to participate in our sorrows and suffering. If he was the chosen one of God, the Word incarnate, why did he suffer and die? That question appears in the New Testament and throughout early Christian literature. The answer, given without qualification, is that he chose to be for us by being with us. It should not surprise us, therefore, that this suffering with us, in the name of God, is lifted up in the spiritual imagination of Christian communities. We need only consider the Roman Catholic tradition, with its emphasis on the stations of the cross, the crucifix, or the crucified in the arms of Mary. Mary herself is brought into this act of solidarity with those who suffer, since she represents all mothers (and fathers) who grieve the death of their children for righteousness' sake. Mary the Mother of God thereby connects

with all who suffer and grieve. In her suffering, she symbolizes the very suffering of God, who grieves for the innocent lost in the violence of the world. If this appears overstated, one should step back and remember that for most people in the world — past and present — human life consists of bearing natural catastrophes, sickness and death due to disease, and the violence of persecution and war. The European Holocaust in Germany was one of many in the twentieth century! Against the background of such suffering, the affirmation of the suffering of Christ is a powerful declaration.

These three affirmations are at the heart of Christian views of the saving power in Jesus Christ: his opposition to sin, death, and moral evil; his fidelity to the Rule of God on earth; his participation in our life. All three affirmations involve direct relations to the cross. In his opposition to the powers and his fidelity to God, be bears the consequences of such resistance; in his solidarity with us he shares our life, but especially the sorrows of those who suffer for righteousness' sake. These connections to the cross must be viewed in the context of the final outcome of his actions, namely, the creation of a community that joins him in his resistance, his fidelity, and his solidarity with those who suffer. Such a community is not the adoration of suffering or the acquiescence to suffering. Rather, Jesus creates a community of those called to live with eyes wide open to the reality of suffering and evil in the world. They are called to join him in solidarity with those who suffer, to resist evil, and to work and hope for the peace and justice of God. These ideas appear again and again in atonement theories in crucial ways: in the affirmation of sanctification (holiness) and not simply justification (forgiveness); in the emphasis on God's purposes for the entire creation and not simply the satisfaction of our personal needs; in the emphasis on a cosmic view of salvation and not simply salvation of individuals. To borrow a phrase from Irenaeus and Athanasius, how *fitting* it is that the community created by Christ to pray, work, and hope for the final salvation of the world comes into being through the sharing of bread and wine, broken and poured out, in remembrance of his life given for us.

All of this brings to mind the time-honored phrase that Jesus does something for us that we cannot do for ourselves. Such a confession can apply to each of the three affirmations just made. His resistance, fidelity, and co-suffering are accomplished in ways that transcend the limitations of our minds and wills. There is saving power in Jesus. But in speaking of Jesus in this way, we are confronted with the twofold character of statements about Christ: the affirmation of saving power in Jesus' life, death, and resurrection leads directly to affirmations about God. For the early church it could not be otherwise. How could there be saving power in his life, in a horrifying death, and even a claim to resurrection, if these events were not connected to God? Thus the three affirmations about Jesus become affirmations about God: it is God who opposes sin, death, and moral evil; it is God who is faithful; and it is God who suffers with us to reconcile us. We are drawn, therefore, into an expansion of the basic thesis about Jesus to statements about God. In effect, Christology becomes theology. To suggest that what is to follow is a second thesis, or something added on to statements about Christ, would only raise the question of how the two are connected. To the contrary, they are parts of the one thesis: Jesus Christ means salvation, and this means Incarnation and Trinity. We are thus led to the conclusion that Incarnation and Trinity are simultaneously the presupposition and the consequence of the proclamation that Jesus is the Christ, our Lord and Savior.

F. Jesus Christ the Saving Power of God

The thesis presented here is this: Jesus Christ is decisive because he reveals saving power, which can only be explained as the saving power of God. From another perspective, if Jesus does not possess or actualize saving power against all that afflicts humanity and divides humanity from God and one another, then he is not significant. But if he does possess such saving power, then it is such only as the presence of the saving power of God. Here again we are reminded of the fact that the language of Incarnation was always rooted in soteriological affirmations. The fact that the doctrine of the person of Christ was not finalized until 451, after the adoption of the Nicene Creed, should not confuse the logical and temporal order of Incarnation and Trinity. The entire debate at Nicea assumes the presence of God in Jesus Christ. Without that there would be no need for the Trinitarian discussion. Thus the starting point is Paul's affirmation that God was in Christ, as well as John's affirmation of the Word made flesh. Both are answers to the question posed by Mark: Who is this Jesus? To say that the Spirit of God is in him, or that he is the Word of God, is to explain how it is that saving power can flow from him as well as to declare after the fact that he stands as the presence of God against us, among us, and for us. It is in this sense that Incarnation is both presupposition and conclusion. Jesus makes no sense if it is not God working through him and present in him. Because God was in him, therefore our thinking about God and Christ are forever changed. It is for good reason, then, that theories of atonement rely upon Incarnation as both presupposition and conclusion. Each event in the story of Jesus is given new meaning because of this claim about God's presence, in Jesus and in the Spirit bestowed upon the community.

Once this declaration of God's presence in Jesus Christ and the Spirit is established, the community is drawn to further declarations regarding the unity of God and God's revelation. This next step, while implicit in the earliest message regarding Christ and the Spirit, was far more complicated and contentious. As discussed in connection with Athanasius (Chapter Five), I proposed that there were two approaches to the concept of Trinity leading up to Nicea. One was what I term a *historical Trinity,* which confesses that God is the Father of our Lord Jesus Christ and the one who through Jesus Christ bestows the Spirit. This view is present in doxological statements in the New Testament and confesses what has happened. It does not assign functions to the three members, and for this reason I do not refer to it as an economic Trinity. This view is monarchical (i.e., gives priority to the Father), has little interest in explaining the relation of Father, Son, and Spirit, or the relation of divinity and humanity in Jesus. While it is grounded in New Testament confessions, it finds unfortunate expression in the popular view that the Trinity is God, Jesus, and the Spirit. The other view is what I call the *Nicene Trinity,* and is largely unknown by most Christians. It is a view of God, not the relation of God to Jesus, involving highly technical terminology. It was forged in the great controversies with Arianism and modalism, wherein it rightly upheld the view that God was indeed in Jesus Christ and that the three personae are truly God, rather than passing modes of being. It was able to connect with both the New Testament and the historical view by employing the personal language of Father, Son, and Holy Spirit. Yet considerable ambiguity remained as to whether the Son referred to the second persona in God, or to Jesus, or to both.

The final Trinitarian doctrine presented a way of thinking about God that could serve as both *presupposition* for the incarnation of the Word and bestowal of the Spirit, as well as a *conclusion* that summarizes the history of redemption. There is but one God, who is from eternity Father, Son, and Holy Spirit. The equality of the three personae was affirmed by insisting that the Son is begotten from the Father and the Spirit proceeds from the Father and the Son. Gathering all these elements together, the final doctrine revealed the inadequacy of beginning with the classical attributes, which abstractly define God as eternal and transcendent, but who belatedly considers the possibilities of creation and redemption. To be sure, God is under no external necessity to create or redeem the world. But the Trinity affirms that God is eternally self-giving (from Father to Son to Spirit), and it is this divine life that constitutes the basis for the creation and redemption of the world (from Father through the Word by means of the Spirit). It is in this way that the Trinitarian view of God becomes the presupposition for the incarnation and summarizes the revelation of God. While the debate over the images of Father/Son is necessary, the unfortunate consequence of it, however, is that it has detracted attention from the fundamental connection between the saving power of Jesus Christ and the affirmations of Incarnation and Trinity. While the doctrine of the Trinity is not *only* a summary, it does in fact gather up the history of salvation in its affirmations of one God, three personae. God can only be God as the source of all that is, the Word revealed in all, and the Spirit that enlivens all. How appropriate it is that the Spirit has been described as the bond of love between the Father and the Son, i.e., God the source of all and the Word revealed in all.

Chapter 12   Christ and the Church

_____

A. Atonement and the Church

In this chapter we shall explore the relations between theories of atonement and the formation of the church — its basic structure, faith, life, and work. The initial assumption is that there is a positive connection between Christology and ecclesiology. But what is the connection? Do theories lead directly to particular forms of the church? The examinations of Anselm and Luther would suggest fairly direct connections: in the former case between a theology of incarnation that connects with a sacramental form of the church; in the latter case between a theology of Word and promise, received by faith in a church formed by a vernacular Bible, sermon (vs. homily), a new hymnody, and a new catechism. But one can also argue that the form of the church, whether established or emerging, may inspire new ways of thinking about Christ. For example, did the experience of oppression and the yearning for liberation inspire a rereading of the New Testament, with the result being liberation theology? Or did the theology name the sufferings and hope of oppressed people in a new way? Whether it is one or the other, or both, there appear to be powerful connections between Christology and the formation of the church.

A somewhat different issue needs to be raised, lest one moves toward a simplistic causal relation between thinking about Christ and the church. Several theories are used widely in different traditions, where the shape, life, and work of the church diverge greatly. For example, one could hear penal substitution preached in Roman Catholic, Presbyterian, Southern Baptist, and Mennonite congregations. This situation suggests that there are obviously other factors affecting the formation of the church besides the dominant image of substitutionary atonement. But what are they and are they Christological in any way?

A variation on the last issue further complicates the relation between Christ and the church. In the current ecumenical interchange, there is a significant level of variety within denominations as compared to the differences between denominations. Some might therefore conclude that there is no connection between theories of atonement and the form of the church, since many denominations now have multiple Christologies within their own house. But I would argue just the opposite. The high level of confusion, disagreement, and at times, outright warfare between factions within a denomination suggests that multiple Christologies do not easily coexist. The reason for this is that theories of atonement do in fact inspire particular forms of the church.[1] Without a conscious attempt to sort them out and resolve the tensions between them, they work at cross-purposes and become the underlying cause for conflict on the basic aspects of ministry: worship, preaching, education, evangelism, mission, and service.

B. Christ and the Church: The Bestowal of Saving Power

One would expect there to be positive connections between Christ and the church. Such an expectation is central to the New Testament, where it is assumed that Jesus did in fact intend to create a new covenant community. It is also supported by the fact that the early leaders saw clear connections between the meaning of Jesus Christ and the faith, structure, and mission of the early church. But as we noted in the introduction above, numerous questions confront us in trying to understand the relations between atonement theories and the church. To explore the complexity of these relations, I shall organize the discussion in response to two pairs of theses. These will provide summary statements to be tested. The first set is:

1. An atonement theory includes both an interpretation of Jesus' life, death, and resurrection as well as some indication of how the saving power of Christ is transmitted to believers across time and space.

---

1. Over the past twenty years denominational meetings have often resembled a multi-denominational or international gathering, with multiple theologies and programs being debated. But since each faction starts from a different principle of authority and/or perspective, there occurs a series of charges and countercharges about how theology is to be done as well as how the church should spend its time and money. The fact that many of these debates deal with highly specific programmatic issues illustrates how different theologies reach quite different views on ecclesial matters.

2. In general, it is the mode of transmission that is determinative for the life and structure of the church.

To understand the first thesis, let us begin with the organization of John Calvin's *Institutes*.[2] In the first two books, Calvin discusses the knowledge of God the Creator and God the Redeemer. Book Three, however, is titled: "The Way in Which We Receive the Grace of Christ: What Benefits Come to Us from It, and What Effects Follow." In Book Four the subject shifts to "The External Means or Aids by Which God Invites Us into the Society of Christ and Holds Us Therein." These titles do more than simply announce that attention will now be turned to the doctrines of faith, justification, election, the church, and sacraments. They state explicitly a connection between what Christ does and how it is received across time and space. While most theologians usually imply such a connection, they do not make this transition as explicit as does Calvin. This distinction between *what* God in Christ does and *how* the benefits of this event are transmitted to us is the key for understanding the connections between Christ and the church. While the distinction should not be overdrawn, it is significant if for no other reason than the fact that most people think of atonement theories as dealing with *what* God in Christ does and neglect *how* Christ's benefits are communicated to believers. Thus the connection between Christ and the church is lost. My purpose, however, is to affirm that *how* Christ's benefits are communicated is a crucial part of an atonement theory because it connects the interpretation of Jesus (what God does in Christ) and church.

The first thesis connects interpretations of Jesus and the church by indicating how believers receive Christ's benefits. But it is the second thesis that suggests a stronger relation, namely, the power to form the life and work of the church. The possibility that atonement theories relate directly to particular forms of the church would connect Christology and ecclesiology in a decisive way. If this were correct, then ecclesial patterns could be seen as the natural and inevitable outgrowth of interpretations of Jesus' life, death, and resurrection. It would mean, in effect, that particular theories contain, implicitly or explicitly, the seeds for various forms of the church. Atonement theories could then be seen as directional signals sending believers in quite different directions when it comes to their corporate life and work. To test such a thesis, let us begin by examining the various ways Christ's benefits are

2. John Calvin, *The Institutes of the Christian Religion,* ed. John T. McNeill, trans. Ford Lewis Battles, vol. 20 of The Library of Christian Classics, ed. John Baillie, John T. McNeill, and Henry P. Van Dusen (Philadelphia: Westminster, 1960), pp. xi-xvii.

shared across time and space. If we examine atonement theories, at least six different transmitters may be identified.[3] The six modes of transmission are:

1. Sacramental participation in Christ. Here the emphasis might fall upon baptism understood as dying and rising with Christ (Rom. 5) for infants or believers, or upon the Eucharist as participation in the new life of Christ by bread and wine.
2. Faith as trust of the heart in response to the grace of God in Christ. If the good news is the grace revealed in the cross of Christ, then the mode of transmission is the proclamation of grace and our response in faith, hope, and love.
3. Rebirth in the Spirit. Here the saving power of Christ is transmitted by means of the new spiritual birth bestowed by the Spirit.

3. A decade ago I developed a typology for the church, assuming that each type claims to be apostolic. (Cf. *Christ the Reconciler: A Theology for Opposites, Differences, and Enemies* [Grand Rapids: Eerdmans, 1996], pp. 31-60.) These types are descriptive of actual forms of the church, but also possess a prescriptive value, i.e., they appeal to what is considered authoritative. In developing this typology, great care was given to presenting positive images based on actual communities of faith. In this respect this typology differs from that offered by Avery Dulles in *Models of the Church* (New York: Doubleday, 1987). In general, Dulles's models are theoretical constructs of theologians rather than actual communities. But more important, Dulles's models do not have equal value. At least three of the five models are either criticized so heavily or finally rejected that the original typology is reduced to several preferred models. A very different approach is found in the instructive writing of Lesslie Newbigin [cf. *The Household of God* (New York: Friendship Press, 1953], wherein he proposes three images of the church, based on the Roman Catholic, Lutheran/Calvinist, and Anabaptist traditions. I expanded the three images of Newbigin to eight, each representing an essential aspect of an ideal ecclesiology. The eight images of the church are:

    1. Sacramental Participation in the Historic Community
    2. Confessing the True Faith
    3. Rebirth in the Spirit
    4. Acts of Love and Justice
    5. Confessing Our Unity in Christ
    6. The Covenant Community or Gathered Church
    7. Pilgrims and Seekers
    8. Solidarity with Jesus Christ and Those Who Suffer.

In this discussion of how atonement theories impact the form of the church, I have named only six modes of transmission. The two images of the church left out are Unity in Christ and Pilgrims and Seekers. I still consider them distinct views of the church, if one approaches the matter from the standpoint of what defines the church. But they do not seem to function that well as forms of transmitters with regard to atonement theories. From the perspective of the shorter list of transmitters, they would have to be classified as variations on either True Faith or the Covenant Community.

4. Participation in the new community of Christ. When God's work in Christ is perceived as the creation of a new, reconciled community on earth, then the connecting link is participation in such a gathered community with its work (discipline) and witness (celebration). Perhaps one way of understanding millennial hope and/or predictions for the coming of Christ is to see it as one manifestation of the importance of participation in a community, defined in this case not by work or witness, but expectation.

5. Acts of love and justice. When God's work in Christ emphasizes the new life demonstrated in Christ's words and actions, then the saving power of God is transmitted by means of engaging in works of love and justice.

6. Solidarity with Christ, who suffers with the oppressed. If Christ is proclaimed to be the liberating power of God, such saving power is received by participation with Christ in the suffering of the oppressed as they struggle for justice and freedom.

To understand this typology, it must be remembered that a typology seeks to identify or isolate that which differentiates the members of a class, even though they share many things in common. All churches may affirm sacraments, but sacramental life is the defining mark for only one type. By contrast, several types emphasize some form of new life and practice, but they vary in significant ways as to how this will be defined: In #3, the rebirth in the Spirit is the defining mark; in #4, participation in the new community is the key; in #5 new praxis is the key; whereas in #6 the community is defined by a liberationist vision of solidarity. Things also become complex when traditions begin to merge these types. For example, Roman Catholic monastic orders combine the sacramental life with a communal discipline. In the case of Mennonites, the communal discipline is combined with works of love, understood as following the example of Jesus. These qualifications remind us that Christian communities are complex, shaped by multiple theological factors as well as different historical and social contexts. But the qualifications do not diminish the fact that such a typology does help us identify how theories of atonement move in different directions regarding the form of the church.

Having named these modes of transmission, let us begin with the fairly obvious ties to particular communions. First, in the early church the conquest of Christ over sin and the devil was connected with baptism as the means of receiving the new life of Christ. Following Romans 6, we participate in Christ's death and resurrection in our baptism. The church was therefore formed as the community that lives in the risen Christ and the Spirit. A second example is the theory of the restoration of the creation in Anselm, which concludes with a direct connection with the sacrament of the Lord's Supper. The benefits of Christ, received from God the Father, are shared with believers who follow the mandates of Scripture and participate in the sacramental life of the church. The crucial question here, however, is whether Anselm's theory generates the impulse to form the church around the sacraments, or does the development of the sacramental system of penance and Eucharist prompt Anselm to reconsider the interpretation of Jesus' death and resurrection in light of the present reality?[4] Since the sacramental system already existed, it is more likely the latter. But in either case, Anselm's theory provides a theological rationale for a particular form of the church and has usually been identified with it. Perhaps the strongest example of how a shift in the interpretation of Jesus' death and resurrection leads to a reformulation of the church is the sixteenth-century use of justification by grace. Once the focus shifts to the proclamation of the gospel as the Word of promise, attention shifts from human works offered to God to the human response of faith as trust of the heart. But to allow such proclamation and response to be at the center of worship and teaching, the shape of the church must be altered. Thus, a vernacular Bible, a new catechism, the sermon (vs. the homily), and a new hymnody come into being to enable proclamation, while the hierarchy of the religious and laity is demolished in favor of the priesthood of all believers. The same kind of analysis can be applied to the liberationist interpretation of Jesus, which finds expression in an ecclesial life marked by solidarity with those who suffer and the expectation for justice and peace in this world.

These examples provide ample evidence for the first set of theses: atonement theories contain implicit or explicit references to a mode of transmission. Without this, an atonement theory would only be an interpretation of Jesus without any indication as to how saving power is accessible to believers across time and space. The examples also reveal how it is the mode of transmission that expresses church-forming power. There is clearly a strong and positive correlation between Christology and ecclesiology. But at this point we need to explore a major complication. Many churches, with radically different forms of church life and structure, rely upon the same interpretation of Jesus. Stated in another way, the same interpretation of Jesus can be linked to more than one mode of transmission. For example, Roman Catholics, Presbyterians, Baptists, and Mennonites all rely upon the theory of penal substitution. But while Roman Catholics connect this interpretation of Jesus with the Mass, Protestants move in other directions: Presbyterians rely on

---

4. Cf. the general thesis of George H. Williams, *Anselm: Communion and Atonement* (St. Louis: Concordia, 1960).

true faith as the transmitter, Baptists claim believers baptism with its emphasis on rebirth of the Spirit, and Mennonites add to believers baptism the
strong emphasis on participation in the community, as well as works of love
and justice. This suggests the second set of theses:

3. Interpretations of Jesus may be connected to more than one mode of
   transmission.
4. The connection between interpretations of Jesus and modes of transmission is variable, depending on the selection of key ideas and the context
   of communities of faith.

The second set of theses does not contradict the first. They do, however,
prevent us from adopting a simple causal theory, namely, that atonement theories necessarily move from an interpretation of Jesus to only one mode of
transmission. If this were the case, a particular atonement theory would be irreversibly tied to one form of the church. There is no doubt that this restriction goes against our hope as well as our traditional assumptions. It works
against our hope that things might be simple, resulting in permanent patterns.
But instead, it overturns the traditional assumption that a particular interpretation of Jesus must find ecclesial expression in only one form of the church. It
should be admitted that this is difficult to accept, because by tradition we are
accustomed to connecting them in this way. How could Anselm's theory find
expression in any other ecclesial form than the sacramental? Or, as suggested
above, Luther's affirmation of justification by grace moves, so it appears, so
naturally to the response of faith. But as hard as it is to imagine, we need to recognize that Anselm's affirmation of the faithfulness of God in restoring the
creation to holiness could be connected with the transmitter of true faith or
even those modes that emphasize the new life of love and justice. The high attention in Roman Catholic traditions for morality and the holy life support
this suggestion. Likewise, as some Lutherans imply by their advocacy of high
church forms and practices, Luther's interpretation of Jesus could find expression in a church organized in terms of bishops, sacraments, and tradition.

The fact that modes of transmission possess a certain fluidity should not
be taken to mean that the connection between interpretation and transmission is arbitrary or simply in the mind of the beholder. Just the opposite is
suggested by the history of this interaction between atonement and
ecclesiology. On the one hand, a particular mode of transmission can be
linked to an interpretation by the continuity of crucial ideas. In this sense,
one can make a case that it grows naturally out of the interpretation. For example, if Jesus participates in our life to restore the creation, then our sacra-

mental participation in his life is a natural and reasonable mode of transmission. Such an argument can be made even though there may be other crucial ideas in this interpretation of Jesus. It is interesting to note that while Anselm's reference to the Eucharist is suggestive regarding the sacramental mode of transmission, he also refers to the importance of Jesus as an example of holiness as well as to Scripture, both revealing how we might share in the benefits of Christ. In the case of Luther, justification by grace received in faith certainly provides a direct link to one mode of transmission. By contrast, Wesley uses wondrous love to move from the love of God in Jesus Christ to the love in us by our life in Christ and the Spirit. Wesley's confidence regarding growing in grace rests entirely upon the power of the Spirit in us. The mode of transmission (i.e., justification and sanctification) arises directly from interpretation of Jesus to the presence of Christ and the Spirit in us.

On the other hand, we should not overlook the fact that context affects the advocacy for a new interpretation of Jesus and/or a new mode of transmission. A case in point would be twentieth-century liberationist theology. It does not in any way denigrate the value of this theological movement by saying that it arose in the context of oppressed persons. Therefore, the interpretation of Jesus as liberator and the emphasis on solidarity as the mode of transmission speak directly to this context. The impact of context can also be seen in the differences between Latin American and North American liberationists. While both share the affirmation of Christ the liberator and solidarity with oppressed persons, the Roman Catholic liberationists in Latin America retain a much stronger emphasis on Incarnation, Trinity, and sacraments in the way solidarity is defined. Another example of the impact of context would take us back to Luther in his quest for a gracious God, or even Anselm in his attempt to provide a theological foundation for what is the new spiritual life, based on penance and sacraments. For both Luther and Anselm, interpreting Jesus and reflecting on the mode of transmission involved highly contextual decisions.

What we have then are a set of conclusions that appear to diverge, but in fact support one another. The first set is: Interpretations of Jesus are usually linked with a mode of transmission, which has decisive consequences for the life and form of the church. The second set is: A mode of transmission may be tied to more than one interpretation of Jesus, and conversely, an interpretation may be connected to multiple transmitters. While this suggests considerable fluidity in the connection, it should not minimize how transmitters either grow quite naturally out of interpretations of Jesus or appear quite responsive to certain contexts. Most important, the second set of conclusions still supports the idea that atonement theories (as interpretations and modes of transmission) are formative for the church.

Given this complex set of relationships between interpretations and modes of transmission, to what extent is there a gravitational pull between certain interpretations and modes of transmission? Some associations are sealed forever in historical patterns. For example, the interpretations of sacrifice, renewal (Athanasius), and restoration (Anselm) are tightly linked to sacramental transmission. These associations are so strong that it is difficult to decide whether it is the historical association or a truly natural link between interpretation and mode of transmission. If *natural* means that there is a legitimate theological rationale for connecting them, then this certainly is the case, though it does not preclude the possibility that these interpretations could be connected to other modes of transmission. Theories that focus on the paradox of sin and grace (e.g., justification, penal substitution, the true knowledge of God [H. R. Niebuhr], and reconciliation in 1 Corinthians) are linked to proclamation of the Word and the response of faith. Those theories that emphasize new life gravitate toward modes of transmission where this is actualized in some definite way: rebirth in the Spirit, new community, acts of justice, or solidarity with those who suffer. Thus, from a historical perspective, these lines of connection can be drawn quite easily. But given the way theology and spiritual life are being reconfigured, it is not impossible to see all sorts of new links. We already have high church Lutheran and Reformed clergy who place just as much emphasis on sacramental participation as faith, as well as Roman Catholic Pentecostals, social activists, and liberationists. The impact of this is not simply variety within a single tradition, but the advocacy for radically different forms of the church stemming from the same interpretation of atonement. (There is, of course, the other form of plurality, where members shift from the more traditional view of atonement within a tradition to another theory, as for example, Lutherans advocating a sacrificial or liberationist view of atonement.)

Does this mean that one can change the form of the church by simply changing the theory of atonement or mode of transmission? In theory this should follow. A Reformed pastor or lay leader could easily be moved to take up a liberationist view of Christ and the church after reading Gutiérrez and/ or visiting Latin America. But if leadership is based on shared values, the change in the theology of leaders will not automatically change congregations or ecclesial bodies — as many leaders have discovered to their grief. Thus a change in perspective only on the part of leaders leads to what we have in so many situations, namely, serious fractures with people either wondering why they do not agree or engaging in all-out warfare. A more likely possibility is that other perspectives on Christ and the church could be added onto the dominant patterns, based on Bible study, worship and preaching, fellowship and community service. Such a process would in effect expand and enrich the shared values of the congregation or ecclesial body, emphasizing both continuity with the past and the openness for new growth into the fullness of Christ.

Any attempt to align the ten interpretations of the cross to the six modes of transmission must take into consideration the distinction between justification and sanctification (i.e., grace and power), which cuts across all of these categories. At a first estimate, certain interpretations appear to rely more on the affirmation of justifying grace as the sole basis for acceptance of the sinner and as the sole foundation for the church. Here the theories of sacrifice, justification, penal substitution, and the three theories based on reconciliation can be mentioned. But even here a close reading of church history would surely find groups affirming one of these theories of atonement that also practice a call to the disciplined life of holiness as part of justifying grace. On the other hand, other interpretations appear to rely more on the affirmation of sanctifying power that gives rebirth to individuals and/or draws them into the new life of holiness. To cite examples, consider the general impact of the theories of liberation, Athanasius, Anselm, Schleiermacher, and the composite found in the Wesleys, where the love of God in Christ opens the possibility of love in our lives. If we look carefully at the list of modes of transmission, the last four lean toward this emphasis on actualizing the new life. Thus, when one or more of these is added to any theory, it can lead to the disciplined life. Roman Catholic monasticism merges the interpretation of sacrifice with the disciplined community as the mode of transmission; Anabaptists have no trouble merging penal substitution with the disciplined community that follows the commands of Jesus.

This tension between grace and power, superimposed on all of the theories, is probably the most decisive issue in current ecclesial debates. No matter what theory one advocates, if it is cast in the language of grace (justification), then the basis for the church will be seen in terms of the Word of promise and sacraments; but if the language of power (sanctification) is the basic vocabulary for interpreting the cross, then the church will be based on some combination of faith and practice. The corruptions of these two poles are well known: the one has found expression in what Bonhoeffer called cheap grace, where the church takes comfort in the unconditional love of God without actualizing the new life; the other finds expression in the demands for agreement in faith and practice (i.e., the church of agreement), producing the inevitable problems of legalism and division. While certain denominational traditions lean toward one of these poles, it is also the case that within each denomination the two poles are engaged in a vigorous struggle.

C. The Gift of Pentecost

The possibility of living with multiple views of Christ and the church has in fact become a reality in the last decades. We have seen the emergence of radical complexity within each denomination regarding interpretations of Jesus and modes of transmission. Instead of general uniformity and consensus within denominations, we now find that most of the atonement theories are present in each communion. Furthermore, given the fluidity of the way modes of transmission are utilized, even more variation occurs. Thus a gathering of Lutheran or Reformed pastors might include the traditional Lutheran/Calvinist emphasis on justification by grace and true faith, but also emphases on sacraments, spirituality and rebirth, and works of justice, love, and liberation. These categories might then be further subdivided. For example, the church formed around true faith might be understood in Luther's sense of trust of the heart in the grace of God, or the demand for acceptance of a literal Bible, or in doctrines and social policies. This polyphony of voices within denominations produces tension and even divisions precisely because different atonement theories (interpretations and transmitters) impact the formation of the church. To think of the saving power of Christ as being transmitted by means of sacraments, proclamation received in faith, communal participation, rebirth by the Spirit, works of love and justice, or solidarity sends different directional signals. Each signal will ultimately lead to different answers to questions regarding the nature and purpose of ordained ministry, worship, education, evangelism, stewardship, fellowship, and acts of service. It is little wonder that at every level of church life, from congregation to regional bodies to national gatherings, there is vigorous disagreement. People are speaking different languages, but unlike Pentecost, they do not understand one another and there is no gift of unity.

Before one descends into expressions of lament and loss regarding this pluralism, we need to place this development in the broader perspective. The attempts to maintain the purity and authority of denominational traditions have largely been undercut by the ecumenical theology and biblical studies of the twentieth century. Ecclesial unions and cooperation have been one expression of this new state of ecumenical religion, but one can also see it at work in the ecumenical character of seminaries, where new generations of leaders are nurtured in more inclusive ways. We also need to note, lest religious leaders take all the credit, that these ecclesial developments were preceded by the grass roots ecumenism of families (i.e., the marriage of someone different) and life together in neighborhoods, public schools, and work places. Living in America has always meant the triumph of experience over dogma. In this case, it has meant that people learned to live together across religious lines, often in spite of religious disapproval. I am prepared to say that God has been mixing things up for a long time, prior to formal denominational unions. What we now have within denominations is another form of that divine impatience with denominational dogmatism. This does not mean, necessarily, the end of denominations, since they have a certain resiliency that allows them to adapt and endure. What it does mean is that denominations now have the opportunity to experience the fullness of theological expression regarding interpretations of Jesus Christ. This can lead to a much richer understanding of the Christian life. But it does require historical and theological understanding of the Christological options at work in this mix. If one lacks consciousness of one's own interpretation of Christ, it will be hard to evaluate other views of Jesus as well as modes of transmission, which send powerful directional signals for the formation of the church.

The point is illustrated in a dramatic way if we consider the vigorous and complex debates regarding strategies for renewal and church growth. There is a striking parallel between many of these proposals and what has been listed above as modes of transmission. In the great debates over strategy now taking place, one finds proposals for renewal by means of: (1) worship, sacraments, or new music; (2) preaching and Bible study; (3) the practice of spiritual disciplines; (4) the use of small groups or new forms of community; (5) programs to involve people in social witness; (6) service and solidarity with the poor and oppressed. Viewed from the perspective of American church history, these struggles are the latest round of debates over *new measures*. But what is too often missing is serious reflection on the question: What is the theology that undergirds the proposed strategy? Stated in the language introduced in this chapter: What interpretation of Jesus Christ is linked to the strategy as a means of transmitting saving power?

The question needs to be asked, since proposals for religious renewal are tempted to let means become ends in themselves. Since the Great Awakening, those planning strategies have known that certain strategies can produce desired results. This triumph of technique reappears in the multitude of practical manuals and testimonials on how to plan, organize, and achieve success in renewal and membership growth. Thus, at a very elementary level one needs to ask if the strategic plan is connected in any way to a theology, or is it another example of a borrowed technique. But even when the underlying theology is stated, one still finds more concern about the techniques and success rates than the theology.[5] The problem is not that the techniques fail to

---

5. The emphasis on technique creates two different problems for ecumenical Protestant traditions: one is that the techniques can be borrowed from general organizational theory and

achieve stated goals. The problem is that they often do! But the question is, Are these stated goals the cause of Christ and the advancement of the Rule of God? Such a word of caution ought to prompt us to fill the measures or strategies for renewal with the retelling of the saving power of Christ.

In atonement theories, the mode of transmission grows out of and relates to a vision of the saving power of Jesus Christ. We have seen that in some cases it can be decisive in the formation of particular churches; in other cases it is quite flexible and can become the means of conveying more than one message of saving power. But it is never the mode of transmission itself that saves, but Jesus Christ and the Spirit. The inordinate attention to new measures runs the risk of achieving the appearance of success without any substance. One is brought back to the affirmation of Luther that the only treasure of the church is Jesus Christ.

The basic thesis of this entire study has been that the gospel of Jesus is far greater and richer than what can be contained in only one theory of atonement. The recognition that interpretations of Jesus' life, death, and resurrection span a wide range of human needs as well as issues relating to the world and God's purposes should be good news for churches. An individual congregation, or a denomination, is made up of quite different members and groups of people who experience life and the world in very different ways. They also speak of sin and grace in very different ways. The multitude of interpretations therefore becomes an opportunity to proclaim the gospel to all of the people, that each might hear a word of grace spoken to them. The church lives, grows, and is faithful in witness and service, when it declares in clear and confident words that Jesus Christ is God's saving power. That requires that we think clearly and faithfully about the many ways Christians have interpreted the life, death, and resurrection of Jesus Christ. To do that opens the possibility, by the grace of God, that people with very different needs and interests might hear in their own way good news.

---

marketing strategies and have no goal other than meeting people's needs as a way of expanding membership. This opens the door to the great debate over what are legitimate and illegitimate needs for religious communities to meet. While Jesus Christ does in fact meet our heartfelt and deepest needs, in America the gospel too often has become a technique for self-improvement and personal happiness. The other problem is that many of these techniques for achieving new community and church growth carry with them quite conservative and/or fundamentalist theology, for example, compare the Promise Keepers movement as well as church-growth movements like Willow Creek and the writings of Rick Warren (cf. *The Purpose-Driven Church: Growth Without Compromising Your Message & Mission* [Grand Rapids: Zondervan, 1995]).

Index of Names and Subjects

Index of Scripture References